Remembrance and Imagination

Patterns in the Historical and Literary Representation of Ireland in the Nineteenth Century

Joep Leerssen

University of Notre Dame Press
in association with
Field Day

Voor Ann

Published in the United States in 1997 by
UNIVERSITY OF NOTRE DAME PRESS
Notre Dame, Indiana 46556
All Rights Reserved.

and in Ireland by
CORK UNIVERSITY PRESS
University College Cork, Ireland

*The paper used in this publication meets the minimum requirements of the
American National Standard for Information Sciences–Permanence of
paper for Printed Library Materials, ANSI Z39.48–1984*

Library of Congress Cataloging-in-Publication Data

Leerssen, Joseph Th. (Joseph Theodoor), 1955–
 Remembrance and imagination : patterns in the historical and
literary representation of Ireland in the nineteenth century / Joep
Leerssen.
  p. cm. — (Critical conditions : 4)
 Includes bibliographical references and index.
 ISBN 0–268–01655–0 (alk. paper)
 1. English literature—Irish authors—History and criticism.
2. Literature and history—Ireland—History—19th century.
3. English literature—19th century—History and criticism.
4. National characteristics, Irish, in literature.   5. Ireland—
History—19th century—Historiography.   6. Ireland—Historiography.
7. Ireland—In literature.   I. Title.   II. Series.
PR8718.L44 1997   96–42459
820.9'9415'09034—DC20   CIP

CONTENTS

ACKNOWLEDGEMENTS

Some portions of this book have been argued previously, in different form and sometimes in a different language, in *Comparative criticism*, 8 (1986): 91–112; the *Dutch quarterly review*, 18 (1988): 209–228; *Eighteenth-century Ireland*, (1988): 7–24; *Irish University magazine*, 20, #2 (1990): 251–263; *Modern language review*, 86 (1991): 273–284, *Handelingen der Koninklijke Zuidnederlandse Maatschappij voor Taal- en Letterkunde en Geschiedenis*, 47 (1993): 55–67, and the collection *History and violence in Anglo-Irish literature*, ed. J. Duytschaever and G. Lernout (Amsterdam: Rodopi, 1988).

This book was finished during a research sojourn in Dublin, where I was Visiting Academic at the Department of English at Trinity College; this was made possible by the support from the Department of European Studies at the University of Amsterdam, and the friendly welcome I was given by Nicholas Grene and Terence Brown at TCD. I was kindly allowed access to the library of the Royal Irish Academy, despite major refurbishing closures, by the Academy's librarian, Siobhán O'Rafferty. Colleagues like David Fitzpatrick and Seán Ó Cearnaigh aided me with their expertise.

I have profited greatly from, and this book has been deeply influenced by, the stimulating conversations and wide learning of my friend Luke Gibbons.

Most importantly of all, there have been the many comments, suggestions and constructive criticisms from Ann Rigney, who helped me in her capacities both as scholar and as spouse. To her this book is affectionately and gratefully dedicated.

ABBREVIATIONS

DNB   Dictionary of national biography
FDA   *The Field Day anthology of Irish writing* (see bibliography under Deane)
MID   *The modern Irish drama: a documentary history* (see bibliography under Hogan and Kilroy)
MIFG   *Mere Irish and Fíor-Ghael* (see bibliography under Leerssen)
RIA   Royal Irish Academy

Anachronism — n'importe.

C.R. Maturin, *Melmoth the wanderer*
(1820); chapter XXX, author's footnote

We find it to be not wholly a conceit or a paradox to say that the distinction between the Present and the Past disappears. Sometimes the Past *is* the Present; much more often it is removed from it by varying distances, which, however, cannot be estimated or expressed chronologiccally.

Henry Sumner Maine, *Village-
communities in the east and west* (1871), 7.

L'oubli, et je dirais même l'erreur historique, sont un facteur essentiel de la création d'une nation.

Ernest Renan,
Que'est-ce qu'une nation? (1881)

Time must not change the Irishman.

Ancient Order of Hibernians,
Installation ceremony (1907)

En un mot, l'histoire ne s'écrit pas sur une page blanche: là où nous ne voyons rien, nous supposons qu'il y avait l'homme éternel; l'historiographie est une lutte incessante contre notre tendance au contre-sens anachronique.

Paul Veyne, *Foucault révolutionne
l'histoire* (1978)

The transition from myth to history was an uncomfortable and often painful process which involved very centrally the questioning of assumptions about universality and permanence.

Philippa Levine, *The amateur and the professional.
Antiquarians, historians and archaeologists in
Victorian England, 1838–1886* (1986), 4.

INTRODUCTION

The subject-matter

In terms of the period covered and the methodological approach applied, this book on cultural reflection and national thought in nineteenth-century Ireland more or less picks up where my earlier *Mere Irish and Fíor-Ghael* had left off. That earlier book was intended as a pre-history of Irish national thought; this book attempts to give a historical profile of Irish national thought as it developed in the climate of European Romanticism, European nationalism and the constitutional union with imperial Britain. I have found it necessary to refer back to *Mere Irish and Fíor-Ghael* occasionally, so as to establish the interface and transition between the pre- and post-Union phases of Irish national consciousness. In thus picking up the thread, occasional reiterations and reminders of points made in the earlier book were unavoidable, for which I apologize to the reader. I felt that it was necessary to specify why there is, in my opinion, a distinctive difference between nineteenth-century developments and their eighteenth-century antecedents.

But despite the shared methodological approach and the chronological contiguity, this book does not set out to be a straightforward sequel to *Mere Irish and Fíor-Ghael*. The earlier book was intended to be virtually a compendium of Irish national and cultural reflection before 1800, with some attempt towards completeness or at least representativity in its selection of source material; in the nineteenth century, discursive activity is so very much more productive, and materials are so much more completely preserved, that it would be a Casaubon-style folly to attempt to cover the field. What is more, the period has been studied much more extensively by a great many scholars, both in general overviews and in specialized in-depth studies, and there is therefore no need of a compendium-style presentation – certainly not since the appearance of the immensely valuable and inclusive *Field Day Anthology of Irish Writing*. My treatment is therefore much more selective and aims at highlighting and interpreting significant details and incidents rather than presenting and commenting the textual record.

Another difference is that the native tradition in the nineteenth century is almost silent, having at long last been pauperized into virtual illiteracy, and therefore the interaction between Ireland's two languages after the Union, and certainly after the Famine, becomes far more one-sided than in previous centuries. There is, quite simply, almost no native, Gaelic-language material to scrutinize for its national attitudes. Instead, there is in the nineteenth century a

1

growing middle-class tradition of antiquarian and revivalist cultivation of the language, but this material reflects, by and large, the attitudes of metropolitan intellectuals and their brand of national thought, rather than the attitudes of those whose first language was Irish.[1]

This book concentrates on the mid-century, for it is in the decades following Catholic Emancipation that I have found material which appears best to illustrate the formative development of a national preoccupation with Ireland's culture and Ireland's past. These cultural and literary developments I approach by way of the contentious appearance of two important works: Petrie's essay on the Round Towers of Ireland, which opened a wide-ranging debate on the question as to how Irish people should see their past; and the cultivation of oral native material (with Hardiman's collection of Irish verse and song for a fulcrum between Thomas Moore and W.B. Yeats), which placed on the agenda the matter of Ireland's senior tradition, especially in its oral (and still living) transmission. Between them, those points of interest define the area in which a sense of Irish cultural identity came to be located: antiquity and peasantry, past and peasant.

The relatively detailed, heavily contextualized and to some extent evenemential treatment of the progress of mid-century cultural (historical and literary) debate is bracketed (and, I hope, placed in perspective) by more analytical sections on the opening and the closing decades of the century: the decades following the 1798 rebellion and the decades preceding the Easter Rising. These periods are dealt with by way of critical analyses of significant and representative literary texts such as Lady Morgan's *Wild Irish girl* and Synge's *In the shadow of the glen*, and authors like Thomas Moore and Yeats, situated as they are on the intersection of poetical (formal–literary) and ideological tensions.

This book attempts, then, to negotiate between a literary and a historical study; it moves in the realm of the history of mentalities and the history of ideas, and even touches upon the history of science and of history-writing; but it does so with special attention to literary sources. In part, this bespeaks my conviction that it would be misleading to isolate literature, by virtue of its artistic nature and 'regulated' formal conventions, from related discursive spheres of intellectual and cultural activity. Historians can get only a partial idea of intellectual patterns and issues if they avoid literary sources; literary scholars frequently arrive at crudely simplified notions as to the context of the texts and authors they study, if they do not place novels, poems and plays against the sounding board of other, contemporary discourse such as history-writing, cultural or political controversial essays. Literary texts float like icebergs in a sea of discourse, are nine-tenths submerged in a larger discursive environment which is chemically (if not physically) identical to their own substance, out of which they have crystallized and into which they melt back.

Another, more important reason to bring literary and historical interests and sources together was dictated by my topic. That topic is the way in which Ireland was imagined during the nineteenth century; this book is not so much a history of ideas or mentality (let alone a literary, social, economic or political history) as an essay towards a history of imagination. The imaginative processes studied here took shape in a cultural environment whose participants (the reading public and those who addressed them) did not restrict themselves to narrowly defined discursive genres. Opinions and debates were engaged and disseminated, attitudes projected and commented upon, in texts which, whatever their different formats (poetry, pamphlets, history books, periodicals, novels, criticism), addressed a largely overlapping readership. That reading culture embraces the National Tale as practiced in the early century and the National Story of the late century, regardless of the fact that the former belongs to the genre of the novel, the latter to that of history-writing, and equally regardless of the fact that these two genres are nowadays the exclusive provinces of different academic disciplines.

An example may help to bring out the issue more clearly. In the dissemination of national thought and of an Irish national, cultural and historical awareness, a very important role was played by the Dublin publisher James Duffy.[2] Born in 1809 in County Cavan or County Monaghan, Duffy began business as a trader in devotional Catholic tracts, and set up a bookshop in Dublin *c.* 1840. Making use of new typesetting technologies and stereotype print, he specialized in cheap sixpence editions for the lower end of the market. Within a few years, he became the main publisher to the Young Ireland movement, especially after the enormous success of the anthology *The spirit of the nation* and of 'The Library of Ireland' series. Duffy's publishing company survived a financial crisis caused by the economic depression of the Famine years, and came to dominate the nationalist and Catholic Dublin book trade in the second half of the century; in the somewhat gushing journalese of a later biographer,

> Here all manner of books relating to Ireland were turned out at white heat – classics from the pens of Davis, Mitchel, Mangan, D'Arcy McGee, D.F. McCarthy, Gavan Duffy, Carleton, Dalton, Williams, Martin Haverty, the Banims, Gerald Griffin, Father Meehan, and later, the matchless stories of Kickham, and the scholarly hagiological works of Cardinal Moran, Bishop Comerford, Canon O'Hanlon and others.[3]

The firm survived Duffy's death in 1871 and continued publishing well into the present century. Its list consisted of a mix of Catholic-devotional, historiographical and novelistic works, as indicated in the names cited above,[4] and confirms the impression that this publisher was a major force in the development and spread of Fenian-style Irish nationalism. The reading public for which Duffy catered would have read Irish-interest texts by these authors regardless of genre difference, and indeed the individual authors in their different works combined literary and historical or discursive prose. To study this reading culture, it is necessary to transcend the compartmentalization of the academic disciplines of literary criticism and historiography. Indeed, as this study hopes to show, some developments in these decades can only be charted properly if they are followed across the divides of neighbouring discursive fields.

The nineteenth century, between the Union and the Great War, beween the risings of Tone and of Pearse, sees the birth, growth and spread of modern

Irish nationalism. That nationalism, unlike its eighteenth-century precursor, Patriotism, relies crucially on an awareness that Ireland is distinct and distinctive, culturally individual and discrete, and therefore deserving of political autonomy. What is more, this cultural individuality is linked specifically, and with increasing emphasis and exclusiveness, to the nation's Gaelic roots. In other words, a Gaelic-oriented cultural and historical self-image takes shape which is quite literally central to the Irish drive for self-determination.

It is this self-image which I set out to investigate. How was Ireland seen in the nineteenth century? How was Ireland's cultural and historical profile silhouetted against other nations and, primarily, against the neighbouring isle? What specific individuality was ascribed to it? In tackling such a topic, it became clear that this self-image was something far more important and fundamental than a mere stereotype as to the Irish national character or similar commonplaces and clichés. 'Imagining Ireland' involved assessing and indeed constructing the nation's history, and also involved the development of a historical awareness which situates Ireland, not just synchronically amidst the other nations from which it is distinct, but also diachronically in a historical development out of which it has grown and by which it has been shaped. As I argue in the following pages, the quest for a national sense of identity was twofold: it was national in its trans-partisan agenda, attempting to work out a shared sense of identity applicable to all Irishmen and transcending their internal sectarian and social differences; it was also national in that it attempted to distil such an invariant and universally shared awareness out of a contentious and conflict-ridden past, transcending thereby the violent vicissitudes of history and extracting from them an essential and unchanging principle of Irishness. The nineteenth-century history of the Irish imagination is characterized by a long and widespread quest for a Hegelian, authentic, trans-historical answer to the old question, 'What ish my nation?'

There is always the temptation to speculate whether or not such imaginings of Ireland were 'true' or 'false', or to pronounce judgement as to whether they were 'right' or 'wrong'; that, I believe, is a misguided and misleading approach. The various imaginings of Ireland were, first and foremost, contentious; they formed part of a contemporary debate, evoked important and diverse reactions, and should therefore first and foremost be studied as part of that debate. Multiple ideas were advanced in many ways by different authors; the first task is to bring a sense of order into this chorus of voices, to see who echoed whom, who was contradicted by whom, and how the various patterns of imagination were distributed and transmitted, disseminated, received and licked into shape along different channels of communication. What we are dealing with is a manifestation of the imagination; to comment upon it in terms of its 'truth' or 'falsity' places the historian in a spurious position of quasi-superior insight into the nature of things 'as they really are'. The imagination does not move in channels of truth or falsity. Is Wordsworth speaking the 'truth' when he states that there is blessing in this gentle breeze? Is it any use to establish whether or not the newspapers were *really* right in claiming that snow was general all over Ireland? By the same token, it seems more useful to establish which images and imaginative patterns were most effective, most influential, most formative in later developments; at best, it becomes possible on that basis to spot inner tensions and rhetorical stratagems which to a latter-day reader may be more obvious than to contemporaries – i.e., to analyse the strategies of the discursive verbalization and expression of certain images.

This last point is where the most interesting interaction takes shape between the textual analysis of (literary) texts and the historical investigation as to the development of cultural tenets and ideas. An important, shaping influence on ideological developments was exercised by literary texts, from Lady Morgan's novels and Thomas Moore's *Melodies* to Davis's poems and Yeats's plays. The fact is universally acknowledged by historians and literary scholars alike; it is also widely recognized that Moore, Davis and Yeats were political essayists as much as poets; but the necessary inference was not always drawn: that such literary texts must therefore be situated in their wider intertextual, discursive and ideological environment, while the literary nature of their verbalization and verbal texture must be taken into the historical analysis of the wider development. This does not merely mean to see texts in their historical and social context (indeed, such an approach may become simplistic and gravitate towards one-dimensional determinism, where cultural activity is seen as 'output' and the only satisfactory interpretation is that which 'explains' it in terms of the underlying socio-political 'input'). The challenge, as it appears to me, is to study the movement of ideas and attitudes, images and perceptions within the cultural sphere, from journalistic to historiographical to literary to critical discourse, and to assess the specificity of the traffic around the specific and somehow special genre of imaginative literature. Literary texts can be studied in the extent to which they engage with ideas that are doing the rounds at the time, expressed in other non-fictional genres, and in the extent to which they disseminate and transform such ideas and feed them back, in a specific form and rhetoric, into the cultural–political system.

In so doing, and in contextualizing imaginative literary source-material inter-textually, in its ramifications with other genres and other cultural spheres, one also avoids the danger of seeing literary activity anachronistically, selected and set apart by a latter-day sense of canonicity. The reader will find that my selection of literary texts has not followed the standards of the canon of Anglo-Irish literature as presently current in academic circles. It may be useful to remember that Leopold Bloom had only two works of Anglo-Irish literature on his bookshelf: the poems of Denis Florence MacCarthy and Allingham's *Laurence Bloomfield in Ireland*, neither of them now in print, neither particularly popular with critics or literary historians. In this book, there is only a little Edgeworth, no Mangan, little Lover or Lever, the merest nod to Carleton, and more renowned authors may often be represented by 'uncharacteristic' excerpts from their work. That is because I am not concerned with the assessment of their artistic achievement, or the progress of literary art over the century, but with the development of a pattern of imagination. I can only hope that this method will occasionally throw fresh light from unaccustomed angles on familiar authors, place their individual achievement in the context of contemporary praxis, and indicate what influence they exerted in contemporary terms and beyond the literary sphere.

The method

The oppositional thought which characterizes nineteenth-century ideologies is deeply embedded in my source material, which involves distinctions, not only between images of Ireland and England, but also between peasantry and ascendancy, Catholic and Protestant, Celt and Saxon. It is important from case to case to see with what rhetoric and discursive strategies those oppositions are conceptualized and verbalized, and (at the larger scale) to see how these diverse patterns of cultural or political identification overlap or interact, or how, through time, they resemble, echo, repeat, vary or contradict each other. In order to bring such discursive strategies to the surface, I have applied a variety of tools in the form of conceptual distinctions. To list them here unremittently, cheek-by-jowl in their theoretical abstraction, may have a disheartening effect; but I ask for the reader's indulgence by pointing out that these theoretical tools have been used *ad hoc*, almost eclectically, as the occasion warranted, and that it may be useful at this preliminary stage to give advance notice on the meaning and background of some technical terms, and on the theoretical and methodological ramifications of the historical analysis as applied in the following pages.

The fundamental method applied in this book is that of imagology, or image studies, which is specifically designed to deal with the discursive manifestation of cultural difference and national identification patterns.[5] Image studies analyses its source materials (encompassing literary artworks and other forms of discourse) for the formulation of notions of domestic and foreign, and of the character of national–cultural 'selves' and 'others'. Its central preoccupation is with the dichotomy between the images of the other and the self-image.

This book is specifically concerned with the creation of an Irish self-image. Self-images have both a synchronic and a diachronic aspect, what Paul Ricoeur, in discussing the human identity, has called *mêmeté* and *ipséité*, 'selfhood' and 'sameness'.[6] 'Selfhood' refers to the fact that we are distinct from others, circumscribed in our individuality synchronically, at any given moment. 'Sameness' refers to the fact that our individuality is maintained through time, diachronically, and that we are from moment to moment linked to our earlier existence, by way of memories and the continuing effects of our previous actions and undertakings.

In imagological terms, the notion of 'sameness' implies that it is important to study traditions, historical consciousness, and the relations with past history. The nineteenth century was particularly insistent on the necessity for historical continuity and historical remembrancing: public monuments were erected in great number, public ceremony came to occupy an important place in political life, festive commemorations of public figures and important occurrences grew in number, size and symbolical importance, and old traditions were assiduously cultivated, revived or even invented. Owing to the tumultuous and fractured nature of Irish history, the diachronic aspect of an Irish self-imagination was particularly fraught in the nineteenth century, and I pay particular attention to it in this book. In doing so, I take my cue from those fields in cultural and ideological history which deal specifically with the matter of historical consciousness and its cultivation.[7]

Another way of bringing the complex Irish relation between selfhood and sameness to light is to apply to textual representations a distinction which was first made by Lessing in his *Laokoon* (1766), and which was echoed by Stephen Dedalus in *Ulysses*: the one between *Nacheinander* and *Nebeneinander*, consecutiveness and contiguousness. Artistic representations can concentrate either on the spatial arrangement of objects into a spectacle, or the temporal concatenation of events into a narrative.[8] Interestingly, as we shall see, one way of unifying history proved to be to rearrange its consecutive events from a narrative order into a spectacle, a conspectus of juxtaposed 'freeze-frame' images.

The distinction between present-day, large-scale society and traditional small-scale community permeates much of nineteenth-century thought and accounts for much of the *imaginaire* of idyllic nostalgia. It was most clearly formulated and made famous by Ferdinand Tönnies in his *Gemeinschaft und gesellschaft* (1887). Irish self-images of this period likewise tend to contrast a timeless and unchanging peasant community with the whirl of political antagonism in the metropolitan centres of contemporary society. Moreover, to the extent that the metropolis constitutes a sociopolitical, cultural and economic centre, while the rustic community is stereotypically (albeit not always in geographical reality) located at the margins of the country, Tönnies's opposition feeds into the modern sociological distinction between the *centre* and *periphery* of a given social system. That concept, overworked though it may be of late, still can yield interesting insights when applied to socio-cultural developments and attitudes – i.e., when applied according to the intentions of its original theoretician, the sociologist Edward Shils.[9]

Finally, two other analytical concepts, which have been applied at various points in this book, should be given advance mention: Gérard Genette's exploration of the shadow zone at the edge of textuality, the *paratext*, and Mikhail Bakhtin's correlation between the imagination of locale and of time in his notion of *chronotope*.[10] *Paratext* is defined by Genette as all typographical material which 'surrounds' a text without forming a fully integrated part of it (footnotes, illustrations, chapter headings, titles etc.); I have found that precisely at these frayed edges of the text, it engages most interestingly with its social and ideological environment. *Chronotope* is the conjoined imagination of spatial and temporal patterns in the literary imagination. The notion offers a crucial insight that fictional time is non-Newtonian, and runs unevenly and at different paces in different parts of the narrative landscape, the distribution patterns of imagined time across imagined space being often highly revealing. As we shall see, Ireland as experienced and imagined in the nineteenth century was not so much a real country as a chronotope, bent in political space and warped in historical time.

AROUND THE UNION:
Patriotism into Nationalism

Political and ideological change

Maria Edgeworth's *Castle Rackrent* (1800) is an epitaph for eighteenth-century Ireland. It describes rakish squires and wily Milesians, much as those rakish squires had been described by earlier travellers like John Bush and Arthur Young, and dramatists like Charles Macklin and Richard Cumberland had peppered their comedies with amusing but crafty Gaels.

Recent criticism has rightly challenged the long-received view that sees *Castle Rackrent*, with its much-imitated theme of the 'Big House' in decline, as the *ab ovo* beginning of post-Union Anglo-Irish literature. Such a view offers an overly comfortable conflation between the beginning of the Anglo-Irish novel, the portentous year 1800 and the constitutional integration of Ireland into the United Kingdom.

That conflation is distortive. As W.J. Mc Cormack has pointed out, *Castle Rackrent* was written and even published before the Act of Union was passed, and cannot therefore be seen as a cultural repercussion of that political event.[1] What is more, the novel's central concerns should be seen in their proper context: that of late Enlightenment Patriotism and the gradual re-emergence of a Catholic middle class. To see *Castle Rackrent* merely in the light of its later epigons (Somerville and Ross or Jennifer Johnston) is anachronistic and denies the novel's pre-1800 cultural roots.

And yet Maria Edgeworth herself realized that her book dealt with a bygone chapter in Irish life. The novel does, even in the author's mind, seem to mark a caesura in Irish history, and her preface already looks forward to the Act of Union and to a new dispensation:

> The Editor hopes his readers will observe, that these are 'tales of other times'; that the manners depicted in the following pages are not those of the present age: the race of Rackrents has long since been extinct in Ireland, and the drunken Sir Patrick, the litigious Sir Murtagh, the fighting Sir Kit, and the slovenly Sir Condy, are characters which could no more be met with at present in Ireland, than Squire Western or Parson Trulliber in England. There is a time when individuals can bear to be rallied for their past follies and absurdities, after they have acquired new habits and a new consciousness. Nations as well as individuals gradually lose attachment to their identity, and the present generation is amused rather than offended by the ridicule that is thrown upon their ancestors. Probably we shall soon have it in our power, in a hundred instances, to verify the truth of these

observations. When Ireland loses her identity by an union with Great Britain, she will look back with a smile of good-humoured complacency on the Sir Kits and Sir Condys of her former existence.[2]

What about this 'good-humoured complacency' that Edgeworth predicted in 1799 would result from the Union? That prediction (which, as the masculine persona in the quoted fragment already indicates, need not reflect Edgeworth's personal belief or political ideals) strikes a present-day reader as odd. The Act of Union is usually seen as a polarizing and antagonizing moment in Irish and Anglo-Irish relations: a measure to suppress the increasingly vocal and radical demands for a recognition of Ireland's separate identity as voiced from Molyneux to Swift to Lucas to Grattan to Tone.

Irish reactions to the Union (or rather, those reactions which have been canonized and transmitted in national Irish history) were overwhelmingly negative. The writings of Curran, Barrington, Thomas Moore; the passionate histories by men with United Irish sympathies such as Mathew Carey; the rising of Robert Emmet and the widespread popularity of his speech from the dock, denouncing Ireland's loss of nationhood; and even the sillier interludes such as young Shelley's Dublin pamphleteering venture: all this illustrates that the Act of Union was seen as a muzzle imposed by a reactionary British government, and that as a conciliatory measure it backfired. This was exacerbated when the emancipation of the Irish Catholics, which had been held out as part of the deal, failed to materialize.

The Act of Union had been intended as a fresh departure; it came to stand for a wrong turn in Irish history. From 1800 onwards, we see a sudden increase in the tendency to view Irish history as unfinished business, as a set of outstanding grievances waiting to be redressed. The year 1800 marks the beginning of what Oliver MacDonagh has memorably studied as an 'Irish habit of historical thought'.[3] This means, in MacDonagh's analysis, that topical political problems carry a whole burden of historical remembrances with them. In nineteenth-century Irish historical consciousness, bygones are anything but bygones, and the past continues to carry an immediate ideological relevance for current attitudes and current affairs. Thus, earlier Irish struggles against foreign encroachment, at various periods and among various opponents, are lumped together into a unified lineage or filiation: the timeless, almost Hegelian ideal of the Irish cause. Witness the way in which Mathew Carey drew the historical roots of his own nationalism: his *Vindiciae Hibernicae* of 1819 invoked 'the same glorious cause as Leonidas, Epaminondas, Brutus, the Prince of Orange, William Tell, Fayette, Hancock, Adams, Franklin and Washington', and was accordingly dedicated to

the immortal memory of the Desmonds, the O'Nials, the O'Donnels, the O'Mores, the Prestons, the Mountgarrets, the Castlehavens, the Fitzgeralds, the Sheareses, the Tones, the Emmets, and the Myriads of illustrious Irishmen, who sacrificed life or fortunes [. . .][4]

The tendency for Irish leaders to emphasize 'the apostolic succession of nationalism by identifying themselves with specific evangelists from the country's past'[5] is one manifestation of historical thought; but, *pace* Foster, it is not specifically Irish. Historians in France, who wrote under the shadow of the Revolution's failed agenda, the defeat of Napoleon, and the European vogue of Romanticism and Hegelian idealism, had a similar tendency to praise the past and not to bury it; to view the events of the past in terms of the timeless ideals which had actuated them. As a result, the events of the past could still command continued political engagement.[6]

The refusal to lay the past to rest, the reduction of history to timelessness, and the idea that past histories endure as a living force in the present: all this is one of the hallmarks of *myth*. I use that term, not in a supercilious or derogatory sense, but in a technical one, and take my cue from Raoul Girardet's *Mythes et mythologies politiques*. Girardet applies the structural notion of myth as developed by Lévi-Strauss to political thought when he sees myth as 'un récit', a narrative:

> récit qui se réfère au passé ('En ce temps-là . . .', 'Il était une fois . . .'), mais qui conserve dans le présent une valeur éminemment explicative dans la mesure où il éclaire et justifie certaines péripéties du destin de l'homme ou certaines formes de l'organisation sociale.[7]

Thus, to feel that one shares the task earlier shouldered by Brian Ború or Red Hugh O'Donnell is, properly speaking, mythical. Romantic historiography tends to view the past as motivated by Hegelian ideals such as the cause of liberty, equality or nationality. Romantic historians, impressed as they were with the evocative descriptions in Walter Scott's novels, were also explicitly concerned with bringing the past to life, and with making the past's immediate presence sensible to the reader.[8] On both these counts, there is a tendency for the romantic historical imagination to veer towards a mythical view. But that tendency was particularly strong in post-Union Ireland. Thomas Davis's position combined the thwarted rebelliousness and patriotism of a United Irishman like Mathew Carey with the romantic idealism of French historians like the Thierry brothers or Michelet, whom he much admired.[9]

Nineteenth-century images of Ireland are situated in this contradictory idea of Irish culture: as a political timebomb or as a picturesque idyll; and in the following pages I propose to chart the tension between Carey's indignation and Edgeworth's 'indulgent smile'; between Edgeworth's prediction that old grievances will be forgotten and Carey's insistence that they shall not. I aim to do so in part by tracing the mythical presence of the Irish past, and in part by tracing the views of an authentic, native Ireland which was stereotypically situated in the wilder parts of the countryside and among the native peasantry. My concern, therefore, is to study the image of a Real Ireland which is partly situated in the past and partly in the peasantry. I propose to trace this nineteenth-century image of Ireland not so much in its party-political impact as in its literary and cultural manifestations and development.

Mathew Carey and Thomas Davis did not 'look back with a smile of good-natured complacency', as Maria Edgeworth fondly predicted, nor were they ready to 'lose attachment to their identity' or to be 'amused [. . .] by the ridicule that is thrown upon their ancestor'. Indeed, Irish literature and culture are usually concerned with precisely this refusal to acquiesce. Matthew Arnold, though he erred in his ethnic essentialism, did have a point when he viewed Irish culture in terms of its 'stubborn rebellion against the despotism of fact' (this being a nineteenth-century Anglo-Irish attitude rather than, as Arnold thought, a timeless Celtic trait). Lady Morgan phrased it better when, under the very shadow of the Union, she wrote in her *Patriotic sketches* (1807):

> A passion for enjoying a twofold existence, independent of actual being; of tracing back genealogical honours, and anticipating a perpetuated life in the hearts of those they leave behind; is a passion incidental to the native Irish character of every rank; and though in the world's language it may be deemed a romantic passion, yet romance, like heroism, is never a national *trait* of a corrupt or base people [. . .][10]

Thus, the actual course of events is rejected as a betrayal of 'what should have happened', as a Wrong Turn; this rejection opposes Myth (or, in Morgan's terms, romance) to reality. That can happen in two ways: either as an act of resistance, a refusal to acquiesce in the status quo, or else as an escape from political tensions. Numerous literary and cultural historians have, from a variety of ideological and methodological perspectives, demonstrated how literature and culture in Ireland were saturated with political preoccupations. My particular interest is the oblique way in which a True Ireland is sought away from the immediate fractiousness of politics: in the glorious, pre-Norman past, or in the idyllic or picturesque community of the native population. Both reflexes, the antiquarian and the idyllic, turn to myth or romance; both are a denial of realism; but both became an important feeding ground for the imaginative iconography and outlook of Irish nationalism.

The background to these developments is a long-term shift in historical consciousness between 1760 and 1890: a shift in which Ireland's social elite, originally English in ethnic background, cultural outlook and political allegiance, redefined its self-image and began to place itself under Gaelic auspices. An upper-class, land-owning or urban, English-speaking Irishman would in the early-to-mid-eighteenth century still celebrate his 'English blood and Irish birth'; in the conflicts between native Irish and English government, the natives would be 'them' and the government 'us'. The English conquest of Ireland was celebrated as a Good Thing, both in history-writing and in drama like Shadwell's *Rotherick O'Connor* (1720) or Phillips's *Hibernia freed* (1722). Sixty years later, by 1780, it had become possible for a variety of Protestant, establishment authors to view Ireland's pre-Conquest Gaelic past in the first person, as their own. This vogue for Gaelic antiquity as constituting one's own national antecedents is part of the pre-romantic Celtic revival of the later eighteenth century as analysed by Snyder and leads into a widespread adoption and application of 'Gaelic' design and iconography as analysed by Jeanne Sheehy; it can be seen as what since Hobsbawm and Ranger's book has become known as an 'invention of tradition', and to some extent it certainly was: a spurious pseudohistorical contrivance, pretending that latter-day concerns were legitimated by counterfeit roots reaching into the past.[11] The Gaelic past that was discovered and appropriated by the Anglo-Irish elite in these decades was, it is true, distorted by faulty scholarship and a romantic idealization; but it was not, properly speaking, an invention or deliberate fake. What happened was that Anglo-Ireland decided to write itself out of its English-oriented ancestral history and instead to trace its cultural origins in a nationally Irish, and therefore aboriginally Gaelic, frame of reference. The fragmented and ill-understood remains of Gaelic history had been collected, and disseminated for a non-Gaelic public, in a slow and painstaking process from c. 1620 to c. 1770; and as relations worsened between the Anglo-Irish elite and the British government, this Gaelic history was slowly absorbed into the national narrative.[12]

These developments gather momentum around 1760 and come to dominate the Irish historical and political self-image in the nineteenth century. To be sure, historiography in the professional and larger British forum is dominated by the altercation between the anglocentric views of Froude and the Anglo-Irish vindications of Lecky; but within Ireland, the dominant narrative of pre-1600 Irish history has by 1890, especially in the popularizing histories aimed at a general readership (see below, pp. 151–6), become so Gaelic- and Catholic-oriented that it antagonizes the Presbyterian population of the northern counties into a still-active stance of Protestant, Ulster particularism.

In all these developments the Union plays a momentous but highly complex role. Did it mark a decisive shift in Irish affairs and attitudes, or does it obscure from our view the many continuities across the turn of the century? We have already encountered that question at the beginning of this introduction. In what follows, I want to offer some considerations on the impact of the Union both in political ideology and in the field of cultural discourse and historical consciousness. I shall argue that, while the Union was perhaps not an absolute watershed dividing Irish history cleanly and naturally in a 'before' and 'after', and while many developments move from the eighteenth century into the nineteenth with some continuity,[13] the 1798 rebellion and the Union of 1800 do form a set of rapids in the flow of history.

The abolition of the Dublin parliament signals the end of the ideology known as Patriotism. What ultimately took its place was the ideology of nationalism. It would be wrong to see the two as cognates: although they have some rhetoric and phraseology in common, and although present-day usage will sometimes conflate the concepts (patriotism counting as a mild, non-virulent form of nationalism), they are, historically speaking, two quite different ways of viewing human society and solidarity.

In order to understand the distinction, we must place the term 'Patriotism' (which in its historical sense I shall spell with a capital P) in its ideological and political context, and attempt a brief exercise in *Begriffsgeschichte*, terminological history. This will demonstrate that, in eighteenth-century Ireland, Patriotism meant something other than 'political and moral loyalty to one's fatherland' such as we understand the term nowadays. Patriotism is neither national chauvinism nor proto-nationalism. True, the Anglo-Irish Patriots militated against foreign, British control over Irish affairs; true, they defended the constitutional prerogatives of the Kingdom of Ireland against the hegemonist encroachment of Westminster, in that often-celebrated tradition which comprised Molyneux' *Case of Ireland stated*, the Drapier's letters, and the efforts of Flood, Grattan and the Volunteers. Indeed, did not the Patriots, or at least the most enlightened among them, move towards a political and economic conciliation with Ireland's oppressed Catholic majority, and was not this an effort to forge national solidarity out of sectarian divisions? Was not Grattan the John the Baptist to the messianic mission of Wolfe Tone?

It is easy to take that view, and it has traditionally been taken. It can draw on the homonymy of the ten-letter word 'patriotism' and (as I hope to show, anachronistically) interpret its eighteenth-century usage through nationally tinted, twentieth-century glasses.[14] This tendency is reinforced by the fact that, in speaking of eighteenth-century Irish Patriots, one refers almost exclusively to a part of the population which is traditionally known as the 'Anglo-Irish': a group of men whose historical presence is, again traditionally, situated between two momentous English-Irish conflicts, the Battle of the Boyne and the United Irish uprisings; whose very name invokes their status as a hyphenated English-Irish hybrid or middle nation; and who are therefore usually seen in a binary polarity of England versus Ireland – between, on the one hand, pro-English/anti-native-Irish Ascendancy interests and, on the other hand, anti-English/pro-Irish national interests.[15] If their political, Patriotic stance is at all seen in a context other than this paradigmatically, inescapably *national* polarity, it is usually compared to the political stance of the American Patriots; and in this way, too, the momentum of their political ideas is linked inherently to a national ideal, to the notion of national independence – since that is what the American Patriots formulated in 1776 and achieved in their ensuing struggle with the antagonist they shared with Ireland.

I wish to clear the deck by addressing some basic issues. I will adduce some examples of the eighteenth-century usage of the term 'Patriotism', so as to show that a nationalist flavour is, by and large, absent; and I shall do so in a European, rather than a narrowly Irish context. This will bring out an ideological distinction between eighteenth-century Patriotism and nineteenth-century nationalism. On the basis of that distinction, the similarities in rhetoric (e.g. the invocation of a nation or fatherland) can be adequately assessed. The path is then open to see to what extent the invocation of an Irish nation or national past differed according to its (Patriotic or nationalist, pre- or post-Union) context, and to what extent post-Union Irish nationalism constituted a fresh ideological departure.

Terminological history: patriotism as a (European) concept

Let us begin with a brief glance at the lexical evidence. The *Oxford English Dictionary* and Littré both give substantial entries *sub verbo* 'Patriot(e)' and its derivations, as does that invaluable treasure store, Larousse's *Grand dictionnaire universel du XIXe siècle*;[16] all these amply illustrate the fact that the Patriot's original object of allegiance was not his nation but rather his society of fellow-citizens. (That differentiation between nation and society may seem overly subtle but is, as we shall see, crucial.)

The root sense of *patriot* seems to have been merely that of inhabitant of a *patria*, fellow-citizen, com-patriot. Much as the term *citizen* derives from membership of the free and politically emancipated population of a *city*, so too the notion of *patriot* seems to be, analogously, intended originally as signifying the citizenship, not of a city, but of a country at large.

The notion thus seems conspicuously to reflect an attempt to express civic appurtenance, not in the usual feudal terms of the lord whose subject one was, but rather in terms of a society of fellow-men, to which, or to whose geographic area, one belonged. If this seems far-fetched, I may draw attention to the fact that, other than in the case of the collocation 'an American citizen', the nationality of a Briton will be expressed by the collocation 'a British subject' rather than 'a British citizen' – a late echo of the a-monarchial overtones which inhered in the notion of 'citizenship', borrowed as it was from Roman-republican ideals.[17] The title-page of Rousseau's *Contrat social* stated with some emphasis that the author was 'Citoyen de Genève'. Similarly, there is the anti-monarchist usage of the terms *patriote* and *citoyen* in Republican, Revolutionary France.

In the root sense of the term, then, *patriot* seems to have been semantically close to *citizen* and to have meant, either 'compatriot', or else 'citizen of a country' (as opposed to 'subject of a sovereign'); the term's ideological connotations must be sought in a bourgeois or anti-feudal direction, i.e., concerning the relations within, and between, classes of society.

The *OED* goes on to paraphrase Littré in remarking that the term was frequently used in collocation with adjectives such as 'good', 'true', 'worthy', and that, as such, it came to refer to one who would function well as a citizen, who would perform his civic duties and live up to his responsiblities towards his compatriots. Indeed, in the 1680s, the decade leading up to the Glorious Revolution and simmering with the barely-contained hostility between Catholic Stuart absolutism and Protestant post-Cromwell republicanism, the term Patriot was 'often applied to one who supported the rights of the country against the King and court'.

It is in this direction that the word's meaning develops henceforth. In 'Absalom and Achitophel', Dryden, that staunch royalist, called a Patriot 'one that wou'd by Law supplant his Prince'. In fact, that was an apt enough description of what John Locke was all about in his *Treatise on government* of 1690, which was to establish a new movement in political thought. The

Enlightenment notion of society as compact or contract, to be regulated by laws rather than status, was formulated most impressively by Montesquieu's *L'esprit des lois*.

The anti-absolutist notion of Patriotism remains in force throughout the eighteenth century, at least in Britain. A Patriot is, in a way, a Whig, a defender of the rights of parliament against those of the crown. He will say that his cause is that of freedom; and among his shining examples are Patriots who served their country by liberating it from absolute or arbitrary power and oppression: men like Brutus, like Gustavus Vasa, like William the Silent and selected other worthies.[18] It is in this light that we must read, for instance, Bolingbroke's essays on Patriotism and on the Patriot King.

But there was a less party-political meaning as well, one which concentrated on the notion of disinterested service to one's country and which began to equate the notion of the Patriot with that of the good citizen, the loyal, responsible member of society. This de-politicized meaning (Patriotism as the virtue of social responsibility and selfless devotion to the common weal) seems to have come to the fore in the early-to-middle eighteenth century. Bishop Berkeley gave a studiously neutral (but tellingly non-national) definition when he said that a Patriot was 'one who heartily wisheth the public prosperity, and doth not only wish, but also study and endeavour to promote it'. Indeed the leading light in this type of Patriotism seems to have been a kind of *political philanthropy*,[19] which often appears to have manifested itself, characteristically, in the many useful public societies that were established at this time. In Ireland, the Dublin Society is the most famous example, of course: its devotion to the practical aims of improving husbandry, manufacture, economy as well as the arts and letters is a typical example of a Patriotic devotion to the public benefit, and one which was eagerly copied throughout Europe at the time. The improvement of the Irish infrastructure by the digging of the Grand and Royal Canals is another example; the establishment of a public maternity hospital in Dublin yet another one. All of these things were seen as endeavours to the public benefit, and, as such, Patriotic in nature. This essentially philanthropic nature of Patriotism is borne out *a contrario* by a passage in a letter from Swift to Pope, where the Dean disclaims the appellation of Patriot; for, he says, the motivations behind his public stance are anything but philanthropic, but rather inspired by his *saeva indignatio*:

> I do profess without affectation, that your kind opinion of me as a Patriot (since you call it so) is what I do not deserve; because what I do is owing to perfect rage and resentment, and the mortifying sight of slavery, folly, and baseness about me, among which I am forced to live.

It was Swift, however, who gave Patriotism its formula for public usefulness, when he let the wise king of Brobdingnag exclaim

> that whoever could make two Ears of Corn, or two Blades of Grass grow upon a Spot of Ground, where only one grew before; would deserve better of Mankind,

and do more essential Service to his Country, than the whole Race of Politicians put together.

This was not only a rhetorical flourish which writers were to echo gratefully time and again; it also reflected, in very practical terms, the concerns of the Patriotic tradition of agricultural improvers – a tradition which goes back to none other than the radical 'commonwealthman' Molesworth[20] (*Considerations for the promoting of agriculture*, 1723), which included Dublin Society co-founder Arthur Dobbs (*An essay on the trade and improvement of Ireland*, 1729–31), and which influenced Arthur Young (best known to Irish historians for his agriculturally oriented *Tour in Ireland, with general observations on the present state of that kingdom*, 1780).

But there is more to it than that: for the term was to get caught-up in party-political developments in the course of the century, and was slowly to move towards a more radical, republican meaning. The Molesworth of the agricultural improvement is also the Molesworth of the subversively anti-absolutist *Account of Denmark* (1694), the Molesworth to whom Swift chose to address, in courteous terms and by way of invoking protection, one of the Drapier's letters; and the Dean's dismissive snarl against the apparent uselessness of 'the whole Race of Politicians' was not uncharacteristic of the general attitude of those improvers who undertook their non-partisan, practical attempts to benefit society. The political system had ground into stagnation with the Whig stranglehold that had established itself along with the Hannover dynasty; it is, significantly, at this time that the term 'Patriot' begins to lose some of its Whiggish connotations and veers in the direction of non-governmental political philanthropy.[21] Patriotism can be seen in this light as well, then: as a disenchantment with a political system that functions according to vested interests, where advancement is due to patronage and not to merit, where public accountability is wholly forgotten and the politi-cian rules the public rather than representing it. It was against the amorality or immorality of that political power play (denounced in various ways from Swift's Lilliput satire to Fielding's *Joseph Andrews*) that Patriots opposed the notion of virtue, of merit, the ideal (Roman-based of course) that political power be entrusted to men of virtue and merit, to the worthiest candidate *quamdiu se bene gesserit*. Franco Venturi quotes from *L'esprit des lois* to the effect that 'Virtue was [. . .] the political ideal *par excellence*';[22] and it is thus, once again, that the notion of Patriotism shows its Lockean roots and Montesquieu-ramifications. I will develop the particularly Irish dimension of this complex later on; for the moment, it might suffice to indicate the Irish background of Molesworth and Toland (overlooked by many historians of the period, even by Venturi), and to recall the fact that one of the earliest controversial pamphlets to draw on the *Treatise on government* was the *Case of Ireland stated*, by Locke's friend Molyneux.

The Revolution of 1688 had situated the notion of Patriotism at the Whiggish end of the political spectrum; the Whigs lost that monopoly in the course of their dominance under the first Georges; and when new revolutions, the American and the French ones, were to re-politicize the notion of Patriotism, it was to be into a republican, democratic, even Jacobin direction. The traditional anti-absolutist reference of Patriotism, its connotations of liberal parliamentarism, became anti-monarchist *tout court*. The 'public good' coincided once again with its Latin and older English synonyms: *res publica*, common-wealth – the *salut public*, eventually, with which a *comité* of virtuous and meritorious men like the Incorruptible Robespierre was entrusted. The early years of the French Revolution opposed, in an interesting terminological polarity, the aristocratic party and the patriotic party,[23] and slowly but surely a Patriot, during the last decades of the century, could come to mean, quite simply, a republican revolutionary – a supporter either of the American Revolution or of the French one, more or less ardent, more or less radical or extreme, but a *revolutionary*. This must be recognized as the cause of Dr Johnson's manifest dislike of Patriotism, 'the last refuge of a scoundrel', as evinced in his imputation that 'the Patriotick tribes' ardently desired the return of the Cromwellian Protectorate. English Jacobins of the 1790s frequently gave themselves, or their pamphlets, Patriotic names, in what appears a deliberate equivocation between that term's democratic and philanthropic connotations.[24]

This outline may suffice to indicate that the Patriot label in the eighteenth century was applied to a political stance on constitutional and societal issues, on economic improvement, and the relations between public and authority. In such matters, Patriotism referred to an essentially liberal position which later spawned a more radical democratic movement to its left. That definition seems to apply to the situation in various north-west European countries. Berkeley's above-quoted definition of a Patriot as 'one who heartily wisheth the public prosperity, and doth not only wish, but also study and endeavour to promote it' was echoed, in more political explicitness, by the Dutchman Jan Wagenaar in his pamphlet *De patriot of politike bedenkingen over den staat der Verenigde Nederlanden* (1747). I quote from I.L. Leeb's English translation:

> A Patriot has such a strong and upright feeling for the welfare of his Fatherland, that, in order to advance the interest of this, he puts not merely his own interest in the balance, but, if needs be, dares to put it entirely on one side. He considers his fellow countrymen and himself as members of one body. His highest wish is that he himself and all the individual members of the Civil State be happy and work together for each other's good. [. . .] He never presses his own interest to the disadvantage of the common cause. [. . .] A Patriot doesn't grumble about the present government, as long as it maintains the Law, and leaves Liberties and Privileges unrumpled.[25]

The similarity between Berkeley's and Wagenaar's ideal of a Patriot is one of many striking parallels between Anglo-Irish and, for instance, Dutch Patriotism.[26] Of course, the Dutch situation was fundamentally different from the Irish one: Holland was a fully independent country, with a republican tradition that was often compared to Venice or Geneva, and with no foreign domination against which Patriot opposition could develop (even to later eyes) a rhetoric of national independence.

The political struggle in Holland was, rather, an internal one. On the one hand, there was the House of Orange, which had laid claim on national gratitude with William the Silent and William III, and which since the days of the latter statesman had obtained strong claims to a hereditary, and thus wellnigh monarchical, stadholdership; and, on the other hand, there were those who looked back to the more truly republican, anti-monarchic and non-Orangist past of the United Provinces, embodied in the no less inspiring statesmen Oldenbarneveldt, Grotius and the De Witt brothers. These anti-Orangists had a vested footing in the municipal or provincial governing bodies (traditionally jealous of their considerable local autonomies) or in the forum of the umbrella parliament, the States General – constitutionally the ultimate locus of political power, and theoretically the appointers of the stadholder. They had also accrued the majority of all public offices, of which they had become the possessors rather than the incumbents; and they had thus developed into something which has been called both a republican aristocracy and an oligarchy.

It was this oligarchy of republican patricians (regenten) who co-opted the Patriot discourse and the appellation of Patriots. Their position in this respect was in line with the situation in Europe generally, as it has been painted on a broad canvas by R.R. Palmer in his The age of the democratic revolution. It is easy to discern parallels between these republican aristocrats in Holland, for example, and the noblesse de robe which in France were rising from the bourgeoisie by way of their hereditarily-owned incumbency in the various regional parlements. The latter, too, came to stand in sometimes open conflict with the centralist, absolute power claims of the royal court (in what Palmer considers a mid-century warming-up exercise for the revolution of 1789). They, too, defended their various regional heteronomies and privileges; and like the Dutch and, for that matter, the Anglo-Irish Patriots, they, too, invoked an opposition between court-inspired corruption and favouritism on the one hand and, on the other hand, a parliamentary policy of power-delegation on the principle of candidates' virtue and merit.[27] Interestingly enough, also, (but I shall come back to this point) they invoked a mandate that was based in the nation, the people-at-large; and that argument recalls the 'consent of the governed' and can count as a litmus-test for the Locke–Montesquieu tradition of political thought – that line of thought which in Holland and Ireland came to be called Patriotic.

It is important to realize that these mid-century Patriots were not yet the revolutionaries of the late 1780s and 1790s. They were, by and large, jealous of their own social prerogatives, and politically conservative. The regenten in Holland, the Protestant landowning class in Ireland, the noblesse de robe in France: for all their opposition to the unfairness of an autocratic, centralist government, they had vested interests in the closed shop of the national economy and were understandably reluctant to give power to the people, to undercut the basis of their own social and economic privileges.[28] On the whole, it can be said that the Locke–Montesquieu line of thought of these Patriots was not so much all-out republican or democratic, as that it continued the seventeenth-century ideal of mixed government, parliament holding a balance of power between the court and the people. That parliament should be partyless, elected freely, such as Swift had given it to the Brobdingnagians, and such as it had been proposed, for instance, in the anonymous *Patriot's proposal to the people of England concerning the ballot, the best way of choosing representatives in parliament* (1705).[29]

Thus it is possible for a more radical, democratic and downright republican movement to arise to the left of the Patriots: the United Irishmen in Ireland; those who, in France, were inspired by Rousseau's *Contrat social* rather than by Montesquieu's *L'esprit des lois*; those who, in England, continued the more radical aspects of Molesworth and Toland; and those who, in the United Provinces, adopted that radical English tradition in the wake of Johan van der Capellen tot den Poll (1741–84). Van der Capellen published in 1781 a radical pamphlet directly addressed to 'the people of the Netherlands' (*Aan het volk van Nederland*), which attacked the arbitrary nature of existing power structures and called on the people to form local representations of 'upright, virtuous, pious men' and 'reliable Patriots'.[30] Van der Capellen also translated the writings of English radicals such as Priestley (*Essay on the principles of government*) and Price (*Observations on the nature of civil liberty*).

During the 1780s, this more radical anti-Orangist Patriotism, concentrated mainly in the urban heartland of Holland, spawned a militia which (by Dutch standards) was relatively powerful. The Patriots, in a remarkable parallel to the role of the Volunteers in Ireland, could use this extra-parliamentary force to carry out their bid for power. The stadholder, William V, was effectively shut out of the County of Holland and his wife was debarred from entering their traditional residence there, The Hague. When William's brother-in-law, the king of Prussia, eventually retaliated against this insult by invading the United Provinces, a sizeable number of Patriots (whose militia were anything but powerful by Prussian standards) fled the Provinces and took refuge in France. They only returned in the wake of the French republican army which conquered Holland in 1795 and founded the French-style Batavian Republic (forcing the stadholder in his turn to take refuge in England).[31]

From such European parallels, an ideological profile of Enlightenment Patriotism begins to emerge. It is a stance we would nowadays call liberal or democratic; it stands for popular sovereignty, a political mandate emanating from the people and vested in a legislative representation of accountable and trustworthy fellow-citizens; or it stands for the independence of parliament against the might of the king; or it stands for a Montesquieu-style separation of powers.

More pertinent to my present argument, Patriotism appears to be characterized by its tendency towards heteronomy: the constitutional acceptance of local particularisms and of legal diversity between the state's different regions, for instance in a federal or confederal system. Patriotism is anti-centralist as well as anti-absolutist and tends to favour a devolution of power, not only in a vertical, hierarchical sense (bringing power closer to the governed) but also in a geographic, regionalist sense (bringing power to subsidiary regional centres). The French *parlements* defended privileges and prerogatives that were both local and parliamentary; the struggle of Flood and Grattan was for *Irish* parliamentary emancipation as well as for Irish *parliamentary* emancipation; and the republican ideal of the United Provinces was concerned to defend regional heteronomy against Orangist aspirations towards a nationwide monarchist power. In that respect, one of the ideological heirlooms of Patriotism that still enjoys widespread currency nowadays is the political ideal of a federacy or confederation as a just and open form of state organization.[32]

In all these respects, Patriotism is essentially different from nationalism. What Grattan aimed to achieve for Ireland was heteronomy rather than autonomy. The Patriots' agenda invoked arguments of equity and just representation of interests rather than an essential, national difference between Ireland and England. Their concern was the fair distribution of power within the state, rather than opting out of the state altogether; their stance was closer to constitutional monarchists like Mirabeau and Lafayette than to a Jacobin like Wolfe Tone. And most importantly, their aspirations, in Ireland as among other European Patriots, were wholly focused on the parliamentary forum. The removal of the Irish parliament was therefore a veritable guillotine to Irish Patriotism.

This is one momentous, immediate and disruptive effect of the Union: it pulled the parliamentary rug from under the ideological feet of Irish Patriotism. The failure of Patriotism in Ireland is, I think, one direct cause of the later absence of an effective Irish liberal party:[33] incipient liberalism was to be transmogrified into Home Rule movements and nationalism, whereas its ideological opposite number, the anti-revolutionary ideology which elsewhere in Europe was to develop into various brands of conservatism, took the guise, in Ireland, of Unionism. Thus, in the ideological field, one of the long-term consequences of the Union was a violent jolt in the alignment of a party-political spectrum: what elsewhere in Europe was to become a left–right polarity turned, in Ireland, into a unionist–nationalist one.

Tenets and rhetoric: nation, fatherland

Some authors and politicians, rooted in the decades of the Grattan parliament, testified to Patriotic ideals even after the Union. The post-1800 career of Henry Grattan still awaits a proper historical appreciation. There is also that great wit and man-about-town, Sir Jonah Barrington, whose *Personal sketches of his own times* are (after Swift) the finest and cleverest prose to come out of the Anglo-Irish *ancien régime*. More important still is the case of Thomas Moore, who had made his début, as a young poet, in the Patriot-oriented *Anthologia Hibernica*, and whose *Irish melodies* continued, not only Grattanite ideals, but also (as Mary Helen Thuente has admirably shown[34]) the United Irish tradition of political verse. And there is the case, to which I shall pay more specific attention in the next chapter, of Lady Morgan. Most importantly, the opening decades of the nineteenth century continued in unabated intensity the conflicts and unease of peasant restiveness. The dispossessed peasantry, which had rocked the Irish political system with its Whiteboyism before the Union, continued to do so after 1800.

But despite the fact that such patterns, as well as individual careers and concerns, straddle the two centuries, the change in ideological climate is unmistakable, in Ireland as well as in the rest of Europe. The philanthropic and virtuous ideals of Patriotism had been discredited in the French *terreur* and the Irish 1798 rebellion; middle-class democratic ideals survived, outside Ireland, under the name of liberalism; but in Ireland as elsewhere a more potent and more radical ideology, which took over some Patriot rhetoric and phraseology, arose in the shape of nationalism.

The character and early development of European nationalism has been much studied in recent years[35] and therefore requires less space here than my sketch of Patriot thought. Suffice it to say that notions of different characters or temperaments, each particular to a given political-ethnic community called a nation, had been current from the Middle Ages onwards; that these national characters had become an object of attention for Enlightenment philosophers like Hume, Montesquieu and Voltaire; that with Herder and in the shadow of approaching Romanticism, each *Volk* or nation came to be considered as a specific personality, each with its unique contribution to the variety of human culture; and that the idea ultimately was developed in Romantic Idealism, with men like Fichte and Hegel, to the point where each *Volksgeist* or national character was seen as a nation's cultural and moral DNA: a blueprint for each ethnic group in its historical destiny.[36] This is how Thomas Crofton Croker in 1824 defined 'the' Irish character:

> The present Irish character is a compound of strange and apparent inconsistencies, where vices and virtues are so unhappily blended that it is difficult to distinguish or separate them. Hasty in forming opinions and projects, tardy in carrying them into effect, they are often relinquished before they have arrived at maturity, and are abandoned for others as vague and indefinite. An Irishman is the sport of his feelings; with passions the most violent and sensitive, he is alternately the child of despondency or of levity; his joy or his grief has no medium; he loves or he hates, and hurried away by the ardent stream of a heated fancy, naturally enthusiastic, he is guilty of a thousand absurdities. [. . .] The virtues of patience, of prudence, and industry seldom are included in the composition of an Irishman: he projects gigantic schemes, but wants perseverance to realize any work of magnitude: his conceptions are grand and vivid, but his execution is feeble and indolent: he is witty and imprudent, and will dissipate the hard earnings of to-day regardless of to-morrow: an appeal made to his heart is seldom unsuccessful, and he is generous with an uninquiring liberality.[37]

Such clichés and stereotypes had been current for centuries, of course, and Croker (who even cites Giraldus at some point) echoes rather than invents them; but Croker, unlike earlier commentators, sees these characteristics as the motivating force of history (the quoted excerpt is contained in a chapter entitled 'History and National Character'), much as a man's character might be seen to motivate his actions. This national essentialism is all-pervasive in the nineteenth century. For a unionist like Croker, it defines the problem that a nation with this type of character is unfit for self-government and must be led and constrained, difficult as that may be, by a superior (British-based) government. The alternative conclusion was the nationalist one.

As a political ideology, nationalism is nowadays usually defined as the desire to organize political unity on the basis of (perceived) ethnic-cultural identity. In the nationalist view, each nation should have the right to incorporate itself in a sovereign state of its own, and ideally each state should incorporate one unified national group. Nationalism abhors multi-ethnic states and the possibility that regional minorities with a separate culture may be ruled from, and marginalized by, an alien, uncongenial and unsympathetic government. The chosen remedy is to redraw political borders so as to fit the cultural population patterns, or to claim autonomy for each cultural-ethnic group.[38] Moreover, in a nationalist view the individual's most natural and fundamental allegiance should be to one's fellow-nationals and to the state in which one's nationality finds its political manifestation.

It is in terms like these that national thought is usually presented in recent studies. It would be a challenging task to assess when and how nationalism (in the above, precise sense, as opposed to the looser sense[39]) developed in Irish cultural and political thought: Thomas Davis would certainly be a nationalist in this European sense, but the case of Daniel O'Connell would be more doubtful. That is not to say that men like O'Connell did not share the nineteenth-century propensity to argue from history: on introducing his parliamentary motion for Repeal of the Union, he 'implacably entered upon a disquisition about Irish history from the year 1172, which takes forty-six columns of Hansard before coming anywhere near the present'.[40] The difference between O'Connell and ethnic nationalists is rather that, as MacDonagh points out, the Young Irelanders, unlike O'Connell, 'placed the emphasis on the race rather than the person, the group rather than the individual, instinct and emotion, rather than reason, cultural rather than constitutional liberation, and a subjective and creative rather than a formal and negative concept of independence'.[41]

That Herderian-cum-Hegelian pattern of ethnic nationalism is firmly entrenched in Irish politics from *The Nation* and the mid-century onwards. Gavan Duffy cited as the guiding principle of Young Ireland a line of reasoning which reflects this new ideology very clearly.

> When a people have the boundaries and history, the separate character and physical resources, and still more, when they have the virtue and genius, of a nation, they are bound in conscience, in prudence, and in wisdom, to assert their individuality no matter how conciliation may lure or armies threaten.[42]

The emphasis on linguistic particularism is an outstanding index. Thus, the magazine *The Celt*, which was published by the Celtic Union in 1857–1858, not only carried appreciative articles on the sanguinary German nationalist poet Körner, and discussed Irish-English politics in the racial terms of 'Celt' and 'Saxon', but also has things like this to say about 'Our national language':

> The merest tyro in politics percieves the importance of language to a nation. [. . .] language alone traces the geographical limits of Italy, and is the only preservative of German unity [. . .] In our own time Greece has received independence solely from the literary interest which invested every mountain and valley and rivulet of that classic land. With these facts before us it is strange that we have so long neglected the cultivation of our national tongue. [. . .] To sing to a free people the glories of our old race, whose pride is prouder than Guelph of Ghibelline; – to lisp in the language of Tyre and Sidon, as Tasso did in the language of Pisa and Genoa – to accomplish for Ireland what Dante accomplished for Italy, what Goethe accomplished for Germany [. . .] is a destiny greater than the destiny of Homer, or Virgil, or Milton, and which none but one greater than any of these may be called on to fulfil. And it shall be fulfilled, – so sure as the fragments of that race shall gather to their native soil to build up a young nation from their old traditions [. . .][43]

Such sentiments were to characterize the final wave of ethnic nationalism leading up to 1916. William O'Brien was reported in *Irishleabhar na Gaedhilge/Gaelic Journal* as having given the following political speech in Cork in 1892:

> [. . .] in the matter of languages as in the matter of nationalities there is a marked tendency in our time to cherish those distinguishing characteristics of blood, of language and tradition which constitute the individuality and stimulate the genius of nationalities, and which are to nations what domestic life is to individuals (*applause*). [. . .] lost were the nation which should forget that the sacred passion of nationality, which is the driving force and vital breath of all our struggles, [. . .] has its origin deep in the recesses of the past, among the old associations of which the Gaelic language is the very living voice and soul (*cheers*). [. . .] it should be necessary to brave the charge of tediousness to claim a kindly thought for that National language which is the oldest of our national possessions, and the inalienable title-deed to the individuality of our race (*cheers*).[44]

This may help to distinguish between Patriotism and nationalism. As the above quotations may illustrate, the nineteenth century witnessed an intensifying conflation between the concepts of nation and of race. The racial Celticism of the Irish literary revival, exemplified by writers like William Larminie, Alfred Nutt and Mrs Green, was prepared by publications like the Rev. J. O'Leary's *Ireland among the nations: or, the faults and virtues of the Irish compared with those of other races* (New York & Boston, 1874), by the Aryanism of Ulick Bourke and of Standish O'Grady in the 1870s, by the racial frame of thought of Matthew Arnold in the 1860s, and by the ethnic essentialism of publications like the above-quoted *The Celt* in the 1850s. Again, the point of incipience was doubtless *The Nation*, which, for all that it preached a national reconciliation between Saxon and Celt (witness Davis's poem of that title), nevertheless, by that very gesture, acknowledged the meaning-fulness of those ethnic categories.[45] When *The Nation's* trans-ethnic nationwide reconciliation ideal broke down in the late 1840s, the Catholic side of Irish nationalism had no reason to shun the self-appellation Celt or Gael. What F.S.L. Lyons calls the 'triumph of denominationalism' in Irish national politics[46] may also mark the triumph of ethnic essentialism. Such ethnic nationalism, in Ireland as much as in other European countries, had its unsavoury aspects. The *Gaelic Journal*, which in 1895 had become an official Gaelic League organ, carried an advertisement in March 1908 which testifies to a strong spirit of anti-semitism, as strong as anything that is exposed in the fictional scenes of *Ulysses*:

> Several Gaelic Leaguers have complained to us recently that they were informed we employ Jewish labour, we now offer the above [£50] to any person who can prove that we are not an exclusively Irish firm, with Irish capital, Irish manage-ment, and employing none but Irish labour.[47]

Unlike this later, ethnic nationalism, then, pre-Union Patriotism aspires towards heteronomy rather than autonomy, will tend towards a federal rather than a unitary state. Both Patriots and nationalists derive the government's mandate ultimately from the volition or consent of the people at large, but Patriotism looks to a society consisting of the pragmatic association of individuals with common interests, whereas nationalism looks to a nation tied by the natural bonds of com-mon descent and a common cultural heritage. What the distinction ultimately boils down to is that nationalism sees the state as the embodiment of a pre-existing national individuality, which in turn gives a moral legitimacy to that state's existence. That idealistic aspect (the material institution of the state is founded on an abstract idea, that of the nation's individuality) is absent in Patriotism.

To draw up such a black-and-white contrast between Patriotism and national-ism is, of course, to polarize and to exaggerate the historical gradations and various shades of grey. Wolfe Tone was not a Hegelian idealist who derived Ireland's claim to independence from cultural arguments; though he did believe in Ireland's title to self-government as a *natural* right, and he did feel that all Irishmen should have a natural, shared and exclusive loyalty to their country.

But even though there was an ideological discongruity between Patriotism and nationalism, there was also a certain form of historical continuity. Whereas in other countries, Patriotism developed into liberalism, in Ireland it left a void that was filled, sometime between 1795 and 1840, by nationalism proper. Some tenets, slogans and types of rhetoric were handed on from Patriot into nationalist discourse, across the conceptual gap that separates the two. I have already mentioned two such discursive heirlooms in passing, which now deserve to be scrutinized a little more closely: the idea of a political mandate arising from the people at large, which would often be called the *nation*; and the idea of *love of the fatherland* as a political imperative.

Patriotism developed the ideology of a parliament's *national* mandate. Originally, the monarch's mandate was derived from dynastic or even divine charisma; what mandate could the Patriots oppose to that? The answer had been given, of course, by Locke. Human political society was based on a consensus of born equals who implicitly agreed to yield some private freedom for the sake of mutuality and social organization; who delegated power to authorities, but (and this is where Locke improved upon Hobbes) who nevertheless kept the fundamental right to accord or withhold their consent. Law-making was entrusted to an authority but subject always to the public benefit of the laws (the above-quoted fragment from Wagenaar echoes this point, as did Molyneux's *Case*, as did the Drapier's Letters), and laws were binding on the governed only insofar as they served the public interest and received public sanction.

Accordingly, it is the public, and the public benefit, which is invoked by Patriot thinkers as the mainspring of any political mandate. Van der Capellen brought the case for popular sovereignty before the *Volk van Nederland*; Palmer describes very well how the American Patriots came to voice their claims, and enact their decisions, in the name of 'We the People';[48] and he points out, in the French case, that the anti-court opposition of the mid-century *parlements* 'put a good deal of incipient revolutionary language into wide circulation: *citoyen, loi, patrie, constitution, nation, droit de la nation,* and *cri de la nation*' (1: 449).

It so happens that the name applied to this mandate-giving public was often, as in the above quotation, that of *nation*. But then again, the invocation of the nation by the Patriots should not be misunderstood in a latter-day nationalistic sense. The nation was not the mystic, supra-individual, organic whole that it became in the wake of Romanticism, in the sense of Young Ireland: a diachronic community with its own character, temperament or personality determining that nation's collective personality and historical horoscope. The concept of the nation in eighteenth-century usage, though it may occasionally invoke a subliminal idea of a shared history and descent, denotes primarily a political, economic, societal concept, the community of persons sharing the same government and the same capital (to recall Montesquieu's definition[49]), the citizenry of a state, society at large. The abbé Sieyès, in his influential tract *Qu'est-ce que le tiers état?* of 1789, even went as far as to state that the nation consisted exclusively of the Commoners, and that the nobility were an external parasite, battening on, but separate from, the nation's body politic.

Such notions of nationhood are societal and constitutional, and differ in emphasis from the meaning of ethnic individuality which terms like nation acquired in the later, nineteenth-century context. Yet, be that as it may, the term itself, in all its semantic variability, had been brought into currency in the Enlightenment and does provide a discursive link between Patriotism and nationalism.[50]

Something similar holds for the notion of *love of country* or *love of the fatherland*. That was to become a central slogan of nineteenth-century nationalism, and as a political argument it can be traced back to the Enlightenment Patriots. Yet again, under the surface of phraseological continuity, there are some important differences. To begin with, love of country was not something which had become the exclusive dogma of one particular political party. There was nothing specifically Patriotic about loving one's fatherland, except perhaps that the *amor patriae* of monarchists would focus more on the person and charisma of the king. But there was something equivocal about a possible cult of the fatherland. Wagenaar in 1747 may have felt that a true Patriot should care about the welfare of the Fatherland (cf. above, p. 17); but Shaftesbury voiced some reservations on that score. Shaftesbury's attitude to love of country has been aptly summarized by Franco Venturi:

> [Shaftesbury's Patriotism] is also opposed to that instinctive sense of love and attachment to one's native land. This was a passion of 'narrow minds', 'of a mere fungus or common excrescence to its parent-mould or nursing dunghill'. The new patriotism is cosmopolitan and indissolubly linked with freedom. It cannot be conceived, or at least would be absurd, without it. It cannot be felt except by those 'who really have a country and are the number of those who may be called a people, as enjoying the happiness of a real constitution and policy by which they are free and independent'. All kinds of absolute power deny and destroy the very base of true love of one's country. 'Absolute power annuls the publick, and where there is no publick, or constitution, there is in reality no mother country or nation [. . .] A multitude held together by force, tho' under one and the same head, is not properly united, nor does such a body make a people. 'Tis the social league, confederacy and mutual consent, founded in some common good or interest, which joins the members of a community, and makes a people one.' As we see, the word patriotism itself conveys, in terms of enthusiasm, passion and ethics, exactly the sense of equality and freedom of those who considered themselves the people and the nation in the ancient republics.[51]

But the very fact that Shaftesbury should feel the need to transcend a narrowly chauvinistic love of the fatherland implies the presence of such an affect. Indeed love of the fatherland is not a latter-day invention: we can encounter it in sources dating back as far as classical antiquity.[52] Yet what we should realize is that, from Roman times onwards, that instinct was considered a general human virtue which ideally was to be felt by everyone, regardless of their political stance and circumstance. Love of the fatherland, as a virtue, was as a-political and non-partisan as other virtues like honesty, charity, filial piety or marital fidelity. It is true, yet again, that Patriot thought made more of *virtue* (and, by implication, of the virtue of *amor patriae*) as a political quality; but it is equally true that non-Patriot and even anti-Patriot writers laid equal claims to those virtuous ideals.[53] In Holland, for instance, though there were many Patriots who waxed fulsome on the *Vaderland*, there were as many Orangists who displayed equal attachment to their native soil.[54]

Even in those cases where the Patriot discourse invoked love of the fatherland, we can see that it did so in terms which had nothing to do with national chauvinism. Johann Georg Zimmermann, a Swiss author of international repute, had in his widely-read essay *Of national pride*[55] warned that national pride was only virtuous to the extent that it was a form of philanthropy, of love of one's fellow-man. An exclusivist national pride, which denigrated or rejected the merits of other nations, was firmly ruled out. Love of country was, then, a general and non-exclusivist virtue with political implications, and was often cited in connection with the love of liberty. A telling example is the sermon given in 1788 by Richard Price, entitled *A discourse on the love of our country*, which famously incurred the criticism of Edmund Burke. Price is quick to point out that 'love of our country' should not be equalled to 'any conviction of the superior value of it to other countries, or any particular preference of its laws and constitution of government'.[56] The same Richard Price, who worked with a club called the London Revolution Society (the revolution being that of 1688, whose centenary Price's *Discourse* commemorated), worded an address of congratulation to the French National Assembly, which began with 'disdaining national partialities, and rejoicing in every triumph of liberty and justice over arbitrary power'.[57]

Neither the idea of the nation, nor that of love of the fatherland were, then, the specifically nationalist slogans they could later come to be. The bronze was there, and it rang; but nationalism had not yet arrived on the scene, like an occupying army, to commandeer those bells and recast them into cannons.[58]

The political invocation of the national past

The most important discursive link between the late eighteenth and early nineteenth centuries – and the one which provides, I think, the clearest indication of the ideological and cultural continuity and discontinuity between Irish Patriotism and Irish nationalism – is provided by the invocation of the national past.

The tendency can be observed throughout Europe: to deploy national ancestry myths for the purpose of political debate. In Holland, P.C. Hooft had, as early as 1610, invoked the origins of the ancient tribe of the Batavi (inhabitants of the Rhine estuary in Roman times) in order to inculcate a message of ancient liberty and virtue, thereby canonizing this tribe into ancestors. In England, the myth of the Anglo-Saxon tribes with their democratic liberties and assemblies of free men gave a racial-historical patina to the arguments of Whigs and commonwealthmen. The same pattern was followed in Germany, which came to invoke its Teutonic past, especially the successful anti-Roman resistance of Arminius (Hermann). After the Revolution, a Gaulish ancestry myth was to play a similar role in the French historical consciousness. As a result, the city squares and historical *lieux de mémoire* of Europe are now peppered with statues to national heroes who resisted the Roman legions: Queen Boadicea on Westminster Bridge, Vercingetorix in Clermont-Ferrand and elsewhere in France, the *Hermannsdenkmal* or Arminian Monument in the Teutoburg Forest, and the Eburonian chief Ambiorix in Tongeren (Belgium). Indeed, at least three republics set up under the shadow of the French Revolution adopted a name which harked back to such ancient national tribes mentioned in Caesar or Tacitus: the Batavian Republic in what had been the United Provinces, the Belgian Federation in what had been the Austrian Netherlands and the Prince-Bishopric of Liège, and the Helvetian Republic in what had been the Swiss *Eidgenossenschaft* (named after the Batavi, the Belgae and the Helvetii, respectively).[59]

Similarly, there was an increasing, albeit more equivocal tendency among Anglo-Irish Patriots to invoke a nationally *Gaelic* ancestry myth. The adoption of a Gaelic past was a complex process winding its slow and sometimes contradictory course through the entire eighteenth century.[60] Originally, for men like Molyneux and Swift, the past was that of the English-style parliaments established by the English crown for the English conquerors in Ireland; an eminent historian of the Enlightenment like Venturi can fruitfully discuss Molesworth and Toland in an English context, without bothering with their Irish background; early eighteenth-century Ascendancy men continuously clamoured for English sympathy on the basis of their loyalty to England; and the Anglo-Irish attitude towards Gaelic (Catholic) Ireland was one of fear and loathing.

But the Anglo-Irish invocation of their English connections got the Patriots nowhere. It did not stop the Woollen Act against which Molyneux stated his *Case of Ireland*; it did not stop the Declaratory Act against which Toland wrote his *Reasons offer'd to the honourable House of Commons*. Indeed, this is understandable; for there was a contradiction, a dilemma at the heart of the stance of early eighteenth-century Patriots like Molyneux. In a way, the Anglo-Irish Patriots tried to have their cake and eat it: for although they took care to dissociate themselves from the disloyalty of the Gaelic Irish and Old English, and stressed their English origins and English commitment, they yet associated themselves with the political institutions which the English had set up in Ireland in earlier times – and which had, in the sixteenth and seventeenth centuries, become the constitutional base from where English supremacy had been challenged. Whilst the early Patriots invoked their Englishness and their roots in the Whig revolution of 1688, they also invoked an Irish jurisprudence, a set of political arguments, institutions and claims, which had their roots in the Confederation of Kilkenny and the Jacobite parliament.[61] Thus, for their arguments on their position in the British constitution, the Anglo-Irish Patriots had to look back to the constitutionally murkier parts of Irish history – and, what is more, to a pre-Williamite Irish history which they called foreign to themselves.

In the course of the eighteenth century, the nationally Irish past presented itself with ever more cogency as that of the Anglo-Irish, too. The history of the country of Ireland came to be adopted as the history of that country's most recent settlers, leading ultimately, to the Anglo-Irish acceptance of a Gaelic past. The Gaelic past had been studied as an alien, exotic culture, made suspect by the hysterical remembrance of the 1641 rebellion and of the reign of James II, as well as by the contemporary squalor of Gaelic Ireland; but it gradually developed towards a national Gaelic iconography which was retroactively invested with Patriot ideals.

That process took place, not in the field of political discourse, but in that of antiquarianism, philology and literature. The Gaelic past had little to offer, either by way of anti-Roman resistance or in the way of a historical tradition of parliamentarism, on which the Patriots could draw; unlike the Gaulish, Gothic and Batavian past, the struggle for freedom of the ancient Gaels had been against those English-based oppressors who had introduced the institution of Parliament in Ireland. But it could happen that the Gaelic past was invested with lofty ideals of a Patriot hue, that the image of Old, Gaelic Ireland could be ameliorated by instilling into it contemporary, Patriot virtues.

The process can be traced in a number of textual traditions: the philological and antiquarian for instance, from Vallancey to Joseph Cooper Walker and Theophilus O'Flanagan, who all drew on historical and linguistic evidence to construct an image of a refined, literature and civilized culture of virtuous kings advised by venerable councillors and revered poets.[62] The idea that Ireland's past was a Gaelic past, that the Gaelic tradition lay at the root and the core of Ireland's historical development, gained currency in a Patriot climate. How that invocation of a nationally Gaelic past changed with the Union can be traced by turning from political to cultural developments.

The literary invocation of Irish identity before the Union

The advent of romanticism and the ideological change from Patriotism to nationalism can nowhere be better traced than in literary texts. In order to trace that development, a few preliminary qualifications must be made.

According to traditional periodization, eighteenth-century Anglo-Irish literature is a merely bio-bibliographical category, a part of English literature written by authors born or resident in Ireland, but undistinguishable in outlook or substance from mainstream English literature. Goldsmith and Swift may have been Irish, the latter may even have penned strenuously anti-English political discourse – but their literary texts, their Gullivers and Vicars of Wakefield, are as much part of English literature as Tom Jones and Clarissa Harlowe. According to traditional periodization, again, it is only after the Union that Anglo-Irish literature becomes recognizably Irish in its contents; it begins, especially in the newly-introduced genre of the novel, to display a conscious regionalism, begins to address Irish topics, begins to draw on an Irish local colour.

I want to suggest that this periodization, though not without a certain overall validity, is based on a partial and simplified view of the literary sources and their concerns.

The distinction between pre-1800 and post-1800 writing can be overemphasized because we ourselves apply distortive criteria to these two periods. There is, to begin with, a tendency to see late-eighteenth-century writing in terms of an anachronistic notion of literature, deeply influenced by the poetics of Romanticism; moreover, we employ fuzzy and changeable criteria when we distinguish Anglo-Irish writing from English-language writing at large. Between them, these two factors can obscure from our view that a thriving and specifically Irish culture of *belles lettres* flourished in late eighteenth-century Dublin.

Historical and antiquarian works were published with lists of subscribers that usually included Patriot public figures and were often dedicated to such Patriots. The authors of such works were, in reviews or elsewhere, praised for their intellectual exertions on behalf of the fatherland's reputation and civility; there were magazines like the *Anthologia Hibernica*. Even before *Castle Rackrent* and well before the Union, there was such a thing as a distinct Anglo-Irish literature. We would have to look for it in the corpus of largely forgotten or neglected texts. Most of these would be ephemeral poems on topical occasions, in indifferent heroic couplets or hackneyed blank verse; but there are more interesting productions,[63] some of them overlooked even by the *Field Day anthology*;[64] and it is to these that I now turn. In particular, I want to draw attention to two historical, Irish plays from the years 1773 and 1774.[65]

Gorges Howard's *The siege of Tamor* (1773) and Francis Dobbs's *The Patriot king; or, Irish chief* (1774) represent a struggle for liberty and independence and are set in the wars of the Gaelic kings against the Danes. What is more, that struggle is presented as a nationally Irish one, where the Gaelic clans become representatives of Ireland as a whole – a typical example of the appropriation of a national Irish, Gaelic-rooted past, which, in a Patriot climate, was undertaken by the urban, English-speaking theatre audiences of Dublin. The urban, Anglo-Irish audience is made to sympathize and even to identify with the cause of the Irish Gaels against the foreigners.[66] Indeed, the cause of the Gaelic freedom fighters is delivered with the rhetoric of Grattanite Patriotism (liberty, national reconciliation, democracy); a discursive, phraseological bond is thus created between the pursuits of national liberty by the medieval Gaels and by the Enlightenment Anglo-Irish Patriots. A title like Dobbs's *The Patriot king, or Irish chief* is significant in itself, as are lofty Grattanite speeches in that play, like the one where King Ceallachan refuses to 'resign / A loyal nation to tyrannic sway', and invokes

> the flame of patriot fire
> Whose purifying blaze ennobles man,
> And banishes each base, each selfish thought,
> Far from the breast wherein it deigns to dwell [. . .]

Howard's *The Siege of Tamor* is even more specific in establishing a filiation between the Gaelic cause and Anglo-Irish Patriotism. His king of Dublin indirectly exhorts his future progeny (that is: the audience, the gallery which is being played to) in terms like these:

> O! may th'almighty arm at once o'erwhelm
> This spacious isle beneath the circling main,
> Its name and its memorial quite efface,
> And sink it from the annals of the world,
> Ere the last remnant of her free-born sons
> Stretch forth their willing necks to vile subjection!

Again, the play's Prologue uses a significant first person when it denounces the destruction of Gaelic literature 'While gothic fires attack'd us as their prey'. Obviously the identification value is pro-Gaelic even to the point of disavowing the English (aye, gothic) roots of the Anglo-Irish population. Accordingly the audience is exhorted to identify affectively with Gaelic Ireland, as follows:

> O Shame! not now to feel, not now to melt
> At woes, that whilom your fam'd country felt;
> Let your swol'n breasts, with kindred ardours glow!
> Let your swol'n eyes, with kindred passion flow!

Small wonder that a play like Dobbs's *Patriot king* never even made it onto the London boards: it was rejected by Covent Garden and by Drury Lane before it was performed at Dublin's Smock Alley theatre.

We may sum this up as follows: by Irish authors, on Irish themes, for an Irish audience, with Irish sympathies. Even when Charlotte Brooke, in her *Reliques of Irish poetry* (1789), aims to present old Gaelic literature to an exoteric audience, she does so in a discourse that is primarily intra-Irish, employing (again) that tell-tale first person plural for an Irish readership. The English readership is addressed only at one remove, in the third person:

> As yet, we are too little known to our noble neighbour of Britain; were we better acquainted, we should be better friends. The British muse is not yet informed that she has an elder sister in this isle; let us introduce them to each other! [. . .] Let them [the joint muses, JL] entreat of Britain to cultivate a nearer acquaintance with her neighbouring isle. Let them conciliate for us her esteem, and her affection will follow of course. Let them tell her, that the portion of her blood, which flows in our veins is rather ennobled than disgraced by the mingling tides that descended from our heroic ancestors.

Brooke does, it is true, allow for the possibility that her translations may be read by a British audience, and indeed she evinces a hope that they may thereby contribute to better Anglo-Irish relations; and a similar concern will be encountered with early nineteenth-century novelists. But unlike her nineteenth-century successors (who, as we shall see in the next chapter, aimed to explain their country, Ireland, to an English readership) Brooke's intended readership is obviously Irish. The *Reliques* only address a possible British audience indirectly; in the first instance, they constitute an Irish text aimed by an Irish author at a target audience of fellow-Irishmen. This is subliminally expressed through her blood and ancestry metaphor, and particularly through the personal pronouns therein. Some of the blood in the above-quoted veins may be third-person English – but the veins themselves, and the ancestors, are first-person Irish. Brooke's bold self-assurance in adopting and addressing an Irish position in this polarity is remarkable. It ties in with another noteworthy characteristic in the quoted passage: for her idea of bringing Gaelic culture, in the second instance, before a British audience is based on a sense of equality and reciprocity. She does not merely represent one passive, silent party to another, active one, but aims to introduce the two 'to each other', looking forward to the mutuality of an acquaintance between the two.

All this was to become very different after the Union; and it is to post-Union developments that we must now turn.

THE BURDEN OF THE PAST:
Romantic Ireland and Prose Fiction

The literary invocation of Irish identity after the Union

There is a general consensus in Anglo-Irish studies that regional Irish fiction of the early nineteenth century is directed towards an exoteric readership, an English audience to whom Ireland is an exotic place, a foreign country. Numerous authors from the period, beginning with Maria Edgeworth, testify to that English orientation in the *destinataire* (the intended, targeted audience) of much Anglo-Irish fiction, and Thomas Flanagan, almost forty years ago, already observed astutely that the concerns of Anglo-Irish literature were 'usually couched in the language of explanation'; Flanagan quotes *Castle Rackrent* to telling effect when he continues:

> That is to say, most of the Irish novels were addressed to an English audience, and most of them offered to explain and interpret the sister kingdom. The supposed 'editor' of the history of *Castle Rackrent* places his story 'before the English reader as a specimen of manners and characters, which are perhaps unknown in England. Indeed, the domestic habits of no nation in Europe were less known to the English than those of their sister country, till within these last few years.' Nor is this novel an exception [. . .][1]

Small wonder if, as Flanagan notes elsewhere, 'Irish novels were invariably reviewed by British journals on the assumption that they had been written to please English taste or to shape English opinion' (39). Indeed, Flanagan might have adduced statements similar to that from *Castle Rackrent* from other authors. Charles Maturin, in the preface to his *The wild Irish boy* (1808), announces that 'This novel from its title purports to give some account of a country little known' (1: 5); Mrs Hall, in her description of Ireland, expresses a hope that the Irish character may be 'more justly apprehended, more rightly estimated, and more respected in England'[2] and a further list of examples would only furnish additional verification. The pattern is almost universally present in the Anglo-Irish discourse of the century's early decades: a bias towards an exoteric (in this case: English, non-Irish) audience, a readership of foreigners.

Most scholars since Flanagan have contented themselves with merely registering the non-Irishness of the intended readership; few have attempted to explain it – beyond the fact that it probably has something to do with the Act of Union, Ireland's lost nationhood, or some other such general comment. Alternatively, one might be tempted to invoke the auspices of Sir Walter Scott or the romantic movement in general, and explain it as a generally current interest in picturesque and distant places and lifestyles, cashing in on the international vogue of exoticism.

Such explanations are plausible and useful, and I shall argue these matters at greater length below. To begin with, however, we should take into account that there did exist, as we have just seen, a consciously Irish literature before the Union, and that it was characterized by a striking absence of any exoteric bias. Did the romantic movement only hit Ireland after the passing of the Union? Surely not – for one thing, Maria Edgeworth is as un-romantic an author as Jane Austen, whereas Charlotte Brooke and Gorges Howard are as romantic as Gray or Macpherson; furthermore, there are many links and continuities across the centennial divide, between the novelists and poets of the early nineteenth century and their eighteenth-century precursors; and the main activity of authors like Edgeworth, Morgan and Maturin antedates the publication of Scott's first novel.

It seems necessary, then, to take a closer look at the relationship between the Anglo-Irish author and the Irish *couleur locale*.

What I find striking is not just Flanagan's point that the authors' target audience should be English; after all, although the London scene refused playwrights like Howard and Dobbs, eighteenth-century antiquarians like Charles O'Conor and Sylvester O'Halloran (important sources for later Anglo-Irish fiction) had already tended to write against English prejudice and English misrepresentation, working towards an amelioration of the Irish image in England. We have seen a similar concern in the quoted passage from Brooke's *Reliques*.

Rather, I find it at least equally remarkable that (unlike O'Conor and O'Halloran; unlike Charlotte Brooke and Gorges Howard) the *representandum*, Ireland, should now be described in the third person rather than in the first. Schematically, one may put it as follows:

	authors	primary target audience	subject-matter
pre-1800	Irish	Irish	we-the-Irish
post-1800	Irish	English	they-the-Irish

What we see here is a paradoxical dissociation of the Irish author from his/her Irish subject-matter. The destinatory vector towards an English audience is so strong that the author no longer identifies with the country which is represented, but becomes an intermediary, an exteriorized, detached observer. A similar exteriority of representation has been pointed out by Edward Said in his well-known book *Orientalism*, which for its motto invokes Marx's dictum, 'They must be represented, they cannot represent themselves', in order to describe how the garrulous discourse of representation interposes itself between the curious reader and the silent (silenced) subdued/passive Orient. Similarly,

Ireland as a *representandum*, as subject-matter, does not speak in its own voice but is spoken for; the author speaks, not as an Irish person, but as an intermediary on behalf of Irish people, adopts a (puportedly neutral) mid-way point between readership (English) and topic (Irish). That was the position taken up by Mrs Hall, who, as we have seen, gave a description of Irish character so as to render it 'more justly appreciated, more rightly estimated, and more properly respected in England' – and who, concomitantly, places herself at a stand-offish, third-person distance from her subject-matter. Her book becomes a type of 'The Irish peasantry: a user's manual'.

> [. . .] no good will ever be effected by flying into the face of their [the Irish's] prejudices; they are a people that must be led, not driven. Preconceived ideas cannot be hammered out of their heads – but they may be directed to other objects; though you cannot stop the source of a river, you may turn its course.[3]

Auto-exoticism: the strangeness of Ireland

A number of stylistic features of post-Union Anglo-Irish fiction reflect precisely this point. The auctorial voice in these novels, or the focalizer (i.e., the character through whose eyes scenes are represented, with whose perspective the narrative identifies) is almost invariably non-Irish, tracing an approach *towards* Ireland from outside (rather than describing Ireland from within). Examples to this effect abound; let me mention a few, taken predominantly from the most romantic authors of that generation, Lady Morgan and Charles Maturin.

In Lady Morgan's *The wild Irish girl* (which I shall scrutinize in greater detail below) the first-person narrator and sole focalizer of the story is English; he approaches Ireland as a strange, uncouth country in a direction that takes him from the familiarity of his domestic English background to the increasing exoticism of the West of Ireland. The novel's title page adopts, by way of a motto, a characterization of Ireland as seen by a non-contemporary non-Irishman, a fourteenth-century Italian traveller (much as the motto to Maturin's *The wild Irish boy* is taken from Spenser's *View of the state of Ireland*). Similarly, an Ireland-bound but England-based vector governs Morgan's novel *O'Donnel*, where the storyline and focalization are tethered to the English characters of Lady Singleton and her circle, and the main Irish hero is represented as an exotic stranger in their midst. Again, Maturin's novel *The Milesian chief* (1812) uses a non-Irish focalizer, Armida, to whom Ireland is a foreign place:

> To Armida, accustomed only to the sunny regions of Italy, or the cultivated fields of England, the effect of such a scene [the west coast, JL] was like that of a new world. She shuddered at the idea of becoming the inhabitant of such a country; and she thought she felt already the wild transforming effects of its scenery (1: 55).

Morgan's other 'national tales', *Florence MacCarthy* and *The O'Briens and the O'Flahertys*; Banim's *The Anglo-Irish of the nineteenth century*; Lever's *The*

O'Donoghue; Lover's *Rory O'More*; one could go on and on. It is almost *de rigueur* for an Anglo-Irish novel from this period to have, for its hero, narrator or focalizer, a cosmopolitan, non-Irish (usually English) character, whose progress westward, towards an acquaintance with Ireland, provides the main basis for plot and incident. In Barry Sloan's words, 'bringing a sophisticated, reluctant and bored stranger into a romantic Irish setting and then permitting a love affair with a native to develop' is a 'formula'.[4] I would add to this that the formula obviously reflects the book's intended effect on the English reader – who is 'sophisticated, bored and reluctant' concerning Irish matters, the reader whom the novel hopes to convert, indeed to seduce, into a more appreciative attitude. Thus, the perspective of this type of regionalism is always a perspective *on* Ireland *from outside*; no matter how sympathetic that perspective may be, no matter how much the propagandistic intent of the novel may be to create a positive understanding for Ireland, Ireland is a passive object of representation.

It is only within the metropolitan frame of reference provided by a non-Irish protagonist that the author can introduce Irish characters who explain their native culture and history from within, as their own heritage. Besides the many incidental and often nameless 'extras' who fill the exoticist pages with minor brogue-ridden interludes and anecdotal sketches of local colour, more prominent 'real' Irish characters would include the Prince of Inismore in *The wild Irish girl*; the abbé O'Donnel, uncle to the title hero of *O'Donnel*; Connal O'Morven's grandfather in Maturin's *The Milesian chief*; De Lacy in his *The wild Irish boy*; Count O'Halloran in Edgeworth's *The absentee* and King Corny in her *Ormond*. What is striking is that even they are never the focalizers in the story. Indeed, they are generally marginal to the central action, an Ulterior Ireland dimly glimpsed at one remove. They are rarely the Irish characters with whom the central characters deal directly; rather, they are friends of friends, acquaintances of the hero's Irish contacts. In other words, there is always a buffer of mediating Irishness between the English point of view and such typical, 'real' Irishmen as may voice an authentic, unmitigated Irish outlook. This buffering character mediates between Irish exoticism and English domesticity.

The degree of Irish exoticism or English domesticity in this mediating character may vary, but often the most central Irish character is de-Irishized to a large extent. It may be said of the Irish hero of Maturin's *The wild Irish boy*, Ormsby Bethel, that he is neither particularly wild nor particularly Irish. Something similar holds for the eponymous hero of *O'Donnel*; as Flanagan points out, 'his "foreign" and "Irish" airs are visible only to Lord Glentworth and his creator. To the reader, he seems a solemnly intended caricature of an English gentleman, whom the inscrutable gods have chosen to disguise as an alien'.[5] Glorvina in *The wild Irish girl* is exceptional in her heightened nationality – but then again it should be pointed out that the role of mediation is not so much performed by her as by the first-person narrator, Horatio, who stands between the Real Ireland and his private English audience: for the novel is, after all, in the form of letters written by Horatio to a friend in England.

Thus the narrative of romantic Anglo-Irish fiction will tend to marginalize its most Irish characters. A variety of narrative and stylistic devices converge into this tendency: the actorial configuration of the story's characters, the tendency to employ footnotes and digressions in order to represent a 'real Irish' local or historical background, and (what may be most relevant for the present purpose) a tendency towards a spatial arrangement which marginalizes and quarantines the Real Ireland: Real Irish characters exist only in the furthest corners of the country, often in spots that are inaccessible and somehow separate from the normal world. They live in remote glens, on islands in lakes, on the shore or even off-shore, in crumbling ruins that are leftovers from the past, almost as if they do not really belong to the same time-scale as the other characters. Anachronisms are frequent when they are described: they continue a lifestyle, not of the previous or even pre-previous generation, but something quite archaic. Morgan's Prince of Inismore, that walking antiquity from a dozen different periods in Irish history, is a case in point.

The typical plot movement in romantic Anglo-Irish fiction is that of a cosmopolitan character moving towards Ireland; but that authentic Ireland is mostly encountered through intermediaries, by hearsay, at one remove. The ontological remoteness, the liminal shadow-existence of an ideal, true Ireland means that the westward progress towards Ireland will never really culminate in an arrival; it will be like one of Zeno's paradoxes, where A never gets to B, because one must first get towards the mid-way point between A and B, or rather: first to the half-way mark between A and the mid-way point. Two inferences remain to be made. First: if there is an ineluctable, impassable mid-way point between the English point of view and the ultimate *representandum*, the Real Ireland, then that mid-way point is taken up by the representation itself: the text, which, as we have seen, purposefully exteriorizes itself from Ireland in order to mediate, to represent. Like an importunate tourist guide, the text says 'Ireland is there; I am here to show it to you.' The self-consciousness of the description (which devotes a good deal of space and attention to establishing its own credentials) interposes itself between reader and subject-matter, hides Ireland from view, indeed pushes it beyond the horizon. In this manner (and that is my second inference) Ireland is *made exotic* by the selfsame descriptions which purport to represent or explain Ireland. Ironically, it is the Irish author who is responsible for the fancy exoticism of the Princes of Inismore and Counts O'Halloran, in a constant play where the request, 'see how interesting Ireland is, how deserving of your attention', shifts into 'see how unusual Ireland is, how strange, how exotic'. That is the direct consequence of a regional literature which tries to establish its discreteness, its regionalism *vis-à-vis* an exoteric readership by means of local colour. It is in this aspect also that nineteenth-century (romantic) Anglo-Irish fiction distinguishes itself radically from eighteenth-century (Patriot) literary practice.

I have called this procedure one of *auto-exoticism*, a mode of seeing, presenting and representing oneself in one's otherness (in this case: one's non-

Englishness). This auto-exoticism is, I contend, essentially post-Union, marking a sensible difference between eighteenth- and nineteenth-century discursive practice, marking a real shift in the articulation of an Irish cultural identity. It is perhaps the most important heritage which romantic Anglo-Irish fiction has bequeathed to subsequent Ireland-related discourse, which, whatever its cognitive or political paradigm, from Romanticism to Postmodernism, has consistently seen Ireland primarily in terms of an anomaly, a riddle, a question, a mystery: something to be explained, an *explicandum*. The heritage of auto-exoticism (what Stephen Dedalus, quoting Burns, called 'To see ourselves as others see us') is still with us, from tourist brochures to postmodern scholarly or journalistic discourse. If, in Wittgenstein's serenely commonsensical words, the world is all that is the case, then auto-exoticist Ireland coquettishly begs to be excused. As Eileen Kane wryly puts it, 'Ordinariness is not distinctive';[6] and accordingly, Ireland is all that is the question; Ireland, if it is to exist at all, must exist *sui generis*, distinctively, un-ordinarily.

The heritage of auto-exoticism is noticeable in three important discursive commonplaces which can be traced back directly to romantic fiction. The first of these may be mentioned merely in passing: the extraordinary preoccupation, still noticeable in today's media and public life, with self-analysis. To a non-Irish observer like myself, it is quite remarkable how much speculative energy and zest is invested, by journalists from Gay Byrne and Gerry Ryan to Fintan O'Toole and John Waters, in discussions of national psychology, in finding collective-emotional explanations for social phenomena, in the question 'why do we Irish behave in such-and-such a manner?'.[7] The other two manifestations of auto-exoticism will figure more prominently in the following pages. One is the constant automatism of explaining Ireland in terms of its past, as if the Real Ireland is somehow unfinished business from bygone ages, or has a privileged relation with a past that here is more immediate than elsewhere; the other lies in the tacit but by no means self-evident presupposition that Ireland is most itself in those aspects wherein it is most un-cosmopolitan, most unlike other nations.

Romance and novel

The main literary repercussion of the collapse of Patriotism in Ireland was, then, the auto-exoticist reflex. To put it crudely: Ireland, if it cannot be a nation in its own right and is reduced to a province, is increasingly described in the discourse of marginality and in terms of its being different or picturesque. The implied audience for Irish literature is English rather than Irish, and the choice of an Irish setting shifts increasingly to the wilder, more peripheral and distant parts of the country. Paradoxically, the most peripheral areas of Ireland are canonized as the most representative and characteristic ones.

However, it would be overly simplistic to trace this process solely as a result of the failure of Irish parliamentary emancipation. An important added factor was the development of the novel: a genre which was adopted by Irish authors under the very shadow of the Union and in the climate of Romanticism. It seems in order, therefore, to see how the change in a political/ideological climate played into the development of the new genre and its conventions.

In 1824, Sir Walter Scott contributed an essay on 'Romance' to the fifth edition of the *Encyclopaedia Britannica*, in which he attempted to make a generic/typological distinction between the two popular forms of prose fiction: the Romance (which would, we may assume, include its Gothic subgenre represented by names like Ann Radcliffe and 'Monk' Lewis) and the Novel (represented by names like Richardson and Burney). Scott pointed out that romance (with its roots reaching back to the chivalric tales of the Middle Ages) relied on colourful incident to the point of disregarding the dictates of plausibility. Following Dr Johnson's Dictionary, he defined the romance in terms of its 'wild adventure'. Plot consistency and realistic recognition value are secondary considerations in the genre of the romance; in contrast, the novel deals with the more ordinary course of human events: it is more sedate in the incidents it relates, describes tea parties rather than dungeons and dragons, and represents a world which lies closer to the reader's own experience. In Scott's own words:

> We would be rather inclined to describe a *Romance* as 'a fictitious narrative in prose or verse; the interest of which turns upon marvellous and uncommon incidents;' being thus opposed to the kindred form of the *Novel*, which [. . .] we would rather define as 'a fictitious narrative, differing from the romance, because the events are accommodated to the ordinary train of human events, and the modern state of society.'[8]

The difference between novel and romance, then, lies in the notion of *vraisemblance*. Unlike romantic fiction, the novel is read under the proviso of its plausibility, its being true to life – more precisely, true to 'life as we know it', true to the conventionally established mode of representing life.

But this generic border also, unavoidably, created borderline cases; indeed, some remarkable instances in Scott's own prose fiction testify to that effect. The Waverley Novels as a whole are called just that, 'novels'. Yet *Ivanhoe* is called 'A Romance' in its subtitle, *Quentin Durward* ditto in the opening words of its 1831 preface; and most of the other titles are given the guardedly neutral name of 'Tales'. The most interesting case is that of *Waverley*, with its ambiguous preface and the equally ambiguous reference in the 1829 preface to *Guy Mannering*, which mentions 'The Novel or Romance of *Waverley*'. The distinction Romance/Novel is not wholly unproblematic and draws a conceptual divide across then existing fictional practice. Although most contemporary prose fiction fits effortlessly into either of the two categories, the early novel in Ireland appears uncomfortably hybrid if viewed against the background of this genre distinction.

Lady Morgan's *The wild Irish girl* (1806) and her *O'Donnel* (1814), and Charles Robert Maturin's *The wild Irish boy* (1808) and his *The Milesian chief* (1812) appeared before Scott's own Waverley Novels, which they anticipate in some respects. The question thus poses itself: what type of fiction were Morgan and Maturin trying to write, and to which extent do their tales reflect a tension between the poetics of the prose Romance or the poetics of the Novel?

Of course, the distinction between Romance and Novel was not wholly of Scott's making. Scott invoked Dr Johnson's Dictionary (as he might also have invoked the more famous generic distinction made in *The Rambler*, no. 4, 31 March 1750), and did not so much invent these generic divisions as that he succinctly and successfully formulated them.[9] The two Irish authors share with Scott the same set of audience expectations and the same literary-historical circumstances. More importantly, Morgan's and Maturin's Irish tales share an important characteristic with some Scottish tales of Scott himself as regards their choice of setting: the local background can invoke a polarity between an 'English' and a 'Gaelic' part of the country: Highlands versus Lowlands in Scotland, Catholic Gaels versus Protestant Ascendancy in Ireland. What is more, that division seems to have led to parallel modes of representation.

In the opening decades of the nineteenth century, the most pronounced literary connotation of a Gaelic setting was Ossianic. After Macpherson's fraudulently fabricated pseudo-translations in the 1760s, Ossian had profoundly influenced the current image of Gaeldom. Described in the ponderous and sublime diction of prose-poems, Macpherson's Ossian evoked mountains, dark and stormy nights, tragic heroes and hoary sages sadly strumming the harp – in short, an iconography evoking (to use Burke's aesthetic distinction) sublimity rather than beauty, and harking back to medieval Romance as well as foreshadowing the onset of Romanticism.

The sublime/Romantic register is reserved, both by Scott and by his Irish counterparts, for their Gaelic settings. However, it must be said that Scott drew his local Scottish colour but rarely from the Highlands – *Waverley* and *Rob Roy* being the most notable examples. In *Waverley*, for instance, the Scottish Highlands are the setting for a Romantic interlude where Flora MacIvor sings an old Scottish ballad for Waverley, accompanying herself on the harp. That song is itself overtly reminiscent of Ossian ('There is mist on the mountains, and night on the vale, / But more dark is the sleep of the Sons of the Gael!'), and so is the setting: the waterfall is called 'romantic' set in a 'sylvan amphitheatre' described as 'the land of romance'. Also, Waverley himself is likened to 'a knight of romance,' and Flora is 'like a fair enchantress of Boiardo and Ariosto'. The narrative, in short, has moved from a novelistic to a romantic register, which is underscored by the words with which Flora introduces her performance:

> To speak in the poetical language of my country, the seat of the Celtic Muse is in the mist of the secret and solitary hill, and her voice in the murmur of the mountain stream. He who woos her must love the barren rock more than the fertile valley, and the solitude of the desert better than the festivity of the hall.[10]

We may safely translate this into generic terms: the Romance is the genre of the mist of the secret and solitary hill, of the mountain stream, of the barren rock, of solitude and the desert; the novel is, rather, the genre of the fertile valley and of the festivity of the hall. In fact, Scott's own description of Flora's performance near the waterfall was considered, by contemporaries, a breach of novelistic plausibility and an indulgence in picturesque romance-kitsch. Maria Edgeworth made this comment on the scene:

> in the first visit to Flora, when she is to sing certain verses, there is a walk, in which the description of the place is beautiful, but *too long*, and we did not like the preparation of *a scene* – the appearance of Flora and her harp was too like a common heroine, she should be far above all stage effect or novelist's trick.[11]

Such a sublime/Romantic register also tends to be used when Morgan and Maturin describe Gaelic Ireland. The most striking instance to this effect is found in the trail-blazer for this type of setting, *The wild Irish girl*. Here, as in Scott's *Waverley* (which it predates by eight years), the hero moves from a more-or-less mundane background into an uncouth region beyond the pale of civilization, where he becomes involved in what Dr Johnson would have called 'wild adventure': young Henry Mortimer, splenetic English socialite, winds up in the west of Ireland where he expiates his gambling debts. Close to his family's Irish estate he finds a crumbling Gothic castle still tenanted by one of the old Gaelic nobility, the Prince of Inismore, who like Ossian is a living fossil of the bygone greatness of Gaeldom, bewailing the fading of its ancient glory. This prince, however, has a beautiful and intelligent daughter, Glorvina, whose manifold accomplishments change Mortimer's *ennui* into romantic infatuation; and so the tale moves, through the meanderings of improbable incident and extensive descriptions of local colour, towards a happy marriage. I shall pay more specific attention to *The wild Irish girl* further on. For the moment, it may suffice to point out (a) that to locate the main body of the story between the initial meeting and the final understanding of the amorous protagonists tends, in Mikhail Bakhtin's analysis of the pre-realist novel, to situate the incidents in a suspended time-enclave (which Bakhtin calls a 'chronotope': a separate, non-Newtonian 'in-between' time, or, in Bakhtin's terminology, 'adventure time');[12] and (b) that *The wild Irish girl* and *Waverley* both revolve around a cultural-cum-political polarity mapped onto the boy-meets-girl storyline. In *Waverley*, beautiful Flora MacIvor is dedicated to the romantic but hopeless cause of the Pretender, and the love affair between Mortimer and Glorvina is fraught with difficulties because they represent inimical national camps: English settlers and ousted Gaels.

Indeed, even more so than in the case of Scotland, an Irish setting implies wild adventure, painful social divisions and political antagonisms. Although the more benevolent, paternalist Patriots had taken some initiatives towards the conciliation between the two Irelands, and Wolfe Tone had even based his entire ideology on the principle of national and nationwide solidarity, the 1798 rebellion had, if anything, widened the gulf between natives and settlers.[13]

Thus, when middle-class, urban, English-speaking Anglo-Irish authors began to use Ireland as a literary topic, they were dealing with an inherently ambiguous theme, riddled with antagonisms and burdened by the memory of recent civil war and by still-continuing agrarian unrest. Was Ireland the country of Anglo-Irish society, of the circles in which these novelists moved, the circles to which the novel, that most bourgeois of genres, inherently belongs – or was it the more exotic Other Ireland, with its more sublime scenery, its picturesque folkways and different, Gaelic culture, its fresh potential for interesting *couleur locale*?

Sublime scenery and high society

Irish fiction of the early century reflects this dilemma. Some tales, like *The wild Irish girl*, opt whole-heartedly for the register of the Romance; others, like Maria Edgeworth's 'Tales of Fashionable Life' (including *Ennui, The absentee*) are set in drawing-rooms of country houses and castles, and are as novelistic in plot as they are genteel in their setting, following, on the whole, a Burney/Austen mode. Those cases testify, then, to a split in the treatment of an Irish setting: the 'festivity of the hall' of upper-class Anglo-Ireland will be the setting for novelistic fictions, whereas misty hills and mountain streams are the domain of Gaelic Ireland and Romantic plots.

But the ambiguity of an Irish setting will necessarily manifest itself, and the political irreconcilability of Ireland's dividedness will pose itself as a generic dilemma to the author. Edgeworth's novels, though novels they essentially are, do contain echoes of a Romantic Gaelic Ireland: secondary characters like Count O'Halloran in *The absentee* and King Corny in *Ormond* add touches of local colour and intercultural tension which would have been unavailable in an English setting. Conversely, although the main body of Morgan's *The wild Irish girl* is Romance pure and simple, its hero's background (which is emphasized in the 'Introductory Letters') recalls the novelistic mode of upper-class England. Fanny Burney's novel *Evelina* or Ann Radcliffe's romance *Udolpho* are unambiguous in their settings: domestic and sedate in the one case, sublime and spine-tingling in the other. The heterogeneous Irish setting, be it deployed towards Romantic or novelistic ends, necessarily entails the uncomfortable proximity of the chosen genre's opposite number. The generic ambiguity for which Scott's *Waverley* was criticized in an isolated instance is all-pervasive and fundamental to Irish novels.

That this could be felt as a problematic dilemma between the contrary dictates of genre poetics is illustrated by two cases: Maturin's *The wild Irish boy* and Morgan's *O'Donnel*.

Maturin, now remembered chiefly for his *Melmoth the wanderer*, had already testified to his taste for Gothic romance with earlier work in fiction and drama;

and with *The wild Irish boy* (1808) he wanted to try his hand at something that was both Irish and a novel. However, he found that Irish local colour was irreconcilable with the novelistic genre, and stated as much in his preface:

> This novel from its title purports to give some account of a country little known. I lament I have not had time to say more of it; my heart was full of it, but I was compelled by the laws of this mode of composition to consult the pleasure of my readers, not my own. The fashionable materials for novel-writing I know to be, a lounge in Bond-street, a phaeton-tour in the Park, a masquerade with appropriate scenery, a birth-day or birth-night, with dresses and decorations, accurately copied from the newspapers. He who writes with an hope of being read, must write something like this.[14]

And something like this is what Maturin wrote – a novel of fashionable life. Despite its Morgan-derived title, the book is not at all 'Wild Irish'; almost all of the action is laid among the upper classes to which the hero belongs, and the only shadow of Gaelic Ireland is vested in the minor characters of the chieftain De Lacy and his chaplain, who are dealt with much like Edgeworth's Count O'Halloran and King Corny.

Morgan herself ran into similar problems when she followed up *The wild Irish girl* with her tale *O'Donnel* (1814). She began this book as an attempt at a fictional treatment of Irish historical materials, intending *O'Donnel* to be a historical novel set in the times of Red Hugh O'Donnell and the Elizabethan wars. However, Morgan found that the theme was too violent, too hot to handle, and like Maturin she stated her failure to deal with the topic in her preface; she 'found it necessary to forego [her] original plan,' because the violence of Irish history involved 'events which the interests of humanity require to be for ever buried in oblivion'.[15] The re-worked version accordingly goes easy on violence and passion and opts for a more sedate novelistic register: like Maturin's *The wild Irish boy* it is essentially a novel of social manners. The action revolves around the vapid character of Lady Singleton and her circle, an English noblewoman who visits Ireland and lures the eponymous hero, heir to the O'Donnell chieftaincy, to her coterie in London, where he is ridiculed by snobbish socialites.

In such cases, Morgan and Maturin describe (with varying degrees of irony and jaundice) a high-life of fashionable intercourse, parties and flirtations, thus further establishing a genre which eventually culminates in the 'silver fork' school of Thomas Hook, Mrs Gore, Lady Blessington and Bulwer-Lytton's *Pelham*. Such settings (where Morgan and Maturin sometimes all too enthusiastically indulge in lavish descriptions and evocations of the high life which they purport to denounce or mock) make little distinction between fashionable scenes set in Britain or in Ascendancy Ireland. If there is any local colour at all, it often boils down to the fact that the Irish upper circles are less truly aristocratic and somehow shabbier than the English nobility which they imitate, and that their titles are more blatantly obtained by political venality.

Yet again, we can see Maturin and Morgan straining against the dictates of the novelistic register. Their choice of an Irish setting unavoidably calls into play their fascination with that Other Ireland which is set amid scenes of sublime natural splendour, populated by pauperized but picturesque peasants and by descendants of the ousted Gaelic nobility living out a life of remembered greatness and contemporary squalor. The Romantic Ireland which Morgan had celebrated in *The wild Irish girl* does find a surreptitious way into *O'Donnel*, for instance, notwithstanding that novel's socialite setting. Morgan sets the scene when Lady Singleton and her retinue travel into the Irish countryside and end up in the house of the last surviving heir to the O'Donnell chieftaincy:

> The wanderers now issued from the gloom of the mountain ravine into a glen formed in the midst of an amphitheatre of rocks, which, by an abrupt opening, admitted a full view of the noble estuary of Lough Swilly. The drifting winds, which swept over the waters, had scattered away every vapour from before the face of the heavens; and the moon, broad and resplendent, threw a flood of silver light upon a scene indescribably wild and romantic. On the summit of one of the shelving rocks, a ruin of some extent was visible, and underneath its shadows, and almost of one substance with the cliff of which it seemed a part, a small house or cottage was rendered most distinguishable by the smoke of its chimney. It was a formless but picturesque structure, evidently raised out of the materials of the ruins which mouldered about it, and within view of the steep torrent, which descending from the mountains, dashed from point to point of the rocks over which it flowed, and formed a small but noisy stream, on its passage through the glen to Lough Swilly (1: 269–70).

Such a set-piece of Romantic interest and sublime landscape description within the more mundane context of a Novel recalls, even in various points of phraseology, the above-mentioned scene from Scott's *Waverley* where Flora performs next to her waterfall; and the parallel can be followed further. Much as Waverley sees the Highlands as they are evoked in Flora's song, so too do Lady Singleton and the others encounter Old Ireland by way of quotation. For in O'Donnel's house (the one sanctuary of romantic interest in what is otherwise a contemporary, quotidian social novel) they find a manuscript book containing the O'Donnell family history, which is interpolated as a series of digressionary chapters – a stratagem which allows Morgan to make use of the historical materials around which (as she admitted in her above-quoted preface) she was unable to centre her narrative.

But the most widespread strategy of including Gaelic Romance in the novelistic context is provided by the fact that the main focalizing characters tend to be of a non-Irish metropolitan background. In almost all the books under review here, the central character, narrator or focalizer, enters Ireland as a genteel and cosmopolitan *ingénu* from abroad; his/her journey into Ireland takes the narrative from fashionable life towards 'wild adventure.' It is thus in *The wild Irish girl*, in *The wild Irish boy* (whose hero Ormsby Bethel moves from England to Ireland), in Morgan's *The O'Briens and the O'Flahertys* (whose main hero returns to the scenes of his youth after a military career in the Austrian service). That pattern has been described by one critic as follows:

> A person of eminence arrives in Ireland; he (or she) possesses every qualification for a rich and interesting life, yet nothing noteworthy has ever happened to him, and he is full of spleen until, once there, he is dragged into a whirl of undreamt-of adventures, his former habits, prejudices and ways of thinking suddenly give way to an all-absorbing passion, which irresistibly hurries him towards bliss or destruction, as the case may be.[16]

The most telling example here is Maturin's *The Milesian chief* (1812), which can be seen as the fulfilment of a 'Wild Irish' novel which Maturin was unable to produce in *The wild Irish boy*. The central character in *The Milesian chief*, through whom most of the narrative is focalized, is a young woman called Armida, who after a polished and artistic upbringing in Italy moves with her family to Ireland. (Her first impression of the exotic wilderness of Ireland has been quoted above, p. 35). Here, she acquires two suitors: one, a fashionable officer in the military service of the government, the other a brooding, Byronic young Gael raised in a Gothic ruin by his old, fanatically anti-English grandfather. Thus Armida's amorous dilemma occasions an oscillation between high-society soirées on the one hand, and sublime stormy landscapes on the other. The incident in each case matches the setting: the soirées are full of dialogue, wit and snobbery, and the Gaelic landscape engenders near-fatal accidents and daring rescues, or chance encounters like a wandering blind bard on the beach, obviously cloned from Ossian and anticipating Flora's performance in *Waverley*:

> She heard the sound of an instrument, faint, tremulous, and wild. It was the Irish harp, touched by a native on his own wild shores, and accompanied by a voice, which, though broken by age, sounded like music in despair. [. . .] The instrument was defective, and the hand of the performer weak with age; but Armida forgot all science while she listened to him, and felt the effect of the scenery united with the sound. The music, though unlike any she had ever praised as excellent, had a charm superior to that excellence: it had a character impossible to define, but impossible to resist: it appealed from rules to the heart, and its simplicity made the appeal resistless, as the inarticulate cry of infancy affects more deeply than the utmost eloquence of distress. Armida, nursed in the classic elegance of Italian melody, wept as she listened to the rude song of the Irish bard.[17]

Of her two suitors, Armida prefers the young Gael: Connal O'Morven, the book's tragic hero – and his fate gives the book its more gloomy hue. When Armida and Connal meet the bard again, his Ossianic traits (use of the descriptive genitive, prophetic prescience, Aeolian effects on the harp-strings being treated as the playing of ghosts) begin to overshadow the course of future events:

> 'Daughter of Beauty!' he exclaimed in the impassioned language of his country, 'the sound of your voice makes me bewail the loss of my sight again. Oh! if my

harp had but one string left, that one string should be alive with your praise.'
[. . .]

He again touched his harp, and Connal said with animated fondness,

'Give us, Cormac, the sweetest song that ever was inspired by love and beauty.'

At the moment the old man bent over his harp in a trance of feeling, a loud blast of wind swept across the strings, and the sound, deep and mournful, resembled a human groan as it passed along the heath.

The old man shuddered: he dropped the harp, and his sightless eyes rolled in their sockets with a force that seemed stronger than actual sight.

'The hand of death is on my harp!' he exclaimed: 'there is a spirit in the air – the voices of other days strike my ear – there is a spirit in the air! I feel his touch on my heart! I see him though I am blind! O'Morven, he whispers, "No song of youth or love!" O'Morven, he bids me sing of woe and death!'

[. . .] And with the inspiration, the solemn fury of a prophet, he struck the chords that for centuries past had summoned the funeral procession to the grave of an O'Morven, and echoed the dreadful cry that was raised over the corpse (2: 99–101).

The Milesian chief from this point onwards becomes a fey tale of tragic rebellion, Connal O'Morven (heir to an ousted Gaelic chieftaincy) being involved in a hopeless uprising against the authorities. Gothic touches are added in increasing profusion: witness the introduction of a stock character from the Gothic iconography in the figure of the evil Italian priest Morosini, who attempts to debauch Armida during confessional. Eventually the tale progresses to a lurid catastrophe when, amidst the ruin of Connal's rebellion, Armida is led away from the battlefield by a less than trustworthy servant, who clearly has evil designs on her chastity, and is brought to a cavern on the beach where Connal's grandfather lies, quite mad, and on the point of expiry. He thinks that Armida is Queen Elizabeth and wants to revenge all old grievances of the Gaels on her. Between the raving madman and the lecherous menial, Armida in her cavern is in dire straits indeed – a far cry from the salons and parties in the capital where she used to move, or those which were visited by splenetic Ormsby Bethel in *The wild Irish boy*. Armida has moved from the here and now of fashionable life to the warped, anachronistic 'adventure time' as studied by Bakhtin, where all periods of the Irish past are conflated into an undifferentiated 'erstwhile', an eternal, primeval conflict. It is also the time-warp of the Protestant Irish political imagination of 1812, which saw 1798 as a direct re-enactment of 1641, and which constantly feared a new flare-up of the papist peasantry's genocidal fury.[18]

The Milesian chief, before it succumbs to the author's more lurid Gothic proclivities, offers a remarkable solution to the Novelistic/Romantic ambiguity which seems to be pre-inscribed in the choice of an Irish setting: it explicitly evokes the polarity between the two Irelands, oscillates between them and between their attendant generic registers. Characters move back and forth between drawing-rooms and craggy glens, from eyebrow-raising witticism to hair-raising adventure.

A similar mode of encompassing both Irelands in the same narrative was followed by Lady Morgan in her later book *The O'Briens and the O'Flahertys* of 1827. In one aspect, it re-enacts a stratagem which she had already used in *O'Donnel*: that of the interpolated manuscript found in an old, Gaelic-owned house, quoted at length as digressionary chapters furnishing local colour. But at the same time, Morgan also uses the technique of deliberate oscillation between, and juxtaposition of, the two Irelands. There are frequent and violent scene-changes from parties at the perimeter of the viceregal court to nocturnal adventures in medieval chapels, gloomy mansions or wild mountains, from ironical descriptions of witty flirtation to Gothic evocations of inexplicable apparitions in the dark. A lively traffic takes place between Dublin and Connaught, and even within the capital there are haunts which require a Gothic treatment. For example: the hero receives a ring as a love-token from Lady Knocklofty (a pearl with in its setting the motto 'Qui me cherche me trouve'); on leaving the fashionable salon in Dublin Castle he falls asleep, exhausted, in the Castle's Gothic chapel; and upon his awakening from a dreadful nightmare, he finds that the ring has been replaced by another one – 'not the pearl of Lough Corrib, with its pretty device – but a death's head on a dark onyx, with the well-known device of the Jesuits engraven in black characters on its circlet – *Sub cruce latet*.'[19]

The contrast between novelistic and romantic setting is further emphasized phraseologically. Lady Knocklofty and her friends lard their discourse with French and Italian expressions, whereas in the west people speak in a strong Irish brogue peppered with Gaelic phrases. Thus, for example, a one-page dialogue between two guests at a masked ball in Dublin gives occasion for the expressions *taillé à l'antique*, *On ne joue pas aux échecs avec un bon coeur*, a friendship *à l'Allemande*, and other friendships *hérissées de si, et de mais, et de sous-entendus*; someone seems *désorientée*, and a rival is described as follows:

> For her beauty, *passe*; and pass it will of itself before long: and for her wit, it is *l'esprit d'anti-chambre, – très-gai, et un peu polisson*. But people of the world are not nice. *Tromper leur ennui en le divertissant* is their aim [. . .] There is nothing in the wit of Lady Honoria; *c'est une flamme sans feu*. (3: 146)

Other fashionable scenes are equally lavish in their use of Italian ('I hear! *guardi il cielo!* [. . .] such *rifacciamenti* are not for ears like mine.' 3: 151).

Gaelic Ireland in the west harbours a different kind of glossolalia, and allows Morgan to show off her error-ridden smatterings of Gaelic; e.g., when O'Brien reminisces about his boyhood education with his foster-brother Shane:

> 'And there was a spirited controversial dialogue, too, between St Patrick and Osian,' continued O'Brien [. . .]
>
> '*Ossin agus St Phaedrig*,' repeated Shane, making the sign of the cross.
>
> 'And that sweet old air, of which the burden was, "I am asleep, do not awaken me."'
>
> '*Ta mi mo hoolah, na dushame*,' interrupted Shane, not now touched, but rapt.

'And Carolan's receipt, sung by old Donogh!'
'Ay, Musha,' chuckled Shane, 'a great *abra, Donogh an abhac*, a great *gramog.*'
(2: 314)

In contrast to the various foreign (French/Italian) phrases from the salons, those Gaelic terms are all glossed in footnotes and thus almost rendered exotic (because deemed incomprehensible) by the very act of explanation. The contrast thus once again becomes that between urbane cosmopolitanism, shared by author and reader, and archaic uncouthness, where the author becomes a mediator and translator, explaining a foreign, alien culture to the readership. The most striking, and influential, instance of this auto-exoticist stratagem is given in *The wild Irish girl*. For the moment, I mention the habit of footnoting mainly to illustrate the tension between the contrary dictates of Romantic local colour and novelistic *vraisemblance*.

For these authorial interventions do reflect the ambiguity between a novel-istic and a Romantic intent. Although the romance requires colourful incident and a sublime setting, here purveyed by Gaelic Ireland, the novel-readership requires a mode of relating the setting to known experience and available information. The curious result is that in texts like these, the narrative is encum-bered with a great deal of explanatory footnotes, at precisely those moments where it is most Romantic. At such points, the exoticism of the sublime setting over-strains the novelistic proviso of *vraisemblance*, and the author will tend to back up implausible descriptions with attesting, by way of a footnote, the truth-value of the representation, thus accommodating the presence of Romance-like passages to the realistic expectations of a novel-audience.[20] Such footnotes abound throughout early Anglo-Irish novels wherever they begin to draw on the romantic exoticism of their *couleur locale*. As we shall see, *The wild Irish girl* simply teems with notes where Morgan says that she is relying either on personal experience, or else on the trustworthy testimony of historians and antiquarians; and in Maturin, too, one comes across footnote-comments such as 'taken from life'.[21]

Thus the political dividedness of Ireland, between fashionable life in viceregal circles and picturesque primitivism om the Atlantic cliffs, is reflected in the generic ambiguity of Irish romance/novels. As Maturin put it in his preface to *The Milesian chief*, Ireland was

> the only country on earth, where, from the strange existing operation of religion, politics, and manners, the extremes of refinement and barbarism are united, and the most wild and incredible situations of romantic story are hourly passing before modern eyes.[22]

In this schizophrenic situation, the footnotes function almost like rivets joining together the contradictory modes between which Irish narrative oscillates.

A world apart: the pastness of Ireland

I return to Scott's distinction between Romance and Novel. It is striking that almost surreptitiously he smuggles into the definition of the novel a temporal element, in that it deals with 'the modern state of society'. Something similar occurs in Scott's essay 'On the supernatural in fictitious composition',[23] where a belief in supernatural occurrences is correlated with the genre of the romance, with the earlier stages of individual development (childhood), and with the earlier stages of Western literature (folk literature, the Middle Ages). Obviously, then, in such a scheme, the novel, which follows ordinary human experience, will tend towards the quotidian and indeed contemporary scope of the audience, whereas the wild adventures of the romance will more easily be set in remoter times.

Accordingly, there is also a temporal distinction between Novelistic plausibility and Romantic adventure. The books under review here show that, indeed, their novelistic content deals with contemporary manners and the 'modern state of society'; so far, however, we have not seen the characters time-travel into the past when they move from their salons into the countryside. Or have we? For we did encounter the curiously time-warped cave where Armida confronted Connal O'Morven's grandfather . . .

It can be said that Romantic exoticism will work on a chronological as well as on a geographical axis: that the exoticism of distant and picturesque places frequently goes together with the exoticism of distant and picturesque historical periods. The existence of such a link between spatial and temporal exoticism has been convincingly illustrated by the anthropologist Johannes Fabian, who has elucidated the tendency of ethnological discourse to situate its object in the past: witness the use of ambiguous terms like 'primitive' or the currency of clichés like 'such-and-such a Papua tribe still lives in the Stone Age'. Fabian calls this 'the denial of coevalness' and explains it from Western conceptualizations of time and from a view of history characterized by an ethnocentrist teleology.[24]

The tendency to view alien/foreign culture as reflecting older periods in human history also marked the iconography of Gaelic Ireland in English-educated minds. Antiquarians had investigated the Irish past and created an image of Gaelic Ireland that was inherently characterized by its pastness: the most genuine and least adulterated form of Gaelic culture was that of the past, before the contamination of the English presence in Ireland. Accordingly, Gaelic Ireland is inherently a matter of the past, a survival of bygone ages, a living fossil of older times, existing only in those places where it has not yet been adulterated by the influence of contemporary European civilization – and this mode of representing Gaelic Ireland once again ties in with the romance's general, Gothic proclivity for ancient ruins and archaic settings.

We can register various repercussions of that principle in the Irish tales of Morgan and Maturin. To begin with, Gaelic Ireland is not just the counterpart of Anglicized middle- and upper-class Ireland, not just one of the two Irelands.

Anglo-Ireland is seen as a part of contemporary life in general, part of Europe, participating in the cosmopolitanism of genteel refinement and drawing on a stock of European manners (witness the English or Continental upbringing of various heroes, and the currency of French and Italian in the Dublin salons). From this European appurtenance, Gaelic Ireland is excluded, exoticized, rusticated. Anglo-Ireland is domestic, Gaelic Ireland is foreign, alien. To go into Gaelic Ireland means leaving Europe, leaving civilization as we know it.

Another result is the fact that Gaelic Ireland, characterized by its pastness, exists only in certain discrete areas cordoned off from the normal world. The natural amphitheatre in *Waverley* where Flora sings her old song is echoed in Morgan's description of the setting of O'Donnel's residence; inaccessible mountain ranges, glens and valleys, castles in liminal settings like islands or the seashore, gloomy and almost collapsing old mansions in deserted, no-longer-fashionable parts of Dublin: such ectopic places apart are the locations where Gaelic Ireland is also situated. Characters have to perform an almost liminal transgression to cross from the 'modern state of society' into 'the land of romance'. In these places, the acme of local colour or pastness is encountered, either in the form of living fossils (the Prince of Inismore in *The wild Irish girl* being the Ossian-derived prototype) or else in the form of a text: the song Flora sings to Waverley, the bard's gloomy croonings in *The Milesian chief*, the family history in *O'Donnel*, the chronicle in *The O'Briens and the O'Flahertys*.

Finally, what is remarkable is the ahistoricity of Gaelic Ireland: such local colour evokes, not so much a recognizable heritage from the past surviving in the present, but rather a mishmash of antiquarian items from the most diverse periods. The desire to furnish local colour means that the Irish past is ransacked for whatever is unusual, uncouth or picturesque, and the result is rampant anachronism. Both Morgan and Maturin are fond of introducing characters wearing 'the old Gaelic dress' and the old Gaelic hairdo (cf. *The Milesian chief*, 4: 127–129; and below, p. 68) – whereas the dress and hairstyle thus described vanished no later than 1600; the Shane-figure in *The O'Briens and the O'Flahertys* is described as a surviving 'rapparee'. The Irish past as it comes to the surface in these representations is not really a history but rather an ill-organized museum of antiquarian curios and collectibles.

All these factors essentially reduce the notion of Irish history to a stasis, an undifferentiated pool of diverse mementos and memories. The Irish past is arranged into an extratemporal iconography where St Patrick, the eleventh-century Brian Ború and the sixteenth-century Red Hugh O'Donnell exist cheek by jowl with medieval Round Towers, Ossianic harpists, and contemporary Gaelic-speaking peasants, in sublime landscapes dimly visible on the horizon. The extreme, and most telling instance is the time-warped, liminal setting of the catastrophe of *The Milesian chief*: the cavern on the sea-shore, where (in the eyes of a dying, mad Gael) modern Armida becomes Queen Elizabeth. Peripherality, liminality and allochrony are piled up in melodramatic overdetermination: the setting is between earth and open air, between land and sea, old O'Morven between life and death, between reason and delirium; Armida between historical and contemporary catastrophe.

The use of an Irish setting – or more particularly: the inclusion of a Gaelic setting in contemporary narrative – drives authors like Morgan and Maturin unavoidably towards anachronism and generic ambiguity (between Romance and Novel, as well as between Fiction and Footnotes). As both state in various prefaces, they found themselves unable to situate their tales in other than contemporary settings, and as a result had to perform odd twists and turns to incorporate Gaelic Ireland, which they viewed in terms of its pastness, within their contemporary narratives. To the extent that authors call upon the genre of the romance, they also call upon that genre's chronotope, its characteristically plastic stretch-and-shrink treatment of how time passes. Gaelic Ireland is set both in a spatial and in a chronological distance, neither in the present nor in the past, but in adventure time, in an anachronistic time-warp.

How could the novelistic and romantic registers come to place such a Procrustean dilemma to Irish writers? Morgan, as we have seen, found herself unable to write a historical or realistic novel, and her failure becomes paradigmatic for the century as a whole. Edgeworth wrote in a letter that 'it is impossible to draw Ireland as she now is in a book of fiction – realities are too strong, party passions too violent to bear to see, or care to look at their faces in the looking-glass.' Samuel Lover felt that the 1798 rebellion was 'too fearful a subject' for him to deal with, 'too tempting to the passion of party, or too forcibly appealing to the gentler feelings of human nature, for mortal pen to be trusted with'; Samuel Lever could only glancingly refer to the realities of destitution and despair.[25] It was Thomas Davis's 'great unfulfilled ambition' to write a historical novel, much as it was Gerald Griffin's ambition to write a history of Ireland – which, however, would dauntingly consist of 'a miserable and shocking succession of follies, excesses and tyrannies', 'centuries consumed in suffering, in vain remonstrance, and idle though desperate struggles for change', and 'the convulsions of a powerful people labouring under a nightmare for ten centuries'.[26]

There was, then, the burden of the political tensions of a country that was still under the shadow of civil war and violent agitation. Scott found, in writing *Waverley*, that he was treading on thin ice when he evoked the radical enmities which were clustered around the rebellion of 1745, then seventy years ago; and the enmities in Ireland were far more radical, far more ingrained, far more alive. Novelists or would-be novelists found that both the poetics of their genre and the politics of their time disallowed too close a preoccupation or identification with Gaelic Ireland: and therefore it may be said that their unresolved problems in creating within English conventions an Irish historical novel represent, not just an interesting case history in the early development of a new fictional genre, but also a remarkable instance of interaction between literary and political developments. Accordingly, Terry Eagleton argues that 'The problem of form [. . .] is also a problem of politics':

> Two quite disparate discourses, the one romantic, the other realist, inhabit Morgan's texts without ever fruitfully interlocking; and since romance signifies an ideal, and realism an actual ruling class, this shift and clash of linguistic registers is the site of a genuine ideological dilemma.[27]

In this light, it is interesting to contrast the failure of Morgan and Maturin with the success of Scott; on the one hand, the difference between the Irish authors and their Scottish counterpart might be explained from the fact that Scott brought more historical integrity and reliability into his novels: that, in a manner of speaking, Morgan and Maturin deal with the past like antiquarians, and Scott does so more like a historian. But there is more to this. The problem for Morgan and Maturin lies in the fact that they set their tales in a contemporary framework, in which the romantic and archaic appeal of Gaelic local colour must inevitably become anachronistic; whereas Scott situated the entire actions of his novels in past periods. Upon closer reflection, it appears that the contemporary setting forcibly imposed itself in the Irish case, that the historical option à la Scott was politically unfeasible in the Irish context: for the Anglo-Irish upper classes in Ireland were essentially unrooted in Ireland, had no past in that country.

Moreover, if Scott wants to draw on Scottish local colour, he can find a plethora of it within the Lowlands of Scotland, with its racy speech à la Meg Merrilies and its quaint customs. It is, strictly speaking, not necessary for him to locate Scottish national colour in the Highlands or to draw on Celtic, Highland material for it: the un-English and characteristically Scottish nature of the Lowlands and the Border provides sufficient store of it. Outside of *Waverley*, *Rob Roy* and *The fair maid of Perth*, Highland exoticism is a relatively rare occurrence in Scott's oeuvre.

The Irish case is far different. There was no Irish local colour except in Gaeldom – because Anglo-Ireland, rootless as it was, had to rely on its close British links to maintain its hold in that country, and constantly conformed itself to its mainstay, the Mother Country, England. Thus, a tale that is both Irish and a Novel is, in a way, a contradiction in terms: a novelistic setting means Anglo-Ireland, means something cloned from, and indistinguishable from, England itself, means something imported and without national Irish past; and an Irish setting means Gaeldom, means straying from a novelistic into a romantic register, means something dispossessed, disaffected and without a present or future. In a way, then, the difference between Scott and Morgan/Maturin reflects the historical difference between Scotland and Ireland within the British national system: Scotland as England's sister kingdom, Ireland as England's colony.

The hybrid vacillation of Morgan and Maturin between a novelistic and a romantic register seriously flaws their Irish tales, often to the point of ludicrousness. As Luke Gibbons has pointed out, the wild irregularity of Irish novel-writing in these years reflects the wild vicissitudes of the course of Irish history.[28] But in the development of the literary representation of Ireland, their treatment of local colour had important effects: it perpetuated, and translated into the field of prose fiction, a form of Celtic exoticism which has not yet lost its currency or its appeal. The Ossianic-Romantic timeless, view of Celtic culture as being lost on the edges of the world and on the fringes of history, beyond civilization and the passage of time, was perpetuated by them and was to prove influential in the subsequent development of Celtic stereotype, with its impact on Anglo-Irish literature and politics. Morgan and Maturin, with their use of Bakhtinian adventure-time-chronotopes interspersed with realistic descriptions of society life, were essentially the first to voice the literary/political formula that Ireland is a country tragically caught between its past and its present.

These Romantic Irish novels could not fit the poetical requirements of the novel as these were crystallizing at the time in metropolitan Britain. That very fact reflects the predicament of post-Union Ireland. Some characteristics we would now consider awkward in terms of novelistic technique indicate how such novels incorporated an older, pre-Union mode of looking at Ireland as it was expressed in other genres: travel description, antiquarian discourse, sentimental comedy.[29] For that reason, such flaws in *novelistic* technique indicate the incorporation of older genres, pre-Union discourse. In order to illustrate this, I shall now turn one last time to *The wild Irish girl*.

Morganatic Ireland: the case of *The wild Irish girl*

I attempted to speak, but my voice faltered, my tongue was nerveless, my mouth dry and parched. A trembling hand presented a cordial to my lips. I quaffed the philter, and fixed my eyes on the face of my ministering angel – that angel was Glorvina! – I closed them, and sunk on the bosom of her father.

'Oh, he faints again!' cried a sweet and plaintive voice.

'On the contrary,' replied the priest, 'the weariness of acute pain, something subsided, is lulling him into a soft repose! for, see, the colour re-animates his cheek, and his pulse quickens.'

'It indeed beats most wildly,' returned the sweet physician – for the pulse, which responded to her finger's thrilling pressure, moved with no languid throb.[30]

The pair who are here playing doctors and nurses, Horatio and Glorvina, are the two protagonists of *The wild Irish girl*, which appeared in 1806. Highly successful when it first came out, the novel inspired Maturin's counterpiece *The wild Irish boy* (or at least its title), and attracting the attention of the reviews, of Mme de Staël, and of a wide and fashionable readership; nowadays, however, it is seen usually as a low-brow spin-off of the more important work of Maria Edgeworth. Glorvina, the female physician in the above-quoted passage, whose pulse-feeling sets the patient throbbing, is the novel's epony-mous heroine. The swooning swain, Horatio, is the novel's narrator. Their story is the standard type, as analysed by Bakhtin on the basis of Hellenistic, medieval and early-modern examples, of 'boy meets girl, and although they have to overcome difficulties and clear up misunderstandings they end up happily married'. In such a story, it is obvious that the main body of the plot and most of the incidents must be furnished by those difficulties and misunderstandings which intervene between the pair's first meeting and their eventual wedding. In the case of *The wild Irish girl*, all these are occasioned, more or less directly, by the fact that boy and girl represent two different and even hostile national traditions: Horatio is English, Glorvina Irish; and Glorvina's ancestors have been ousted from their princely estates by those of Horatio. Not for nothing does the novel carry the subtitle *A national tale*. Morgan was to give the same specification to her later works like *O'Donnel* and *The O'Briens and the O'Flahertys*.

If the sexual polarity between Horatio and Glorvina attracts them towards each other, the political one is of a more divisive nature. It is the cross-purpose between these two polarities which generates most of the novel's action, and which also provokes an allegorical reading, suggesting a pattern of political symbolism in the personal fate of two youngsters. The ultimate happy ending of a harmonious union in the bonds of wedlock is held up as an example for the political relationship between the two countries: old grievances should be forgotten, worn-out prejudices should be abandoned, and England and Ireland should co-operate in a happy, loving partnership. That ideal reflects, and transmutes, the Patriot outlook of a few decades previously, and its agenda to develop an equal and equitable partnership between the sister kingdoms of Ireland and Great Britain. Indeed, as we shall see, Morgan herself was firmly rooted in the intellectual and ideological climate of pre-Union Ireland. Her start in public life was made under the auspices of her father, a well-known Dublin actor who was himself a native speaker of Irish and who was especially celebrated for playing the funny but endearing and commendable Stage-Irish characters of late-eighteenth-century sentimental comedy. Morgan's own attitude is evinced by her tellingly named *Patriotic sketches of Ireland written in Connaught* (1807), which vindicates a national ideal midway between English hegemony and native insurrection.

But whereas Charlotte Brooke, in the Preface to her *Reliques*, had spoken of England and Ireland as sister kingdoms (above, p. 31), the relation in *The wild Irish girl* is explicitly genderized in the protagonists Horatio and Glorvina – a symbolic actorial pattern that was to prove succesful until Brian Friel's *Translations*.[31] In this respect, *The wild Irish girl* fits into a long-standing tradition which had personified Ireland as a female, and had represented her colonial relationship with England as one of sexual exploitation or oppression. That tradition goes back to Gaelic poems of the early seventeenth century, in the Stuartist or Jacobite symbolism of the Kathleen Ní Houlihan and Roisín Dubh figures; an early Anglo-Irish adaptation being Swift's *Story of the injured lady*.[32]

In this respect as in others, *The wild Irish girl* occupies a pivotal position, and marks a turning point in the literary representation of Ireland. This may sound surprising. In the emergence of nineteenth-century Anglo-Irish literature, the status of Morgan is subordinate to that of Maria Edgeworth, and her novel, though its initial success usually guarantees its mention in more specialized literary histories, or elsewhere in parentheses or in a footnote, is subject to severe critical strictures. Indeed, as my opening quotation may have indicated, much of that severity is justified. *The wild Irish girl* as a novel constantly hovers on the edge of unconscious self-parody, where people quaff philters and, while in a faint, throb. The form (an epistolary novel) is ill-fitting, the narrative is ramshackle, and the characters are performing puppets. But, with all its flaws, *The wild Irish girl* offers a cross-section of discursive genres in transition, and its mongrel heterogeneity is like an unblended accumulation of superimposed discursive sediments, testifying to incipient changes in the Irish image and in Irish discourse; and it is as such that I would here like to review and reassess the novel.

In my discussion of *The O'Briens and the O'Flahertys*, I pointed out how Morgan was given to glossolalia, 'speaking in tongues': dialogue in metropolitan circles is larded with French or Italian, in the west it is shot through with Gaelic. That tendency is not quite so pronounced in *The wild Irish girl*, though it is by no means absent. Rather, the contrast here is between speech and silence, between narrative action and discursive explanation. In order to describe this contrast, as well as other features of this remarkable novel, it might be useful to invoke the notion, coined by Bakhtin, of *heteroglossia*. By this is meant the tendency for the primitive, pre-Realist novel (Bakhtin's test case being Rabelais) to adopt a variety of narrative voices, to anchor itself in discursive genres of more established and reputable genres.[33]

The wild Irish girl is in precisely such a position. The Anglo-Irish regional novel was a new genre, born under adverse conditions. We have seen what repercussions this had on the writings of Morgan and Maturin. One effect was a pronounced tendency to combine narration and explanation, and to invoke towards that end all sorts of textual traditions and source materials from other genres. *The wild Irish girl* is a very uneasy blend of fictional narrative and referential discourse. The narrative, the fiction, is a love story. As we have seen, it is the story of faltering voices, trembling hands, faintings and throbbings. But in the midst of all this passion there is also a discursive element which offers observations on Irish life and antiquity, matters of curiosity and political relevance. These discursive digressions from the fictional storyline obviously represent the novel's real interest. *The wild Irish girl* is less concerned with the two ostensible protagonists than with a colourful representation of Ireland and Irish claims to positive interest. Indeed, it often becomes a sort of tourist's guide to Ireland, the charms of the Irish landscape, the pleasant and pathetic character of the poor but honest Irish peasant, the impressive and fascinating history and antiquity – and not in the last place, the great cultural accomplishments of Ireland. In each of these interests, Morgan sets out to contradict English prejudice, focused in Horatio, who visits Ireland full of reserve and who is gradually brought to see what a wonderful country it is. He goes through a similar process, by the way, when it comes to his relation with Glorvina, for at first he cannot believe that anyone could be so accomplished, let alone someone living so far away from urban society; but in stages he must confess that Glorvina is indeed everything she is praised for.

The wild Irish girl is a piece of pro-Irish propaganda disguised as a novel. Clearly, those two elements are difficult to reconcile, and Morgan, who is in constant danger of losing her love story from sight amidst her historical or anthropological digressions, has to resort to various stratagems to keep her narrative and her digressive discourse together. Thus, the priest (whose medical commentary we encountered in the earlier-quoted passage) is used as a foil to Horatio's sceptical curiosity (embedding cultural and political arguments into the parameters of the fictional plot). Also, one of the most striking characteristics of this text is the unusual predominance of its paratext.[34] *The wild Irish girl* is remarkably generous in its use of mottoes, quoted material and, in especially lavish profusion, footnotes, and it is by way of this paratextual layering of the text that I want to approach the historical position of *The wild Irish girl*.

A rough calculation would indicate that its paratext accounts for the greater part of *The wild Irish girl*. In a way, that is part of the novel's maverick charm. Morgan can crowd out her actual narrative by extremely lengthy digressive footnotes, and she does not hesitate even to add footnotes to her footnotes. The relationship between the narrative and the footnotes is an interesting one, and indicates the complex nature of this work and of its position in Anglo-Irish literary history.

The footnote usually appears at points of heightened local or antiquarian colour. At such 'authentic Irish' points an asterisk will suspend the fictional narrative and interpose some explicative comment. Ironically, then, the footnotes, by the very act of explaining such points, presuppose the need for such explanation and underline the exotic and alien nature of the *explicandum*. What is more, the explanation usually invokes, either geographical, extra-diegetic reality (e.g. 'A waterfall like the one described here really exists, a few miles north of such-and-such a place'), or else the testimony from other, written sources. It is at this latter point that a Bakhtinian heteroglossia can begin to sound through the novel's narrative.

In the footnotes, Morgan is free to address her readers directly, *in propria persona*, in her own voice. At times this digressive interest, the interest in Ireland itself rather than in the girl who metonymically personifies it, takes over to such a degree that the story is a mere thread on which Morgan strings the beads of her footnotes. Morgan exploits to the full the nature of the footnote as a textual shadow zone between the fictional narrative and the first-order reality of author/reader, where one can comment and elaborate upon the fictional text without rupturing the skein of fictitious make-believe, the integrity of the diegesis. Thus we can make one preliminary distinction: the footnotes are used as an overflow to save Morgan's plot from a fatal overdose of discursive digression. Although there is a good deal of discursive observation within the story as such, the passion of trembling hands and meaningful looks is reserved for the narrative core text, the footnotes being the exclusive reservoir for antiquarian argument and informative digression.

But the footnotes have a second, perhaps less obvious, function, since they absolve Morgan from describing the indescribable, and function as guarantors of veracity backing up the story's faulty *vraisemblance*. The novel's exoticist claims to (re)present the Real Ireland must inevitably fall short of their mark, and it is as a back-up in precisely that contingency that the footnotes play their role.

The unspeakable, the indescribable and the footnote

The wild Irish girl is less concerned with its hackneyed love story than with its setting, Ireland, which Morgan aims to introduce, in all its exotic and unsuspected beauty, to a British audience. However, the signified Ireland is deferred in a typical telescoping of exoticism. The really exotic must by definition be indescribable, since the presence of an observer, or the act of description, would taint its exotic quality. That which is visible, accessible, that which can be mediated, to an English audience, has lost the pristine quality of being truly exotic. The truly exotic is hidden from view, just as Glorvina's family was hidden in a Hidden Ireland (to use Corkery's phrase), a picturesque ruin where life went undiscovered, untainted, it would seem, by English presence. Untainted? Well, not quite. Whenever such purportedly pristine, untainted instances of exoticism are described, it will sooner or later be conceded that perhaps this is not the Perfectly Exotic after all, since there have been some previous instances of de-exoticization, of contacts with Civilization.

Typically, pristine exoticism is, almost necessarily, watered down at some point,[35] and so it is in this book which genderizes exoticism into the suspense between jealousy and virginity. For we learn that Horatio's father had visited the spot (incognito, like his son) and had even won a promise that Glorvina would be given to him as his wife. That is also one of the graver misunderstandings which temporarily bars the two young people from a happy union. Horatio speculates jealously that there has been some Other in Glorvina's life: another man, or indeed a prior non-Irish contact adulterating her pristine Irishness. The fact that Glorvina may have felt amorous passion before meeting him, is a direct threat to Horatio's desire that Glorvina should be a virgin (in an emotional rather than a crude physical sense); and that traditional masculine desire for virginity in one's beloved is a parallel to the exoticist desire to see Ireland as it really is, before it was ever exposed to foreign admixture, an identity which can be observed without being exposed to, defiled by, the proximity of an Other.

This is the book's leading desire: to represent a Real Ireland whose identity is untainted by foreign presence. But that, of course, is an impossible paradox. The true, the real, the genuine, cannot submit to the process of being represented without thereby losing its pristine authenticity.

A parallel of this predicament is given by Morgan's treatment of the passion between Horatio and Glorvina. As my initial quotation already illustrates, the two tend to be speechless in each other's presence whenever it becomes emotionally charged. They cannot communicate their feelings to each other except through faltering voices and mimic gestures. 'Could my heart have lent its eloquence to my lip – but that was impossible; very imperfect indeed was the justice I did to my feelings' (49); 'It is a sigh, a glance, a broken sentence, an imperceptible motion (imperceptible to all eyes but our own) which betrays us to each other' (155); or this:

> Besides, she never *said* she loved me. *Said!* – heavens! were words necessary for such an *avowal*? O, Glorvina! thy sweet glances, thy insidious smiles, thy ready blushes, and delicious tears: these, these are the sweet testimonies to which my heart appeals (217).

And yet Glorvina – whose name, as Morgan herself is careful to gloss, means 'sweet voice,' *glór bhinn*, in Irish – is not an incoherent, inarticulate person. She displays great eloquence when it comes to vindicating her country's accomplishments, playing the tourist guide, dispensing antiquarian information to Horatio. It seems that in such a scheme (which is also to be encountered in the sentimental novel of the later eighteenth century, e.g. Mackenzie's *The man of feeling*) language functions as the expression of *knowledge*, while the expression of *feeling* must take a non-verbal, pre-discursive form. The vexed vacillation between rapturous outburst and choked silence is quite unlike the cool, composed language of Edgeworth, but might indicate a similar predicament differently resolved. Terry Eagleton points out that in this generation of Anglo-Irish novels,

> Language is weapon, dissemblance, seduction, apologia – anything, in fact, but *representational*; it is in a perpetual condition of untruth, and truth can thus only be imported from the outside, by those disinterested enough to represent the people accurately both to others and to themselves. But such a viewpoint must naturally repress the conditions of its own representability, which is why Edgeworth's crisp, judicious, eminently reasonable prose is a politics all in itself.[36]

The wild Irish girl contains an ironic play on this dilemma between the discursive communication of cultural interest and non-discursive communion of feeling. When Horatio learns Gaelic, language can for once express passion because, paradoxically, the avowal of love is couched in the meaningless language of a grammatical exercise:

> The other evening, as we circled round the evening fire in the great hall, the Prince would put my improvement to the test, and taking down a grammar, he insisted on my conjugating a verb. The verb he chose was '*to love*.' – 'Glorvina,' said he, seeing me hesitate, 'go through the verb.'
> Glorvina had it at her finger's ends; and in her eyes swam a thousand delicious comments on the text she was expounding.
> The Prince, who is as unsuspicious as an infant, would have us repeat it together, that I might catch the pronunciation from her lip!

'I love,' faintly articulated Glorvina.

'I love,' I more faintly repeated.

This was not enough – the Prince would have us repeat the plural twice over; and again and again we murmured together – *'we love!'*

Heavens and earth! had you at that moment seen the preceptress and the *pupil!* The attention of the simple Prince was rivetted on Vallancy's grammar: he grew peevish at what he called our stupidity, and said we knew nothing of the verb to love, while in fact we were running through all its moods and tenses with our eyes and looks.[37]

The only possible reconciliation between eloquent silence and thwarted speech lies in the medium of song, when the linguistic discourse of speech is redeemed by the non-linguistic emotional magic of music; Glorvina is at her best when she sings and plays the harp. Of course, in Thomas Moore's *Irish melodies*, which began to appear two years after *The wild Irish girl*, the icon of the harp as the true voice of the real Ireland was to gain immense importance; and fittingly so, since Moore culled his initial melodies from Bunting's collections which dated back to the Belfast harpers' festival of 1792. The United Irishmen, who had chosen the badge of the harp as their emblem, had, as it were, lifted the image from heraldry to turn it into the sign of a national voice refusing to be stifled; and Moore elaborated this notion in manifold ways in his *Melodies*.[38] But in the years between the United Irishmen and Moore, it was surely the string-tugging Glorvina who co-opted the harp icon most powerfully. Morgan herself was an enthusiastic strummer, and one of her best-known portraits depicts her as a real-life *glór bhinn*, with the instrument. Olivia Desmond, the heroine of *St. Clair, or the heiress of Desmond* (1807) was a harp-player like Glorvina. Again, in 1807 Morgan also published a volume of society verse entitled *The lay of an Irish harp*, which featured for its title poem something that closely foreshadows Moore:

> Why sleeps the Harp of Erin's pride?
> Why with'ring droops its shamrock wreath?
> Why has that song of sweetness died
> Which Erin's Harp alone can breathe?[39]

Indeed, one may speculate that there was some rivalry between Moore and Morgan over the question as to who could claim to be the principal player of the national harp. Morgan herself left a bequest for a marble plaque to the memory of Carolan to be put up in St Patrick's Cathedral, Dublin, where it is still to be seen, linking her name to the premier iconic representative of the native bards.

It is, then, in the medium of song and balladry that *The wild Irish girl's* opposites between speech and speechlessness are reconciled, that Glorvina becomes a true personification of her country, and that her identity becomes truly that of her name, the Sweet Voice; it is then, also, that she is first espied by Horatio, who promptly falls in love with her and tumbles from his hiding-spot, thus propitiating their acquaintance and nurse-patient relationship.

Here, too, *The wild Irish girl* occupies a seminally important position: for as we shall see, the entire nineteenth century was to look for true native genius in the medium of oral verse, song and balladry (below, pp. 173–7).

Let me reiterate, for the present, two observations: (a) the narrative core text is the medium for the love story while the footnotes are the medium for discursive referential discourse; (b) verbal discourse in *The wild Irish girl* often breaks down in its referential function. We have seen that incapacity of reference, of description, with regard to the narrative fiction of the young people's passion; but it can also be observed with regard to the representation of that other passion in the book, the almost infatuated fascination with what is exotic and interesting in Ireland. It is at this latter point that the footnotes can begin to play their role, already hinted at above, of guarantors of the uncontrollable veracity of the novel's exoticism.

Much as the centre of the narrative fiction, the passion between Horatio and Glorvina, is something unspeakable, so too the ultimate reference of the Irish-related digressions is indescribable and out of the reach of linguistic communication. These discursive digressions point towards a notion of the Real Ireland, the True Ireland, the ineffable, as yet unknown or misunderstood Ireland – the Ireland, in short, for which the main narrative text cannot find words and for which the author paratextually invokes the authority of other sources. On such occasions, the footnotes' referential function becomes bibliographical: Morgan's text refers to (that is to say, invokes the credentials of) other texts about Ireland. The footnotes, characteristically, tend to be of an intertextual nature and invoke, not so much a Real Ireland as previous discourse about Ireland. Thus, the footnotes can come to the rescue whenever Morgan's plot becomes ensnared in the paradox of its aim: to represent, and mediate for an uninitiated readership, the perfectly exotic, undivulged Ireland, as it was never seen by strangers. As soon as it becomes apparent in the story's exoticism that an Ireland which is representable must be less than perfectly exotic, the footnotes invoke ulterior authorities backing up Morgan's pointers to a Real Ireland, which thus remains outside her own ken, beyond the horizon of her own representation. It is here that *The wild Irish girl* sheds its fictional trappings and begins to quote from, or to comment upon, other texts, source texts.

The remarkable heteroglossic and, to a twentieth-century reader, 'un-novelistic' aspect of *The wild Irish girl* is its explicit invocation of non-fictional sources. In a way, this novel which pretends to be about Ireland in fact is about other texts about Ireland; and the central narrative is really a unifying central junction from which references are thrown out to different discursive traditions in the anchoring footnotes. If we want to find out the novel's relationship with Ireland, or better, with the image of Ireland which it invokes, then we must approach this relationship by way of the footnotes.

Heteroglossia, footnotes and source traditions

Let us now turn to Morgan's source texts, since these are such a conspicuous presence in her novel. I can see three main textual traditions underlying the novelistic narrative of *The wild Irish girl*. The most important of these is antiquarian discourse, on which many of Morgan's footnotes are explicitly grafted. (The other two, to which I shall return, are the genres of sentimental comedy and travel description.)

Elsewhere, I have paid more particular attention to that tradition of eighteenth-century Irish antiquarianism, to the issues it addressed and the stance it took through the course of the eighteenth century. In my view, the antiquarians constituted an interface between the Anglo-Irish, Protestant élite and Ireland's Gaelic sub-culture, and they did much to formulate a Gaelic iconography of Ireland's national identity – thus indirectly preparing the stock of images on which cultural nationalism like that of Davis and Pearse could draw. That tradition includes names like Charles Vallancey, Joseph Cooper Walker, Sylvester O'Halloran or Thomas Campbell, whose work has deeply influenced our image of ancient Ireland, though their names may no longer be common currency. But those names are all there, in the footnotes of Lady Morgan – their last discernible presence in the realm of literature, perhaps, before they disappeared from sight under new sediments and in a new stratification of discursive practice.

The division of discourse into literary (artistic) and non-literary (i.e., referential) fields is to some extent an invention of the nineteenth century. Morgan's novel gains its interest in that it shows almost the exact incipience of that division; for here referential discourse is not yet fully banished from the realm of literature, but it is only half admitted, relegated to footnotes, half-submerged under, and quarantined from, the fictional main text. As I shall discuss in the next chapter, the names of Vallancey, O'Halloran, Walker and the others were to lose their currency in these post-Union decades. In the realms of archeology and philology these men were eclipsed by more scientific successors, and were dismissed for being too fanciful, while from the realm of literature proper they were dismissed for being too referential, too academic. Yet with Morgan they are still there, half-hidden at the bottom of the page, in the small print. If one wishes to contend that the antiquarians of the late eighteenth century more or less fixed the iconography of a Gaelic Ireland, then the mediation of Morgan – a mediation across the gradually widening divide in the field of *belles lettres*, between referential discourse of the Enlightenment and the fictional 'literature as art' of the nineteenth century – is of cardinal importance. *The wild Irish girl* marks the introduction, the translation of the antiquarian iconography into Anglo-Irish literature.

I think that this applies more to Morgan than to Maria Edgeworth. Edgeworth, who is rooted in the pre-Union Protestant gentry of Anglo-Ireland, marks the beginning (rather than a transition, as in Morgan's case) of a genteel tradition of

Anglo-Irish fiction often focussing on the Ireland of the Big House, stretching to Somerville and Ross, to Synge, to Yeats and Lady Gregory; and the less genteel or polished author of *The wild Irish girl* should perhaps be seen, not so much as a minor, *manqué* contemporary of Edgeworth than as a minor successor of Charlotte Brooke, continuing the tradition in Anglo-Irish literature of a romanticization of Gaelic Ireland which stretches to Mangan and Davis, and ultimately to Patrick Pearse – and indeed to the programme of Gaelic revivalism as it inspired the early Gaelic League and early neo-Gaelic literature.

The difference between Edgeworth and Morgan is also related to that between their respective family backgrounds, especially in respect to their fathers. Edgeworth's father was a well-regarded Anglo-Irish gentleman with a town named after his estate, a member of the Irish parliament and of the Royal Irish Academy; Morgan's father was an actor. Owenson senior was perhaps the most famous actor of Irish parts of his day, hugely popular with audiences for his interpretation of quaint Irish roles. His special forte was his knowledge of Gaelic and he often threw into his performances a Gaelic song or two, thus heightening nationality and local colour; and it is reported that he also sang Gaelic songs over his daughter's cradle when she was still a baby. Morgan describes in her *Patriotic sketches* how in early childhood her imagination was 'warmed into feeling' and 'kindled into ardour, by the pensive legend of national woe, or the romantic tale of national heroism.' She is proud to have 'caught from the paternal lip, the transmitted "song of other times", breathed in the native strains of my native country' (1: i–ii). The identification between Gaelic song and True Irishness goes back a long way in Morgan's life – as does the notion that True Irishness must be sought Elsewhere, as the *representandum* behind the mimesis, as the folk-ways which the actor theatrically invokes and impersonates; what we see can only be the mere representation.

It is a matter of record that Owenson senior had in Morgan a dutiful and affectionate daughter. She appeared on the stage with him, organized benefit performances for him when his star began to wane and took care of him in his old age.[40] Many critics agree that she gave a fond, sentimental picture of her father in her portrait of Glorvina's father, the old but powerful and dignified Gaelic prince.

For one thing, we see here an affiliation with the native tradition, partly mediated by the antiquarians, partly invoked directly through her father (whose original name was McOwen – Mac Eoghain or Mac Eóin – rather than Owenson). But as her father was, first and foremost, an actor, we may also interpret these indications to the effect that *The wild Irish girl* translates yet another genre into the medium of novelistic narrative: namely, that of the sentimental comedy with its sentimentalized Stage Irishman. This stock character is a phenomenon in English literature whose existence was short-lived but remarkably intense. Unlike the despicable or buffoon-like Stage Irishman of earlier tradition, the sentimental comedy as it became popular in the second half of the eighteenth century gradually ameliorated the image of the Irish stock character until he became endearing, artless, a bit of a wastrel or vagrant, perhaps, but likeable and full of the most commendable emotions.[41] This type disappeared from English literature after the 1798 rebellion and with the eclipse of the sentimental comedy as such, that is to say, after Macready; one of his last stirrings is in a brief benefit performance organized in 1807 as a showpiece for Owenson. In this 'prelude', entitled *The Irish actor, or the recruiting manager*, Owenson played the Stage Irishman Phelim O'Guffinocarrollocraneymacfrane.[42] But the type was to drop out of theatrical practice until it was revived, in a more national-heroic sense, by Dion Boucicault in pieces like *The shaughraun*. Moreover, as I shall argue further on (pp. 170–2), sentimental verse throughout the century was to celebrate 'colourful peasants' who in themselves are a straightforward continuation of the Stage Irishman; Morgan's own verse 'Kate Kearney' being an early case in point.

What I said of Morgan's novelistic adoption of antiquarian discourse also applies, I think, to her relation with the earlier, now gradually obsolescing genre of the sentimental comedy with its sentimentalized Stage Irishmen. It was a genre and a discursive convention with which she had, one might almost say, close family ties; and a case can be made for a reading of *The wild Irish girl* as a novelistic adaptation of a sentimental Irish comedy. The fact, for instance, that most of the incident of plot is generated by the incognito disguise and assumed identity of the hero, and the fact that the happy end coincides with a re-establishment of the hero's true identity, indicate narrative structures taken directly from the English comedy tradition, for which there are few previous examples in earlier novels. Besides, Morgan's descriptions frequently hover on the edge of describing pantomime and have the 'acted' quality of a *tableau vivant* or a stage climax:

> 'Merciful Providence!' exclaimed the bridegroom, and lowering his face, sank on the shoulder of the priest. That voice pierced to the heart of his rival; who raised his eyes, and thus clung to the railing of the altar, faintly uttering, 'Oh! God, my father!' – Glorvina, released from the nerveless clasp of her lover, sunk on her knees between the father, and the son, alternately fixing her wild regards on each; til suddenly turning them on the now apparently expiring Prince, and throwing her arms around his neck, she frantically exclaimed, 'It is my father they will destroy!' and, sobbing convulsively, clung closer to him (p. 242).

A third textual tradition which is introduced into the novelistic discourse by *The wild Irish girl* is that of the travel description. Irish travel descriptions as a genre can be followed back at least as far as the year 1699, when the London bookseller John Dunton travelled into Connemara; and though the genre gradually developed into the still-existing one of scenic descriptions of Ireland (e.g. Heinrich Böll), it became particularly influential in the dissemination and discursive formulation of Irish attitudes during the second half of the eighteenth century. Indeed, a correlation may be made between the type of imagery which was used for travel descriptions of those decades (Bush, Young, Twiss, authors who have been quoted widely ever since) and that of the contemporary Irish comedy. The late eighteenth-century travel description, too, did much to change received images of Ireland, for whereas the Gaelic Irish had universally been seen, until *c.* 1750, as benighted barbarians, and the Anglo-Irish settlers as the upholders of European civilization, the travel descriptions of men like Bush and Young did much to invert that view and to represent the Anglo-Irish upper class as duelling, profligate, loutish colonialists oppressing the honest, long-suffering Gaelic peasantry. *Castle Rackrent* would have been impossible without the precursorship of Young's *Tour in Ireland*.

Morgan's storylines recall the source tradition of travel description. Horatio describes in letters to an English friend his journey to, and his experiences in Ireland. What is more, many episodes describe Horatio's adventures while he travels, the places he sees and the people he meets. And once again, the footnotes testify to Morgan's debt, for the names of the most illustrious travel writers are all there, italicized and often extensively quoted, Young, Bush, La Tocnaye, etc. Again, it is these travellers' assessments of the relationship between English landlord and Irish peasant, set amidst glowing evocations of the scenic background, which Morgan invokes and adopts. Indeed she does so to a far more simplistic degree than Maria Edgeworth, whose view of that relationship is more ironic and less ready to reconcile conflicting interests in the optimism of a happy-ever-after marriage. As Robert Tracy has rightly pointed out, Morgan's version of the Anglo-Irish–Gaelic conflict is too pro-Gaelic, too appreciative of the claims of Gaelic history, to be adopted by Edgeworth.[43]

The failure of these novels to achieve the realist plausibility, cohesion and self-contained evenemential consistency of, say, Jane Austen proves to be directly linked to the fractured nature of their source traditions, their Irish settings and their Irish historical background. This is perhaps one of the more fundamental elements which such romantic Irish novels bequeathed to later representations of Ireland: a deep-seated suspicion that no cohesive, ordered narrative could be mapped onto the sublime and unpredictable wildness of the Irish chronotope and its adventure time. To quote Bakhtin,

> Whenever Greek adventure-time appears in the subsequent development of the European novel, initiative is handed over to chance, which controls meetings and failures to meet – either as an impersonal, anonymous force in the novel or as fate, as divine foresight, as romantic 'villains' or romantic 'secret benefactors'. Examples of the latter one can still find in Walter Scott's historical novels.[44]

That goes, *a fortiori*, for Morgan and Maturin; and it will persist, not only in the failure of a realist Irish novel to emerge after 1830, but also in the pervasive commonplace of a nightmarish, paranoid history driven by blind chance and by invisible plots.

The National Tale between narrative and spectacle

There is that Anglo-Irish literature which is Anglo-Irish in class background as well as in the fact that it comes out of Ireland in the English language; there is that Anglo-Irish literature which comes out of the Protestant gentry of Ireland, which often sees Ireland through the focus of the Big House, and which often mirrors the perplexities of the Anglo-Irish social predicament – the literature of George Moore's *A drama in muslin*, of Somerville and Ross, of Yeats, Jennifer Johnston or Helen Wykham's *Ribstone pippins*. That tradition takes its cue, obviously, from Maria Edgeworth. This is not, however, the romantic tradition of Anglo-Irish literature, the tradition of Mangan, Davis, Pearse; the tradition also of Griffin and Kickham, of Boucicault. It is my contention that that tradition goes back to Lady Morgan. To be sure, her *oeuvre* was not the profound source of inspiration to later writers that Edgeworth's was – in fact, people were almost eager to relegate the Whiggish, eccentric, flamboyant and vaguely unrespectable actor's daughter Morgan to oblivion.[45] And yet it seems that *The wild Irish girl* is a type of clearing-house through which most pre-romantic appreciations of Ireland, its inhabitants and its antiquities, passed from out-of-date modes of discourse into the realm of literature, where they were given a new lease of life. The wild Irish girl stands at the crossroads between pre-romantic and romantic Ireland; and she marks the beginnings of political romance and romantic politics. Thomas Flanagan already observed that *The wild Irish girl* 'gave first form to the rhetoric of Irish nationalists';[46] Tom Dunne, who situates *The wild Irish girl* in the 'shadowy boundary that then existed between the two related forms of literary discourse', history-writing and fiction, points out that 'Through such writings, at least in part, the work of antiquarians and historians entered the arena of political discourse.'[47] I would add that its characteristic heteroglossia could instill literary appeal into political rhetoric, and into the literary imagination a nationalistic iconography of past greatness. As I shall argue in the following chapters, her successors in this respect were not so much the early to mid-century historians, but rather the poets of *The nation*, who inherited Morgan's fondness of Old Gaelic exoticism and of explicative antiquarian footnotes. Tom Dunne rightly stresses the fact that Morgan, in the preface to a 1846 re-edition of *The wild Irish girl*, mentioned the 'exquisite literary historical essays' of Thomas Davis among her novel's ablest successors.[48] After the Famine, and under Davis's influence, Morgan's vision was to re-emerge in history-writing – particularly in the populist historiography which, in an interesting echo of Morgan's 'National Tales', set out to relate 'The Story of Ireland' (cf. below, pp. 150–6).

The wild Irish girl makes it obvious how recalcitrant the Matter of Ireland was to straightforward narrative. Time and again, the narration is interrupted in order to give digressive explanations, to fill in the historical background, to argue the rights and wrongs of the country. Indeed there is a pronounced tendency for the action to be stopped or frozen: either in arresting 'scenes', arranged like genre paintings, with fraught characters frozen in affecting poses; or else in the constant possibility that the *place of the action* (Ireland, its landscapes, its buildings and *lieux de mémoire*) takes over from the action itself, and that the vicissitudes of the characters are neglected in order to present the reader with a picturesque canvas.

Here we recognize the tendency towards *spectacle*. Ireland is a *spectacular* country, a place to behold. This spectacular quality has been analysed by Peter Brooks in his study on *The melodramatic imagination*,[49] and the link between spectacle and melodrama will come as no surprise to those who have tasted the theatrical and high-strung flavour of *The wild Irish girl*, with its antecedents in sentimental comedy. What is more, the *spectacular* can also count as an echo of the Ireland of magnificent scenery as described and engraved in travel descriptions: an accumulation of landscapes and sights to be seen. In both these respects, the spectacular quality is at odds with Morgan's basic concern, namely to provide a *narrative*. Spectacle, by its very nature, must punctuate and suspend narrative; spectacle is the presentation of a discrete situation rather than the setting forth of a train of events. Spectacle represents objects in space as opposed to narrative which represents events in time: the opposition was made famous in Lessing's *Laokoon*, which opposes *Nebeneinander* to *Nacheinander*, the plastic principle of spatial arrangement as opposed to the dramatic principle of temporal-evenemential arrangement (cf. above, p. 7). Thus, ironically enough, use of local colour and the heteroglossic echoes of Morgan's textual source traditions stifle the possibility of creating a novel such as that genre was to develop elsewhere in the course of the nineteenth century. It comes as no surprise to find that no Great Tradition of novel-writing is to be encountered in nineteenth-century Ireland. After a few decades, the representation of Irish identity in literature was to turn to other genres: poetry, narrative history and (towards the end of the century) drama. As we shall see, Morgan's heritage to the nineteenth century was not the creation of a viable Irish Novel, but rather the transmission of earlier modes of representation, and the urge to add explanatory footnotes to the description of pathetic scenes – and, of course, the auto-exoticist reflex.

The Gaelocentric tradition of cultural nationalism, which we can trace from Morgan through the nineteenth century, was not the product or even the specific outlook of Ireland's Gaelic population. For Gaelocentric or Gaelophile cultural nationalism is, is the final analysis, an Anglo-Irish projection or invention – or at best an Anglo-Irish transmogrification of Gaelic raw materials. It is largely motivated by an exotic fascination with an alien culture: the fascination of the eighteenth-century antiquarians and of the travellers, the fascination of the actor's daughter two generations removed from native, Gaelic-speaking roots and married to a knighted Ascendancy physician. In that respect, too, Irish cultural nationalism, grown as it has out of a culturally and politically divided country, is to a large extent an interiorized form of exoticism, auto-exoticism. The fascination with things Gaelic is a nostalgic and an exoticist one. Gaelic antiquity proves to have unsuspected riches, to have mysterious links with other ancient civilizations like the Greek (constantly invoked by Glorvina), it is interesting in that it is completely different from familiar culture. The fascination with the Gaelic past and with the Gaelic language is a fascination with the unknown. For authors like Edgeworth and Yeats, who see Ireland in terms of its inner divisions between Gaels and Anglo-Irish, this exoticism remains vested in what is the alien alterity of the native Gaels. But when Morgan consecrates a marriage between the two traditions in the persons of Horatio and Glorvina, thus uniting the Gaelic and the Anglo-Irish poles, English-language discourse can begin to identify with that exotic culture, can begin to see itself as somehow belonging to it.

Here is another facet of that mind-set which I term auto-exoticist. Not only does it involve the reflex to 'see ourselves as others see us', or in the 'cracked lookingglass of a servant', or in an amused fascination with one's own quaintness; it is also an exoticist preoccupation with the curious, unknown nature of Ireland's other, Gaelic culture, while at the same time enshrining that culture as a central part of one's national identity. Irish cultural nationalism as a form of internalized exoticism takes its initial shape in a romantic atmosphere, as expressed most powerfully for the first time in *The wild Irish girl*. Perhaps Horatio finds a new meaning in life, a healing for his *ennui*, his spleen, his prejudice, through the tender ministrations of Glorvina and in the interesting world of Irish life. But he is not only the taker in this bargain, for he has something to offer too. He is an audience. He is someone, at last, to whom the incestuous preoccupation with the past and with national traditions can be divulged; he is someone who does not yet know, someone for whom the Irish identity is still unfamiliar. It is he who makes Ireland interesting, who makes Ireland exotic, to whom everything can be told and explained. Here at last is someone to whom the Gaelic Irish tradition can show how very quaint it is; and he marries into that tradition. The onlooker whose standards define quaintness becomes part of the family, and the value of exoticism can be interiorized.

As I have pointed out, there are two attitudes to discourse in the character of Glorvina. There is the Glorvina who holds forth, who garrulously vindicates the accomplishments of her country, who is as loquacious as an enthusiastic tourist guide; and there is the Glorvina whose communication is non-verbal: song at best, and otherwise mere sighs and glances. Similarly, there is that Gaelic Ireland which needs to vindicate its case, to claim understanding and sympathy, to make its accomplishments and grievances known to the world; and there is the Gaelic Ireland which remains mysterious, exotic, hidden, other and unknowable. The former sets out to convince us, the latter allures us; the former speaks the discourse of nationalism, the latter hushes the silence of exoticism. The importance of Morgan in the literary iconography of Ireland is that she is the first to fuse these two elements, the ideological and the idyllic, and that she enshrines, as an adopted national identity, the fascination value of Gaelic exoticism within the discourse of Anglo-Irish literature.

THE CHALLENGE OF THE PAST:
History and Antiquity

Antiquarian and historical views of the past

The wild Irish girl's father, the venerable Prince of Inismore, was ousted from his land and possessions because 'he would neither cut his glibbs, shave his upper lips, nor shorten his shirt' (I:114); if the reader is to take this seriously, this means that a forfeiture enforced in the later eighteenth century was based on late-medieval legislation against the *sylvestri Hiberni*.[1] Such an anachronism is remarkable. It presents the past, not in its historical development and in its own dynamism, but as an undifferentiated reservoir of 'Old Things'; it collapses the diachronic disparities between the fifteenth and the eighteenth centuries and merges it all into an undifferentiated 'long ago but not forgotten'. This approach to the past I call *antiquarian* and I oppose it to a *historical* approach, which takes due note of the transitions, changes, disruptions, developments, causalities and filiations which between them differentiate the past into a succession of events. The distinction goes back as far as Francis Bacon, who opposed *historia* to *antiquitates*.[2]

The past as a succession of events and developments, or the past as a storehouse of facts and curiosities: that opposition between the historical and the antiquarian assessment coincides fairly neatly with the one I have demonstrated above between the registers of narrative and spectacle. The deep structure underlying such binaries is probably the distinction, made famous by Lessing's *Laokoon*, between the plastic and the dramatic arts in terms of the use that is made of space and time: narrative arranges its constituent elements in time, and forms a *succession* (what Lessing called a *Nacheinander* or 'one-after-the-other'), whereas spectacle arranges its constituent elements in space and forms a *Nebeneinander* ('one-next-to-the-other'; cf above, p. 7).

The study of antiquity, as opposed to the writing of history, had traditionally dealt with objects, artefacts, remains of ancient buildings and structures of ancient languages, which it tried to describe accurately and fit into a plausible background. Such antiquarianism – the forerunner of the more modern scholarly discipline of archaeology – was concerned with the past's artefacts and heirlooms rather than its changes and developments.[3] Its activities in the eighteenth century had been severely vitiated by the fact that no reliable historical information existed by which north-European artefacts from early-medieval or pre-Christian times could be plausibly contextualized. The main framework of interpretation was based on the Bible and the semi-fabulous references in ancient geographers like Strabo or Plinius. As a result, the antiquarian analysis of the ancient past turned around in speculative circles trying to explain national origins in terms of the migrations of the tribes descending from the sons of Noah or the nations vaguely described as Celtae, Scythae or Hyperboreans by Roman or Greek sources.

The early nineteenth century witnessed the crisis of antiquarianism in a process which recalls Thomas Kuhn's model of scientific revolutions. The Biblical/classical frame of reference collapsed under the weight of ethnographical and philological information which reached European scholars, and antiquarianism underwent a paradigm shift. The speculative lucubrations of the eighteenth century, which used to be admired for their ingenuity (a frequently used appreciative qualification) became the province of amateurs, marginal to serious scholarship (which would now tend to be praised rather for its painstaking and rigorous and critical qualities). Antiquarians became figures of good-humoured fun, fanciful old fogies riding amusing hobby-horses, as in Sir Walter Scott's novel *The antiquary*. The crisis of antiquarianism resulted in the break-up of what had once been a highly-regarded scholarly pursuit in its own right. Its penchant for etymological explanations was taken over, on a more scientific footing, by the new science of comparative linguistics; its collection and study of the artefacts and non-discursive remains of ancient civilization was conducted in the form of archaeology; and to the extent that antiquarian study failed to become scientific, it was marginalized into a pursuit for more-or-less fanciful amateurs and eventually was exiled to the far reaches of occultism or the lunatic (or at least non-academic) fringes of scholarship: those who studied the Great Pyramid of Egypt for its symbolism comprising all knowledge of ancient humanity, or those who attempted to prove that the British nation descended from the Lost Tribes of Israel and could therefore lay claim to the status of God's Chosen People.[4]

Besides the division into comparative linguistics, scientific archaeology and unscientific speculation, antiquarianism, at the moment of its demise, let forth a spark of inspiration to the nascent phenomena of the historical novel, historical monuments, and the historical museum. Monuments and museums afforded a possibility of witnessing, in a public and accessible place, the past in its immediate 'hands-on' presence, redeemed from its transience and inaccesibility in an unretrievable preterite, present for us to behold as spectacle and contemporary *Nebeneinander*; a psychological need which previously had actuated the antiquarians was thus satisfied. Similarly, in the historical novel, picturesque detail and titbits from life in the past could fulfil a useful function as background colour, giving the narrative greater period authenticity. That is the antiquarian impulse as we have observed in Lady Morgan; it is also to be observed in the novels of Walter Scott.

To see the development of the scholarly investigation of the past in these terms will, as I aim to show in the next pages, throw interesting light on Irish cultural reflection, which ranged from scholarly debates in the Royal Irish Academy to ardent poems in *The nation*. The Irish national past was obscure and imperfectly understood, neglected or misrepresented by previous generations of historians, accessible only through the medium of scarce sources, which were themselves only beginning to be inventorized and which were couched in the hermetic medium of the Irish language. Moreover, the nature of the national past had become a politically fraught topic, the study of which could not be undertaken in any degree of ideological neutrality. It is highly instructive, therefore, to trace the development of the study of Gaelic antiquity in the decades after the Union, and to do so with reference to the scholarly and political context of that time. The political climate was dominated by national tension and the scholarly climate was dominated by the rise of a critical, scientific-comparative methodology. Shaped by such influences, these developments of historical investigation came to a crisis in the 1830s and 1840s, when a great controversy concerning the origin and use of the Irish Round Towers dominated the intellectual scene.

Native learning and antiquarianism after the Union

Irish antiquarianism had had its heyday in the second half of the eighteenth century. After the comparatively peaceful passing of the Stuart *coup* in 1745, sentimental primitivism could come to attenuate the anti-Gaelic stance of the Anglo-Irish élite. The investigation of Irish history was adopted by scholarly societies of Enlightenment vintage and came to rely more and more on native sources and native help; witness the way in which Charles Vallancey collaborated with Charles O'Conor of Belanagar, and Joseph Cooper Walker and Charlotte Brooke made use of the services of Theophilus O'Flanagan. Native learning was slowly beginning to be adopted by the Anglo-Irish intelligentsia, in a pattern that was to persist after the Union and into the nineteenth century. Sir William Betham relied on the help of Edward O'Reilly and Owen Connellan, and the expertise of Eugene O'Curry and John O'Donovan was made accessible in the public domain initially because these men were enlisted by Larcom and Petrie as assistants in the Ordnance Survey of Ireland. Connellan, O'Donovan and O'Curry made a greater name and a better career for themselves in the world of learning than O'Conor, O'Flanagan or even O'Reilly had done (though O'Conor and O'Reilly had been allowed into the ranks of the Royal Irish Academy). Connellan was appointed Irish historiographer-royal by George IV, William IV and Victoria, and obtained the chair of Celtic at Queen's College, Cork; O'Donovan received an honorary doctorate from Trinity College, Dublin as well as a (meaningless) appointment to the chair of Celtic at Queen's College, Belfast; and for O'Curry there was eventually the professorial chair in Newman's Catholic University. Indeed the emancipation of native-born scholars in terms of professional career prospects is closely linked to the educational facilities open to Catholics in Ireland. O'Flanagan worked in Trinity College and in the Royal Irish Academy as a mere assistant or amanuensis, and could not hope to do any better than to set up a private academy in Limerick. A Catholic scholar like John Lanigan, author of the *Ecclesiastical history of Ireland* (1822) could only reap academic laurels by going to the Continent: he was given a chair at the Italian university of Pavia before returning to Ireland in 1796 with at least the prestige of a professorial title. Academic status was an important thing in the gradual professionalization of the historical sciences, and until the establishment of Newman's Catholic University (which finally brought academic recognition and security to Eugene O'Curry) the only Irish institution offering career possibilities to native scholarship was the seminary at Maynooth, founded in 1795 as a conciliatory measure by the government to cater for those Irish aspirants to the priesthood whom the French Revolution had barred from pursuing their call on the Continent. Maynooth was a vitally important institution in the life of Catholic Ireland; not only were the meetings of its governing council in fact tantamount to bishops' conferences (banned as such under the existing legislation),[5] it also became an important scholarly focus for an Irish Catholic intelligentsia. It afforded a professorial chair for Lanigan when that scholar was driven from the Continent by the tide of revolutionary wars (Lanigan was later deprived of his Maynooth place by the malicious rumour that he had Jansenist sympathies); it gave employment to the Gaelic scholar Paul O'Brien, author of an Irish grammar. Yet even O'Donovan never managed, for all his widely-acknowledged learning and vastly valuable contributions to scholarship, to keep destitution at bay; his tokenist appointment to a chair of Celtic at Queen's College, Belfast, was poorly remunerated (indeed, there were no students forthcoming to follow his courses there) and he had to work exceedingly long hours to make a living by his pen; after his death, a charitable fund had to be set up for his widow and children.

Later nineteenth-century trends towards professionalization aside, the pattern set in the Patriot decades was to persist until well after the Union: that the investigation of Irish antiquity and the Irish language and literature was a matter for Anglo-Irish gentlemen gathered together in clubbish societies and assisted by scholars with a native knowledge of Gaelic culture. On the whole, such Anglo-Irish antiquarianism had flourished under protection of the Patriotic political climate.[6] The investigation of the nation's past was considered a philanthropic, public-spirited effort to improve the state of general knowledge and to enhance the nation's standing by elucidating its ancient origins, and the subscribers to the learned volumes of these decades include a preponderance of Patriotic public figures; it was, also, the Patriot politican Henry Flood who, in his testament, bequeathed funds to Trinity College towards the establishment of a professorial chair in Irish. Flood, moreover, stipulated that the first incumbent of that chair, 'if he should be then living', was to be Charles Vallancey, the most celebrated anti-quary of his day, whose enthusiasm was behind a multitude of scholarly initiatives: he was one of the founding members of the Royal Irish Academy, had started and conducted a scholarly review entitled Collectanea de rebus Hibernicis, and was a helpful patron to many men who, like Lanigan, O'Flanagan and others, had more learning than he but less financial security.

Vallancey's name has by now become a by-word for hare-brained fancy. He read dictionaries as modern critics would read Finnegans wake, based elaborate theories on comparisons between languages of which he was utterly ignorant – Gaelic and Algonquin, or Gaelic and Chinese. He could blithely assert that the great Gaelic sixth-century legislator Cenn Faeladh was known in China under the name of Confulus, erroneously rendered as Confucius.[7] A modern reader may marvel that this man was regarded, by all but a few, as the leading antiquarian of his day; but on closer scrutiny the case appears less bizarre. Vallancey, after all, worked in a context where the central model of cultural antiquity was provided by the Old Testament. In that biblical context, it makes perfect sense to see kinship between Gaelic and Hebrew, or Gaelic and Chinese, since all linguistic difference dates back only to the Tower of Babel, and all the world's nations are related in that all descend from the three sons of Noah: Sem, Ham and Japhet. The model was, to adopt a phrase from early ethnology, monogenist, tracing human diversity back to a single common origin. Etymology – the study of linguistic derivations and similarities – was conducted on a purely lexical basis: languages were seen simply as collections of individual words, which in turn were combinations of radical syllables; grammatical structures governing the morphology of word-formation were not taken into account. To demonstrate similarities between Gaelic, Hebrew and Chinese by reducing them to their constituent syllables was perfectly permissible and followed established linguistic practice; it was as if one could demonstrate architectural similarities between the Parthenon, the Alhambra and the Great Pyramid by reducing all three edifices to lookalike piles of rubble, mortar and broken stones. In that context, Vallancey's fallacies become less idiosyncratic and less egregious, and his antiquarian heritage, which threw its shadow well into the nineteenth century, begins to warrant closer scrutiny.

According to the paradigm in which Vallancey worked, the nations of Northern Europe were all descended from Japhet, son of Noah (while as the Semitic nations and their languages were derived from Noah's son Sem, and the black races were considered to be descendants of Noah's son Ham). In particular, the European continent was held to have been populated by the offspring of Japhet's progeny Gomer and Magog.[8] The link between the prehistoric inhabitants of the British Isles (Scoti) and their biblical ancestor was often sought in the similarly-named Scyths mentioned by classical Greek sources. Thus, a model which we may call Scytho-Celtic was arrived at, which traced the Celtic Scoti back by way of the north and east European Scyths to, ultimately, Japhet and Noah. There were, however, variations on this model. Various antiquaries were convinced that the Celts had reached the British Isles, not through the heart of the European continent, but by the circuitous sea route leading from the Middle East to Carthage and pre-Roman Spain to the British Isles; and in order to bolster this model they could point out the evidence for ancient Phoenician tin trade mentioned by classical authors, as well as the version propounded by native sources: for the Lebor Gabála Érenn, followed by all native scholars including Keating, held that the original Gaelic ancestor to settle Ireland was Míl Easpáine, the Spanish one, whose ancestors had come to Spain by way of Egypt. Against the Scytho-Celtic model, then, was placed the Phoenician model – a debate in antiquarian linguistics that goes back as far as the mid-seventeenth-century confrontation between the Phoenician-oriented French scholar Samuel Bochart (friend of Sir James Ware) and the Scytho-Celtic champion, the Dutch scholar Marcus Boxhorn (who influenced Edward Lhuyd and Gottfried Wilhelm Leibniz).

In Irish antiquarian practice, a certain political flavour inhered in the choice of historical model. Those who took a positive interest in Irish antiquity, who relied on native amanuenses and were willing to envisage a prestigious, highly civilized origin for the country's native inhabitants, tended to favour the Phoenician model; it was this school that had closest ties with the Patriotic element in public life (witness Flood's choice of Vallancey for his endowed Trinity chair). More conservative, anglocentric scholars who preferred to believe that Ireland was primordially a barbaric country where all traces of culture were introduced by outside influences such as the Vikings or the English, naturally rejected the Phoenician model and endorsed a Scytho-Celtic one. The main representative of this school was the Irish antiquary Ledwich, supported by British colleagues such as Pinkerton.

The decades between 1775 and 1800 saw increasingly vituperative altercations between the two schools. Ledwich and Vallancey, who originally had collaborated in *Collectanea de rebus Hibernicis*, began to use that forum to excoriate one another. The case of Ledwich is interesting. He exercised considerable critical sense in debunking Vallancey's Phoenician fancies, but became every bit as heedless and headstrong when it came to expounding his own Viking-oriented ideas.[9] Among the Irish Patriotic audience which took a sympathetic interest in the origins of their native country, Vallancey's party (including in its ranks scholars like Sylvester O'Halloran and the somewhat more sedate Joseph Cooper Walker) kept the upper hand in the debate; in Britain, the Scytho-Celtic approach of Pinkerton and Whitaker was in the ascendant. In addition, a competing model should be mentioned which had some influence in the nineteenth century: the British antiquary Jacob Bryant published a massive book in 1775, reprinted in 1806, entitled *Analysis of antient mythology*. In its three weighty tomes Bryant drew up a Casaubon-style Key to All Mythologies and explained the cultures and religions of the Middle and Far East as vestiges of a Hamitic complex, derived from Noah's third son Ham and reaching from ancient Egypt and Assyria to India, the defining characteristic of which was the worship of the serpent (or serpent's egg) and of sexuality and fertility. Bryant called this cultural stratum 'Cushite' or 'Cuthite' after Ham's son Cush.

Irish antiquarianism was plunged into a crisis by a combination of political and scholarly events. In scholarly terms, the rise of the Indo-European model exercised a considerable destabilizing influence on Irish speculations on the national origins, and in political terms, the rising of 1798 and the Union of 1800 placed the estimate of the national past under a great political mortgage. Conservative opinion saw in 1798 a re-enactment of the traumatic rebellion of 1641: a conclusive proof of the irredeemable barbarism of the native Irish. In the conservative view, Anglo-Irish Patriots were accused of culpably conniving, through their sympathy and laxity, with the disaffection of this nation which could obviously only be held under control by repressively authoritarian government. This conservative, unionist backlash against the rebellious Gaels and their Patriotic fellow-travellers naturally embarrassed those antiquarians who had taken a rose-tinted interest in the exotic and interesting antiquity of the Gaels; it vindicated the negative estimates of Ledwich and Pinkerton and placed the entire Phoenician school under a cloud. J.C. Walker wrote to Pinkerton to confirm the latter's malicious suspicion that 'Vallancey must [. . .] be hurt at the conduct of those whose champion he has been', and could only offer the following limp defence of the embarrassed savant, which implausibly conflates moral character, ethnicity and linguistic knowledge:

> the rebellion began amongst, and was for a considerable time confined to, the des-
> cendants of the English and other nations that settled in the counties of Dublin,
> Wicklow, and Wexford. I do not believe it would be possible to find one hundred or
> even fifty people in those three counties who understand and speak the Irish
> language.[10]

This makes more sense if we realize how strong the anti-English subtext was that ran through the Phoenician model. The presupposition was that ancient Ireland had had a native tradition of high civility, which was now lost owing to the violent destruction and wholesale ruin that was brought upon the country in modern times. In the opposition between civility and barbarism, the Anglo-centric view saw the Irish as savages and the English presence as a force of civility; the Phoenician hypothesis turned the tables, and predicated civility on the native Gaels while bracketing the English presence with the Viking spolia-tions, seeing them as violent disruptions. This implicit valorization was subliminally reinforced by the fact that the link between Phoenicia and Ireland was usually traced by way of Carthage, and that a similar pattern was detected in Carthaginian-Roman relations as in Irish-English ones.[11] Thus, Vallancey (himself a general officer in the Engineers, a staunch member of the establish-ment and certainly not subversively anti-English) could write:

> Almost all Carthaginian manuscripts were committed to the flames, and the
> History of this brave and learned People, has been written by their most bitter
> Enemies, the Greeks and Romans; in this too they resemble the Irish.[12]

Indeed the pattern was imposed on all obscure parts of Gaelic pre-history: the Irish were successively derived from all the ousted races and lost civilizations in world history, whose names only entered the record as they encountered their overthrowers and vilifiers. Ultimately the line of descent is traced back from Phoenicia to the Holy Land, and Vallancey speculates that the Phoenicians (of whom Carthage was indeed a colony) were originally 'in all probability [. . .] no other than the indigenae of the Land of Promise, the *Chanaanites*', driven thence by Joshua and his chosen people.

One may see why men like Ledwich, an ordained minister in the Established Church of Ireland, had strong reservations about such an approach to the Irish past; and one can see why it abruptly ceased to be fashionable after 1798. Irish history-writing in the opening decades of the nineteenth century on the whole steered clear of the airy realms of antiquarian speculation – the field was left to Ledwich, whose *Antiquities of Ireland* was reprinted in 1804, and to Walker, whose more pro-Gaelic *Historical memoirs of the Irish bards* was reprinted in 1808. Historians proper abandoned the late-eighteenth-century ambition to give philosophic accounts of Irish history and tended, in the opening years after the Union, to address the conflicts of the 1790s, to assess the causes and effects, the rights and the wrongs, of the United Irish rising and the enforced Act of Union.[13] The study of Gaelic antiquity fell under a cloud, lost its fashionableness in the salons of Dublin as that city itself, deprived of its metropolitan status and of its parliament, sank into provincialism.

A good indication to that effect is the sudden inertia of the Royal Irish Academy on the antiquarian front. It had produced six volumes of *Transactions* in the decade between 1787 and 1797, each of which included a section of antiquities, with contributions by Vallancey, O'Halloran, Walker and O'Flanagan among others. In contrast, the next six volumes, published over the period 1800–1815, had little or nothing of Irish interest in their antiquities sections, and although men like Caesar Otway and James Hardiman began to take up antiquarian topics again thereafter, the publication rate as a whole stagnated badly: only two additional volumes appeared between 1815 and 1828. Whatever did appear in these decades was reticent and matter-of-fact, dealing with the description of archaeological finds, and deliberately refraining from wild theories about the prestigious or barbaric origin of the Gaels. Thus, Thomas Wood, in his essay, 'On the mixture of fable and fact in the early annals of Ireland, and on the best mode of ascertaining what degree of credit the ancient documents are justly entitled to', studiously avoided the very mention of a Phoenician or Vallanceyesque model,[14] and J.C. Walker concluded his essay, 'On the origin of romantic fabling in Ireland', with the following disclaimer:

> I might have urged the probability of the Irish bards being descendants of an Oriental colony; and inheriting, of course, the inventive faculties peculiar to the East; but I have studiously avoided every assertion, or conjecture, that could lead to controversy. I have no system to support.[15]

But the Patriotic, orientalizing model of Irish antiquity, though not often openly propounded, was tenacious enough; significantly, though few antiquarians endorsed the now largely discredited Vallancey, they all shared an intense and openly expressed disgust with regard to Vallancey's adversary Ledwich; indeed, it may be said that, whatever differences of opinion prevailed among antiquarians in the first half of the nineteenth century, they all concurred in excoriating Ledwich. Vallancey himself was still alive and did publish two additional volumes of *Collectanea de rebus Hibernicis*, by now a highly eccentric one-man venture; he was occasionally championed against his critics, largely on the basis of his earlier charisma in the field of learning. In his 'Remarks on the Irish language, with a review of its grammars, glossaries, vocabularies and dictionaries', James Scurry defended Vallancey against the strictures of Edward O'Reilly.[16]

This O'Reilly, in turn, was perhaps the most important Gaelic scholar prior to John O'Donovan. He was amanuensis to the Ulster King of Arms, Sir William Betham, whose genealogical researches he assisted; his Gaelic studies are among the most valuable of the early century.[17] With O'Reilly, a tenuous tradition of native scholarship and antiquarian interest begins to reinvigorate the world of Anglo-Irish scholarship. The Iberno-Celtic Society, of which he was the assistant secretary and whose sole volume of *Transactions* he edited in 1820, was itself a revamped continuation of Theophilus O'Flanagan's Gaelic Society of Dublin.[18] But unlike the Gaelic Society, which had been modest in its membership's social standing, O'Reilly's Iberno-Celtic venture stood under the august presidency of the Duke of Leinster, and its membership included, not only four former members of the Gaelic Society, but also eight peers, six baronets, two MPs and two Roman Catholic bishops.

The overall impression one gets from recorded activities and publications in the years 1800–1825 is that a great deal of continuing antiquarian and cultural zeal still persisted among the Catholic and (lower-)middle class intellectuals (many of whom came from native hedge-school milieus), but that this interest could no longer count on the overt support and patronage of a Patriotic Anglo-Irish élite in the troubled political climate. Men like Theophilus O'Flanagan, Peter O'Connell, Edward O'Reilly and (in his early career) Owen Connellan had little official, prestigious backing for their Gaelic expertise,[19] and the great number of Irish language primers and grammars that were produced in this time were much more modest in presentation than Vallancey's *Grammar of the Iberno-Celtic or Irish language* of 1773. They were practical grammars rather than scholarly linguistic analyses, aimed for everyday usage rather than academic consultation;[20] Paul O'Brien's *Grammar* was a textbook for his courses at Maynooth. With the person of O'Reilly, however, we see how Irish learning, linguistic and antiquarian knowledge, slowly regained a degree of social acceptance.

This process was helped by the high reputation of a few native, Catholic scholars who in spite of their religious disadvantage had managed to carve out a respectable scholarly career for themselves: Lanigan, author of the well-regarded *Ecclesiastical history of Ireland* (1822) or the great archivist Dr Charles O'Conor, whose massive conspectus *Rerum Hibernicarum scriptores veteres*, published in 1814,[21] was never mentioned but in awe – and rightly so, as in discussing important manuscript sources it lay the very foundation for later scholarship in Gaelic philology and ancient history. There was also the less academic, but very widespread influence of the hugely successful *Irish melodies*, in which Thomas Moore recalled the romance of bygone Gaeldom in numbers appearing, successively, in 1808, 1810, 1811, 1815, 1818, 1821, 1824 and 1834 (a collected edition first appearing in 1820). Moore himself showed considerable antiquarian interest in his choice of topics, and handsomely acknowledged the work of O'Flanagan in a note accompanying the song 'Avenging and Bright', which was based on the story of Deirdre and the sons of Usnach – first made available to the English-speaking world in O'Flanagan's translation as published in the *Transactions of the Gaelic Society* of 1808. Moore concluded his source reference with the remark 'Whatever may be thought of those sanguine claims to antiquity, which Mr. O'Flanagan and others advance for the literature of Ireland, it would be a very lasting reproach upon our nationality, if the Gaelic researches of this gentleman did not meet with all the liberal encouragement they merit.' O'Flanagan's Deirdre edition also provided the source text for Ferguson's 'Death of the children of Usnach', which appeared as part of Ferguson's *Hibernian nights' entertainments* and sparked off all subsequent interest in the Deirdre theme from Standish O'Grady to Synge.[22]

Prince, poet, peasant chief: George IV, Thomas Moore and Captain Rock

The 1820s opened amidst sectarian politics and the continuing burden of post-1798 recrimination. The decade was rung in by the deaths of Henry Grattan and of George III; it ended with the passing of Catholic Emancipation, the death of George IV, the impending Reform Bill, and a fresh start in cultural and scholarly life in Ireland. Catholic Emancipation, that British promise which had been held out even during the passing of the Act of Union, had failed to be secured by the British government against the opposition from ultra-conservative quarters and the monarch himself. The failure to deliver Catholic Emancipation had embittered Irish political feelings and had given O'Connell his first great campaigning platform. Irish politics in the early 1820s were sour indeed, as becomes obvious from the visit that was made in 1821 by George IV. This was the first time (not counting 1688–90) that an English king set foot in the Irish capital since Richard II's expedition of 1399, and it was a highly equivocal success. George III had clung to life, 'an old, mad, blind, despised and dying king', until 1820, and it was not until 1821 that the Prince Regent, 'the dregs of his race', could fulfill his long-standing desire to mount the throne. His earlier Liberal and pro-Emancipation sympathies had by then dissipated, and the transition from regency to royalty took place amidst the universal disgust of his people.[23]

George immediately proceeded to do what leaders usually do when they face unpopularity at home: he went on a foreign tour so as to bask in ceremonious welcomes and (for once) enthusiastic crowds lining the streets. George's tour as newly-crowned king took him, first to Dublin, then to his Hanover dominions and finally to Edinburgh; and it is the Edinburgh leg of this visit that is best remembered, stage-managed as it was by Walter Scott and marking the new love affair of the British royals with their colourful, romantic Scottish lands. The Edinburgh visit marked a triumphant end to the foreign tour, which had, however, begun under a cloud. The Edinburgh visit marked a kingdom's gracious acceptance of its new monarch and new dynasty;[24] the visit to Dublin was seen as an exercise in servile ingratiation to a bloated, drunken rake.

As George was about to leave Holyhead for Ireland, on 7 August, he learned that Queen Caroline, taken ill shortly after her mortification at the closed doors of Westminster Abbey, had died. Was the entire vacation to be called off? Was it to take place in solemn and cheerless mourning? By no means; true to form, George spent his crossing in merrymaking and arrived at Howth speechlessly drunk, having instructed the authorities that he did not want to see anyone in deep mourning (black crepe around his sleeve was as far as he himself went to mark his bereavement).

This turn of events marred the Dublin visit (which lasted until 3 September 1821). On the one hand, there was the excitement and honest, though short-lived enthusiasm of the Irish population, who genuinely seem to have welcomed the visit as the occasion for an end to sectarian bitterness and a fresh start with a well-disposed king; on the other hand, the cheers and festivities had from the outset an uncanny and artifical ring to them. Things got worse when it became clear to observers and gossips that Lady Conyngham, George's mistress, was also in Ireland and spent much time in the company of her widowed paramour. All this gave great offence and proved to be counter-productive. Satirical pamphlets and poems (which were dogging the vastly impopular monarch throughout this stage of his career) appeared in great number:

> Pray why are these untimely sportings hurried,
> Whilst England mourns an 'Injured Queen', un-buried?
>
> . . .
>
> As Nero fiddled whilst proud Rome was burning,
> So Pat rejoices whilst poor John Bull was mourning![25]

After the feverish round of 'processions, and feasting, and loyalty – boiling-over loyalty' was finished, and George left from Dunleary (which on the occasion was renamed 'Kingstown' in his honour), the hangover was all the greater, and it became apparent that the visit had been only superficially successful in papering over the cracks and divisions. 'The noise of the shout of welcome had [. . .] scarcely ceased to sound in men's ears, when matters fell back in their former state'.[26] The visit had failed to establish any deep sense of unified loyalty. True, the king had courted popularity by ostentatiously sporting a huge shamrock cockade, but from hindsight that appears like a mountebankish finger exercise for his appearance in tartan and kilt at Edinburgh. True, Peter O'Connell hailed the monarch with an address in Irish,[27] and the king's polite letter of thanks to his host, Lord Talbot, was published in English with a parallel Irish translation by Thaddeus Connellan; but such efforts were largely sponsored by proselytizing Protestant bodies like the Irish Society, who wanted to use Irish as a vehicle for the conversion of the Irish natives to Protestantism.[28] True, Dublin's Orangist City Corporation and Daniel O'Connell unified for the purpose of a gracious joint address; but this show of obsequious loyalty disgusted more critical spirits to such an extent that it backfired badly.[29] The fact that O'Connell knelt when presenting a laurel to George was regarded as particularly servile. Some satirists imputed that

Dan was flirting for a knighthood or a baronetcy; Curran (in terms that were taken up by Byron) was reminded of 'a bastinadoed elephant kneeling to receive the paltry rider';[30] and Thomas Moore especially, when noting the visit in his diary entry for 10 September 1821, was outraged at 'the worse than Eastern Prostration into which my countrymen have grovelled during these last few weeks'. His only excuse for this sycophancy was that 'they have so long been slaves, they know no better [. . .] it is not their own fault if they are ignorant of any medium between brawling rebellion & foot-licking idolatry'.[31] At a commemorative dinner to celebrate the happy conclusion of the visit, the Orangist Lord Mayor of Dublin proposed a toast to the 'glorious, proud and immortal memory' which antagonized the Catholics present, and sectarianism was back where it had started.[32] The following July Orangist attempts to decorate the statue of William III on Dublin's College Green led to fresh conflict.

Throughout the 1820s, disaffection and sectarian difference continued; so did the continuing agrarian unrest which formed the strongest point of continuity between pre-Union and post-Union Ireland: the spasmodic resistance of a pauperized, disenfranchised and semi-illiterate peasantry, loosely associated under names such as Whiteboys and venting their threats and grievances with anonymous letters signed by invented leaders like 'Captain Moonlight' or 'Captain Rock'. The effect of this continuing tension can best be registered in the career of Thomas Moore. Moore, already highly popular as a national poet owing to the *Irish melodies*, seems in the 1820s to have come to remember with increasing intensity his radical Patriot origins, his friendship with Robert Emmet and with the United Irishman Lord Edward Fitzgerald (whose biography he published in 1831; cf. also p. 249, n. 36). The *Irish melodies* have often been seen as lightweight subsidiary ditties alongside his Anacreontic verse and his narrative, exoticist *Lalla Rookh*: twee, syrupy drawing-room sentimentalities. However, some of them did pack a political punch and evinced an uncowed and enduring sense of Irish national separateness. Of the 124 melodies, some 85 are primarily anecdotal or sentimental in nature; but the rest do have a political or national thrust.[33] A number of Moore's poems invoked, indeed cultivated, Irish antiquity, Gaelic myth and historical events. 'Avenging and bright' is based on the Deirdre story, 'Silent, O Moyle' evokes the fate of the Children of Lir, 'The wine-cup is circling' describes the Fianna; 'Remember the glories of Brian the brave' celebrates Brian Ború; 'Let Erin remember' invokes a historically unspecific, but pre-Norman period of ancient glory, 'The valley lay smiling before me' addresses the prelude to Strongbow's landing, 'Though the last glimpse of Erin' deals with anti-bardic legislation in the sixteenth century. Some five poems deal with eighteenth-century history: 'As vanquish'd Erin' (on post-Boyne sectarianism), 'Forget not the field' (given away by the air as a poem on the Battle of Aughrim), ''tis gone, and for ever' (celebrating the brief splendour of Patriot independence in the 1780s); 'O breathe not his name' (on Emmet), 'She is far from the land' (on Emmet's lover Sarah Curran), and 'Shall the harp then be silent' (elegy on the death of Grattan).

The historical information in such poems is derived (as the footnotes acknowledge) from antiquarians like Keating, Charlotte Brooke, O'Halloran, Walker, Warner or O'Flanagan; and while the opening lines are usually innocuous enough (and the opening lines, or the opening stanza, is usually all that is remembered of these verses), the political, topical allusions are usually delivered towards the end.[34] Dermot Mac Murrough's adulterous career, leading to the Norman invasion, is evoked blandly enough in 'The valley lay smiling before me', but the concluding lines are:

> They come to divide – to dishonour,
> And tyrants they long will remain.
> But onward! – the green banner rearing,
> Go, flesh every sword to the hilt;
> On *our* side is Virtue and Erin
> On *theirs* is the Saxon and guilt.

Similarly, the 'Song of the battle-eve' is equivocal until the final stanza as to which battle may be meant – it could be Waterloo. But then comes the fourth, final stanza:

> Let those who brook the chain
> Of Saxon or of Dane
> Ignobly by their fire-sides stay;
> One sigh to home be given,
> One heartfelt prayer to heaven,
> Then, for Erin and her cause, boy, hurra! hurra! hurra!
> Then, for Erin and her cause, hurra!

Again, 'Like the bright lamp' may start off in an anodyne way on the persistence of hope through difficult times, it becomes clear as the poem progresses that its true topic is the 'national cause'. The 'spirit of Erin' appears 'thro' the tears of a long night of bondage', and hope is held out for its eventual resurgence:

> The nations have fallen, and thou still art young.
> Thy sun is but rising, when others are set
> And though slavery's cloud o'er thy morning hath hung
> The full noon of freedom shall beam round thee yet.
> Erin, O Erin! though long in the shade,
> Thy star will shine out when the proudest shall fade.

It is hard to think of this being sung to piano accompaniment by gentle young ladies in drawingrooms in London or Bath.[35] The diction of Moore's Regency verse should not obscure the straightforward, and often radical political message that was being delivered. References to 'tears in the eyes' may at first sight disqualify a poem as an effete, inconsequential nullity (Deane feels that 'Moore's elegance was frequently reduced to enervation', FDA, 1:1056); but it would be wrong to let a first line like 'Erin, the tear and the smile in thine eye' evoke the kitschy picture of an artless, charming Kathleen bravely smiling through her tears: this poem employs, with almost Wordsworthian simplicity, a clever dialectic to evoke the vacillations of faction-ridden, sectarian politics and the confused memories of glories and defeats.

But the true political importance of the *Melodies* lies in their cultivation of remembrance. To 'remember' is constantly held out as an ethical and political imperative ('Remember the glories of Brian the brave', 'Forget not the field', 'Let Erin remember', 'Remember thee! [i.e. Erin]'). Such remembrancing is now a political necessity, because Ireland between Union and Emancipation is at the nadir of its national destiny and needs the commitment and patriotic zeal of every true Irishman (Deane speaks of 'the heroic-sentimental refusal to allow any force to conquer the undying spirit', FDA 1:1054). Historical consciousness is cultivated, not (as in Lady Morgan) out of antiquarian or explanatory interest, or as a marker of Irish separateness and particularism, but for purposes of agitation; in that respect, Moore is closer to Davis than to Lady Morgan. Accordingly, the leading opposition on which many of the patriotic *Melodies* are structured concerns the contrast between silent oppression and mute despair on the one hand, and 'speaking out' or 'bursting forth in song' on the other. The most complex and powerful treatment of this opposition is, of course, his elegy on Emmet, 'Oh breathe not his name', using between-the-lines allusion in order to hint at a political radicalism which had become unmentionable. Emmet's speech from the dock ('Let no man write my epitaph') is reworked into a mode of remembrancing that uses silence and allusion rather than explicit mention.[36] Moore constantly likens himself, metaphorically, to a bard[37] or, metonymically, to the Irish harp – which once sang of Irish glories, was then silenced, its strings broken by English tyranny, and is now repeatedly taken up again in these melodies.[38] Moore the bard, Moore the harpist or even the personified harp, struggles against silence and against the muzzling effect of the national eclipse. Like that other harp-playing Irish author, 'Glorvina' Lady Morgan (who likewise is preoccupied with the struggle between silence and speech, cf. above pp. 58–9) Moore turns naturally to a symbol which since the Patriotic Harpers' Festival of Belfast had stood, not only for the country at large (the harp had been the heraldic badge of the kingdom of Ireland since Tudor days), but also for its cultural self-expression in speech, song and music. Moore and Morgan could draw on harp-imagery that had been popularized by radical Patriots of the previous generation. As Mary Helen Thuente has shown, United Irish circles had made frequent use of the image – especially in the song 'Hibernia's harp strung to liberty', which came to provide an emphatic sub-title to the oft-reprinted songbook called *Paddy's resource*. Robert Emmet had himself penned a ballad beginning 'Genius of Erin, tune thy harp'.[39] (It may be added that another phraseological echo from United Irish antecedents lay in the use of the name *Erin*. This interesting neologism, ungrammatically borrowed from the genitive case of Gaelic *Éire*, had come into fashion as denoting something that encompassed both the ancient Gaels and the modern state of the country.)

The insistent use of harp imagery should also be placed against the important sense of orality in early-nineteenth-century Anglo-Irish verse, to which Seamus Deane (FDA, 2: 1–9) has rightly drawn attention; harp symbolism thus feeds into the theme (popularized most effectively by Moore) of a struggle against muteness and cultural amnesia, which adds an ideological sounding-board to the vogue for songs and ballads as the authentically Irish genres of verse and poetry. Indeed, one of the important words in the *Melodies* is 'Oh'. No less than sixteen melodies begin with that ejaculation, which in most cases would have been a superfluous *Flickwort* if it were not for the fact that as a little upbeat-vocalization it facilitates musical performance. The orality of the *Melodies* thus reinforces both the sentimentality of their diction and the idea that they are so many escapes from pent-up silence.[40]

No surprise, then, that the *Melodies* were used in nationalist rhetoric (e.g. by O'Connell), or that there were contemporary accusations as to the politically mischievous nature of Moore's poetry. The Orangist clergyman John Graham denounced Moore's predictions of freedom and the end to bondage as pernicious in their effects upon the peasantry; and Robert Southey, in the *Quarterly Review*, warned against the inflammatory effects of these songs.[41] Moore countered by repudiating the tendency to 'identify nationality with treason, and [to] see, in every effort for Ireland, a system of hostility to England' (FDA 1:1054) – but in so doing, he only stressed his refusal to conform to the standards of an anglocentric ideology. Poems like 'The harp that once through Tara's halls' or 'Remember the glories of Brian the brave' draw contemporary political national zest from Gaelic antiquity in a manner that closely foreshadows Davis and the other *Nation* poets, and should redeem Moore from those critics who have chosen to focus on sentimental poems about friendly meetings and partings, roses at the end of summer, and similar trifles. The *Irish melodies* were recognized for what they were (straightforward nationalism) by a perspicacious outsider, the French historian Augustin Thierry, who wrote a fan letter in 1839 astutely hinting at the common anti-English grievances of France and Ireland:

> Votre poésie patriotique me parut, il y a bien des années, non seulement le cri de douleur d'Irlande, mais encore le chant de tristesse de tous les peuples opprimés. C'est de la vive impression qu'elle fit sur moi après nos désastres de 1815, qu'est venu, en grande partie, le sentiment qui domine dans l'Histoire de la Conquête de l'Angleterre.[42]

Two years after George IV's visit to Dublin, in August 1823, the author of the *Irish melodies* made a trip to Kerry where he wanted to gather material for a book that he was then preparing on Whiteboyism and agrarian unrest. In Kerry, Moore came across the name of the Protean pseudonymous Whiteboy leader, Captain Rock, and heard that it was sometimes considered an acronym for 'Roger O'Connor, King' (*Journal*, 6: 664, 6 August 1823). This was an ironic coincidence because the individual to whom that nomenclature applied was an ex-United Irishman and one of the most colourful mountebanks of the period. Roger

O'Connor (1762–1834) had been imprisoned during the 1798 rebellion, had since then embarked on a career as a con-man, fraudster and petty criminal, and had also come to see himself as the rightful king and champion of 'his race' (*mar dh'ea*: his real name was, aptly, 'Conner', but, true to form, Roger donned the O and styled himself O'Connor Ciarraighe).[43] Here was life imitating the art of Morgan and Maturin, a real-life Irish rebel living out the fantasy characters of the Prince of Inismore and O'Morven. Moore gratefully seized on the coincidence for satirical effect, adding a jocular aside in his *Memoirs of Captain Rock* where the hero himself comments upon his name, its notoriously fraudulent and fantastical real-life analogue, and thus, indirectly, upon his own fictitiousness:

> With respect to the origin of the family name, *Rock*, antiquarians and etymologists are a good deal puzzled. An idea exists in certain quarters that the letters of which it is composed are merely initials, and contain a prophetic announcement of the high destiny that awaits, at some time or other, that celebrated gentleman, Mr. Roger O'Connor, being, as they fill up the initials, the following awful words, – Roger O Connor, King![44]

There is something highly symbolical in the encounter between Moore and the reputation of Captain Rock alias Roger O'Connor; between them, they covered the entire spectrum of Irish national letters. Moore was a poet and balladeer and a budding historian; Captain Rock the floating signifier on crude blackmailing letters from the disaffected, silenced Irish peasantry; O'Connor himself a living reminder of 1798 and an inventor and manufacturer of the country's native roots. Moore's trip to Kerry and his growing anti-English resentment culminated in the publication of his *Memoirs of Captain Rock* (1824); O'Connor was in 1828 to reappropriate the sobriquet by publishing his unabashedly radical *Letters to his majesty, King George IV, by Captain Rock*; but his notoriety in 1824 rested chiefly on his latest publication, in 1822, of the fraudulent and even lunatic *Chronicles of Eri*. All these texts are worthy of notice.

The *Chronicles of Eri* are a prime example of the mystification, fraud and fantasy that can flourish in the absence of proper factual material. It should be borne in mind that in 1822, the older native annals and chronicles were by and large in private hands and, by the standards of knowledge of the day, almost undecipherable and unused as materials for the writing of Irish history; Irish historians only came to rely on native annalists after the great work of inventory, cataloguing and publication had been undertaken by scholars like Charles O'Conor of Stowe, John O'Donovan and Eugene O'Curry. In 1822, *The Chronicles of Eri*, though a palpable imposture to modern eyes, could not easily be proved false. They claimed to be literary translations from the Irish, which in turn was given a fanciful, sort-of-Vallanceyesque derivation. The subtitle specified that the *Chronicles of Eri* were *the history of the Gaal Scot Iber: or, the Irish people* and that they were *translated from the original manuscripts in the Phoenician dialect of the Scythian language*, by an author who, in noble fashion, omitted his first name and signed himself 'O'Connor'. A further clue as to that savant's identity is furnished by the portrait opposite the title page, showing the noble profile of 'O'Connor Cier-rige head of his race and O'Connor, chief of the prostrated peope of his Nation. Soumis pas vaincus'. A heady concoction of national pride and imposture, the former evidently functioning as a *captatio benevolentiae* for the latter.

The *Chronicles* themselves are balderdash from beginning to end, describing ancient tribal peregrinations, the institutions of noble, rational and humane laws, and similar heroic anachronisms. They do not acknowledge debts to any other antiquaries – why should they? After all, they are translations from what purports to be a primorial, authentic Irish source-text – but evidently follow in the mode of the Keatingesque/Vallanceyesque, Phoenician model, tracing the ancestry of the Gael back to the Mediterranean, indeed to a patriarch called Aeolus (who was apparently adopted in Greek myth to become the god of the winds, but involving a pun on the Gaelic word for knowledge or learning).

As a fraud, the *Chronicles of Eri* are part of a penchant, widespread across Europe and across the centuries, for falsification and counterfeit history, ranging from Ossian to the Protocols of the Elders of Zion. O'Connor's case is more interesting, however, in that it appeared when factualist historical and philological scholars were just beginning, with great difficulty, to extricate themselves from antiquarian speculation, and for a long time could not provide a definitive falsification of this fictitious trumpery. If General Vallancey and Sir William Betham were respectable scholars in the mainstream of academic debate, who was then to prove these *Chronicles* wrong – especially if authentic sources were as yet, at the time, all but inaccessible? We shall see the same problem resurface when the Round Tower controversy broke loose in 1828–1832 and George Petrie had to stave off the competition of Henry O'Brien's obviously deranged fantasies. It is no surprise to see that the *Chronicles of Eri* maintained a tenacious existence on the fringes of mainstream scholarship. The somewhat eccentric German antiquary Von Donop, who himself held Phoenicianist theories, accepted them as genuine, communicated his notions and his endorsement to the Royal Irish Academy in 1837 (he was a corresponding member) where his communications were read out by Sir William Betham; O'Connor's book inspired (or intoxicated) a Viennese geographer named W. Obermüller during the 1860s and 1870s, and was eventually republished in a German translation in the early century. Proto-Nazi and Nazi Germany provided a congenial climate for such speculative pseudo-scholarship, and the respected geographer Leo Herrmann (under the pseudonym of L. Albert) decided to propagate the 'buried truth' of O'Connor's book (which he had translated and annotated in German) in the 1930s. His Eri-Revival was taken up in Britain in 1939 by the British Israelites.[45] We shall see a similarly tenacious afterlife for the theories of O'Brien concerning the Round Towers, which, after they were proved false among scholars, continued to appeal to a more-or-less lunatic fringe of Rosicrucians and other speculative system-builders.[46] Such phenomena testify to the scantiness of hard factual knowledge concerning the Irish past and to the deep-seated need to glorify and embellish that past, to see it in the rosy hues of romance and exoticism. It is also a measure of the refusal to acquiesce in the mundane and the straightforward. That attitude (a loyalty to fancies and a rebellion against the despotism of fact) has been ascribed specifically to a Celtic temperament, which is, of course, untenable; it would be closer to the mark to say that it is an attitude which seems to prosper in a climate where the continuity of history has been disrupted and stigmatized, and people attempt to reconstitute and revalorize it on the basis of scant data. That model would account for the forging of national source-texts in areas where genuine records have become unavailable in a climate of political tutelage and cultural self-estrangement: Macpherson's Scotland in 1760, Russia and the 'discovery' of the Song of Prince Igor in 1800, Bohemia and Václav Hanka's 'discovery' of the Königinhof and Grünberg manuscripts in 1817–18, Brittany and the 'construction' of *Barzaz Breizh* by Villemarqué in 1839, Finland with the compilation of the *Kalevala* by Lönnrot in 1835–49, etc.[47]

Moore's *Memoirs of Captain Rock* is perhaps his most felicitous historical or controversial work and contains some of his most effective satire. Its main purpose is to give a survey of unrest, rebellion and agitation in Irish history and to explain it as a direct result of the ham-fisted and insensitive way in which the English government has historically persisted in mishandling Irish affairs. The dialectic of 'English misrule and Irish misdeeds' may seem straightforward to us nowadays, but it came as a novelty in 1824 when the historiographical scene was still dominated by simplistic sectarian denunciations back and forth; and Moore could brilliantly suit his satirical mode to his dialectics. He adopts, for the initial frame-story (how the manuscript of the Captain Rock autobiography was found) the persona of an English Protestant travelling to Ireland on an evangelist mission, sent thither by a tractarian society of ladies in a small English West-Country town, 'directed to the conversion and illumination of the benighted Irish'.[48] The narrative scheme thus echoes, not only the mode of explanatory travel description, but also the familiar framework of many Anglo-Irish novels of the preceding decades. English fatuity is satirically contrasted with Ireland's violent conflicts.

> From Roscrea I turned off the main road, to pay a visit to an old friend, the Rev. Mr. ———, whom I found comfortably situated in his new living, with the sole drawback, it is true, of being obliged to barricade his house of an evening, and having little embrasures in his hall-door, to fire through at unwelcome visitors.[49]

It is here, in the Wild West, ridden by tithes, evictions and Whiteboys, that the English hero meets (by moonlight, of course) the Captain, who hands him his autobiography, containing a satiric overview of how the various generations of Rocks have continuously been goaded into action by English misrule and blundering misgovernment. There are repeated attacks on the Established Church and its exaction of tithes,[50] but on the whole the history aims to tell the story of Irish violence as a mode of resistance and reaction triggered by bad government. The succeeding generations of members of the Rock family form a way of tying the various historical episodes together into a continuous narrative and to bring out the structural pattern that persists from case to case: the interdependence between violent unrest and insensitive government. Rock becomes an avatar, a transindividual principle active throughout Irish history.

> As the Law and the Captain are always correlative in their movements, the state of the *one* during any given period will always enable us to judge of the activity of the *other*. It has been said, that 'you may trace Ireland through the Statute-book of England, as a wounded man in a crowd is tracked by his blood' – and the footsteps of the Captain are traceable, in like manner, through the laws that have prevailed during the last four-and-twenty years (pp. 367–8).

The story ends with the emigration of the Captain (involving a bitter, satirical comment on transportation measures, 373), after having invested his son as Captain: the story of oppression and resistance is not yet at an end. In creating the figure of Captain Rock, Moore deployed a stratagem that was to be popular throughout the century with historians aiming to make the silent masses of the population their protagonist. Among French historians, the figure of Jacques Bonhomme was to become a device to narrate the amorphous history of the oppressed nation in the convenient terms of a transindividual, multicentury biography;[51] something similar is attempted by Moore in this satire. The vicissitudes and violent disruptions and discontinuities of Irish history are reduced to a unified, tellable tale; here as in other instances we see the desire at work to subdue the disparate *Nacheinander* of the Irish past into a conspectus, the enactment of an invariant formula. 'Thus, *semper eadem* (and generally according to the *Irish* translation of it, "worse and worse",) is destined to be the motto of Ireland to end of time' (31n.).

Of the partisan, partial small-scale histories that were written in the aftermath of the 1798 rebellion and the Union, *Memoirs of Captain Rock* is perhaps the most interesting achievement. O'Connell thought that it was 'to the struggle for Catholic Emancipation what *Uncle Tom's Cabin* was to the abolition of slavery'; commercially, it was a runaway success, going through at least five editions in 1824, a French edition appearing in 1829.[52] The basic formula (Irish history as a continuous resistance, never successful but likewise never abandoned) was to have enormous influence on the development of later nationalism. It had been heralded by W.H. Curran's *Life of John Philpot Curran*:

> For centuries Ireland had been in a state of miserable bondage. Her history is but the disgusting catalogue of her sufferings, exciting to unprofitable retaliation, from which she regularly sank, subdued but untranquillized, into a condition of more embittered wretchedness, with the penalties of rebellion superadded to the calamities of oppression. From the period of her annexation to England in the twelfth century, down to the close of the seventeenth, she had thus continued, barbarous and restless; too feeble and disunited to succeed, too strong, and proud, and irritated, to despair; alternating in dreary succession between wild exertions of delirious strength and the troubled sleep of exhausted fury.[53]

Moore translated this deep structure (a continuous, invariant tension between oppression and resistance) into the motif of a family history, where each generation takes over the struggle from the preceding one (in other words, a veritable *tradition* of rebellion). Such an idea of a dynastic filiation of anti-English resistance was to become the guiding principle of Persian nationalism. Moore in some manner even foretold the relentless continuation of the struggle by his deliberate open ending, and indeed in his private moments seems to have sensed the need for a cataclysmic, revolutionary disruption in the stagnated Anglo-Irish entwinement. Witness this entry in his journal, November 1832:

> So hopeless appeared the fate of Ireland under English government, whether of Whigs or Tories, (the experiment now having been tried thus with both, and the results of both being the same) that, as the only chance of Ireland's future resuscitation I would be almost inclined to run the risk of Repeal even with separation as its too certain consequence, being convinced that Ireland must go through some violent & convulsive process before the anomalies of her present position can be got rid of and thinking the riddance well worth the price, however dreadful would be the paying of it.[54]

The engagement between Moore, Rock and O'Connor did not end with the *Memoirs*. Captain Rock did not cease his literary career when Moore was done with him: O'Connor grasped the momentum of Moore's book and adopted the persona of Captain Rock explicitly for his own when he brought out, in 1828, the *Letters to his majesty, King George the Fourth, by Captain Rock*. Moore's satirical persona is kidnapped, or emancipated, from its author, and the ex-United Irishman O'Connor/Rock delivers a magnificent piece of effrontery in his own voice. He continues the conceit of *Memoirs of Captain Rock* by opening the book with an Introductory Letter from New York, 1 June 1826 (where we may suppose Moore's fictional persona to have arrived following his emigratory farewell at the close of the *Memoirs*). That introductory letter is addressed, in sham Irish, *Do Uia Morda* (read: *do Ua Mórdha*: To Moore), and pays Moore a back-handed compliment for having presented the Captain's memoirs to the world in such a stylish manner.[55] (It is important to remember that *Memoirs of Captain Rock* came out anonymously and that Moore's authorship was at best a matter of public conjecture.)

Nor is that all. O'Connor's *Captain Rock* has footnotes added to his letters to George IV (who, in noble fashion, is addressed affably as 'Sir, My Cousin' – one king to another); and these footnotes are all signed with the initials 'U.M.' Are we to construe that, following the introductory letter, as 'Ua Mórdha'? Even to entertain the mere suspicion is to fall victim to O'Connor's mystifications. In these anonymous and pseudonymous books, using half-mythical personae linked vaguely to real-life persons, who is to say what identity is authentic or false, assumed or imputed for purposes of legal anonymity or hoaxing trickery? Even O'Connor's authorship of the *Letters to George IV* is something we must infer from textually circumstantial evidence.[56]

The discourse of political satire and agitation here reaches a veritable aporia of shadowy identities and authorial appurtenances, and the borders between truth and fiction become very muddled indeed. As we shall see further on, Moore was to become embroiled in another, quite similar, shadow fight over Henry O'Brien's Round Tower theory, when Father Prout (himself a living fictional persona inhabiting the mere mortal shell of Francis Mahony) took Moore to task for being, not the author, but a mere plagiaristic translator, of the *Melodies* – of which Prout damningly provided the Latin and Greek 'originals'! In such instances, the tensions and humours of Anglo-Irish political and literary life reach a complexity worthy of Nabokov or Borges.

But even without the sounding board of the borrowed persona of Rock (partly the mythical Whiteboy leader, partly the half-mad impostor Roger O'Connor), Moore's *Memoirs of Captain Rock*, part satire, part history, is by far the most interesting interaction between literature and politics in Ireland in the 1820s. The mythical Whiteboy leader Captain Rock; the larger-than-life Roger O'Connor, ex-United Irishman and fraudster; and the poet-cum-pamphleteer Moore: these three between them seem to sum up the political and ideological shadows that lay over Irish culture and scholarship. The Union, which had exacerbated sectarian and social conflict; the memory of 1798; the view of antiquity as a dark glass where shades can be called up at will by antiquarian speculation; the view of history as legacy of disruption and chaos, a storehouse of grievances and unsettled scores: all that placed a heavy mortgage on the Irish historical imagination of the first quarter of the century.

There were, of course, attempts at serious history-writing. Hardiman's *History of Galway* of 1821 is an early, outstanding example; another being Lanigan's *Ecclesiastical history of Ireland* of 1822. Yet even Lanigan's history could not avoid religious sensitivities, since it was, since the days of archbishop Ussher, a hotly debated question whether the first introduction of Christianity in Ireland had taken place under Roman, papal authority or as a locally independent initiative (the latter model evidently being a preferable antecedent for Protestants, the former for Catholics); insofar as Lanigan came down, naturally enough, in favour of a papally sanctioned mission, his history was obnoxious to Protestants.[57] The 1820s, after all, were the decade of intense tithe unrest and Whiteboy/Rockite agitation fanned by the government's tardiness in grasping the nettle of Emancipation. The broadsheet ballads of the period mix old-fashioned, *aisling*-style messianism with the names of Bonaparte and O'Connell, and an end to Protestantism was foretold by the widely popular prophecies of Pastorini.[58] This in turn gave Irish Orangist Protestants a sense of imminent Armageddon, another re-enactment of 1641 or 1798 – witness the apocalyptic evidence given by Church of Ireland clergymen to a parliamentary committee of inquiry in 1825, on the subject of Rockite unrest (quoted in FDA 1: 1135–8).

A new departure in this post-Union climate, though heralded by isolated achievements like O'Conor's *Scriptores*, Hardiman's *History of Galway* or Lanigan's *Ecclesiastical history*, did not take place until the 1820s were almost over. A cardinal figure in the re-emergence of Irish antiquarianism after 1828 was George Petrie, who began his career as a landscape painter but was already in 1820 among the members of O'Reilly's Iberno-Celtic Society. In 1828 he was elected to the Royal Irish Academy, and it was in that forum, which Petrie helped to shake from its decades-long stupor, that he began to promulgate his great archaeological knowledge acquired during his work for the Ordnance Survey. But if we see Petrie as the Prince Charming who woke the Sleeping Beauty of Irish antiquarianism, we should realize that not all the world of scholarship had stood still in the intervening years; and that the re-emergence of the antiquarians into the field of learning in the very late 1820s was by no means a question of picking up where Vallancey had left off. Things had changed since 1798, and Irish antiquarianism had some catching up to do.

New developments: linguistics and ethnography

The Phoenician model had, if only for patriotic reasons, maintained a certain prestige in antiquarian circles. The anti-Phoenician Ledwich was universally execrated by all antiquarians and the Oriental model was endorsed by well-regarded scholars like O'Conor, Walker and Lanigan, even though Vallancey had done much to discredit it by his increasingly eccentric flights of fancy. Anyway, in a country positioned like Ireland, on the westernmost fringes of the Old World, where could antiquarians look for their origins except in a generally easterly direction? It accorded with geography and with the ingrained biblical model; and, ironically enough, it also accorded with the information that was beginning to come in respected Oriental languages like Iranian and Sanskrit. Sir William Jones had, in the preceding decades, made the supremely important observation that Sanskrit showed many similarities with Greek and other European languages; work on the Zendavesta and old Iranian tended toward similar conclusions; the building blocks of the Indo-European model were being added to scholars' linguistic knowledge.

Among antiquarians, however, the radically novel nature of this material was not obvious. Links with the east were nothing new to those who derived all humanity from Noah and who traced all the world's languages from Hebrew. Ironically, the scholarly and philological testimony coming in from the Far East, which in the long run was to clinch the argument for an Indo-European language family, tended in the short run to bolster the Phoenician model against the Nordic-Scythic one. Bryant's mythological system of 1775, with its theory of a pagan Cushite civilization spanning most of the ancient Orient, was republished in 1807 and continued to influence later scholars even as its implicit presuppositions were being eroded by the advent of the new Comparative Linguistics.

The true importance of the work of men like Jacob Grimm and Franz Bopp was that they systematized the methods of etymological analysis, and that they began to emphasize, in linguistic comparison, the importance of grammatical and structural analogies over verbal and incidental similarities. This could provide, in the words of a later scholar, 'safeguards against illegitimate ingenuity and eccentric conjecture; against all those unsatisfactory uncertainties which have brought discredit on the study of most languages, and on that of the Keltic most especially'.[59] It was only on the basis of Grimm's and Bopp's groundwork in the methodology of linguistic comparison that scholars could arrive at confident assessments of the relative relations between languages, and structure these into a genealogical family tree. This led to a general acceptance, by the early 1820s, of a complex of Indo-Germanic or Indo-European languages, which included the Germanic and Romance languages as well as Greek and Sanskrit, but excluded Hebrew and its cognates.

Unfortunately, the similarities between the Indo-European languages and the Celtic ones were so un-obvious that for a while it was a moot point whether Irish resembled Hebrew or German most. As long as doubts remained on that score, the Phoenician model remained viable. The first of the new comparative scientists who attempted to establish the link between Celtic and Indo-European was the great Welsh ethnographer, Samuel Evans Prichard, who, in a supplementary study to his earlier *Physical history of man* (1813), discussed the point at great length in his *Eastern origin of the Celtic nations* of 1831.[60] Prichard drew mainly on Welsh data, but it was obvious that a proven Indo-European appurtenance of Welsh would also clinch the argument on Gaelic. It was only in 1837 that the matter was settled with any degree of authority: in that year, Pictet published his essay *De l'affinité des langues celtiques avec le sanscrit*, which was taken up and elaborated further by Franz Bopp the following year in his lecture *Über die celtischen sprachen*. Pictet was obviously unaware of Prichard's work and was actuated by Schlegel's doubts as to the relatedness of the Celtic and the Indo-European languages;[61] but Bopp's essay of 1838 did refer to Prichard.[62] Zeuss' *Grammatica Celtica* of 1854 eventually gave the definitive summing-up in the case.

All this adds ups to the fact that almost until 1840 there was abundant evidence for some vague Oriental background in the ancient past of the national language, but little reason for Irish antiquarians to realize the paradoxical notion that this Oriental background, given its Indo-European nature, excluded the possibility of Hebrew, Phoenician or Semitic origins. The linguistic debates of the Continent took place with little active involvement from Irish scholars – the one exception being Nicholas (later Cardinal) Wiseman, who began his distinguished career with public lectures delivered in Rome in 1835 on recent scholarly developments. Wiseman's lectures on the *Connexion between science and revealed religion* opened with two surveys 'On the comparative study of languages'. In the course of these lectures, Wiseman criticizes the way in which British scholars had continued to work in an outdated fashion and had fallen behind the insights of recent German scholars; he only made a favourable exception for Prichard, whom he credited with the important discovery that the Celtic languages belonged to the Indo-European family. To Prichard, Wiseman opposed the useless lucubrations of old-fashioned scholars like Sir William Betham, whose Phoenician speculation Wiseman demolishes.[63] It was probably because of this unflattering treatment of Betham that Betham's adversary, George Petrie, took cognizance of Wiseman's espousal of Indo-Europeanism and came to propound it himself. Petrie was later to quote Wiseman's criticisms in a pamphlet against Betham published in 1840, and in early 1838 went on record as opposing popular Druidic theories in favour of the scholarly investigation of 'The history of the Indo-European race'.[64]

The Irish involvement in the unfolding Indo-European paradigm was limited to Wiseman and (marginally) Petrie. But Continental scholars for their part were by no means heedless of Irish learning. It is instructive to see what linguistic material was used by the early Continental comparatists. Pictet used the eighteenth-century work of the poet and scholar Hugh MacCurtin,[65] but relied more heavily on O'Reilly's dictionary and grammar, as well as on O'Brien's grammar of 1809. Pictet even wrote to O'Reilly in January 1835, requesting further linguistic and philological information.[66] Bopp, like Pictet, uses MacCurtin occasionally but relies most heavily on O'Reilly; and Zeuss, again, used MacCurtin, O'Reilly and O'Brien, but was by 1854 in the more fortunate position of also having O'Donovan's grammar of 1845 available.[67] It is strikingly obvious that the speculative antiquarian tradition of Anglo-Irish savants contributed little or nothing to the scholarly advances in linguistic insight, whereas the tenuous and struggling tradition of native scholarship proved to be of greatest value. Pictet, for one, specifically singled out 'le bel ouvrage publié par le docteur O'Connor, aux frais du duc de Buckingham, et intitulé: *Rerum hibernicarum scriptores veteres*', praising O'Conor of Stowe for having been 'le premier qui ait porté, dans les études de l'ancienne Irlande, un esprit de critique sage et éclairée' (IX).

But all this was largely a one-way interest; with the exception of more or less isolated figures such as Prichard, Wiseman and Petrie, British and Irish scholarship took little notice of the Celtological advances in Continental philology. In Ireland, this backwardness would lead eventually to the explosive clash of the Round Tower controversy, to which I shall pay greater attention further on; in Britain, another and no less explosive development took place as that country adopted, in the Victorian period, an ethnological sense of cultural identity which relied on a partial knowledge of comparative philology, emphasizing the alleged Germanic racial origins of the English nation to the exclusion of possible Celtic elements. Scholarly backwardness in Ireland led to a tenacious persistence of Phoenicianism; in England it led to Teutomania. The one cannot be understood except in relation to the other.

Irish Phoenicianism and English Teutomania

There can be no better way of looking at the outdated approaches still prevailing among Irish antiquarians than to look at the work of Sir William Betham, Ulster King of Arms (and as such chief heraldic and genealogical authority in Ireland), prominent member of the Royal Irish Academy and the Royal Dublin Society. Betham may be considered Vallancey's successor to the laurels of Phoenicianist theory – but he was to find out, painfully, that those laurels had wilted. It is easy to poke fun at Betham's fantastical speculations, easier, even, than in the case of Vallancey; for if Vallancey was only following the pattern of his times, Betham belonged decidedly to the rearguard, and his Phoenicianism is so extremely fanciful as to outshine the more sober historians working in that mould, such as O'Conor of Stowe, Lanigan and D'Alton. Yet Betham deserves to be acknowledged, not only because of his fantastical clangers, but also at least for his patronage of O'Reilly, Connellan and Lanigan; it should also be remembered that his genealogical work as Ulster King of Arms was far from worthless. But his speculations on the origins of Gaelic culture firmly stuck to a model which was more and more difficult to entertain. Betham's particular fancy was that the Phoenician ancestry of Irish antiquity formed part of a large Oriental seafaring civilization stretching from Yemen to Siam, with, for its most interesting Western representatives, the Etruscans. And so, where previous scholars had collated their ignorance of Irish with their ignorance of Carthaginian, Betham could set out to hunt for similarities between the Irish language (which he did not understand) with Etruscan (which nobody understood). Betham's test case was the text contained in the Umbrian *Tabulae Iguvinae* or Gubbio Tablets, which he called the 'Eugubian Tables'. His *modus operandi* in this analysis is an instructive sample of antiquarian fancy and of its lack of critical spirit.

Betham decodes this text is such a manner as to make it yield an account of the sea-route from Italy to Ireland. He transcribes the original PUNE CAR NE S PE TUR I E AT I I ER I E A BI E CA TE NA RA C LU M into something that he considers Gaelic: 'Pune car na is be tur i e at i i er i a bi e ca ta na ra ac lu am'. That, in turn, is translated into the literal English – to wit, 'Phoenician to Carne (the turn) it is night voyage in it likewise in knowledge great in it the being away how it is the going with water on the ocean'; and that means, in Betham's idiomatic translation:

> O Phoenicians, this is a statement of the night voyage to Carne (the turn), and of the manner of going, with great science, over the waters of the ocean.[68]

Laughable, of course. The Gaelic that Betham transcribes from his original is utterly fantastical, disjointed quarks and neutrons, elementary particles without structure or cohesion or semantic identity, which could belong to any language.[69] To mention only one example of Betham's radical ungrammaticality: the fact that he can repeatedly, indeed hundreds of times, construe the collocation I E as if the former were the Irish preposition *i*, 'in', and the latter the Irish objective case for *sé*, 'he' or 'it', and blithely translates the twain as 'in it', means that he is unfamiliar with (or heedless of) that basic feature of the Gaelic language, namely that prepositions and personal pronouns are merged into prepositional pronouns and conjugated as such – 'in it' taking the form *ann* or *inti* (mod. *innti*).

Moreover, it is indicative that the process of translation is fourfold: from inscription to transcribed Gaelic, thence into nonsensical literal English, thence into contrived literal English. At the end of his long linguistic journey from Etruria to Ireland, the original is gradually lost sight of in an ever-thickening fog of semantic entropy, in which anything can mean anything else. What Betham calls translation merely imposes on the Rorschach test of an unintelligible original a machinery of telescoping association; the perspective of his free associations always converges into the same vanishing point. A good example of this tendency to schematize an abracadabra into whatever suits his purpose, is given by a 'corrigendum' (297). Betham states at some point that he had made a flawed transcription, but it really turns out to make no difference whatsoever: the alternative reading 'which gives *the distance of the sea* [. . .] instead of *holy one of the sea*' does not change anything. It 'does not [. . .] much affect the narrative', it 'strengthens the evidence' for the identity between Irish and Etruscan, and the reader is left to choose whatever version he prefers, 'as either renderings are perfect' (297). A remarkable example of unfalsifiability, and a good illustration of Karl Popper's tenet that a conjecture ceases to have scientific value as soon as it becomes unfalsifiable.

In short, the Ulster King of Arms is fantasizing, with a great deal of ingenuity and very little critical sense. He develops romantic, adventurous scenarios, and Irish antiquity functions as a mere void which he fills with colourful incidents and adventurous journeys, obviously inspired by Homer, the Aeneid, and Ossian. Thus, a nonsensical toponymical list which Betham draws up by Gaelicizing ancient records yields very little information, but, rather like the free associations triggered by a Rorschach test, does give us an interesting glimpse into Betham's adventurous imagination:

> Thus we find in Ptolemy and other ancient geographers, as among modern discoveries, places distinguished by names which in the Celtic indicate – the *round hill*, the *good market*, the *swampy marshy inlet*, the *happy tribe*, the *welcome*, the *island of gentle showers*, the *fruitful hill*, the *pleasant town on the sea*, the *farthest torrent* or *great river*, the *eastern island fruitful in corn*, the the [sic] *bounteous islands*, the *island of rich earth*, or *fruitful soil*, the *land of love*, the *good harbour for ships*, the *harbour of refuge*, the *fortified depot for goods*, the *highland tribe*, the *narrow district*. Mariners are warned against other places by fearful denominations as – the *coast of death and evil*, the *gulph of the power of death* the *gulph of cruel pirates*, the *deceitful invitation*, or *false bay*, the *land of robbers*, the *unhealthy country*, the *weedy river*, the *muddy stream*, the *quarrelsome people*, the *shipwreck rocks*, the *inhospitable coast*; and many others, all of which are appropriate [of course they are! JL] and descriptive of the places, too palpably to be mistaken, and too obviously Gaelic to admit of question. (28–29)

What pretends to be a list of place-names is more a list of ingredients for an epic adventure story of the Ossian-meets-Odysseus type, set somewhere between 'the land of love' and 'the gulph of cruel pirates'; what Betham enumerates are mythical narrative ingredients rather than philological obervations. Ferguson, in his review of 1845, was scathing on 'the endless rigmarole of "moon", "stars", "steering", "ocean", "night", "day", "knowledge", "science", and "O Phoenician!" that succeed one another in monotonous repetition for [. . .] 200 pages'.[70]

When this appeared in the early 1840s, etymological *bricolage* was no longer the respectable scholarly pursuit it once had been. Ferguson's review was even more scathing than Wiseman's references had been seven years earlier. By now, Betham was (in a process that I shall describe in greater detail below) marginalized in the Royal Irish Academy, had failed to get these conjectures published in the Academy's *Transactions*, and found himself badly out of touch with the prevailing climate, one of the last surviving dinosaurs of a bygone paradigm. At the same time, the stubborn loyalty to exotic national roots remained popular among the dilettanti and amateurs, if not among serious scholars; and the gradual marginalization of Bethamite speculation and Phoenicianism was a process that took decades of bitter controversy which left their stamp on the Irish historical imagination. Meanwhile, the battle over the true nature of Ireland's Celtic roots was given added political edge by the fact that at the same time there was a wholesale dismissal of everything Celtic in England.

Prichard's great Celtological work, *The eastern origin of the Celtic nations*, took up a lone, monogenist stance against the growing polygenist tide of nineteenth-century anthropology, which stressed radical interracial differences.[71] It is remarkable how Prichard's work exemplifies, not only the emergence of comparative linguistics from its antiquarian origins, but also the close links between the emergent disciplines of comparative ethnography and comparative linguistics; Wiseman called these, in 1835, the 'sister sciences' of 'philological and physiognomical ethnography'.[72]

To be sure, many scholars warned against the possibility that linguistic and racial nomenclature might be confused; someone who speaks a Celtic language is not necessarily a member of the Celtic race, and persons who in nineteenth-century ethnology might be classified as Celts could well have a Romance language like French, or a Germanic language like English, for their mother tongue.[73] But at the same time this caveat was more noticeable in the breach than in the observance. The racial classification of humanity became dominant in all spheres of life and was considered a meaningful category both for the measurement of physical appearance (skin colour, facial angle, crania, brain volume) and of cultural refinement; Robert Knox's *The races of men* appeared in 1850, was reprinted in 1862 and became widely popular; a similar fame was later enjoyed by John Beddoe, who did an anthropological survey of English regional types so as to establish the degree of Saxon or Celtic blood in their genetic make-up (*The races of Britain*, 1885).[74] From its beginnings, the science of comparative linguistics was a handmaiden to ethnological history; when the spread of certain languages and language families was traced, this was automatically seen as the spread or retreat of nations and races.

One result of this tendency was the fact that Indo-Europeanism, from its very beginning, could imply a certain sense of the alienness of Jewish and Semitic culture. This is how Matthew Arnold described the case of Humboldt, whose ideas in education he so deeply admired:

> [. . .] we read of a genuine Teuton, Wilhelm von Humboldt, finding, even in the sphere of religion, that sphere where the might of Semitism has been so over-

powering, the food which most truly suited his spirit in the productions not of the alien Semitic genius, but of the genius of Greece or India, the Teuton's born kinsfolk of the common Indo-European family. 'Towards Semitism he felt himself,' we read, 'far less drawn'; he had the consciousness of a certain antipathy in the depths of his nature to this, and to its 'absorbing, tyrannous, terrorist religion,' as to the opener, more flexible Indo-European genius, this religion appeared.[75]

The note of irony is there, to be sure; but Arnold himself goes on to admit that even in the sphere of religion,

the tendency is in Humboldt's direction; tends more and more to establish a sense of native diversity between our European bent and the Semitic bent, and to eliminate, even in our religion, certain elements as purely and excessively Semitic, and therefore, in right, not combinable with our European nature, not assimilable by it. This tendency is now quite visible even among ourselves [. . .] and for its justification this tendency appeals to science, the science of origins; it appeals to this science as teaching us the way our natural affinities and repulsions lie. It appeals to this science, and in part it comes from it; it is, in considerable part, an indirect practical result from it (26–7).

The invocation of science, as both a frame of reference and an inspiring paradigm for racial attitudes, is astute and typical of Arnold's progressivist thought; but the complacent acceptance of growing racial, biological constraints on cultural life is unsettling. It throws an unflattering light on Arnold's life-long cultural crusade, and (for instance in the 'Sweetness and Light' argument of *Culture and anarchy*) his campaigns for the 'Hellenization' of Philistine attitudes against Hebrew religious moralism.

In the context of the quoted fragment (the lecture series *On the study of Celtic literature*, published in 1867), Arnold used his reference to a growing 'Aryanization' of cultural attitudes merely as a rhetorical springboard from which he could launch into his defence of Celtic culture – the Celts had, after all, been proven to be 'our brothers in the great Indo-European family' (27). For if Arnold in 1867 wanted to vindicate the cultural interest of a Celtic heritage, he had to do so against an overwhelming atmosphere of mid-Victorian, anti-Celtic reservations and an exclusive emphasis on the Teutonic roots of England and, by extension, the British empire.

It is not easy to illustrate the prevalence of Teutomania (Arnold's term) or Anglo-Saxonism by referring to one or two important and widely-cited publications. The attitude seems to have been highly pervasive in a diluted, non-explicit way, much as one may find coffee sweet-tasting without being able to pinpoint the sugar in the cup. There are certain egregious (and by the same token, untypically extreme) cases, such as Charles Kingsley's *The Roman and the Teuton* (1864); there is the fact that various writers began to purge their style of Latin-derived words in favour of Saxon ones, dropping 'preface' in favour of 'foreword';[76] but on the whole, the ideology must be reconstructed from implicit assumptions, incidental references, occasional asides and ephemeral sources. Thankfully, that difficult and important work of inventories has been performed by scholars like Faverty, Stepan, MacDougall and L.P. Curtis.[77] From their inventorizations we can gather that many Victorian men of letters in the wake of Carlyle (who was, of course, the great apostle of German learning and culture in post-Romantic England) linked the glory of the nation's past exclusively to its Anglo-Saxon ancestry. It was not a new attitude; the praises of parliament and the English constitution had traditionally been sung with reference to Anglo-Saxon *witan*;[78] eighteenth-century antiquarians like Pinkerton and Whitaker had followed ancient history as an exclusively Anglo-Saxon affair, mocking the barbarity of the savage Celts who had stood in the way of progress. The same Saxon orientation suffused the work of Carlyle. However, in the new century it was no longer described in the old-fashioned terms of 'Gothick Liberty' but rather in those of the linguistic and racial kinship of the Teutons or Saxons who everywhere in Northern Europe had left the stamp of rugged individualism. The Sage of Cheyne Row exercised enormous influence on later men of letters, such as Tennyson (whose attitudes to Ireland we shall encounter further on) and Kingsley. As importantly, Carlyle's historiographical reputation and influence worked deep into the great mid-Victorian generation of historians: Froude (whose anglocentrism with regard to Irish history was famously challenged by Lecky), Kemble, Stubbs, Freeman, Dicey, John R. Green, and their chief forum the *Saturday Review*.[79] Where Carlyle had argued that the Teutonic invaders had driven the Britons 'into the mountainous nooks of the West, whither they were not worth following', Green's hugely popular *Short history of the English people* celebrated the Anglo-Saxon conquest as a veritable ethnic cleansing:

> Not a Briton remained as subject or slave on English ground. Sullenly, inch by inch, the beaten men drew back from the land which their conquerors had won; and eastward of the border-line which the English sword had drawn, all was now purely English.[80]

An ethnic cleansing, to be sure – at least, if not of the British territory, then certainly of the British origin-myth, which as a result, acknowledged only a Saxon ancestry. Small wonder that by 1866 a Welsh critic could complain:

> There are probably few educated Englishmen living who have not in their infancy been taught that the English nation is a nation of almost purely Teutonic blood, that its political constitution, its social customs, its internal prosperity, the success of its arms, and the number of its colonies have all followed necessarily upon the arrival, in three vessels, of certain German warriors under the command of Hengist and Horsa.[81]

In Britain, as in Ireland, the reflection on the nation's ethnic roots was part of national politics of the day; here as in Ireland, matters like the Act of Union and the agitation surrounding Catholic Emancipation helped to give such rarefied scholarly speculations an immediate political barb. Carlyle's Germanocentrism was not only noticeable in amusing eccentricities such as complimenting William

Allingham on his Saxon name and urging him to drop his Irish regionalism;[82] it also enabled him to write an essay of staggering bigotry against 'The repeal of the Union'. The Union between Britain and Ireland is described like this:

> Ireland at this moment and for a good while back, has been invited and is practically invited to become British; to right its wrongs along with ours, to fight its battles along by our side and take share in that huge destiny along with us.

It is instructive to look at the distribution of first- and third-person usage. The Union is described, not as a contract between two equal partners, but ethno-centrically as an admission of a third person party (they-the-Irish) into a first-person (we-the-British, including Carlyle and his intended audience). Carlyle proceeds to draw a parallel with an earlier invitation to 'join us' similarly extended to other savages: Cherokees, Sioux and Chactaws.

> 'Can you, will you, O Noble Chactaws [. . .] join us in this heavy job we Yankee Englanders have got to do here?' [. . .] Alas! the answer was in the negative; the Chactaws would not, could not; and accordingly the Chactaws [. . .] are extinct; cut off by the inexorable gods.

The lesson to be learned from this example: Ireland is to become British, or it shall cease to be. 'Noisy, turbulent, irreclaimable savagery [. . .] is doomed to be reclaimable or to disappear.' Or, in language that would have been close to Carlyle's heart: *Willst Du nicht mein Bruder sein, schlag' ich Dir den Schädel ein.*

Carlyle concludes this essay with a passage that encapsulates the intimate conjunction between racial thought and anti-Irish political and ethnic prejudice at the time. It also illustrates how a purported analysis of British-Irish relations (whether or not the Union should be repealed, and how to deal with the arguments of those who favour repeal) can descend into pure invective 'which curses instead of thinks and considers'. The underlying ethnocentrism is revealed in Carlyle's implicit claim to speak for 'Nature herself' and with the authority of 'the laws of Nature'; it is this superior authority which allows one partner in the Union to confront the other with a choice between 'wholesome *slavery*' and extermination:

> The Celt of Connemara, and other repealing finest peasantry, are white and not black; but it is not the colour of the skin that determines the savagery of a man. He is a savage who in his sullen stupidity, in his chronic rage and misery, cannot know the facts of this world when he sees them; whom suffering does not teach but only madden; who blames all men and all things except the one that can be blamed with advantage, namely *himself*; who believes, on the hill of Tara or elsewhere, what is palpably untrue, being himself unluckily a liar, and the truth, or any sense of the truth, not in him; who curses instead of thinks and considers; brandishes his tomahawk against the laws of Nature, and prevails therein as we can fancy and can see! Fruitless futile insurrection, continual sanguinary broils and riot that make his dwelling-place a horror to mankind, mark his progress generation after generation; and if no beneficient hand will chain him into wholesome *slavery*, and, with whip on back or otherwise, try to tame him and get some work out of

him, – Nature herself, intent to have her work tilled, has no resource but to exterminate him as she has done the wolves and various other obstinately *free* creatures before now! These are hard words, but they are true.[83]

The voice of racism speaks with the assumed authority of natural, biological necessity, and models political choices on the law of the jungle.[84] Carlyle's essay is an extreme example and shows a pitch of anti-Irish invective that could only be reached when anti-Irish prejudice was exacerbated by the party-political passion stirred up by O'Connell's campaigns for Catholic Emancipation and Repeal of the Union. The political climate in Britain was much polarized in the years surrounding Catholic Emancipation and the Reform Bill, and accordingly anti-Catholic and anti-Irish feeling reached a high pitch in the 1830s and 1840s to coincide with the Teutophile influence of Carlyle. This bequeathed to the next generation the 'Celt-hating' attitude which Matthew Arnold attempted to defuse in his famous *On the study of Celtic literature* of 1867. Here, he reflected on the position of his father, Dr Thomas Arnold:

> I remember, when I was young, I was taught to think of Celt as separated by an impassable gulf from Teuton; my father, in particular, was never weary of contrasting them; he insisted much oftener on the separation between us and them than on the separation between us and any other race in the world; in the same way Lord Lyndhurst, in words long famous, called the Irish, 'alien in speech, in religion, in blood' (23–4).

Dr Thomas Arnold was famous as headmaster of Rugby, celebrated in that national boys' classic, *Tom Brown's schooldays*. Whether or not Arnold *senior* was a Teutophile in the mode of Carlyle, Kingsley and Freeman, is not quite clear. The *Quarterly review* in 1868 referred to him as 'that Teuton of Teutons, the Celt-hating Dr. Arnold'; but that qualification may be partly inspired by Arnold *junior's* above-quoted comment, made a year previously – a comment which did not go unchallenged at the time, for Matthew Arnold had to write to his mother and sister to inquire for corroborative evidence and to test his memory against theirs to see if he was correct in remembering his father as utterly abhorring the Celt.[85]

There may even be a slight Oedipal distortion at work. It is well known that Arnold father and son had a fraught relationship. In vindicating the Celt, Matthew was to some extent deliberately challenging his father's values, the more so since in the preceding years he had become acutely aware that his mother's Cornish background meant that there was a Celtic element in his own matrilinear ancestry. Whether or not this may have reinforced his tendency to speak of the Saxon element in masculine terms and to consider the Celts as 'an essentially feminine race',[86] is an open question; but to see English culture as the product of a union between Saxon and Celtic ancestors is certainly an extrapolation of his own personal parentage.[87] In the process, he may have come to see, or to represent, his father's Teutonism in exaggerated terms. Thomas Arnold's own writings offer little justification for such an assessment, and, if anything, provide a wholesome contrast to the Carlylean excesses which I have just quoted.

Thomas Arnold's views were, of course, those of a Tory churchman; but within the scope of that stance he was a liberal, with a firm belief in the progress of freedom and equality. His political attitude may perhaps best be described as that of a Christian Democrat *avant la lettre*, which in the context of early Victorian England made him unusual. He could draw surprisingly honest and open-minded conclusions on the basis of convictions that led others into narrowminded bigotry. His firm belief in the inequality of races never became an excuse for shallow, ethnocentric triumphalism; on the contrary, it imposed on the more advanced races, as he saw them, the duty to help and improve the more backward ones. Such a benevolently paternalist attitude was comparatively enlightened in the context of early Victorian thought and is far removed from the harsh 'submit or perish' attitude of Carlyle.[88] What distinguishes Arnold's racial outlook from that of Carlyle is that Arnold, as a churchman and a practising Christian, held a mono-genistic belief as to human origins. Like Prichard, and unlike the polygenists with their exclusive attention for the differences and inequalities between races, Arnold did allow for a fundamental kinship and common origin embracing all humanity:

> [. . .] they who believe in the common origin of all mankind, must conclude that all moral differences, between one race and another, may be gradually removed as they have been created; and that as unfavourable circumstances made them differ, so a happier system and better institutions may in time restore their original equality.[89]

Arnold made this point explicitly in the context of defending Catholic Emancipation and even the disestablishment of the Anglican Church in Ireland. True, Arnold had little sympathy for Irish Catholics, that 'unpromising race' with their 'dreadful religion': he concedes that the Irish may be every bit as savage as the likes of Carlyle would make them, 'that the Irish race are deeply tainted with barbarism; that they know little of obedience to law; that they are the slaves of passion and feeling, and by consequence deficient in the highest qualification of human nature'; nevertheless, Arnold argues,

> with this unpromising race and this dreadful religion we have chosen to connect ourselves; and we have thus deprived ourselves of the right to regard them with mere disgust and abhorrence; we must endeavour to better them, and the more so as the virulence of the evil is in a great degree to be attributed to our own neglect or absolute ill-treatment (p. 33).

This is very far removed from the harsh stance of Carlyle. The presence of a large population, 'containing in themselves all the different elements of a nation, locally distinct, differing in race, and in a large part of them in language also, from the people of Great Britain, cannot be considered as necessarily forming only a part of our national society, on whom we as the majority may impose what rules we will, while they have no other duty but submission' (31–2). That, coming from the alleged 'Celt-hater' Thomas Arnold, is as forceful a statement of Ireland's right to self-determination as one is likely to encounter anywhere. Arnold also exhibits a much fairer sense than Carlyle of what it means to have contracted (or rather, imposed) a constitutional union:

> We are bound either to treat them fairly, or not to meddle with them at all; and if our constitution must be altered before they can be members of it, we are bound to alter it; as we, by making them subjects unjustly, contracted voluntarily the obligation to make them citizens; or else we are labouring at this hour under the guilt of our ancestors' usurpations (p. 32).

He put it even more bluntly in his private correspondence. '[. . .] the Irish being a Catholic people, they have a right to perfect independence, or to a perfectly equal union: if our conscience objects to the latter, it is bound to concede the former'.[90]

It would be wrong to lump all 'Teutomaniacs' together as an undifferentiated whole. Racial thought was different according to its polygenist or monogenist emphasis and was cited for different political purposes. Also, the argument of racial disposition was usually cited in tandem with other determinist factors such as climate and environment;[91] accordingly, there might be different assessments as to the relative importance, in national characters, of nature and nurture, race or climate, disposition or circumstance. Be that as it may, the cases gathered here do indicate an important field for future study. The two racialist ideologies of Teutomania and Celticism have been largely studied separately, and although many scholars, like L.P. Curtis, have discussed how each of these two ideologies was based on a contradistinction between Celt and Saxon, the interaction or interdependence between the ideologies, the relations, not between Celt and Teuton but between Celtophile and Teutomaniac, still deserve further study.

That being said, this brief digression may help to fill in the background of the developments in Irish historical consciousness which I propose to trace here: how, in the middle decades of the last centuries, there were at least two important incentives for Irish intellectuals to adhere to their Orientalist heritage. One reason was the fact that the advances of Indo-Europeanism might to superficial observers strengthen rather than weaken the case for the notion that Europe's ancient civilizations had Oriental links; the other was that the non-Oriental, intra-European, Teutonic model that was so much in vogue in the neighbouring country, seemed to follow straight in the footsteps of narrow-minded and illiberal Celt-haters like Pinkerton and Ledwich, and seemed to function largely as a discursive means of stigmatizing and denigrating the Celtic past.

New departures: the Ordnance Survey and the Royal Irish Academy

It would, of course, be illusory to think that the granting of Catholic Emancipation brought all political and sectarian controversy in Ireland to a harmonious close; conservative Protestant opinion hardened, as can be seen from the defiant stance of the *Dublin University magazine* which was founded after the first Reform Bill so as to voice the attitudes of Protestant Ireland. Even so, the measure may have helped to defuse the tense legacy of post-1798 feelings. Thomas Moore attempted to express this in his *Travels of an Irish gentleman in search of religion* (1833), which, though it remained stubbornly Catholic in its exegesis and its view on Church history, famously began by stating that after Emancipation, the Irishman's loyalty to Catholicism was no longer an *a priori* matter of political loyalty to a down-trodden religion, in dogged defiance of unjust oppression, but that the two creeds could now be judged fairly and even-handedly on their tenets and merits. But the great importance of Emancipation was that the terms of political debate were slowly being redefined, and that sectarian difference between Orange and Green, Protestant and Catholic, exacerbated by the memories of 1798, was transmuted into a polarity of Ireland versus England, nationalist versus unionist. It is indicative that O'Connell's campaign, having once won the religious, intra-Irish matter of the rights of Catholics, went on to the national issue of Home Rule and Repeal of the Union. It is no less indicative that Anglo-Irish literature gradually abandons the mode of explaining Ireland to an English audience and instead begins to explain native Ireland to an Irish audience: the post-Union climate changes, in the period 1830–1845, to a programme of uniting native and settler into a common Irish national awareness.[92] 1829 did prepare for a minor intellectual and cultural renaissance in the 1830s. After Emancipation, the Protestant élite can no longer consider itself an English colony on the Irish shores and must try to establish its own identity: Irish and unionist. That, as we shall see, is the main issue in the writings of Samuel Ferguson, who resented the idea that Catholics with their nativism could claim an exclusive monopoly on Irish nationality, leaving Protestant unionists implicitly to the outer margins of non-Irishness.

The immediate impact of Emancipation was to highlight the religious differences between Protestant and Catholic Ireland; it would be simplistic, therefore, to see Emancipation in itself as the catharsis or catalyst for a national cultural revival. On the other hand, Emancipation came at a time (long overdue, and conceded by the government with grudging ill grace) when the stagnation of post-Union sectarianism was beginning to crumble and a non-contentious, non-partisan interest for Irish culture and Irish antiquities was spreading once again. A cardinal figure in this development was, without doubt, the landscape painter, music collector and archaeologist George Petrie, with his involvement in the rejuvenated Royal Irish Academy and in the Ordnance Survey.

In the mid-1820s, the Ordnance Survey of Ireland[93] had, after initial triangulation adjustments, been entrusted (under the command of one Colonel Colby) to a young officer named Thomas Larcom; he was to become one of the most commendable examples of British officialdom in Ireland (he was later to organize famine relief as Commissioner of Public Works, was involved in the reform of the Poor Laws, and became Permanent Undersecretary for Ireland in 1853). Larcom, from 1828 onwards, expanded the Ordnance Survey project from a straightforward map-making and gazetteering project into a huge synopsis of the Irish physical and cultural landscape, where each historical landmark was to be described in its physical appearance and antiquarian importance in major archaeological descriptions accompanying each map.

The Ordnance Survey had accordingly started to employ a native scholar to ascertain the proper nomenclature of the Gaelic toponymy. Until 1830, the official employed for those purposes (on very scant wages) had been Edward O'Reilly; upon O'Reilly's death in 1830, he was replaced in that capacity by John O'Donovan.[94] However, whereas O'Reilly had been a poorly paid drudge working in isolation, O'Donovan's activities were placed under the co-ordination of a Historical Department which Larcom had set up around 1828 in order to prepare a 'Historical Memoir', and which had been placed under the care of George Petrie.

The story of the Historical Department, which met at Petrie's house and included, not only John O'Donovan, but also Eugene O'Curry (as yet plain Curry without the restored O) and, briefly, James Clarence Mangan, is well known. The troika of Petrie, O'Donovan and O'Curry has often been celebrated as the rescue team of Irish antiquarianism, the men who set the investigation of Gaelic antiquity on a new, scientific and critical footing, and whose enormous labours laid the groundwork for all subsequent work in the field. At the same time it is important to realize that this work was undertaken for, and for more than ten years largely funded by, the Ordnance Survey project as it was expanding under Larcom's inspired direction. It is all the more important to stress this, since the Ordnance Survey has been heavily distorted in Brian Friel's widely successful play *Translations*. Friel presents the Ordnance Survey as a blunt colonial instrument in the hands of the imperial forces, inflicting cultural self-estrangement on native Ireland by means of billeting English soldiers in rural villages, and imposing uncomprehending and ugly anglicizations of native placenames under threat of eviction. In fact, the very opposite was the case.[95] Although triangulation and measurements may have been undertaken by soldiers, the fieldworkers sent out to inventorize placenames, architectural remains and other cultural artefacts were men like O'Donovan and O'Curry, with a good knowledge of, and a sympathetic interest in, local antiquities and native lore, foreshadowing later folklore commissioners, salvaging the original placenames from neglect or corruption by painstaking inventorization of manuscripts, giving them English transliterations rather than translations, and capturing a great deal of local lore and learning from communities which would fifteen years later be swept away by the Famine. If, today, the Gaelic substratum of Irish culture is most prominently visible in the placenames and the landscape, then that presence is owing to a large degree to the work of the Ordnance Survey of 1824–1841. We may go even further and say that the Ordnance Survey was a major contribution to the cultural nationalism of later decades, in that it equated the very land itself with a Gaelic past and a Gaelic-speaking peasantry, thus canonizing the Gaelic tradition as the very bedrock, the cultural ground under the feet of modern Ireland, making Gaelic culture literally aboriginal and autochthonous to Ireland, a native fruit of its very soil.[97] The Ordnance Survey turned the entire countryside of Ireland into one vast *lieu de mémoire*: topography became replete with historical and mythological overtones, while history and myth became specific and graspable in their topographical locale. As William Stokes put it:

> [. . .] the most ancient history, itself quoting from the most dim traditions, indicated the name, locality, and purpose of a certain monument; its remains are found corresponding in name, place, and obvious purpose with the old account, itself borrowed from sources older still, while its architecture is that of the most remote Pagan period, and so the monument verifies the history and the history identifies the monument, and both become mutually illustrative.[97]

This effect of rendering the historical and mythical past present by describing it in its territoriality, while at the same time historicizing the territory by tracing its records and earlier mentions, is aptly illustrated by the time-warped fancy of a field worker in the Ordnance Survey Historical Section, one Mr Wakeman, who felt that as they became engrossed in the work,

> I felt as if I had a personal acquaintance with Niall of the Nine Hostages, or Con of the Hundred Battles (or bottles, as poor Mangan humorously misstyled the hero), or with Leogaire [. . .][98]

One particularly important result of the Ordnance Survey at the ideological level was, then, that sense of place and sense of past became mutually linked and almost interchangeable, and that Ireland itself, as a geographical space, became inescapably also a vessel laden with the placenames, monuments, memories and cultural cargo of a Gaelic past. In that respect, the Ordnance Survey, although its results were to codify Ireland's national separateness as a primordially Celtic country, closely resembles the antiquarians and regional historians of England who at the same time were engaged on their County Histories. Philippa Levine's description of these English counterparts has remarkable applicability to the enterprise of Petrie, O'Donovan and O'Curry:

> The reconstitution of the past was a means of consolidating and realising place and identity in a landscape increasingly unfamiliar. A historical landscape peopled with events, buildings and figures from the past and verified by historical fact was a triumph of possession. Nostalgia provides an insufficient explanation for the popularity of organised antiquarian pursuits. It was rather an alternative cultural force of amazing vigour, an attachment to local identity [. . .] It asserted a sense of provincial dignity and of distinctiveness and provided a crucial link between past glories and present triumphs.

Levine accordingly characterizes Victorian County Histories in terms that fit the Historical Memoir of the Ordnance Survey precisely: they 'acknowledged the significance of both material remains and of municipal manuscripts. The ideal county history was one which embraced accounts of local superstitions and customs alongside discussions of medieval land holdings, of monasteries dissolved under Henry VIII and transcripts of epitaphs on old tombs.' However, the Ordnance Survey seems also in one fatal flaw to have borne the mark of antiquarian localism as characterized by Levine: 'They revelled in the sheer weight of detail, in "a fanatical obsession with the historical significance of the individual object".'[99] Indeed, the Historical Memoir of the Ordnance Survey badly overshot the mark; and indeed it seems to have taken on Casaubonish proportions. Sixty thousand names of parishes and townlands were surveyed, inch-by-inch in their full cultural and historical dimension, with a tender loving care which found no detail too small or to obscure to warrant full and painstaking investigation.[100] This almost obsessive precision and love of minutiae eventually backfired. In 1835, after ten years of work, the Historical Department of the Ordnance Survey proudly presented its first published instalment: a topographical and historical description of the parish of Templemore (of which the city of Derry formed part). The British government was impressed and horrified by the 'excessive zeal' displayed in what 'from a tactical viewpoint [. . .] was an unmitigated disaster' with its 'enormous sprawling bulk'.[101] The Prime Minister, Peel, inquired later on:

> As the account of that single parish constitutes a work of nearly 400 pages, it is manifest that the labour and expense of continuing a publication for the whole of Ireland would be very great; and, independently of the consideration of labour and expense, it may well be doubted whether the value of the memoir is increased by the great extent and variety of the detail into which it enters on many points of merely local and temporary interest.[102]

Obviously the archaeological tail had begun to wag the cartographical dog; and as a result, the government brusquely stopped funding for the historical project. As the government official in charge formulated it:

> That the ordnance officers should collect and be encouraged to collect much valuable information which cannot be given to the world in the shape of a map is quite true. That this should be published in the shape of a memoir or of *pièces justificatives* I admit. That we should pay for this I agree. But that we should undertake to compile regular county and city histories of all Ireland I cannot assent to.[103]

In the course of 1838, the scheme of the grandiose Historical Memoirs as they had expanded under Petrie and Larcom was drastically cut down. By mid-1840 the project had foundered. The matter was certainly not improved when an anonymous letter in 1842 accused Petrie and his staff of Catholic bigotry and nationalist predisposition; it is not clear though, whether this sectarian venom was instrumental in prompting the government's decision to cut the Ordnance Survey down to financial size.[104]

The suspension of the Historical Memoir was widely felt to be a great pity, as work on other parts of Ireland had progressed a good deal since then, and the work of many scholars and fieldworkers over a ten-year period was condemned to remain unfinished and unpublished even as it was nearing completion. The words of J.T. Gilbert, twenty years after the fact, still echo the frustration:

Government in 1842 unexpectedly stopped the grant for the Historic Department of the Ordnance Survey of Ireland, the specially educated and disciplined
labourers in which were thus dispersed and left to seek other employments just
at the time when they had attained to the high state of efficiency qualifying them
to methodize and give to the world in a satisfactory form the results of years of
combined study and investigation.[105]

There was a good deal of commotion on both sides of the Irish Sea about this
insensitive government measure. The government acted against the recom-
mendations of a Parliamentary Commission; both the British Academy and the
Royal Irish Academy had strongly commended the scholarly importance of the
Ordnance Survey and did not take kindly to its abrupt termination, and there
was widespread agitation (led in Ireland by Petrie's friend Lord Adare – the future
Lord Dunraven – and including William Smith O'Brien) to salvage the project. It
was not to be. The materials collected and sorted principally by John O'Donovan
remain accessible in manuscript only, and the volume on Templemore remains
solus. One shining piece of salvage was George Petrie's great essay on the antiquities of Tara Hill, which incorporated the fieldwork of the Ordnance Survey
and was read to the Royal Irish Academy with the permission of Larcom and
Colby. This great specimen of modern, critical archaeology, collating manuscript
tradition and topographical information with a precise description of the site and
its artefacts, was an outstanding example of the light that modern scholarship
could throw on the Irish past; it received the Royal Irish Academy's Cunningham
Medal and was published in its *Transactions* for 1839.[106]

Petrie's Tara essay apart, the failure of the Ordnance Survey was a bitter
disappointment to those who had hoped to see a new type of critical scholarship
illuminate the dark recesses of Irish antiquity, a non-partisan, factual basis for
future historical investigation. There were, however, consolations. The reputa-
tions of O'Donovan and O'Curry as philologists had been firmly established; the
new methodology of combining physical evidence with native manuscript
sources was now widely accepted as the proper procedure for antiquarian investigation; the movement to dissuade the government from its insensitive budget
cuts had been truly trans-partisan and had united all Irish men of learning into a
common front;[107] and the materials that were gathered, if not published, by the
Ordnance Survey were just in time to salvage the historical folklore and popular
learning of rural Ireland on the very eve of the Famine, with its devastating effect
on rural society and culture.

The cultural and social fabric of Gaelic Ireland was to vanish in 1845–1848
with a suddenness that can only be compared to the disappearance of Jewish life
in Central Europe. This cataclysm added another instance of the notion that history, in Ireland, was a series of disruptions and divorces from the past, rather than
a traditionary accumulation growing out of it. The materials collected by the
Ordnance Survey helped to save something at least from that cultural guillotine,
the Famine. J.H. Todd, then President of the Royal Irish Academy, stated later that

this information has been of singular interest [. . .] In many places it will be found that the descriptions and drawings presented in the collection are now the only remaining records of monuments which connect themselves with our earliest history, and of the folk-lore which the famine swept away with the aged sennachies, who were its sole repositories.[108]

J.T. Gilbert echoed these sentiments in 1849: 'Thus very many ancient remains were identified, which otherwise would have been lost to history; much valuable ancillary information was also derived from the traditions and legends of the natives, since obliterated by famine, eviction and emigration [. . .].'[109] Indeed, the feeling in post-Famine Ireland was that Carleton's peasantry, with its lore and pastimes, had been swept out of existence. Sir William Wilde wrote in the *Dublin University magazine* in 1849:

> The old forms and customs, too, are becoming obliterated; the festivals are unob-
> served, and the rustic festivities neglected or forgotten; the bowlings, the cakes and
> the prinkums (the peasants' balls and routs), do not often take place when
> starvation and pestilence stalk over a country, many parts of which appear as if a
> destroying army had but recently passed through it. The hare has made its form on
> the hearth, and the lapwing wheels over the ruined cabin. The faction-fights, the
> hurlings, and the mains of cocks that used to be fought at Shrovetide and Easter,
> with such other innocent amusements, are past and gone these twenty years, and
> the mummers and May-boys left off when we were a gossoon no bigger than a
> pitcher. It was only, however, within those three years that the *waits* ceased to go
> their rounds upon the cold frosty mornings in our native village at Christmas; and
> although the 'wran boys' still gather a few half-pence on St. Stephen's Day, we
> understand there wasn't a candle blessed in the chapel, nor a *breedogue* seen in the
> barony where Kilmucafauden stands, last Candlemas Day; no, nor even a cock
> killed in every fifth house, in honour of St. Martin; and you'd step over the *brosnach*
> of a bonfire that the childer lighted last St. John's Eve.[110]

This helped to give folklore studies – which burgeoned after the Famine – a sense of combined urgency and nostalgia. As we shall see in the next chapter, the collection of folk culture, which had begun with Crofton Croker in the 1820s, intensified strongly after 1845 to become one of the main feeding grounds of the Yeatsian revival by 1890. The Ordnance Survey, which had worked under the very shadow of the imminent Famine, marked an important step in the development of anthropological interest in Ireland's living native culture.

Even while Petrie was preparing the Historical Memoir for the Ordnance Survey, he was also elected to become a member of the Royal Irish Academy. That august body was just then beginning to wake up from its post-Union stupor, and gained much prestige under the presidency of Sir William Rowan Hamilton, renowned astronomer and mathematician. With Hamilton adding to the Academy's lustre in the sphere of the exact sciences, Petrie was to become the Academy's chief luminary in the field of the humanities.[111] It was Petrie who procured some of the outstanding manuscripts for the Academy's library, chief among which was the holograph copy of the Annals of the Four Masters which he acquired in 1831; it was Petrie who from 1837 onwards laid the foundation for a collection of Irish antiquities which would eventually become the core collection of the National Museum of Ireland.[112] The Academy's Council minutes of the period 1830–1845 illustrate a pronounced trend to acquire manuscripts and artefacts previously held in private hands; this retrieval process from the private domain into a place of well-ordered public accessibility (and the need was soon felt for analytical catalogues) marks one of the more important pre-conditions of the gradual redemption of philological and text-historical studies from amateurish speculation. The same process led to a growing desire to have the more important manuscript materials published in print; indeed, in 1840 the Irish Archeological Society was founded by Academy members Petrie and Todd precisely for this purpose. Petrie was a driving force in this process; and it was Petrie more than anyone else, who introduced, into the Academy of learned and ingenious gentlemen (amateurs and dilettanti for the most part, and not a few of them Freemasons[113]) the precise, critical spirit of new scientific scholarship.

The Royal Irish Academy to which Petrie was elected in 1828 was still dominated by the Phoenician model; this was to change, though not without great friction, as a result of Petrie's achievement, his institutional influence and his critical factualism. The entrenched rearguard held the Academy's key positions: important members on the Council representing 'polite letters' were men like the Ulster King of Arms, Sir William Betham, and the barrister John D'Alton, both of whom had espoused the Phoenician model of Irish antiquity – Betham in the ludicrously speculative way that we have seen, D'Alton in a more sober, conventional vein. D'Alton, his Phoenicianism notwithstanding, was an important figure in the development of Irish historiography. Following the archival work of O'Conor of Stowe and O'Reilly, he was among the first to rely strongly on native annals and chronicles as a source, and on that basis wrote a number of interesting local histories. One work deserving of mention is his *History of Ireland from the annals of Boyle* (1845). D'Alton's work is all the more interesting because it exemplifies a dual tendency, which is often found to work in tandem. On the one hand, there is the reliance on ancient manuscript sources, often accompanied by the desire to see such sources (re-)printed, on the other, a penchant for local history. Another outstanding example of this dual trend is found in the work of James Hardiman, whose *History of Galway* of 1821 was based on extensive use of manuscripts and had been preceded by his 'Catalogue of maps, charts, and plans relating to Ireland'. (*Transactions RIA*, 14).[114] The prevailing English fashion for reprints and publications of ancient sources is matched in Ireland by the activities of the Irish Archaeological Society, founded in 1840 in order to bring important MS sources into print (a move designed to combat fanciful speculations), and its counterpart the Ossianic Society. Indeed, the entire work of John O'Donovan, grounded as it was in the fieldwork undertaken for the Ordnance Survey, shows that it was through the pursuit of *local* history that the use and (re-)publication of MS source material gained a foothold in Irish antiquarian and historiographical practice.

In the very year that Petrie joined the Academy, D'Alton had read, on 24 November 1828, an essay which in its published form was to take up no less than 380 pages of the Academy's *Proceedings*. This 'Essay on the ancient history, religion, learning, arts and government of Ireland', which received a prize of £80 and a gold medal, was in fact the most ambitious and wide-ranging treatment of older Irish cultural history since the days of Walker, and a clear sign that ancient Ireland was once again a respectable topic for scholarly investigation. Like Lanigan six years previously (in the authoritative *Ecclesiastical history of Ireland* of 1822), D'Alton endorsed the Phoenician model of the Irish past, but did so in a more circumspect and sedate manner. Thus, his reliance on the Carthaginian speech in *Poenulus* (cf. p. 245, n. 11) took care to distance itself from Vallancey's eager speculations, and D'Alton preferred to invoke the weighty name of Dr O'Conor, the Stowe librarian, rather than the fanciful Vallancey. This did not preclude him from endorsing the theory that the Round Towers were linked to Oriental fire-worship, citing the Zend-Avesta and other recently disclosed Oriental sources in evidence.[115]

On the whole, then, the Oriental (Phoenician) theory of Irish origins held sway, not only in the complacency of the Royal Irish Academy (which from 1800 until 1830 was hardly on the cutting edge of scholarly developments), and not only in philological circles, but also among historians, represented by Lanigan and D'Alton. And, as D'Alton's work also exemplifies, the single most interesting litmus-test for a historian's or archaeologist's beliefs concerning the nature of the Irish past (Phoenician or otherwise) was his treatment of the Round Towers. This was to become the most burning issue in Irish historical studies for the next twenty years or more. The issue was raised practically immediately after Petrie's accession and D'Alton's essay, for in the same fateful year 1828 the Academy's Council proposed a public prize essay on the 'Origin and Uses of the Round Towers'. Scholars were invited through public advertisement to submit their theories to the Academy in essay form; it was evidently hoped that, in this manner, a satisfactory account could be established as to when and by whom, and for what purposes, these remarkable and mysterious edifices had been erected.

Round Towers

Round Towers occur in some profusion in Ireland (nineteenth-century sources cite anywhere from fifty to a hundred specimens, either still standing or mentioned in the records), but hardly occur in other European countries. They do not have any analogues in the standard typology of mainstream European architecture and are, therefore, largely *sui generis* and practically exclusively Irish. The various comparisons that were made, in the course of the nineteenth century, with other edifices such as the Sardinian *nuraghe* or Oriental pagodas or minarets, are so far-fetched as to illustrate rather the opposite of what they intended to prove: Round Towers, we may conclude, really do not resemble anything else. Nowadays, the consensus is that Round Towers are a primitive form of fortification, current before the introduction of Norman-style castles or late-medieval siege technology, and aimed mainly (apart from possible secondary use as belfry, light-beacon or lookout-tower) to offer monastic communities some form of refuge from marauding bands of enemies. They are usually assigned to a period between 900 and 1100 AD. However, that consensus was only reached after a long and intense battle between two schools of archaeology, which we may call, for the sake of the present argument, the romantic and the positivistic ones. The romantic school took its cue from Vallancey and the Phoenicianists, ascribing to these edifices an origin which, in its exoticism, would match their picturesque and exotic appearance, and on the whole argued that they dated back to pre-Christian times. The positivists, on the other hand, saw them as essentially ecclesiastical buildings, therefore necessarily posterior to the introduction of Christianity and presumably medieval. Among the proponents of the romantic theory were well-regarded scholars such as O'Conor, Lanigan and D'Alton, as well as more fanciful ones such as Vallancey, Betham and (later) Henry O'Neill and Marcus Keane, and a number of downright cranks such as the notorious Henry O'Brien. The positivist school found its greatest champion in the towering figure of George Petrie, whose theories, later endorsed and refined by scholars like Lord Dunraven and Margaret Stokes, form the basis of the present-day consensus.[116]

The debates surrounding the origin and use of the Round Towers lasted throughout the nineteenth century, with peaks around 1830, 1845 and 1870. These debates are of immense importance, as I shall try to point out, for our understanding of the development of historical consciousness and the historical imagination in nineteenth-century Ireland. They do not merely concern a specific topic in the history of architecture, but rather form the main battle-ground for two different ways of viewing the Irish cultural tradition. The Round Towers became a shibboleth by which two conflicting views on Irish antiquities could make their stand; as Ferguson sarcastically remarked in 1845, 'no Irish antiquary can be well supposed to write a complete book without giving his own theory of the round towers of that country'.[117]

This is in itself remarkable. It is a curious question why Round Towers, of all things, should have become such symbolic figureheads in a clash between two historical paradigms. This may have something to do with what I have just described as their peculiarity: the fact that they are largely exclusive to Ireland and do not fit any larger architectural typology or easily classifiable period. More directly important, perhaps, is the fact that they were *there*, physically present in a touchy-feely way.[118] Unlike the mysteries and the irretrievable disparition of ancient Irish culture, lost, inaccessible and largely unknown, the Round Towers were still part of the here and now; they formed a physical link with a past that was so mysterious and unknown that it may just as well have been wholly non-existent. In other words, the Round Towers, in their very presence, were a *lieu de mémoire*, a monument which formed a tangible link between present and past, lending a degree of presence to the past itself. It was this monumental function that could lend them an immediate symbolic importance for the persistence of such a thing as Irishness.[119] Round Towers *per se*, in their picturesque presence, transfigured the *Nacheinander* of past history into a *Nebeneinander* and lent substance to the transitoriness of history. Not for nothing did Round Towers figure prominently and ubiquitously among the symbols representing Ireland, alongside shamrocks, harps, druids and the occasional wolfhound: of all these, and amidst the revolutions, turmoil and conflicts of the period 1795–1845, the Round Towers were the most durable, the most obvious icon of the existence and persistence of a specifically Irish cultural presence. This symbolic importance indirectly informs the theory of O'Conor of Stowe that the Towers were the gnomons of immense sundials, whose shadows at certain times of the years afforded astronomical observations: if the hypothesis is not factually correct, it at least metaphorically satisfying in that it sees them as the still points around which the course of time revolves, immobile in their structure and casting different shadows at different periods. More explicitly, the role of the Round Towers as *lieux de mémoire* is summed up explicitly in a poem by Denis Florence MacCarthy, originally published in *The nation*, which gained immediate and lasting fame (it is still the most anthologized of MacCarthy's poems). The Towers are 'conquerors of time', outlasting other monuments from antiquity, unchanging (like the pyramids) through the movements and vicissitudes of history. Their origins are remote, obscure, forgotten, generations and invaders have come and gone, and through all these periods the towers have remained and (so the poet hopes) shall remain as a symbol of permanence. Insistently the poem opposes the Towers to the notion of historical transience:

> The pillar towers of Ireland, how wondrously they stand
> By the lakes and rushing rivers through the valleys of our land
> In mystic file, through the isle, they lift their heads sublime,
> These gray old pillar temples, these conquerors of time!
>
> Beside these gray old pillars, how perishing and weak
> The Roman's arch of triumph, and the temple of the Greek,
> And the gold domes of Byzantium, and the pointed Gothic spires,
> All are gone, one by one, but the temples of our sires.
>
> The column, with its capital, is level with the dust,
> And the proud halls of the mighty and the calm homes of the just;
> For the proudest works of man, as certainly, but slower,
> Pass like the grass at the sharp scythe of the mower!
>
> . . .
>
> . . .
>
> Two favourites hath Time – the pyramids of Nile,
> And the old mystic temples of our own dear isle;
> As the breeze o'er the seas, where the halcyon has its nest,
> Thus Time o'er Egypt's tombs and the temples of the West!

The names of their founders have vanished in the gloom,
Like the dry branch in the fire or the body in the tomb;
But today, in the ray, their shadows still they cast –
These temples of forgotten gods – these relics of the past!

Around these walls have wandered the Briton and the Dane –
The captives of Armorica, the cavaliers of Spain –
Phoenician and Milesian, and the plundering Norman Peers –
And the swordsmen of brave Brian, and the chiefs of later years!

    . . .
    . . .

There may it stand for ever, while that symbol doth impart
To the mind one glorious vision, or one proud throb to the heart;
While the breast needeth rest may these gray old temples last,
Bright prophets of the future, as preachers of the past![120]

Small wonder, then, that those of a romantic disposition would want to enhance the symbol and its symbolic value by extending their duration as far into the past as possible; that is what we see happen in MacCarthy's poem.[121] A Round Tower of two or even three thousand years' standing was twice as satisfying as one of a mere eight hundred years, and held together a greater part of Irish history. That, I submit, is the reason why these monuments (with some ancillary debates concerning cromlechs and the *Lia Fáil*) became the *casus belli* for the two opposing camps in the Irish historical imagination.

The state of the question *c.* 1830

By 1830 there was already a sizeable body of work and speculation as to the use and origin of the Round Towers. Antiquaries like Peter Collinson and Richard Gough had offered descriptions in the 1760s; and by the end of the eighteenth century there was already a split between a Nordic and a Mediterranean-Oriental hypothesis. The Nordic antiquaries, Ledwich foremost among them, favoured a Danish, twelfth-century origin, and most observers were agreed on the idea that the Towers were at least of Christian date. Daniel Augustus Beaufort, in his *Memoir of a map of Ireland* (Dublin, 1792, pp. 138–41) and Richard Colt Hoare in his *Journal of a tour in Ireland AD 1806* (London 1807, pp. 278–91) concurred in a tentative monastic attribution, as did Weld in his *Illustrations of the scenery of Killarney* (London, 1807). That hypothesis was further supported by a Colonel Hervé de Montmorency-Morres, who published his *Historical and critical inquiry into the origin and primitive uses of the Irish pillar-tower* in 1821. Montmorency-Morres[122] opined that the architecture of the Round Towers bespoke a defensive purpose.

Thus, around 1820, there was a body of opinion which already foreshadowed the explanation later to be established more firmly by Petrie: a monastic origin and intended for defensive use. There was, however, a strong opposite tradition which held that the Towers were of pre-Christian date, were introduced into Ireland from the East through Phoenician intermediaries, and that they had been originally used for Oriental religious practices such as fire-worship. That theory was initally linked to the name of Vallancey and the *Collectanea de rebus Hibernicis*; it had also been advanced by Thomas Campbell in his *Philosophical survey of the south of Ireland* (1777), was adopted by Lanigan in his *Ecclesiastical history* of 1822, and was to spawn a number of similar conjectures throughout the nineteenth century. It had little hard evidence to recommend it,[123] and was usually argued by finding flaws in the more mundane theory of monastic-Christian or medieval origins. For instance: if the Round Towers were situated closely to church establishments, why, in so many cases, did they survive and not the adjacent church buildings? Was not the medieval theory advanced by men whose avowed interest it was to downgrade Irish history, such as Ledwich? If they were built for defensive purposes, were they not much too fragile and unstable for that purpose? This last question in turn gave rise, throughout the century, to claims and counter-claims involving either the remarkable sturdiness or else the remarkable fragility of the Round Towers.[124]

It is striking that, once the Royal Irish Academy began to take on topics of antiquarian interest again in the 1820, the theories advanced in its *Transactions* tended to favour the Orientalizing, Vallanceyesque paradigm. John T. O'Flaherty set the tone in 1824, when he read 'A sketch of the history and antiquities of the southern islands of Arran, lying off the west coast of Ireland, with observations on the religion of the Celtic nations, pagan monuments of the early Irish, druidic rites &c.', which hinted strongly at Persian parallels and Zoroastran fire worship.[125] A similar approach was taken by a woman contributor, a Miss Beaufort, who condoned the fire-temple theory in her prize essay on 'The state of architecture and antiquities, previous to the landing of the Anglo-Normans in Ireland', read before the Academy in 1827. Beaufort's essay repeatedly draws parallels with Sanscrit and Persian, but does so in order to endorse the theories of Vallancey and Betham.[126] An important endorsement was finally given by John D'Alton's aforementioned 'Essay on the ancient history of Ireland', read before the Academy in 1828, and awarded £80 and a gold medal: D'Alton came down strongly in favour of fire worship and Zoroastrian parallels, citing the Zend-Avesta.[127]

The 1830 prize essay: Petrie and O'Brien

We may presume that Petrie, who had become a member of the Academy's Committee of Antiquities in 1829, wanted to overhaul this entrenched Phoenicianist attitude in the Academy when he proposed that the 'Origin and Uses of the Round Towers' be made the topic for a prize essay in 1830. In November 1830, the Council endorsed Petrie's proposal for a prize essay 'on the round towers of Ireland, in which it is expected that the characteristic architectural peculiarities belonging to all these ancient buildings shall be noticed, and the uncertainty in which their origin and uses are involved be satisfactorily explained'.[128] The Round Towers had been cited in a variety of interpretations by generations of scholars and antiquaries, and it was obvious that no progress was being made to reconcile, or advance beyond, the various positions. The prize essay was obviously intended to break through this stagnated *status quaestionis* (indeed in the next decades it was to become a commonplace to refer to the Round Towers as the *vexata quaestio* or 'vexed question').

The result was that matters were brought to a head. Different opinions concerning Irish antiquity, which for decades had coexisted in relative mutual disregard, were now forced into a confrontation. The Academy's advertisement of the prize essay, published in December 1830 and reiterated, for lack of satisfactory submissions, in March 1832, elicited either three or five entries (accounts differ);[129] when the submission deadline expired in mid-1832, the Council found that it not only had to judge authors of varying ability and thoroughness, but that it also had to choose between mutually incompatible scholarly persuasions.

The two contending protagonists were Petrie himself and an unknown young enthusiast by the name of Henry O'Brien, born in County Kerry in 1808, recently graduated from Trinity College, and now based in London. Petrie, in later eyes, stands for painstaking, critical investigation, while O'Brien has come to stand for wild speculation untrammelled by considerations of common sense; but that may have been less glaringly obvious in 1832. Both essays were later reworked by their respective authors: Petrie's *Ecclesiastical architecture of Ireland* appeared in massive form, lavishly illustrated, in 1845, and O'Brien's *The Round Towers of Ireland* appeared in book form in 1834. The differences between the two books is manifest; but it may be argued that Petrie's essay had profited a great deal from being reworked into book form, while O'Brien's essay was greatly disimproved in the reworking by the author's growing frustration and increasingly overwrought paranoia.[130] The differences between the two essays may have been less pronounced than would appear from the published versions. But the main, irreconcilable difference between the two, apparent even in June 1832, was the fact that O'Brien works on the basic assumption of a great Oriental presence in Irish antiquity, whereas Petrie refuses to countenance speculations predating the introduction of Christianity.

In adjudicating the prize, the Council appears to have split along lines of persuasion. The sole partisan in favour of O'Brien's essay was John D'Alton, whose Phoenicianist persuasion obviously predisposed him against Petrie's medieval theory. Remarkably, Sir William Betham seems to have gone Petrie's way, but that need not have been a matter of serious scholarly persuasion; a concept that does not easily fit Betham. Rather, Petrie's standing in the Academy was very high indeed at the time, Petrie having just managed to obtain an original MS copy of the Annals of the Four Masters. Betham seems to have judged according to personal sympathy rather than from considerations of scholarly agreement, and became Petrie's declared enemy only in subsequent years.[131]

In the event, a final decision was reached – with a fatal dose of compromise. Petrie's essay did, indeed, receive the prize medal and money, but a consolation prize was afforded to O'Brien as runner-up and in recompense for the young man's frenetic labour to meet the deadline after having been belatedly informed of the competition.

Matters might have ended there. D'Alton and Beaufort had earlier received medals for *their* version of Irish antiquities, now Petrie had put the more factualist interpretation back on the Academy's agenda by having *his* version acclaimed. But all this failed to take the personality of young Henry O'Brien into account, and the awkward timing of the adjudication.

Almost two years elapsed between the initial advertisement of the prize essay (towards the close of 1830) and the final adjudication (published towards the close of 1832, six months after the expiry of the final deadline in June 1832). By the time the result was announced, expectations had become very highly pitched indeed, and scandal was already brewing. O'Brien had begun to ply the Council with importunate letters, hinting that the extension of the deadline and the renewed call for submissions were ploys to give Petrie a chance of improving his essay. Apparent confirmation of O'Brien's charges appeared in the *Dublin penny journal*, a cultural and historical magazine for the middle classes launched in June 1832, and headed by two members of the Academy's Council: Petrie himself and his friend and collaborator Caesar Otway. (Another important contributor was John O'Donovan, who at the time was working with Petrie in the Historical Section of the Ordnance Survey.)

The *Dublin penny journal* carried an unmistakable Petrie-esque imprint, dedicated as it was to the critical and factualist elucidation of Irish antiquity, against all unfounded speculation. Imprudently, its editors allowed themselves to be caried away by their interest in Round Towers which were now looming so large over the antiquarian and archaeological endeavour, and the *Dublin penny journal* accordingly devoted unusual amounts of space and prominence to Round Towers while their origin and uses were still *sub judice*, subject to the Academy's adjudication and endorsement. The *Dublin penny journal's* second issue included a discussion of 'National Emblems' in a letter from Caesar Otway (writing under the pseudonym Terence O'Toole), in language that was already exuding scepticism concerning 'clever conjectures':

> The Round Tower [. . .] is a prodigious puzzler to antiquarians. [. . .] They have been assigned to the obscene rites of Paganism – to the mystic *arcana* of Druidism – said to be temples of the fire-worshippers – Christian belfries – military towers of the Danish invaders – defensive retreats for the native clergy, from the sudden inroads of the ruthless Norman. But all these clever and recondite conjectures are shortly, as I understand, to be completely overthrown, and the real nature of these Round Towers clearly explained, for the first time, in a Prize Essay, presented to the Royal Irish Academy, by an accomplished antiquarian of our city.[132]

Otway was foolishly spilling the beans. The 'accomplished antiquarian of our city' could be none other than Petrie, and the prize-winning essay was already stated in so many words to be a demolition of previous conjectures ranging from Vallancey to Ledwich to Montmorency. O'Brien (whose essay argued precisely that the Towers, with their phallic shape, had been built for 'the obscene rites of Paganism') was understandably shocked to read this; no other conclusion was possible than that this piece was written on the basis of inside information, that the adjudication of the prize was a foregone conclusion as soon as the deadline was passed, and that the prize was to go to an inner-circle fat-cat of established reputation. In other words, Otway's indiscretion gave the strong impression of an inside job.[133] Chastened, the Dublin penny journal (though it continued to describe Round Towers as ecclesiastical buildings) thenceforward abstained from anticipating the official verdict;[134] but when that verdict came in mid-December, it failed to resolve what was already becoming a scandal. The Dublin University magazine, the new voice of conservative, Protestant respectability, carried the announcement in its first issue (January 1833), in tones congratulating Petrie and the respectable sort of scholarship that he stood for. Yet even here was a potential barb, for there was already, joined to the congratulations, a call for the acclaimed essay to be made public:

> We announce with feelings of sincere pleasure, the success of our highly-gifted fellow-countryman, Mr. George Petrie, in having obtained the first prize, a gold medal and fifty guineas, presented by the Royal Irish Academy, for the best Essay upon the origin and use of the Round Towers of Ireland. We trust Mr. Petrie may be induced to submit speedily to the public, the results of his judgment and experience upon one of the most interesting topics connected with Irish antiquities [. . .][135]

The situation was indeed odd. The Council had, no doubt owing to internal divisions and a sense of embarrassment at the muddled procedure, hedged its bets and given a consolation prize to O'Brien; but meanwhile a prestigious public accolade was given to an essay and a theory which as yet were unknown in their contents and conclusions to the general public. The public was told that Petrie had come and solved the riddle to the Academy's satisfaction; but no details as to Petrie's solution were divulged.

This failure to go public was to take on ridiculous proportions. Petrie could not be 'induced to submit' anything to the public for the next twelve years, for it took that long for him to rework his prize-winning essay into what he considered publishable form, to have illustrations engraved, etc. The Petrie essay reached the public only by way of indirect reference.[136] One person who did go public, meanwhile, was the disappointed rival, Henry O'Brien.

In retrospect, O'Brien can be seen as a pathological obsessive, suffering from paranoid delusions. His wild speculations on the origin and use of the Round Towers are matched by his frenzied controversialism over the alleged conspiracies in the Academy's inner circle. It appears that the controversy he stirred up, and the public humiliation and ridicule he had to endure, ultimately hastened his death in 1835 at the age of twenty-seven. But while O'Brien's essay on the Round Towers was idle speculation taken to extremes, his criticism of the Academy's procedure is not entirely groundless. The aim of the prize essay was undoubtedly to reconcile the conflicting versions and schools concerning Irish antiquity once and for all; in the event, O'Brien was given a bonus prize of £20, Petrie's essay was allowed to share the honours with O'Brien's incompatible counter-version, and initially it was even decided that both essays would be published in the *Transactions* – the Academy thus seeming to have it both ways, endorsing two conflicting versions of Irish antiquity. Although there were precedents for the awarding of bonus or consolation prizes (the Academy had given one in 1828 to Thomas Wood),[137] O'Brien construed it as a sign of bad faith and as an attempt to save the established authority's reputation in the face of his, O'Brien's, incontrovertible and superior essay. And this is the tale that he told before the public.

Even while the issue was still pending, O'Brien grasped an opportunity to present his case independently of the Academy's control. An amiable and slightly eccentric clergyman-scholar in exile from Spain, Joaquín Villanueva, had in the preceding year (1831) published, in Latin, a theory on Ireland's Phoenician origins, deeply indebted to Vallancey (*Ibernia Phoenicia, seu Phoenicum in Ibernia incolatus, ex ejus priscarum coloniarum nominibus, et earum idolatrico cultu demonstratio*, Dublin 1831). It was in part an old man's hobby-horse, subscribed to for charitable purposes by various worthies of the Dublin intellectual scene and endorsing a view of Irish history which at that point no-one took the trouble of contradicting (there are no reviews of Villanueva's book, nor references to him in subsequent antiquarian writings).[138] O'Brien decided to bring out an English translation of this book; and no author was ever more strangely served by his translator. O'Brien translated and edited Villanueva's original much as Charles Kinbote, in Nabokov's *Pale fire*, edited John Shade's poem. The result appeared under the promising title *Phoenician Ireland. Translated and illustrated with notes, plates, and Ptolomey's map of Erin made modern, by Henry O'Brien, Esq., B.A., author of the 'prize essay' upon the 'Round Towers' of Ireland* (Dublin, 1833). Villanueva's name is absent from the title page, mercifully so, because O'Brien is highly selective in what he chooses to translate, and interpolates lengthy passages from his own hand. The result is a farrago of footnotes and digressions with only the most tenuous connection with Villanueva's book (of which it has the effrontery to reproduce excerpts in an appendix as proof of fidelity). To complete the Nabokovian uncanniness, it is couched throughout in O'Brien's insane prose style; a sample from his dedication to the Marquis of Thomond may give an idea:

> And yet, my Lord, will you not commiserate with me the degeneracy? and say 'how are the mighty fallen?' when informed that the individual who has *revived so many truths*, immersed between the rubbish of *three thousand years* accumulation – and that when his researches did not apply alone to *Ireland*,* but took in the scope of

---

* [O'Brien's note:] 'The formation as well as the date of this, the *present name* of our island, I account for in a forthcoming note.'

the *whole ancient world* – has been defrauded of that prize for which his zeal had been enlisted, and his young energies evoked? while – from that system of *'jobbing'* with which our country has been long accursed – he has seen the *badge of his victory transferred* to another, merely because *that other* was a *member* of the *council* of the *deciding tribunal* who disregarded the crying fact, that the *whole texture* of their friend's *essay* must, *inevitably*, be *untenable!** However, my Lord, in the consciousness of *your* countenance I find my consolation; and, soon as my 'Towers' appear, I doubt not, this *wise* (?) *'tribunal'* will reap the fruits, together, of *their own discomfiture and of my revenge.* (x–xi)

Villanueva's Phoenician book is the merest pretext, in short, for a full frontal attack on the Royal Irish Academy. The entire vituperative correspondence between O'Brien and the Academy is reproduced in the Introduction ('To the Public', xiii–xxxii), and the 'Translator's Preface' (i–xxxii) is one long anticipation of the startling, overwhelming and incontrovertible proofs that O'Brien will offer to the astounded world once his Round Tower essay will see the light of day.

The reviewer of the *Gentleman's magazine* already poked fun both at the 'Spanish antiquary' ('an etymon hunter on a full scent') and at the frenetic, italics-ridden prose of the translator.[139] Doubtless, the etymological conjectures of Villanueva deserved to be criticized: any place-name beginning with 'Bally-' he construed as indicating a primordial worship of the god Baal, and he even went so far as to suppose an ancient worship of Astarte from the fact that that goddess's name was still daily on the lips of the Irish populace in the old song 'Molly Astore'.[140] O'Brien himself may have been warned by this patronizing and ironic review that he could not expect to be taken seriously merely because he was so very vehement in insisting on his achievement; but he was to receive worse treatment at the hands of the critics when his book on the Round Towers finally appeared in 1834. Before looking at contemporary reactions to O'Brien's book, however, it may first be in order to look at the theory advanced there and to place it in context.

Round Towers and phallic worship

The appearance of *The Round Towers of Ireland (or the mysteries of freemasonry, of sabaism, and of budhism, now for the first time unveiled)* in 1834 was slightly delayed: O'Brien had initially placed his essay with the printer P. Dixon Hardy, who was a member of the Royal Irish Academy and one of the more prominent Dublin publishers in the field of Irish history and antiquity at the time (he took over the *Dublin penny journal* when that magazine became too burdensome for Petrie and Otway, and was later to publish the works of Sir William Betham). However, Hardy, upon becoming acquainted with the scandalous nature of the work, declined publishing it, and the book appeared under a joint

---

* [O'Brien's note:] 'Of this I give, by *anticipation*, the most *startling* and *overwhelming* proof, even in a note appended towards the end of the 33rd chapter of the present work.' [no such note is appended 'towards the end of the 33rd chapter', J.L.]

London and Dublin imprint. It caused an immediate sensation, though not in the author's favour. The book opened with a ludicrous dedication[141] and was preceded by a lengthy introduction which recapitulated (in more extensive form than in *Phoenician Ireland*) the contentious origin of the text, often in highly derogatory terms, evidently written with much anger, much frustration and little self-control. The main body of the book was no less intemperate. Previous theories were set aside with scorn, exclamation marks and italics, and to the extent that an argument could be detected in the author's ravings, that argument was both far-fetched and shocking.

O'Brien started out from four clues. One was that Round Towers look like erect penises; the second (pointed out by Miss Beaufort also) was that the word 'Erin' looks like the word 'Iran'; the third was that Iran lies in the east, the cradle of Irish civilization, and that in the east there are pagodas, which, to the extent that they look like Round Towers, also look like erect penises; and the fourth one (clinching the matter) was that the Gaelic word for penis, *bod*, looks like the first syllable in the word 'Buddhism', denoting an eastern religion. The rest follows as a matter of course. There was once a Persian civilization, where the creative fertility principle was worshipped under the shape of the phallus, and in phallic-shaped pagodas. This religion, originally taught by Zoroaster, was known as Buddhism or, alternatively, as Sabaism. These Buddhist-cum-Zoroastrian Sabaists were expelled from Persia, settled in Ireland under the name of Tuath-De-Danaans and built pagodas there (the Round Towers) to continue their phallic worship. The hypothesis is given extra clout by the illustrations, which deliberately appear to emphasize the penis-shaped aspect of Round Towers by turning sharp angles into curves and rounding off their conical roofs to give a hint of the *glans penis*.[142]

This hypothesis by itself forms an archimedian fulcrum with which O'Brien unhinges all of ancient and middle-eastern history and re-interprets the entire religious history of the world as a cover-up exercise in effacing the heritage of the noble Sabaists. The serpent and the apple in the Garden of Eden are interpreted as genital symbols; serpent-worship is seen as a derivation of phallus worship;[143] the Hinduist veneration of sexual polarity in the shape of *lingam* and *yoni* is adduced in evidence; and if there are carvings of crucifixes to be seen on Round Towers, then O'Brien immediately explains this by the fact that there was in fact a pre-Christian, Buddhist worship of the crucifix. In other words, this is madness surpassing even Roger O'Connor's *Chronicles of Eri*.

But whereas the *Chronicles of Eri* never gained much serious attention, Henry O'Brien's book became a *cause célèbre*. Nobody endorsed O'Brien's theory, but there were always some who refused to reject it wholly and utterly. For better or for worse, O'Brien's name was made famous by becoming the subject of scandal and ridicule; his theory was given exemplary status by being so memorably unmentionable in polite society; and he remained, if only at the symbolic level, a focus for all those who had misgivings about Petrie's factualism.

To begin with, it must be said that O'Brien's theory was flawed but not wholly without substance. To be sure, it would be ludicrous and plain wrong, a distortion of historical data, to see the Round Towers as sites of phallus worship. No amount of historical relativism or epistemological scepticism should tempt us, merely because we cannot know for certain what is truth, to countenance what we know for certain to be an error. Historians and critics in the last decades have become perhaps too lenient in endorsing, or empathizing with, historical errors and mistakes, merely because they made sense at the time or because they fitted the paradigm within which they were conceived, or because there was some sort of edifying *poiesis* in them, a poetic justice if not a factual correctness.[144] Those who refuse the benefit of hindsight and merely immerse themselves sympathetically in the past or in unfalsifiable conjecture are tourists or dreamers, not historians; for although historians may not claim knowledge of absolute truth with which to measure the endeavours of the past, or a positive knowledge of what things were like, they do have a positive knowledge of what has been falsified in history, what has been proved wrong, what was certainly not the case.[145] We know, positively, what falsification has taught us: that the earth is not flat; that combustion does not proceed by the emission of phlogiston; that the Gaelic language has not evolved from Hebrew, that the Round Towers were not built by phallus-worshippers. To waive such positive knowledge-*quod-non* is to descend into silliness and make-believe.

That being said, O'Brien's thesis is far from insignificant, even though it is factually wrong. He worked, it should be remembered, before the definitive establishment of the Indo-European frame of reference, which he anticipated to some extent.[146] His extensive survey of phallic worship and fertility worship in antiquity, though it is misguided in its application to Gaelic historical myths and Round Towers, invokes material concerning the religious eroticism of Hinduism made available by men like Sir William Jones; such material, along with the surviving traces of phallic superstition in the Mediterranean area, was leading to a new interest in the link between sex and religious ritual, foreshadowing, and paving the way for, important later insights in anthropology and psychology. Although O'Brien never mentions it, the work of Richard Payne Knight (*A discourse on the worship of Priapus and its connexion with the mystic theology of the ancients*, 1786) was certainly an important source, directly or indirectly, for his theories.[147] The embryonic anthropological interest in the link between sex and religious ritual was kept alive by a number of books and tracts which followed in O'Brien's footsteps and helped to pave the way for Freudian thought.

This process was partly fed by the gradual discovery of the cultic religions and mysteries of classical antiquity: those of Orpheus, Bacchus, Demeter or Mithras. Some of these cults and mysteries involved the glorification of sexual energy, and there were syncretic tendencies which brought in Oriental elements or deities. Such factors help to make clear that the religious fringe activities of classical antiquity (of which phallic icons survived) should be conflated with analogous remains of Oriental religions, from Egypt to India, and hence be interpreted collectively as the substratum of a vanished primordial cult spanning the entire pre-classical world. Indeed, that view of primitive religion was to remain operative even in the thought of Sir James Frazer and Sigmund Freud. All this means that O'Brien's views, though intemperately expressed, were not quite as grotesque as might be supposed at first glance. Well-regarded English anti-quarians at the time, such as Godfrey Higgins, held similar phallic theories.[148] Again, an army lieutenant by the name of I. Webber Smith published a pamphlet *An essay on the Round Towers of Ireland as compared with other monuments* (1838), which like O'Brien (but without his paranoid tendencies) made comparisons with phallic or genital symbolism in ancient Egyptian religion and Hinduism. He held that the phallic worship of Baal had also spread to the British Isles in the shape of May fires and maypoles:

> The same superstition had spread itself to England, and was the origin of our May poles, which many a happy and innocent maiden has danced around in the gaiety of her heart. It is a melancholy fact, *sed omnia Priapi haec sunt: altera certè non!* (p. 19)

Webber Smith was led astray by his reliance on Vallancey (he also (22n.) perpetrates the Molly-Astore-solecism noticed with Villanueva, p. 117); but his speculations on the fertility rites underlying May fires and maypoles may for modern anthropologists seem plausible enough. A similar point has been made by Thomas Maurier, in his *Indian antiquities* (7 vols.; 1793–1800), echoed by Godfrey Higgins.[149] Webber Smith was also among the first to draw attention to one obvious and undeniable presence of untamed genital sexuality in Irish ecclesiastical architecture: the Sheela-na-Gig figure.

> I will merely add, that before any one indignantly rejects the theory I have supported, I would advise them to examine the female figures carved on some of the old Irish churches, which, although I have not as yet deemed it necessary to make use of them, strengthen most remarkably my ideas relative to the round towers (p. 36).

The Sheela-na-Gigs (medieval carvings of a female figure, often on or in church buildings, provocatively displaying her genitals with legs spread wide) were also adduced as survivals of a pre-Christian fertility worship in Thomas Wright's *The worship of the generative powers during the middle ages of western Europe* (1866).[150] To be sure, to see Round Towers and Sheela-na-Gigs as mutual counterparts is going too far; but it is obvious that O'Brien's application of phallic religion to Irish architecture was part of a nineteenth-century movement in religious anthro-pology, and that in that development O'Brien was not without impact. Not only were later phallic theoreticians explicit in taking up O'Brien's point,[151] it also appears that O'Brien's book came to stand for all daring, speculative theories which refused to be laid to rest by the mundane factualism of Petrie, even after the publication of Petrie's essay in 1845. Another faithful support group for O'Brien's theories was found among freemasons. There were strong masonic hints in the title, dedication and introduction of the book's first edition, and subsequent reprints seem to have been sponsored by masonic and otherwise hermetic-speculative associations.[152]

O'Brien, Moore and Father Prout

But all this was very much an underground, fringe movement at the time. The scholarly and educated community greeted the appearance of O'Brien's book with loud and unanimous derision and outrage. There were scathing reviews in all the leading literary magazines. These make interesting reading since they set out to demolish a book which prudery prevented them from even summarizing. So unmentionable was O'Brien's theory that it could not even be referred to in plain terms by those who wished to explode it. Recourse was sometimes taken to Latin, in order to shelter the unmentionable topic (witness the quotation from Webber Smith, above), and very occasionally the word 'phallic' was used; but for the rest the reviewers, when they had to explain why they were outraged by this book, had to use very tortuous language indeed. The *Dublin University magazine*, after devoting most of its space to a vindication of the Royal Irish Academy against O'Brien's charges, finally comes to the point:

> We are, therefore, under the embarrassing necessity of stating as we can, that, according to Mr. O'Brien, the round towers of Ireland, beautiful as they appear in the landscape, and interesting to the poet's and antiquarian's taste, were in the first ages constructed to represent a certain particular division of the human anatomy, which the refinement of modern civilization has excluded from decent language.[153]

The reviewer even objects to the fact that he is supposed to *notice* the similarity; if O'Brien thinks a Round Tower looks like a penis, well let him speak for himself!

> This foul and grotesque association of dissimilarities – 'Hyperion to a Satyr' – he maintains [. . .] by a most grotesque appeal to the observation of sense – an incorrect induction, which, if it has any support in fact, cannot extend beyond his own experience. (380)

Similarly, the *Gentleman's magazine's* oblique snigger:

> If the author is correct in his supposition, as to the motive for which these towers were built, conceiving, by looking at the *present population* of Ireland, that their purposes have been fully answered, we humbly suggest whether it would not be desirable to *commence taking them down.*[154]

Indeed, it may be because the nature of O'Brien's theory precluded public discussion that reviews mainly fastened either on his speculative method and fanciful etymologies, or else *ad hominem* on the vexed background and arrogant conceitedness of the book. The *Dublin penny journal* vented part of its irritation in animadverting on the fact that O'Brien, who referred to his opponent as plain Mr Petrie, fatuously styled himself Esq. and B.A. – or 'Big Ass' as the reviewer (Dixon Hardy) glossed it. O'Brien threatened legal action over Hardy's exceedingly harsh review, which was however stoutly maintained, with the exception of an apologetic retraction of the 'B.A.' taunt.[155] The result was to drive O'Brien into insanity; he died within weeks of the altercation with the *Dublin penny journal*, on 28 June 1835.

All this also meant that his book became a *succès de scandale* and a *cause célèbre* before the year ran out: a second edition (with a slightly shorter title and introduction) appeared in the same year. As P.T. Barnum said, there is no such thing as bad publicity.

The paradox is, then, that while the critical and factualist methodology of Petrie was vindicated by the absurdities of his opponent, O'Brien himself gained a curious underdog claim to sympathy. This became apparent in an interesting spin-off controversy around 1835, when Thomas Moore entered the fray.

Moore had been commissioned by the editors of *Lardner's cyclopaedia* to write a three-volume history of Ireland for them, and by 1834 he had made up his mind on the matter of Irish antiquity: he had come to reject the Milesian story as set forth in Keating and felt that Ireland had been settled by North-European Gaels, who received their civility through Phoenician trade contacts and a possible pre-Celtic, Oriental settlement.

> After much thought upon the subject, I have seen reason to abandon entirely the old Milesian story which is not tenable, I find, in any way (except as to the general tradition of an early Eastern colonization) and to adopt very much the views of Pinkerton & others, in considering the Scots as a *Gothic* colony. This is very far from being the popular view of the subject, but much as I like to be popular in Ireland, still '*magis* amica veritas'.[156]

Moore had become, in other words, a sceptic and factualist. Earlier contacts with a starry-eyed Round Tower enthusiast (possibly O'Brien himself) had convinced him of the bizarre nature of these speculations. Thus he wrote in his journal in late May 1833:

> Had a strange letter from a man about the Irish Round Towers saying that he, and he alone has found out their whole secret history and will communicate it to me for my present work, *moyennant une bonne somme d'argent* – a second letter from him offering to come pass a month with me, or more, if occasion should require, during which time he will make me a master of the whole birth, parentage, & *bringing up* of the Irish Round Towers, asking me only (in addition to the honour of his visit) one hundred guineas for the same![157]

Moore was in fact looking for an occasion to establish his position and to disso-ciate himself from the antiquarian, speculative enthusiasts. At first he thought that a vast antiquarian tome by Algernon Herbert, *Nimrod* (1826), would be a good topic for a critical book review, but when O'Brien's book appeared he jumped at the occasion. The *Edinburgh review* for April 1834 carried a sarcastic article on O'Brien's *Round Towers*, with many mocking side references to *Nimrod*, and lampooning the entire enterprise of antiquarian speculation. The final paragraph betrayed the author and the author's self-advertising interest:

> By the work of the late venerable librarian of Stowe, the authenticity of the Irish Chronicles is placed beyond dispute; and the Essay of Mr. Dalton on the religion, learning, arts, and government of Ireland, abounds with research on these several subjects, alike creditable to his industry and his judgment. Let us hope that the same service which these and other sensible Irishmen have achieved for their country's *ancient* history, will be effected also for the *modern*, by the work which is now expected from Mr. Moore (p. 154).

Moore was quite pleased with the review and the humorous stir it caused. *The times* carried an extract of Moore's article, O'Brien was vowing revenge, and letters and journal entries testify to Moore's delight in the scene. Later, in 1842, Moore was to recall with mixed feelings that his review probably hastened O'Brien's death.[158]

But the matter did not end there. In early 1835, Moore brought out the first volume of his *History of Ireland*, which dealt with the nation's origins and antiquity; and he managed to fall foul of almost everybody. The *Dublin University magazine* savaged him for daring to presume that Christianity had been introduced into Ireland under papal authority; generally, Moore's mixture of Orientalism and factualism (the book is closest to D'Alton's 1830 historical essay) pleased no-one. Although Moore steered an even-handed or even equivocal course between the two opposing schools of Irish antiquarianism, the Oriental and the Nordic, he failed to take the scientific innovations of someone like Petrie into account – largely because Petrie, slow-working investigator of massive data, found it difficult to see his studies into a definitive, printable form.

All in all, then, Moore's *History*, though undertaken by the most famous Irish man of letters at a time when there was growing demand for a work like this, left the questions of the Irish past much as it found them. It did elicit, however, a scathing and brilliant satire in *Fraser's magazine* (a conservative quarterly), by the pen of a certain Father Prout.

Father Prout, parish priest of Watergrasshill, County Cork, was the satirical persona of Francis Mahony, himself a Corkman. The persona was an amiable Catholic priest, halfway between Mr Pickwick and Mr Shandy, full of nugatory erudition and with many contacts among the literary world, all of whom he met when they undertook their pilgrimages to his parish so as to kiss the Blarney Stone. Mahony himself had given up the priesthood; he had originally been educated by Jesuits in France and in the Irish College at Rome, and had taught at Clongowes Wood College before settling down to the secular career of journalism. A staunch conservative, he had a great dislike for nationalist leaders of Catholic opinion, such as Daniel O'Connell ('the bogtrotter from Derrynane') and Thomas Moore, author of *Captain Rock* and the *Travels of an Irish gentleman in search of religion*. The death of Henry O'Brien and the appearance of the first volume of Moore's *History* coincided nearly enough to mark the joint occasion of Mahony/Prout's most felicitous satire, amusing and scathing at the same time: 'The rogueries of Tom Moore' (1835).

Prout attacks Moore by satirically vindicating O'Brien. The satire is close-knit and may mislead the inattentive reader: the vindication of O'Brien is, fundamentally, a vindication of O'Brien's utter originality – whereas Moore, in the *Edinburgh review*, had accused him of echoing received speculations. Prout twists this criticism of Moore's around into an accusation of plagiarism, and then turns it against Moore whom he accuses of being a plagiarist himself.

The vindication of O'Brien, is, then, backhanded and highly ironic, part of a multiple satiric inversion:

> [. . .] over Henry O'Brien, as he is young and artless, I must throw the shield of my fostering protection. It is now some time since he called at Watergrasshill; it was in the summer after I had a visit from Sir Walter Scott. The young man was then well versed in the Oriental languages and the Celtic: he had read the 'Coran' and the 'Psalter of Cashil', the 'Zendavesta' and the 'Ogygia', 'Lalla Rookh' and 'Rock's Memoirs', besides other books that treat of Phoenician antiquities.

The mention of Lalla Rookh and Captain Rock is a first hint of barbs to come. Moore's Oriental poem *Lalla Rookh* had been a runaway success, and by alluding to this Prout cunningly places Moore himself in the vicinity of Orientalist minds. Throughout the rest of the piece, Moore is to be described as 'the veiled prophet of Khorasan' and similar references to *Lalla Rookh*; in other words, Moore of all people is not one to mock O'Brien's Orientalism. The point is rammed home with much political innuendo when Prout alludes to the national-political, Irish meaning that was often read into *Lalla Rookh's* episode of the 'Fire-Worshippers':

> From these authentic sources of Irish and Hindoo mythology, he [O'Brien] [. . .] had picked up a rude (and perhaps a crude) notion that the Persians and the boys of Tipperary were first cousins after all. This might seem a startling theory at first sight; but then the story of the fire-worshippers in Arabia [as told in *Lalla Rookh*, JL] so corresponded with the exploits of Captain Decimus Rock in Mononia [Munster, JL], and the camel-driver of Mecca was so forcibly associated in his mind with the bog-trotter of Derrynane, both having deluded an untutored tribe of savages [etc.][159]

Thus the ironic vindication of O'Brien and the sarcastic-satirical attack on Moore kicks off. A multitude of references are marshalled to unflattering effect: that Moore himself used the Round Towers in legendary fashion in his poem 'Let Erin remember'; the sham duel that Moore and Sidney Smith fought with pistols which upon inspection proved to be loaded with blanks. The attack culminates, however, with a splendid controversion of the *Irish melodies* (which 'made *emancipation* palatable to the thinking and generous portion of Britain's free-born sons', 153): Prout accuses Moore (who had been an assiduous pilgrim to the Blarney Stone, and a frequent visitor) of having pilfered his *Melodies* from manifold unacknowledged originals in foreign languages, mainly French and Latin, and having passed off the English,

Hibernified translations as his own work. And this from the one who imputed plagiarism to poor O'Brien!

The substance of the satire, and the chief point around which the fun turns, is Prout providing us with the 'originals' from which Moore 'plagiarized' his *Melodies*. 'Go where the glory waits thee' is shown to correspond line-by-line to a sixteenth-century French song; 'Oh 'twas all but a dream' is juxtaposed with its seventeenth-century French original; 'To a beautiful milkmaid' is pilfered from Prout's own Latin original, 'In pulchram lactiferam', which is duly quoted; 'The shamrock' is denounced by having it placed side-by-side with a French song of the Wild Geese, 'Le Trefle d'Irlande'. 'Wreathe the bowl', to top it all, is derived from the ancient Greek poet Stakkos Morphides. Finally, Prout's own immortal 'The bells of Shandon' is given to the reader as the *Ur*-version of Moore's 'Peterburg air'.

All these translation games are so many clever *jeux d'esprit*, which at the time were a fashion with the men of letters around *Fraser's*.[160] There is, then, a double aim in 'The rogueries of Tom Moore': one, as a setting to show off Mahony's clever reworkings of Moore's *Melodies*; and passing them off, satirically inverted, as the originals taken *by* Moore rather than as the translations taken *from* Moore. The other purpose is to castigate the nationalist, Catholic giant of Irish literature, who, after his specious successes in poetry and controversial satire, was now claiming the laurels of historiography and who had seen fit to exercise his wit on the case of a poor, deluded, young and defenceless visionary.[161]

There is, of course, a natural solidarity between the satirist and the antiquary: both meet near Blarney, both deal in nonsense and absurdities, one deliberately, the other unconsciously so.[162] But 'The rogueries of Tom Moore' was more than that. For the modern reader, it illustrates much the same point as did the case of the ungraspable Rock–O'Connor (who is at the same time an invented persona, a real person, and that person's fantastical self-mythologization): to what complexities and contradictions the historicist cult of authenticity and true identity can lead. By so cleverly inverting the notions of what is original and what is derived, Prout's skit strips the *Irish melodies* of the thing they aimed to celebrate most: Irishness. The *Melodies* turn out to be, in Prout's satiric inversion, Latin, Greek or French – anything but Irish. Their celebration of Irish national values is a sham imposition, much as Moore's Catholic–nationalist vision of the Irish past, as his opponents in the *Dublin University magazine* tirelessly pointed out, is a distortion of the historical record.

For contemporaries, the attack against the canonized national poet went beyond mere fun. It was the first and cleverest rebuttal of Moore's claim to be a historian. It voiced some justified strictures at Moore's fly-swatting exercise against the unfortunate O'Brien, and it may have marked the first indication that Moore's literary career was now past its peak. In doing so, it perpetuated the memory of O'Brien as a pathetic, Chattertonesque visionary, mercilessly crushed by the learned establishment.[163]

And all the time the real debate remained formally unresolved; for Petrie was still reworking, expanding and improving his prize essay, despite the growing impatience of the public, despite the fact that, while the essay was silently being improved, other works like Moore's *History* could not take cognizance of it and were, perforce, driven to the established Oriental model of O'Conor of Stowe, Lanigan and D'Alton. O'Curry was later, in the 1860s, to recall that 1837 was a time 'when the round-tower controversy had attracted a degree of critical examination and public discussion which it never enjoyed before'.[164]

The rift in the Academy: Petrie and Betham

Petrie's dilatory procedure in seeing his Round Tower essay into print was perhaps congenital to his method. The great value of his work lay in the fact that he tackled large topics with painstaking attention to detail; but it also posed a threat to his projects' completion. The discomfiture of the Historical Section of the Ordnance Survey was in part due to this relentless attention to detail; and as the Ordnance Survey foundered towards the end of the 1830s, the portents must have bode ill for the completion of Petrie's other *magnum opus*, the as yet unpublished version of the Round Tower essay. Indeed the misgivings were there almost from the beginning. As the *Dublin penny journal* reviewed O'Brien's book, it already regretted that Petrie's version was not before the public to state the opposite case; and Dixon Hardy (the reviewer, who had taken over the *Penny journal* from an overworked Petrie), remarked sourly:

> Of Mr. Petrie's Essay [. . .] we can say nothing, as it has not appeared, and from the tardy operations of that gentleman, we do not calculate upon having a very early opportunity of criticising it.[165]

That was in 1834. In that year, Petrie read his 'Essay on the military architecture of Ireland' before the Academy. Again, this essay was given a medal; it too was to remain unpublished (definitively so). As the 1830s ground on, with the O'Brien scandal, the appearance of Moore's *History* (vol. 1 in 1835, vol. 2 in 1837) and the collapse of the Ordnance Survey historical memoir, Petrie's absorption in his private perfectionism became less and less creditable. It certainly weakened his position in the Royal Irish Academy as he set out to reform that body (at least its literary and historical section) in the spirit of critical, scientific precision.

   This development eventually brought matters within the Academy to a head, culminating in a public rift between Petrie and Betham. The seed of this conflict seems to have been sown during the adjudication of the fateful prize essay on the Round Towers. Betham cannot but have noticed that the Orientalizing speculations of O'Brien were much closer to his own mode of antiquarianism than the clinical factualism of Petrie, which was highly sceptical of pre-Christian theories; his initial support for Petrie in the adjudication process seems to have been based on personal liking rather than on a careful and balanced comparison of the two essays.[166] Even so, rumour had it that O'Brien had had some encouragement from Betham, and the *Dublin*

University magazine somewhat peremptorily drew Betham's name into the argument, presuming to speak for that august gentleman:

> He [O'Brien] insisted on [. . .] the equivocal inference drawn from a few words attributed to Sir W. Betham, which, if designed for praise, had, by some misfortune, the manner and expression of ridicule [. . .] he cannot perceive any difference between a well-bred sneer and a compliment, or between the gaiety of a playful humour, and a grave assertion of fact. Hence the odd misapprehension of Sir W. Betham's comment; which must have excited a smile at its grave irony when uttered [. . .][167]

Nor was this high-handed appropriation of Betham's name all; a footnote was even more irritating: 'We are informed on very good authority, that Sir William Betham considers the question to be set at rest by Mr. Petrie's essay, an opinion in which most learned men occur.' All this gave the impression of wishing to save Betham from an erroneous slip of the tongue and previous misapprehension; a kind of imposing solicitude which was less than flattering to the beneficiary.

As the 1830s wore on, the once cordial relations between Petrie and Betham deteriorated: Petrie found it more and more difficult to countenance the type of gratuitous, unfounded speculation that Betham loved to indulge in. By 1835 Petrie, himself such a perfectionist, felt that Betham's papers read before the Academy were so ignorant and error-ridden that they should not be printed in the Academy's *Transactions*. Accordingly, the *Transactions* was to become, not so much a record of papers read before the Academy as a screened and refereed forum, submissions to which were to be vetted by a Committee of Publications. In a counterbalancing effort, a new periodical publication alongside the *Transactions* was set up in 1836: the *Proceedings*, which would fulfill the function of recording what papers had been read and what scholarly activities had been undertaken by the Academy.

In this manner, the communications of Sir William Betham were effectively frozen out of the *Transactions*. Betham became exceedingly vexed at this when, between November 1836 and June 1838, he read a series of papers containing his Carthaginian-Etrurian theories and his interpretation of the 'Eugubian Tables', which we have noticed above (pp. 92–3). They were reported in the *Proceedings* but rejected for the *Transactions* by the Publication Committee. This embittered Betham greatly; in 1840, Petrie saw this rejection as the breach of the friendship between Betham and himself. Indeed, Betham was reduced to the less prestigious expedient of having his theories privately printed by Dixon Hardy, as *Gael and Cymbri* and its sequel volume, *Etruria Celtica*; that last work contains a peeved account of how papers read in 1838 before 'a learned Society' had been referred to a committee and rejected for the Transactions (pp. 52–53).

It must have been galling for the Ulster King of Arms to see his essays rejected only a decade after similar pieces by O'Flaherty and Beaufort had been handsomely included in the *Transactions*; rejected, to boot, because of a new climate introduced by a newcomer and erstwhile protégé. For while the *Proceedings* record the discomfiture of Sir William, they record also the simultaneous triumph of Petrie. On the same day that Betham presents his ambitious but misbegotten theory of the Eugubian Tables (24 April 1837), Petrie begins his reading of the essay on Tara, a triumphant piece of archaeology based both on field work and on a philological source critique of native topographical material,[168] which was to earn Petrie his third Cunningham Medal – an unheard-of hat-trick. Petrie seems to have had an unsettling knack of upstaging Betham. While Betham drones on about his Eugubian Tables in early 1838, Petrie reports on cairns and stone circles in County Sligo, concluding with the galling remark that

> their investigation will form an important accessory to the history of the Indo-European race, and also that such an investigation will probably destroy the popular theories of their having been temples and altars of the Druids.[169]

Worse, when Betham landed a scoop by reading, on 25 June 1838, a paper on the recently discovered Cross of Cong and St Patrick's Breastplate, he was sorely discomfited. He offered readings of the inscriptions on these archaeological treasures, which he was induced to withdraw, obviously challenged and mortified by the superior knowledge of Petrie. To cap it all, Petrie countered Betham's lecture with impromptu observations which met with such approval that Petrie was requested to prepare a paper for the *Transactions* on the subject (*Proceedings*, 1: 211–212). This happened at the end of a two-month confrontation occasioned by the discovery of a cromlech in the Phoenix Park. Betham had read (on 9 April 1838) a letter from a correspondent in India concerning 'cromlechs' in Bombay, endorsing the Oriental/Phoenician model of Thomas Moore and older antiquaries like Sir Richard Colt Hoare. Petrie had countered in his usual factual manner by reading, on 19 and 28 May, a detailed archaeological report on the finding. When Betham retorted on 11 June by reading a paper 'On the ancient tomb recently discovered in the tumulus in the Phoenix Park', the positions were already so entrenched that the *Proceedings* washed its hands of the lucubrations of an eminent fellow-member in that it unusually gave his paper, not in a potted paraphrase, but *in extenso* and 'without alteration or abridgment' (196–200) – obviously implying that Betham was damned by his own words.

Thus, by mid-1838, the Royal Irish Academy had become the arena in which two paradigms were fighting a duel to the death: old-fashioned, entrenched, genteel muddle-headed amateurishness as championed by Sir William Betham; newfangled, scientific, pedantic and intolerant factualism as championed by George Petrie. When Thomas Moore visited Dublin in September 1838 he found relations between the two erstwhile friends very tense indeed:

> Called upon Shelburne and took him to Todd's, where we found a rich display of Irish Antiquarianism, Petrie & Betham being added to our host himself. The conversation was accordingly 'germane' to the occasion and Petrie & Betham having got on the subject of the different colonies that settled in Ireland (as indi-

cated by the remains of stone & bronze weapons &c. &c) a breeze was very near
springing up between them which was however got rid of laughingly by my saying
that if there *was* to be a duel between them, the formula must be 'Choose your
weapon, bronze or stone.'- Was little aware, till Petrie enlightened me afterwards on
the matter, of the heart-burnings there have been on the subject of Irish antiquities
lately – Sir W. Betham more especially, having drawn down much ridicule on
himself by endeavouring to show that a certain Etruscan inscription, well known to
scholars, is every word of it Irish. To make this out, he has, it appears, disjoined &
connected syllables without scruple, and what is still worse as Petrie intimated, has
shown nothing so clearly, either Irish or Etruscan as his utter ignorance of both. A
good parody on this paper of Sir William's has been produced by a Mr. O'Donovan
(the translator of the Four Masters) [. . .][170]

Moore had meanwhile (in mid-1837) brought out the second volume of his
History of Ireland, which dealt with the period from the first Danish incursions to
the death of Henry II and Roderick O'Connor. The 1838 visit was a belated eye-
opener for Moore. He had undertaken the *History* as a literary job, to be compounded from earlier authorities and with little original or archival research; it
now became clear to him that he had followed in the well-worn tracks of a disin-
tegrating paradigm. On his 1838 visit, he became friendly with Petrie, used the
library of the Royal Irish Academy with the help of Todd (*Journal*, 5: 1997; the
library was then in the process of being catalogued by O'Curry), and became convinced that he had made a fatal error in not drawing on native MS sources which
were just in the process of becoming available. During his 1838 visit, he made
grateful use, not only of O'Conor's Stowe catalogues, but also of O'Donovan's MS
translation of the Annals of the Four Masters (*Journal* 6: 1906, 2006). There was
even talk that he was to revise some of his earlier statements on Irish antiquity in a
projected fourth volume of the *History*. Witness the well-known anecdote as given
by O'Curry,[171] who intimates that Moore was overwhelmed by the sight of the
great ancient MSS in the Academy library, confessed his ignorance in matters of
Irish history, and contritely admitted his naive presumption in undertaking his
History. The anecdote has gained wide currency because it was reiterated *verbatim*
by Matthew Arnold in *On the study of Celtic literature*. O'Curry misdates this to
1839 (when Moore did not visit Ireland), and his account is contradicted by the
evidence of Moore's journal, which never once mentions O'Curry, never once
mentions a mortified confession of ignorance, and merely records, during the
1838 visit, pleasant and instructive meetings at the Ordnance Survey and the
Academy with Petrie and Todd; the underling O'Curry was evidently beneath
Moore's notice.

Moore indeed wrote a letter to Petrie saying in so many words that he
intended to add a revisionary introduction to volume four, which had in August
1837 been negotiated with the publishers;[172] the original history had been
intended for three volumes. The third and fourth volumes of Moore's *History*
appeared with some delay; volume 3 (1840) dealt with the period from King
John to Henry VIII, volume 4 (1845) with Edward VI to the death of Eoghan Rua

O'Neill and the collapse of the Confederation of Kilkenny. The delay was attributed by O'Curry to Moore's sudden crestfallen humility, but can be more properly attributed to the growing sense that the *History*, which met with little or no acclaim, was a burdensome drudgery to its author, who was increasingly buffeted by private losses and tragic family circumstances. In the event, no critical revision was contained in the fourth volume. Moore had evidently run out of steam and stamina; the third and fourth volumes are uninspired, pale digests of received knowledge organized in old-fashioned manner, reign by reign, monarch after monarch in succeeding chapters, petering out without any conclusion or closure at the end of the last volume. Moore had by 1842 also come to regret that his *History* had acquired a partisan, nationalist reputation (*Journal*, 5: 2263).

Thus the achievements of the new scientific learning and methodology of Petrie remained without public echo; indeed, the sense around 1840 was that they were doomed to remain undivulged altogether. The delay in Petrie's publication of the Round Towers essay became irksome, caused misgivings among the interested public and left the field wide open to opponents like Betham; and this was compounded by the fact that Petrie had shot himself in the foot with his belief in painstaking, critical fact-checking, when the Ordnance Survey Historical Memoir was aborted.[173]

The matter came to a head in 1839. In January of that year, Petrie promised an obviously impatient Council that he would have his Round Towers essay in the press in two months; on 24 June, Petrie was given the Cunningham medal (for an unprecedented third time) in recognition of his essay on Tara, which had been read in 1837 and appeared in the *Transactions* for 1839. The unusually short and snappy publication record (a mere two years for an essay full of maps and engravings), may be partly explained by the fact that Petrie was here presenting the collective efforts of the Ordnance Survey of the area. Once again, Petrie's account was deliberately anti-speculative:

> To expose the errors in the accounts of Tara by O'Conor, Vallancey, and others, would be but an idle combat with shadows. However gratifying they may have been in their day to the Milesian national vanity, they have made but little impression on the cooler minds of the uninterested, or unprejudiced, and are now wholly disregarded.[174]

Instead, Petrie turns to a minute observation of the site itself, compared to authentic native topographical sources such as the Dinnseanchus (of which the relevant portion of the text is given, 105–118) and a descriptive poem by Cuan Ó Lochlainn (119–125). There may well have been some political hidden agenda in awarding the prestigious Cunningham medal to a work which so obviously demonstrated the potential of the Ordnance Survey Historical Memoir, which was then under a death sentence; but, on the whole, Petrie's Tara essay was widely praised as a perfect example of the new, scientific methodology. It will be remembered that Pictet had already praised the assiduous archivist O'Conor of

Stowe for his *esprit de critique sage et éclairée* while chiding Celtomane anti-quarianism for its penchant for *absurdes systèmes* (pp. 91 and 252, n. 61): a similar methodological scientism is obviously what Petrie's essay represented so triumphantly. Sir William Rowan Hamilton, upon presenting Petrie with the Cunningham medal, delivered a eulogy that concentrated on Petrie's 'employ-ment of a manifestly rigorous method of inquiry in what had seemed to many persons a region of fancy and fable' and Petrie's 'evident approach to the character of scientific proof'. Later Petrie's biographer William Stokes likewise praised this essay in particular (of which 'it is not too much to say that it forms the key to all the reliable ancient history of the country') for Petrie's 'severe and scientific method', testing 'the truth of history and tradition by existing remains'.[175] The interesting opposition between sober criticism on the one hand and absurd speculation on the other reflects the values of the new, positive and critical approach to scholarship. What counted was judgement rather than wit, sobriety rather than ingenuity: what was needed was not a flair for projecting models and seeing patterns but the painstaking labour of conscientious fact-checking and impartial weighing of evidence.

All this left Sir William Betham out in the cold. His *magnum opus*, evidently ambitious enough to hope for the Cunningham medal, had even been rejected for publication in the *Transactions*; and, goaded beyond endurance by the mor-tifying triumph of his competitor, he blew the whistle. He withdrew from the Academy's Council (where, almost symbolically, he was replaced by Samuel Ferguson, adept of the new critical-philological method, and Petrie's future suc-cessor as the great antiquarian luminary of the Academy) and published an open letter to vindicate his resignation and impugn Petrie (whose standing in the Academy had, despite the Cunningham medal, been weakened by his continuing failure to deliver his Round Towers essay). In the course of 1839, Betham had already opened hostilities, in that Petrie had been forced to undertake the entire financial responsibility for the outstanding publication; now, Betham had gone further and had attempted to impeach the entire Petrie-friendly Council; but his attempt in that direction was voted down in 1840.[176]

Betham retaliated with his open letter to the Academy's president, Rowan Hamilton. His main argument was that the Academy, with Petrie on its Coun-cil and Petrie prominent in all its activities, was turning into a Petrie fan club, whereas Petrie was in fact doing little to merit this adulation. The limited funds of the Academy were being wasted on the very costly printing of Petrie's essay on Tara Hill (which was not so much his own achievement as that of the Ordnance Survey collectively), while substantial amounts of money were being sunk into the preparation of the printing of the Round Towers essay, which was now in its eighth year of preparation after having been awarded a gold medal, and still nowhere near completion. After impugning Petrie's use of Irish textual material, as translated by O'Donovan, as 'trash' and 'rubbish', he indignantly asked,

Four hundred pounds have already, *in unsuspicious confidence*, been placed in the hands of the Council, *for wood-cuts* for Mr. Petrie's essay on the Round Towers, which we are told is to occupy *an entire volume of the Transactions*, the printing of which will swallow up our little remaining capital. Nearly nine years since I read the MS of this Essay on the Round Towers, which then would not occupy a quarter of a volume. I suppose by the author's powers of amplification, it has grown greatly since, and will most likely *be illustrated with translations* from Irish MSS *as evidence in support of his hypothesis*; and if it be *done as well*, and as *veritably*, as his last *great work* on Tara, it will add another bell to the cap which the Academy has already acquired through his exertions.[177]

Petrie gave as good as he got. He published a response which told the full story of Betham's growing mortification at the steady exposure of his own incompetence, explaining the attack as a peevish and spiteful *ad hominem* explosion rather than serious criticism; true to form, and ever the conscientious scholar giving full account of his sources, he reprinted Betham's entire letter as part of his own reply.[178] This put the matter to rest – for a while at least. Betham's accusations were to reappear, as we shall see, in 1845.

Meanwhile, Petrie's standing was somewhat weakened as a result of all this. His interpretation of the medieval, ecclesiastical origin of the Round Towers was in the unenviable position of having become the officially sanctioned version before it was stated before the public in fully argued form, and thus attracting pre-emptive criticism which weakened his case before it was even made. The most formidable challenge came from antiquarians in Cork, especially John Windele, who discovered funereal remains and skeletons in the groundworks of one Round Tower and therefore concluded that they had been intended as sepulchral monuments. Windele (whose friend and collaborator Matthew Horgan, parish priest near Blarney, had written on the Round Towers, possibly in competition for the Academy prize[179]) published such theories in his *Historical and descriptive notices of the city of Cork and its vicinity* (Cork, 1840) and in regional antiquarian journals such as the *Journal of the Cork Antiquarian Society*, causing Petrie some misgivings; he wrote to O'Donovan in August 1841, mentioning Windele's finds, and adding:

Sir William Betham has been making a great fuss about the discovery of a skeleton in the tower of Ardmore, which he says, wholly upsets my theories as to the origin and uses of the towers, and I believe he is going to publish a book on the subject! I hope sincerely he may.[180]

Sure enough, Betham did seize upon this opportunity to controvert his enemy's theories. Betham's book *Etruria Celtica* of 1842 contained a chapter on Round Towers (2: 189–229), of which the obvious intent was to nip Petrie's theory in the bud:

This long-agitated *questio vexata*, may now be considered as set at rest. The Essay which gained the gold medal of the Royal Irish Academy ten years ago (which has not, and that of Mr. O'Brien, which has been published), are both found erroneous in their conjectures. The delay of the appearance of the former has rendered it an abortion confuted while yet unpublished; if it ever appears, it may be useful as a statistic account of the present appearance of the round towers, but for showing the object for which they were erected, it will be altogether worthless (2: 229).

By 1843, Betham, emboldened perhaps by the continuing failure of Petrie to publish his essay, was back in the Academy. He was instrumental in procuring the Cathach for the Academy's collections, one of its most precious antiquarian treasures, and this apparently gave him a moral right to ride his hobbyhorse once again. The *Proceedings* mentioned, po-faced, that on 24 April 'Sir William Betham made a communication on the antiquity of certain languages'. The interest in phallic worship and sexual symbolism even re-emerged within the ranks of the Academy, with the side effect of lending some oblique, coincidental credit to the theories of Henry O'Brien: in 1844, Clibborn gave a paper on Sheela-na-Gigs, mentioning with a deal of tolerance the opinion of 'advocates of the O'Brien theory of the Round Towers' that Sheela-na-Gigs were the female counterpart to the masculine Tower shape, and airily evoking a mixture of gnostic, Buddhist and pagan religious analogues.[181] And year after year, the commissioners reported that Petrie's essay was still in the process of being prepared for publication.

A re-enactment of the 1840 showdown-by-open-letter took place in 1845, just months before Petrie's essay came off the press (but then again, it had been 'just months' for many years now). A motion, brought forward by Betham, that financial control be removed from the Council was stingingly voted down without a division on 13 January 1845. A week later, the Lord Lieutenant informed the Academy that he had received a letter from Sir William Betham, denouncing the Academy's waste of public funds, and requested clarification. Betham's letter was subjoined and contained in substance the same accusations against Petrie and the Council as had been made five years earlier, all the more compelling now because Petrie (who in the meantime had seen the Ordnance Survey project dashed) had not published anything since that time. The Council gave Petrie an opportunity to reply and obtained financial testimonials from printer and publisher; this was forwarded to Dublin Castle, together with an icily polite letter by the Academy's President, MacCullagh, justifying the Council's trust in Petrie and vindicating its financial probity in the publication of the Round Towers. The letter ended:

> The Council do not find any other charges brought by Sir W. Betham, of a kind proper to be noticed officially. On the tone and manner of Sir W. Betham's statements they refrain altogether from making any comment.[182]

The reader may now imagine what an enormous sigh of relief must have been breathed by Petrie himself and by all the *bien pensants* of the scholarly world, when the *magnum opus* finally did see the light of day in March 1845. It appeared in two editions, both as volume 20 of the Academy's *Transactions* and in its own right, under the title *The ecclesiastical architecture of Ireland, anterior to the Anglo-Norman invasion, comprising an essay on the origin and use of the Round Towers of Ireland, which obtained the gold medal and prize of the Royal Irish Academy*. Much of it (12–109) is taken up by a refutation of the earlier, pagan/Oriental theories, which had been originally brought up by Vallancey and repeated later in various forms by 'Doctors Lanigan and O'Conor, Miss Beaufort, Mr. D'Alton, Mr. O'Brien, Mr. Moore, and, recently, Mr. Windele of Cork' (11–12). Petrie is courteously circumspect in controverting Miss Beaufort and 'the late Rev. Dr. Charles O'Conor [. . .] the only formidable supporter of this hypothesis' (47–66); Moore and Windele are drily dismissed, and some poisoned barbs are reserved for Betham (109, 338–9, 417–421).

This massive quarto volume with its copious illustrations was an even more triumphant vindication for Petrie's critical procedure than the essay on Tara had been. It was rapturously received by the leading intellectual journals.

Round Towers after Petrie

There was remarkable consensus among reviews of all political colourings as to the merits of Petrie's work. The *Dublin University magazine* gave a lengthy and positive review by Petrie's friend Samuel Ferguson,[183] which described at length the vexed background of the publication and the extent to which Petrie had almost overstretched the patience of the public.

> The anxiety of the public to be acquainted with the solution of the original question has latterly manifested itself in a degree of impatience which, however unreasonable on the part of any one acquainted with the vastly enlarged scope of the work, cannot be wondered at in those who are either unaware of the extent of the additional inquiry, or incompetent to judge of its curiosity and value (379–380).

The review emphatically endorses Petrie's findings against the specious speculations of Vallancey, Betham ('whose attempted translation of the Eugubian inscriptions into spurious Irish has given him an unenviable notoriety in literary adventure', 388) and O'Brien. Here, too, the praise is largely concentrated on Petrie's method, 'the characteristic caution and candour with which the whole inquiry is conducted' (389), 'the temperateness of an accurate and calm scholar' (392).

The Catholic counterpart of the *Dublin University magazine*, the *Dublin review*, was no less positive, and carried a substantial review by the prestigious Maynooth professor Matthew Kelly. Kelly seems to have been particularly well-disposed towards Petrie's findings since the monastic-ecclesiastical attribution of the Round Towers coincided with Kelly's own, Rome-centered and ultramontanist view of Irish history.[184]

Nationalist opinion was represented in Thomas Davis's review in *The nation*. Davis frankly admitted that his romantic, national enthusiasm had initially predisposed him towards the Oriental, glamorous theories, and that he had begun his reading of Petrie's essay 'strongly bigoted against his conclusion', in the hope of finding fault with it. Davis's candid admission that Petrie had convinced him and had disabused him from his previous errors, through sheer force of argument and scholarly integrity, was perhaps the most gratifying endorsement of all. Davis, almost in an act of exorcism or self-critique, recounts once again all the erroneous theories which have been disproved by Petrie's final word on the subject.[185]

Final word? Not quite. To begin with, the *Ecclesiastical architecture* (though it was published and greeted as a great task finally brought to conclusion) was in itself, yet again, a proof of Petrie's difficulties in finally bringing great tasks to conclusion. Almost perversely, Petrie demonstrated what Betham had maliciously called his 'powers of amplification' by publishing a book that on closer inspection proved to be only the first half of one. The title page gave the fateful specification 'volume I', and the book as a whole contained only two of a projected three parts: the overview of previous theories, and Petrie's own case for the dating of the Round Towers (and other ecclesiastical buildings); part three, a statistical and historical description of all pre-Norman church buildings in Ireland, was held over for future publication. Those who knew Petrie apprehended that this second instalment was not going to be published in a hurry, and accordingly the Academy's *Proceedings* echo a mixed sense of elation and despondency: elation that the work is finally before the public, despondency that the saga is not yet brought to a finish. Indeed, the Academy seems to have spoken an equivocal *iam satis* on the occasion; witness a Council report from 1845:

> Although it [vol. 20 of the *Transactions*, consisting wholly of Petrie's book] contains only a portion of Mr. Petrie's essay, the Council have recommended, and the recommendation has been adopted by the Academy, that in consideration of its bulk and value, and the numerous and beautiful wood-cuts which adorn it, the volume be received as acquitting Mr. Petrie of his engagement; but they have declined entering into any further agreement with him, as to the publication of the remainder of the essay.[186]

This meant that a number of woodcuts, intended to illustrate the second volume, were as yet unused – we shall see in what form they were to surface later. It also meant that this first volume, which repeatedly referred the reader to further specific details in the second part, left chinks in the armour of Petrie's argument. It would have to be a very biased reader who would want to make use of these flaws, but biases did exist.

As Davis's own admission of initial reservations already indicates, a good part of the public was less than willing to submit to Petrie's authority; and that part of the public appears to have been mainly middle class and nationalistically oriented. Petrie himself expected as much in his preface:

> I have not, however, any very sanguine expectations that either the evidences or the arguments which I have adduced, or those which I have still to submit to my readers [!], will have any very immediate effect on the great majority of the middle classes of the Irish people [. . .] in changing their opinions as to [the Towers'] indefinite antiquity and Pagan uses. Among these such opinions have assumed the

form of a sentiment almost religious, and my dry facts have too little poetry in them to reach the judgment through the medium of the imagination. Neither do I anticipate that I shall be able to convince all those who have written recently in support of those erroneous, but popular theories [. . .] (ix).

It is possible that the failure of Petrie's earlier ventures in popular education, the *Dublin penny journal* and the *Irish penny journal*, is at the root of this attitude; Petrie resigns himself to be élitist. It is remarkable how this strange passage both formulates, and acquiesces in, an apparent gulf between the professional historian and the vulgar opinions of the middle classes. While Petrie may have been correct in his apprehension that his *magnum opus* was not to be the last word, it was badly phrased. Surely the Round Towers were fascinating to others than the professional scholar and the gentlemen-members of the Royal Irish Academy;[187] surely the reason for this widespread fascination was rooted in something broader and deeper than merely academic interest; surely the professional historian, with all his learning and expertise, should have a greater sense of responsibility than to abandon the unenlightened to the errors of their ways? While Petrie may have intended no more than a resigned statement as to how entrenched the opposing theories had become (and he should have realized that his own tardiness was in part to blame for this), he infelicitously and snobbishly seemed to limit the currency of superior insight to a narrow elite. This was later to be held against him: the quoted statement was indignantly cited by men like Henry O'Neill (an illustrative counterpart to Petrie), who also seized on the fact that Petrie did not think it necessary to translate Latin quotations into English for the benefit of the Plain People of Ireland.

> Thus the Doctor fails to convince the grocer, and he goes off soliloquising that he hardly expected to succeed with the middle classes, but he fondly hopes the learned will be convinced.[188]

Of course, attacks like that were themselves slightly disingenuous: what Petrie had written was never meant to be a pamphlet intended for the education of Irishmen and -women at large; it was primarily aimed at the scholarly community, published as an immensely costly learned volume, far beyond the financial reach of the general reading or book-buying public. But the upshot of it all appears to have been that, while Petrie's standing became unassailable among the social and intellectual élite (for whom a benevolent interest in the great Irish past was quite compatible with a mildly conservative stance in politics), the middle classes – the readership of Davis and *The nation* – remained prone to hanker after something more appealing to the imagination and to their national enthusiasm. Petrie spoke to the peers, gentry and professionals who were members of the prestigious scholarly societies like the Royal Irish Academy and the Irish Archaeological Society; these grave and learned men would occasionally address the public at large in an attempt to divulge the insights of proper scholarship and to counteract the persistence of popular errors. Witness the case

of the remarkable 'Nun of Kenmare', Sister Mary Frances Cusack, who published
a popular *Illustrated history of Ireland from the earliest period* in 1868, immediately
after Petrie's death. She received immediate reactions from 'four or five eminent
Members of the Royal Irish Academy', among whom was Dunraven, who
expressed their regret to her 'that I should appear to have adopted, or at least favoured, Mr. D'Alton's view' as to the origin of the Round Towers. Cusack demurely
bowed to such august pressure in the second edition of her book (which
appeared in the same year) by paying lip-service to the Petrie version, but still
cited the pagan theory as a matter of interest – to the point of representing,
almost intact, the version she had been told to retract.[189] Apparently, the public at
large was influenced more by Moore's or Cusack's Histories, by poems like Denis
Florence McCarthy's,[190] pamphlets like O'Neill's furiously anti-Petriesque *The
Round Towers of Ireland* (Dublin 1877), or by a vague sense as imparted by Father
Prout, that alternative models like O'Brien's and Windele's had been blocked out
by a closed shop of bigwigs. The Petrie who had set out to subvert an old-
fashioned antiquarian establishment in 1829 had, after 1845, become the much-
acclaimed figurehead of the establishment himself. The issue was clinched when
he received an honorary doctorate from Trinity College Dublin in 1847.

Throughout the century, therefore, we encouter two opposing streams of
archaeology: those who attack Petrie (mainly provincial antiquarians and men
writing from outside the pale of academia) and those who loftily defend Petrie
against his detractors, like Dr William Stokes (Petrie's biographer) or the Earl
of Dunraven.[191] Generally, a certain contentious rivalry between a Dublin and
a Cork school seems to have made itself felt. Against the Dublin-based troika
of Petrie, O'Donovan and O'Curry there was the Cork-based alignment of
John Windele and Owen Connellan, who were more sympathetic to Betham
and to pagan theories, and whose text-editorial activities gravitated to the
Ossianic Society rather than to the Irish Archaeological Society. Connellan,
erstwhile assistant of Betham, beat his rival O'Donovan in obtaining the chair
of Celtic at Queen's College Cork in 1849 (O'Donovan in turn obtaining the
chair at the Belfast College),[192] and the two men were competitors also in their
respective translations of the Annals of the Four Masters.

Other opponents of the new archaeology, Petrie-style, were a more motley
crew. To begin with, there was the continuing presence of Henry O'Brien, who,
if he had not found general acceptance, had found at least the next best thing:
general notoriety. Few people followed O'Brien; almost everybody loved to cite
him.[193] Moore's journal mentions occasional correspondents volunteering their
far-fetched theories.[194] Throughout the century, eccentric clergymen such as G.S.
Faber or Richard Smiddy intervened in the debate. The aging controversialist
Faber, author of *The origin of pagan idolatry* (London, 1816; itself based on
Bryant), wrote a letter to the *Dublin University magazine* in 1850 attacking Petrie
and supporting 'my valued and talented friend, Miss Beaufort'; Smiddy published
a dotty *Essay on the druids, the ancient churches, and the Round Towers* in 1871
(dedicated to 'the Celtic race, all over the world'); even further out on the lunatic

fringe were Freemasons, Rosicrusians and British Israelites.[195] The timing of all this is not without irony. Petrie had died in 1866; the paganists began to reassert themselves in the years immediately thereafter, with for their foremost champions Marcus Keane and Canon Ulick Bourke.

When Henry O'Neill published his attacks against Petrie, he already hinted at fresh evidence in favour of O'Brien's theory.

> The theory of O'Brien is the one which Dr. Petrie shunned; he sneered at it, as not deserving his notices and 'utterly absurd'. O'Brien's book throws much light on Phallic worship, but the poor fellow wrote it in a few months, and lost his reason and his life after the over-exertion: it bears evidence of haste. We have many proofs in support of O'Brien's theory, but we wish to write at leisure, and will, therefore, not introduce them in the present work. [. . .] And so, reader, these mysterious monuments belong to the night of time [. . .] They tell us of a people of rare practical skill, and of strange creed [. . .] But we can only whisper these secrets now; some other time they may be fully revealed.[196]

The follow-up, in 1877, was disappointing enough: a short 23-page pamphlet, *The Round Towers of Ireland* (Dublin, 1877), purporting to be the first instalment in a series and containing merely a 'Preface' full of accusations against Petrie and his myrmidons in high places; nothing more was published, and no secrets about the mysterious monuments from the night of time were revealed. Meanwhile, however, alternatives to Petrie had been formulated more successfully by Marcus Keane and Canon Ulick Bourke.[197]

Marcus Keane, a member of the Royal Irish Academy, published his ambitious *The towers and temples of ancient Ireland; their origin and history discussed from a new point of view* in 1867, one year after Petrie's death. Ironically, it was in this book that many of the woodcuts of Petrie's *Ecclesiastical architecture* (re-)surfaced; as a result, the presentation, sumptuously illustrated as it is, looked imposing indeed.[198] The text was, however, an unmitigated throwback to earlier speculations. Keane's theoretical framework is that of Bryant's 1775 *Analysis of antient mythology* and G.S. Faber's 1816 *The origin of pagan idolatry*, and accordingly Keane works wholly in a pre-scientific, Biblical frame of reference. Cuthite serpent-worship and phallus-worship is proposed as a religious substratum common to pagan Europe, including the use of later Christian symbols such as the fish and the cross. This allows Keane to perpetrate the most daring antedatings of edifices bearing such (pre!-)Christian symbols. No grist is too outlandish for Keane's mill; not only does the 'Astartification' of 'Molly Astore' make a merry reappearance, but even Captain Rock is among the authorities:

> I am aware that O'Connor's *Chronicles of Eri* is not looked upon as good authority by learned archaeologists, and that some suppose it to have been a composition by Mr O'Connor himself. But to my mind the early portion of it bears internal evidence of authenticity as an ancient composition. I believe it to be the work of Olam Fodla [. . .][199]

Canon Bourke's *Aryan origin of the Gaelic race and language*, which appeared in 1875, was an attempt to reconcile native Milesian mythography, as expounded by Keating, with the insights of modern science and philology. It is best summarized by giving its extraordinary title in full:

> The Aryan origin of the Gaelic race and language, showing the present and past literary position of Irish Gaelic; its phonesis, the fountain of classic pronunciation; its laws accord with Grimm's laws; its bardic beauties the source of rhyme; the civilisation of pagan Ireland; early knowledge of letters; the art of illuminating, ancient architecture. The Round Towers. The Brehon law. Truth of the Pentateuch. Knowledge in pagan times retrogressive, not progressive; the inductive sciences; philology and ethnology confirm the truth of Irish history; Gaelic names of persons and places full of historic suggestiveness; in this respect and in poetic power Irish Gaelic superior to Sanskrit. One thousand unpublished Irish manuscripts.

Bourke firmly believes in the native/biblical derivation of the Gaels from Magog, son of Japhet;[200] at the same time he tries to bring this nativist scheme into accord with the progress of science by calling this Oriental (Jewish!) origin Aryan, and in the process he extensively summarizes the progress of comparative historical sciences as marked by the names of Max Müller, Matthew Arnold, Prichard, Pictet, Henry Maine; within the Irish scholarly framework, Bourke is most fulsome in his praise (paradoxically enough) for the factualist archaeologists and philologists: Petrie, O'Donovan and O'Curry (11, 48–50).

Accordingly, Bourke attempts to square Petrie's ecclesiastical theory with his own Milesian ancestry myth, and advances the notion that the towers were built in Pagan times and later converted to Christian purposes. His book, which comes from a Catholic, populist-nationalist background, is also indirect testimony to the extent to which the middle classes had been left bewildered by the entire tradition of conflicting interpretations. Bourke, an educationalist and well-known propagandist for the Irish language, states his reasons for writing this book in his Preface:

> Ever since the publication of *Easy lessons in Irish*, and the *College Irish grammar*, the author has, time after time, received from amateur scientists, and occasionally from scholars [. . .] questions like the following [. . .] The Round Towers. Which opinion – that of Dr. Petrie or Thomas Moore – is correct? Were the Etruscans Gaels? Were the Children of the Gael of Aryan origin, and not Cuthite or Phoenician?[201]

Here, then, is a book evidently aimed at popularizing knowledge and insights from the historical sciences to a non-professional audience; and we see that that audience is left to acquiesce in the mythical version of Irish history to a far greater extent than was warranted by rigorous scholarship. By 1875, the Catholic middle classes with a national interest (the readership of Canon Bourke) were taking cognizance of the scientific achievements of Petrie without abandoning the colourful imaginative appeal of the Milesian origin-myth as it had been handed on and watered down from Keating to Moore to Denis Florence MacCarthy. This was the type of history that was to be fed to the American-Irish market, with 'Histories' like those of Haverty or A.M. Sullivan; it was also the underlying imaginative mind-set for the revivalist. populist type of cultural nationalism of which Canon Bourke himself was such a prominent representative. Bourke, assistant to that great champion of the Irish language, Archbishop MacHale, was among the more important forerunners of Douglas Hyde in the matter of the cultivation and revival of Irish: he had published self-taught Irish lessons in *The nation* between 1858 and 1863, and kept Irish language interest alive in the provincial Connacht press.[202] Bourke's attempt to accommodate Milesian myth within the terms of positive scholarship is therefore no mere idiosyncrasy; it bespeaks a tendency, with which I shall deal at greater length further on, that pre-scientific thought and mythical lore concerning the past survived their scholarly disestablishment and maintained their currency within Irish historical consciousness and Irish national thought at large. Meanwhile, the malleability of factual hard evidence to the fervent beliefs and enthusiasms of the larger portions of society was amply illustrated by the fact that Round Towers were beginning to be manufactured to suit nineteenth-century taste and attitudes.

Counterfeit towers and the O'Connell monument

Round Towers had their most obvious symbolical importance, not only as enigmas from the past, but also as symbols of Irish cultural individuality; as such, they were used, and overused, as part of the national-cultural iconography, so profusely present on kitschy Victorian title-pages and printers' embellishments, alongside shamrocks, harps, wolfhounds, druids and maiden-icons.[203] If, in the course of the nineteenth century, the model of the ancient (Celtic) High Cross becomes a favourite style of graveyard monument, it should come as no surprise that Round Towers were beginning to be built here and there – not just as miniature icons on graveyard monuments or hotel fronts, but as Victorian follies in a nationally Irish style, picturesque embellishments in corners of country estates. The best effort was made by the parish priest of Blarney, Father Matthew Horgan. A friend of the Cork antiquarian John Windele, Horgan had started to construct a Round Tower at Blarney on Windele's design; the project was aborted at a height of twenty feet, but Horgan later tried again at Whitechurch. Also, Lord Brandon had a Round Tower built near Killarney's upper lake.[204]

All that is to some extent anecdotal, triggering facile quips to the effect that here at least are Round Towers whose date for once is quite unproblematic. But the matter of life imitating art had further ramifications. Windele's theory that Round Towers were sepulchral hero-monuments was borne out by skeletal finds at their base; a theory which was to haunt archaeologists for much of the mid-century until it was established that the skeletal remains were latter-day introductions, planted there partly as a practical joke by graveyard workers willing to take Windele's fancies for a ride.[205] This places us face to face with a highly complex dialectical vortex of historical fact, fiction and counterfeit. If much of the archaeological and historical investigation of the Irish past was implicated in an imaginative recon- stitution or recapture of that past, constitutive of a national historical awareness, then it becomes fascinating to see a feedback mechanism take place, where historical materials are provided to support historical theories and tailored on the model of the theories they are designed to illustrate. The 'construction' of a national past, the 'invention' of a tradition here becomes literal truth, and historical data are manufactured in order to accommodate latter-day images.

A good example to this effect is the mysterious mention of a book in a catalogue by John O'Daly, the well-known antiquarian and bookseller from the mid-century, member of the Ossianic Society. A good bibliographical historian as well as bookseller and publisher, O'Curry published regular catalogues of rare books of Irish interest; and his catalogue for October 1855 featured an item which appeared, from its mere title, to give a strong boost to the plausibility of the pre-Christian Baal-worshipping theory of the Round Towers:

> De Antiquitate Turrum Belanarum Pagana Kerriensi, et de Architectura non Campanilis Ecclesiasticae, par [sic] T.D. Corcagiensi Hiberno, small 4to old calf, with numerous woodcut engravings of Round Towers interspersed through the text, £10 – Lovanii, 1610.[206]

It is a startling coincidence that such a unique book should turn up, after more than two centuries of total obscurity, at precisely the moment when all minds were agitated by its topic. The Louvain 1610 imprint also seems too good to be true, for it appears to tie in with the early printing efforts undertaken by Irish Franciscans at the Louvain College. However, the works produced by Irish Franciscans at that time (not counting the later, Bollandist ones around Colgan) were very modest in appearance. It seems implausible that at the same time an unknown Corkman was to have commissioned a quarto volume with numerous illustrations. Woodcuts of Irish Round Towers in 1610? Done by whom, and how, on whose commission? Surely this is a latter-day fabrication, a counterfeit, making use of nineteenth-century woodcuts originally made for O'Brien, or for Petrie's first (published) or second (unpublished) volume. The book, false or not, in any case is no longer traceable but does provide a useful marker for the tendency of facts and objects (Borges would have called them *hrönir*) to come into existence if people think about them long and hard enough.

The interaction between scholarly thought, ideological charge and kickable buildings is best illustrated by the episode around O'Connell's sepulchral monument in Glasnevin cemetery.

It is indicative of the symbolic power of Irish antiquities, and Round Towers in particular, that the public subscription and commission of a funereal monument to the Liberator should have been given to Petrie. Glasnevin cemetery, where O'Connell was to be interred after his death abroad in 1847, was in itself a testimony to Catholic Emancipation: under previous legislation, no organized

Catholic cemetery was allowed in Dublin, and the drive for a large municipal (indeed, national) Catholic cemetery was undertaken immediately after the enfranchisement of Catholicism. Petrie's design was to encapsulate Irish ecclesiastical antiquity in a nutshell: a romanesque chapel flanked by a High Cross and a Round Tower; a Victorian title-page engraving in three dimensions.

But once again, Petrie seems to have been over the top, and the great work was abandoned halfway through. Funds were not sufficient to complete the entire threefold structure; and eventually only the Round Tower part of it was completed, in simplified form but of oversized dimensions.

Petrie protested energetically against this trimming of his plans. Partly this was because, as a stickler for historical accuracy, he saw the new reduced-budget layout as a loathsome fallacy and distortion of that authentic Irish antiquity, of which he had become the officially sanctioned spokesman. His protest letter to the O'Connell monument committee is eloquent in its regret at not having the sepulchral erection 'a correct memorial of our ancient pillar tower, and a satisfactory one to cultivated architectural taste':

> the O'Connell monument has not that tempting charm to me that it once had when I, perhaps foolishly, hoped it would have been a structure in every way honourable to the country.

Petrie protested at the unhistorical entrance to a crypt through the chapel as 'in every way objectionable or [. . .] barbarous' and urged that 'it should be the business of those who desire the monument to preserve as much as possible the ancient features of the Irish Clogtheach, to conceal this unusual feature'.[207]

But there was more at stake than historical accuracy: any deviation from the 'correct' arrangement as prescribed by Petrie would tend to support indirectly Petrie's adversaries, whose theories might have less to do with 'cultivated architectural taste' but did have a certain popular appeal. To have chapel and High Cross abandoned would make the Round Tower less obviously an ecclesiastical edifice; to have a body interred at its base (even that of O'Connell himself) might tend *ex post facto* to play into the theory of Windele that the Round Towers had been heroic sepulchres. Petrie's faithful friend and biographer, William Stokes, sombrely speculated that the trimmed-down version of the O'Connell monument might have been suggested by other than purely economic motives.

> It may be asked why were his designs so completely departed from? If funds were wanting, good taste would have been contented with erecting one or two portions of the group, in strict accordance with antiquarian truth, and architectural propriety. Did the theories of Vallancey, or of Windele, or the insane speculations of O'Brien, work a change in the minds of the committee? The magnificent tower stands without its basement plinth, and with no church, or sculptured cross in relation to it.[208]

Thus, contemporary monuments to honour the great national dead (becoming an important manifestation of national politics, as Glasnevin was later to become the rallying-ground of Pearse and the republican cult of remembrance) became instilled with the contradictory versions of the Irish past.[209]

Myth, fact and the historical imagination

The Round Towers debate became a flashpoint for the simmering dilemma between historical fact and historical imagination. It is a measure of the discontinuity and fragmentation of Irish historical development (itself caused by its oppression at the hands of the neighbouring isle) that such a wide discrepancy had sprung up between the historical facts and the historical imagination: the facts lost in the ruins and ravages of the past, the imagination cut adrift on swells and currents of speculation and auto-exoticism.

The result was the tendency, especially among nationalists, to look back to a golden primordial Gaeldom brutally ravaged by foreign incursions, to cling to the more mythical or pseudohistorical embellishments concerning Gaelic antiquity, and to perpetuate Milesianisms deriving ultimately from Keating and the *Lebor Gabála*.

An indication to this effect is best provided by the installation ceremony of the Ancient Order of Hibernians in America in 1906.[210] This ceremonial arrangement in itself bespeaks an attempt to recapture the past and to perpetuate a sense of continuity with authentic, Gaelic institutions – such as they were fancifully understood to be by this para-masonic organization. The various officers involved carry titles such as *Ard-Righ*, *Ollamh*, *Bard* and *Brehon*, are dressed in pseudo-antique robes, they address each other in stilted, quasi-archaic formulas ('Be seated, Valiant Chief of Escort and worthy protector of our inner chamber'). The ceremony of induction is a long set of variations of leading people from an amorphous Outside into regulated, ritualized and hierarchical order: into the inner chamber, into the order and into its rules and tenets.[211] This initiation and (literally) induction brings the novices face to face with, precisely, a Round Tower.

> A large fac-simile of the Round Tower ought to be placed on the right of the presiding officer. The tower should be well lit by some style of lamp or gas which would throw the lights through the windows of the Tower. National scenes, or at least a sunburst, should decorate the walls. (p. 22)

The net result of all this (facsimile tower, officers in ancient garb and with ancient titles) is to confront novices with a living, authentic past, kept alive by the endurance of tradition and by the unchanging sameness of ritual. Ancient Ireland is not only evoked by the choral singing of 'The harp that once', 'The shamrock' and 'The pillar-towers of Ireland', but also re-enacted and ritually perpetuated, and fittingly the central element in this is the chief symbol of unchanging permanence: the Round Tower. Novices are instructed in True Gaeldom by an exegesis of that enduring edifice, in terms obviously inspired by Denis Florence MacCarthy's poem:

Mark, my friend(s), the straight shaft pointing heavenward. See each stone laid upon the other in even circle round; see the door placed some distance above the ground; see the whole fabric knitted together by some cement whose composition was known only to the Master Architect of by-gone days, the 'Goban-Saer'. Recall that twice one thousand years those venerable monuments have withstood the attack of time and man. The arches of Imperial Rome, the temples of Classic Greece are gone, but still remain those towers of our sires. Once they were the home of wild pagan custom, and the abiding place of false gods. Purified of error, they became the shelter of Holy Faith, and the treasure house of Mother Church. When the glory of Inisfail was lost in the days of gloom, their deserted columns still remained silent sentinels over the relics of the past. My friend(s), reflect – those towers saw the coming of Milesian, Dane and Saxon. Those pillars witnessed the glory of Con, of McNessa, and of Brian of the Tribune [sic]. Those mystic temples heard the prayers to Bel, the hymn of the Druid, and at last the psalm of Patrick, and since then welcomed no other faith. My friend(s), read the lesson of the Tower. Time must not change the Irishman (pp. 28–9).

Petrie must have turned in his grave. Obviously, volume 20 of the *Transactions of the Royal Irish Academy* carried a lot less clout in the spread of populist nationalism than Oriental paganism and the poems of Moore and MacCarthy.

A measure of this is given *a contrario* by the strenuous efforts of one nationalist, Catholic, middle-class scholar to clinch the debate in favour of factual truth: none other than Eugene O'Curry, one of the erstwhile collaborators of Petrie on the Ordnance Survey, the great initial cataloguer of Irish manuscripts materials in the Royal Irish Academy, the Bodleian Library and the British Museum, and, alongside O'Donovan, undoubtedly the greatest authority on pre-Norman Gaelic Ireland. In 1854 O'Curry had been deservedly appointed Professor of Irish History and Archaeology in the newly founded Catholic University of Ireland, and in the period between his appointment and his death (in 1862) had done much to marshall his priceless expertise into lecture form. His *Lectures on the manuscript materials of ancient Irish history* appeared in 1861, followed in 1873 by the posthumous three-volume lectures *On the manners and customs of the ancient Irish*. In these lectures, O'Curry staunchly stood up for a factualist understanding of Irish antiquity, unclouded by popular misconceptions. He accordingly endorsed Petrie's work in the strongest terms (even hinting repeatedly that he had assisted Petrie in his work on the Round Towers), and concluded that since the appearance of Petrie's *Ecclesiastical architecture* in 1845

> nothing has been discovered – indeed nothing, I believe, ever can – to throw the smallest doubt upon the clear conclusions on the origin and uses of the round towers of Ireland, to which, after long thought and research, he [Petrie] had come.[212]

It is useful to counterbalance populist Catholic historians such as Canon Bourke and Mary Frances Cusack with O'Curry. There were not only those who refused to abandon the colourful myth, but also some who became conscientious champions of truthful fact in setting the record straight and purifying the nation's historical consciousness from error and invention; and both schools were influential in later attitudes. Not only was there a tendency to base political rhetoric and a nationalist frame of reference on the myths rather than the facts; there was also a counter-tendency to adopt a factualist, even pedantic truthfulness in the imaginative or fictional evocation of the nation's past. Tellingly, O'Curry found it 'humiliating to our national pride and degrading to our self respect' rather than amusing

> to read these bold attempts of such ignorant, unscrupulous fabricators of facts, as Ledwich, Beauford, and Vallancey, to impose their audacious forgeries on our presumed ignorance of the written and existing records of our national history (3:321).

A curious polarity results from this: one, a penchant for myth and fantasy when invoking the notion of Gaelic antiquity, the other, contrariwise, a factualist attention to the minute details of historical accuracy, especially when it comes to the literary evocation of the past.

Thus, John O'Donovan wrote a letter to Denis Florence MacCarthy (undated, but evidently at the beginning of the poet's career, i.e., in the early 1840s) where he gently took issue with a historical error in MacCarthy's poem 'The foray of Con O'Donnell'. MacCarthy had based this poem on a report in the Annals of the Four Masters, and had made use of that text in Owen Connellan's translation; O'Donovan wrote to point out that this translation ('made by Owen Connellan, a peasant from Tireragh, *who has as much brains as a "hatching goose"* (Irish)!') had led the poet astray in a point of historical fact.[213] O'Donovan's attempt to tether MacCarthy's poetical imagination to factual correctness makes more sense when we realize how much his poem on the Round Towers did to perpetuate an erroneous interpretation concerning them. How far this concern for factual authenticity went, can best be seen by turning to a revised edition, some thirty years after its original publication in 1832, of Gerald Griffin's historical novels *The invasion*. Griffin had packed his novel with colourful references to daily life in pre-Norman Ireland – as an earlier commentator put it, 'narrative interest is almost wanting, the chief interest being the laborious and careful picture of the life and civilization of the time, the eve of the Danish Invasions'.[214] However, the antiquarian detail as supplied in 1832 had a limited shelf-life, and the publisher James Duffy called upon O'Curry to bring these references into line for the republication.

> The publisher of the present edition of *The Invasion* has thought it right [. . .] to correct, as far as possible, the involuntary errors into which the great Irish novelist was led in a work so likely to be regarded as an authority on Irish Life, Manners, and Customs, two thousand years ago [sic]. Without interfering with the text, then, (save in more correctly spelling the Irish names and words employed in it,) he has shortly referred the reader, at the page foot, to the following Notes, which have been prepared from critical memoranda, kindly made for the purpose by Eugene O'Curry, Esq., MRIA [. . .] A short glossary of the principal Irish words used in the text has also been appended, for the use of readers unacquainted with the language.[215]

The result is an extraordinary conglomerate of detail-laden text and digressive footnotes, as extravagant as anything in Morgan's *The wild Irish girl* but this time perpetrated, not out of the author's romantic, explanatory ebullience but as a positivistic, academic correction and updating. O'Curry's notes are crammed with critical reflections on the previous generations of antiquarians, whose dead wood it is his task to clear. O'Curry objects to an anachronistic mention of the shamrock, the incorrect nomenclature concerning ancient musical instruments, etc. And, of course, there is also a muscular comment on Round Towers. The reader of this cheaply printed popular novel is directed to scholarly tomes such as Petrie's essay on Tara and O'Curry's forthcoming *Manners and customs*.[216] The normal relation between narrative and colourful detail is thus quite inverted. It is not the antiquarian detail which is introduced for the sake of enlivening the tale, but the tale is seen as a battleground for the proper historical education of the readership. Accordingly, the reader is only given a 'guided tour' of Griffin's story, harnessed into a proper understanding by an orthopaedic corset of notes and glosses. The first six pages of narrative are burdened with no less than thirty-two footnotes and nine pages of appended paratext containing O'Curry's explanations and corrections.

Thus, in the mid-century, the national evocation of Ireland's ancient history has come to be highly contradictory. On the one hand, a strenuous attempt to salvage authentic Irish tradition from the ruins of the past, on the other, the currency of over-used, badly understood symbols with much evocative power but embarrassing to prestigious sections of the Irish intelligentsia in their gimcrack trumpery.[217]

This heightens the literary problems under which we have seen Lady Morgan labour. The poetry and song of *The nation* was submitted by Davis and Smith O'Brien to orthographical correction by the inevitable O'Donovan and O'Curry, and the use of Irish orthography and even Irish typeface was insisted upon – in the face of some resistance:

> When [Davis] proposed to form a class to study the Irish language, when he desired to revive the native names of historical men and places, there was vehement resistance. O'Brien seconded both projects energetically, if he did not originate them. 'Accustom every one', he wrote to Davis, 'to write Irish words in Irish character'; and at forty years of age he became a student of Gaelic. A library edition of *The spirit of the nation* with music and illustrations was issued, and Davis procured the assistance of the Irish scholars O'Donovan and Curry to correct the proper names. But the first appearance of the genuine Gaelic patronymics created consternation.[218]

One can understand why. The reader is continuously tripped up by this contradiction between factualism and rhetoric. References to Old Ireland, the Native Sod which claims the audience's loyalty, make use of names and phrases which, for the sake of philological and archaeological authenticity, are given in correct Irish spelling and even in the Irish typeface, necessitating explanatory footnotes and guides to pronunciation. It is as if the crowds in St Petersburg in 1917, on their way to storming the Winter Palace, were given art-historical explanations concerning the metalwork on the gates they were trying to batter down. References to Tara are given in the correct Irish form *Teamhair*, which is then made to rhyme with 'defamer'.[219] An amused Gavan Duffy saw his poem on 'The men of the north', which involved references to Slieve Donard and other places, transmogrified in something as unpronounceable as it was authentic. Romantic national propaganda underwent the Ordnance Survey treatment; and Duffy wrote teasingly to MacNevin:

> The text of the ballads is to be larded with a Celtic nomenclature furnished by John O'Donovan, which sometimes consists of an aggregate meeting of the consonants with scarcely a vowel to take the chair [. . .] You will stare with all your eyes to see what has become of all your old acquaintances. What do you say to the Lee becoming the Laoi, and the Shannon the Sionann, Limerick Luimneach, and Slieve Donard Sliab Domangart?[220]

This episode shows that auto-exoticism was at the heart of *The nation*. Not for nothing had Lady Morgan, in a preface to the 1846 revised edition of *The wild Irish girl*, claimed that Davis's essays continued the tradition of that book. In contrast to other Repeal organs, which dealt with Ireland on the basis of topical urgency (as a set of contemporary political, economic and constitutional grievances), *The nation* emphatically wanted to acquaint the Irish readership with its own history, its own culture, its own roots, and to draw the ideological strength for a nationalist commitment from this historical self-awareness; but on the other hand, the veneration for the genuineness and authenticity of that selfsame national past means that it is kept pristine, unsullied, in its own orthography and typeface, and, by the same token, different and distant from the latter-day, English-speaking readership.

To create an Irish, national historical awareness was the prime objective of Davis and his fellow-workers: to see that Ireland was not a province, some sort of Lake-District-cum-Isle-of-Wight, but a nation. The difference between province and nation, crucially, involves a sense of historical individuality: the fact that Ireland looks back into a past that diverges from the English or British one, that it traces its antecedents through a root system of its own. As long as Ireland is ignorant of this past, it lacks this crucial element in a national consciousness and might as well be a sectarian Yorkshire-*outre-mer*. Davis's task was, then, a dual one: first, to redeem Ireland from what he perceived as an atrophy of historical interest, and secondly, to furnish the historical data on which such an interest could feed. The reader may wonder at this, for over the foregoing pages the notion of an unresolved past, of historical thought, has unremittingly presented itself as a central factor in Irish culture and politics. Why should *The nation* want to preach, not just to the converted, but to a readership with a high degree of historical awareness?

For one thing, some decades had elapsed since the bitter remembrancing of Morgan and Moore; the 1830s and early 1840s had seen a subsidence in agrarian violence, a tempering of sectarian conflict and something like a minor cultural renaissance around the *Dublin University magazine*, led by benevolent, paternalist Unionists like Ferguson and Lover; the mode of evoking Ireland had lost some of its sharp, historical edges and had begun to drift into peasant idyll and folk sentiment (as we shall see in the next chapter). It was not until the Famine radicalized a number of intellectuals, and the tensions of 1847–8 over education created a rift between O'Connell and the Young Irelanders, that a new atmosphere for national agitation appeared, giving space to movements like the Land League and the Fenians. In other words, Davis began his work in a climate that was marked both by a high degree of academic historical interest (as a result of scholarly work like that of Petrie) and by a lull in political antagonism. But *The nation* also marked a new departure vis-à-vis the bitter, agonized remembrancings of the period 1800–1820. For one thing, the exoteric tendency of Morgan and Moore, their implicit assumption that they wrote for an outside readership to whom Ireland had to be explained, was quite reversed in *The nation*: Davis and his staff explained Ireland to the Irish, not to England. What is more, their explanations and evocations, their recourse to the past, were meant to energize and to motivate that readership, in an activist sense. The matter is put succinctly by Gavan Duffy. In discussing the poetry of Moore (another obvious forerunner of *The nation*, to whom Duffy himself had dedicated an appreciative article in one of its early numbers; FDA, 1: 1250–1254), Duffy pointed out the difference between Moore and *The Nation*: 'His melodies dating from the unsuccessful insurrection of '98 and the Union were the wail of a lost cause, while the songs of *The nation* vibrated with the virile and passionate hopes of a new generation.'[221]

The nation's invocation of the national past was exhortatory. The past was to be brought before the public's eyes so as to fan their national ardour and their national self-awareness; readers were to place themselves under the auspices of Brian Ború, Owen Roe, Sarsfield and Tone. Much as the ballads of *The nation* persistently stressed the need for national unity between Celt and Saxon, Orange and Green, Protestant and Catholic, under the common appellation Irish, so too did the historical ballads of *The nation* attempt to effect a diachronic unification, to unify and homogenize the common Irish history, to render it present to the latter-day generations as an ongoing heirloom and tradition of greatness and heroism. Of the ballads in *The spirit of the nation*, forty contain rousing celebrations of the past. Of these, eleven are set in ancient, Gaelic Ireland, five in the Tudor period, five in the 1640s, and eight in a Jacobite or Wild Geese context, while four celebrate the Patriot heyday of the Volunteers, and five hark back to the United Irishmen. The preponderance of Gaelic Ireland is remarkable: with the exception of Griffin's *The invasion*, no historical novel of the early century had chosen Gaelic Ireland for a setting. The 'virile hopes' mentioned by Gavan Duffy came to the fore in the choice of martial topics. Fights, battles, armies, banners and heroism are the order of the day; and it is remarkable how the Wild Geese and other military glories come to occupy a foreground position in the national iconography. Such a martial tendency marks a change from the mellower tones of

Moore and foreshadows the *machismo* of Standish O'Grady; it was reinforced by the appearance, also around the mid-century, of histories such as Matthew O'Conor's *Military history of the Irish nation, comprising a memoir of the Irish brigades in the service of France* (1845), and John Cornelius O'Callaghan's *History of the Irish brigades in the service of France* (1854).[222]

The nation almost willed itself into a virtual historical and social concourse, a meeting place, a *forum* in the Latin root sense of the word. It ran a series of sketches of great Irish figures, under the name 'National Gallery'; historical essays were published as an ancillary series, called 'The library of Ireland'. In so doing, and by the choice of such titles, virtual *lieux de mémoire* were created, libraries, 'Repeal reading rooms' and galleries were projected consisting of printed words, remembrance halls and *salons* were built in ideas and discourse. Interestingly, if press and media are the abstract ties which link a modern society into an 'imagined community' (as per Benedict Anderson's model), *The nation*, in being among the first press organs to claim this role in a particularist Irish context, consistently evokes points of physical congregation (galleries, libraries, reading rooms), almost as if it nostalgically harks back to the modality of a pre-modern community of direct person-to-person contact and unmediated person-to-person information exchange.

The most arresting example of this idealist monument-building-in-the-abstract is doubtless Davis's essay, 'Hints for Irish historical paintings', in which an entire series of canvases is projected into the future, commissioned, listed as if in a catalogue. Themes for future national-historical paintings are given, in chronological order, with indications of the historical and literary sources where the painter may find further information to assist the project. It begins with 'The landing of the Milesians', 'Ollamh Fodhla presenting his laws to his people', 'Nial and his nine hostages', 'A druid's augury' and 'A chief riding out of his fort', invoking the historical detail furnished by sources such as Keating, O'Halloran, Vallancey, Walker, Moore's *Melodies* and *History of Ireland*, and even Griffin's *The invasion*. The list ends with propagandistic topics: 'Father Mathew administering the pledge in a Munster county', 'Conciliation – Orange and Green' and (O glorious prospect!) 'The lifting of the Irish flags of a national fleet and army'.[223] This essay by Davis, above any other text, exemplifies the substitution of *Nacheinander* by *Nebeneinander*, turning a succession of disparate events into a spectacle of juxtaposed objects.

The projected picture gallery did, in the event, materialize in some form: that of the illustrated history. In order to understand the importance of the populist, illustrated history in the second half of the nineteenth century, we must see its emergence as a response to the Davis-style cultivation of national historical awareness. Not only did *The nation* carry ardent national ballads on historical themes (famously collected under the title *The spirit of the nation*, surely a highly meaningful title), the 'Library of Ireland' series had also published an anthology of ballads which had become a runaway success. Edited by Charles Gavan Duffy, *The ballad poetry of Ireland* became one of the greatest best-sellers of the entire century, going through three editions in its first month, and reaching thirty-nine editions by the time Davis reviewed it.[224] Davis accordingly conceived the idea of recycling this poetic ardour into a properly historical-political awareness, in that he hoped to create a 'ballad history of Ireland', with the object of making 'Irish History familiar to the minds, pleasant to the ears, dear to the passions, and powerful over the taste and conduct of the Irish people in days to come'. Davis continued with a portentous comparison between the powers of imaginative literature and historiography, attempting to reconcile the allure of the one with the factual truthfulness of the other:

> Exact dates, subtle plots, minute connections and motives rarely appear in Ballads, and for these ends the worst prose history is superior to the best ballad series; but these are not the highest ends of history. To hallow or accurse the scenes of glory and honour, or of shame and sorrow; to give to the imagination the arms, and homes, and senates, and battles of other days; to rouse, and soften, and strengthen, and enlarge us with the passions of great periods; to lead us into love of self-denial, of justice, of beauty, of valour, of generous life and proud death; and to set up in our souls the memory of great men, who shall then be as models and judges of our actions – these are the highest duties of history, and these are best taught by a Ballad History.[225]

Lady Morgan would have approved: Glorvina's dilemma, between the charm of song and the urgency of explanation, is here transcended. Nay, more than that: for if we add Davis's call for pictorial material to this agenda, we see Irish history *Nation*-style acquire a multimedia presence, the overwhelming immediacy of a *Gesamtkunstwerk*, rendered present to the ear and the eye, the head and the heart, the senses and the intellect all at once. The generation after *The nation* was to take up Davis's call for such an appealing cinemascope approach; especially in the radicalized climate of post-Famine years, following the split over the university colleges. It is necessary to enter into a brief digression concerning this episode.

The college quarrel was essentially a re-enactment of the debate over the National Schools, which had taken place in 1831. The generation of primary-school pupils of that time had now come of age, and the English government attempted to establish a non-denominational set of Queen's Colleges in the provincial capitals. Alongside the Anglican conformism of Trinity College Dublin, a Queen's College in Belfast would cater for the North's Presbyterian population, while colleges in Cork and Galway would provide a secular alternative to Maynooth or Trinity. The Catholic hierarchy, foremost among them MacHale,[226] argued strenuously against this project, which aimed at bringing various denominations together, much as MacHale had fulminated in 1831 against a non-denominational National School system. It would be easy to denounce this as Catholic exclusivism. To some extent it certainly was; but one may sympathize with MacHale's point of view to the extent that the respectable, Anglican, unionist part of the population had co-opted the transpartisan stance, conflated the ideals of Protestantism with the notion of civil improvement generally, and hid a smug Protestant supremacism behind the conciliatory façade of non-denominational civility. Even Ferguson, as we shall see, had argued the need for 'Scriptural edu-cation' among the natives; Trinity College was a breeding ground for the 'Protestant Crusade' which equated improvement with proselytization; and that the Protestant Archbishop Whateley had foolishly but tellingly described the aim of the National Schools as the education of every pupil into a 'happy English child'. National Schools were so non-denominational and so apolitical as to ban all expression of national sentiment, Irish or otherwise, thereby advancing a unionist ethos by default.[227] In the event, the Christian Brothers' schools, vigor-ously supported by MacHale, had become highly successful, both educationally and ideologically. A Royal Commission on Education in 1876 praised the high standards of Christian Brothers' schoolbooks, adding that 'they combine nation-ality and Catholicity in considerable proportions'.[228] Accordingly, the Christian Brothers' schools were a breeding ground for that type of Irish separatism which flourished in the later decades of the century, and which saw the redemption of Ireland from British rule partly as a religious, partly as an ethnic crusade.

This 'triumph of denominationalism' as Lyons calls it (84) was propelled by the fresh instalment of the educational debate over the Queens' Colleges. MacHale, and O'Connell in his wake, denounced their non-denominational set-up which would naturally expose the budding Catholic intelligentsia to the greater social prestige and allure of Protestant, Ascendancy fellow-students; the proposed colleges were called 'godless' and 'infidel', and this drove the final wedge between O'Connell's Catholic Repeal Association and the non-denom-inational liberals in Young Ireland. *The nation*, true to its mission, supported anything that transcended sectarian division and aimed at national improvement. Its anti-Connellite and non-denominational stance over this issue cost it dearly in terms of populist credibility, and made it possible for rival periodicals to break away in a more aggressively nationalist direction, such as Mitchel's *United Irishman* (set up in 1848) or Kickham's *The Irish people* (set up in 1863).[229]

Ironically, it was in these decades after the death of Davis and the discomfiture of Young Ireland, that *The nation's* programme of historical-consciousness-raising came to full fruition. A.M. Sullivan's career is exemplary in this regard. Radi-calized by the famine, assistant editor of *The nation* in 1855 and editor from 1858 to 1876, Sullivan, a Home Rule MP from 1874, clashed bitterly with the Fenians; but he gained much popularity over the fact that he was imprisoned on the account of an article he had written on the Manchester Martyrs, and was instrumental in erecting a statue to Henry Grattan on College Green. He also won fame as a latter-day Curran by defending Land Leaguers. This remarkable man brought Davis's ideals into practice, especially in his massively influential history book for young people, *The story of Ireland; or, A narrative of Irish history, from the earliest ages to the present time, written for the youth of Ireland* (Dublin, 1867). Not only does the format of a story transcend the division, deplored by Davis, between imaginative literature and factual history, the illustrations appear almost like a response to Davis's request for a gallery of 'Irish historical paintings'. The first of the many illustrations in the *Story* deals with the theme which Davis, too, had mentioned as the starting point, 'The Milesians sighting the "Promised Isle"' (11). The final illustration provides a poignant counter-point, and shows the leave-taking of emigrants; the Milesians are forced out of their promised isle ('A scene from the Irish exodus', 561). Sullivan's *Story*, then, in presenting an emotive, gripping, pictorial and literary version of 'exciting history', follows a pattern which we have seen exemplified in the case of Canon Bourke: that the attempt to set the historical record straight involves a continuing acceptance, in the teeth of factual falsification, of Ireland's legendary origins as exemplified in the *Lebor Gabála* and Keating. Sullivan's book situates itself, like many other late-nineteenth-century histories which reach from the Fianna to the Fenians, between myth and history and dovetails one with the other. In subsequent decades, such popular Stories and Tales merged into a popular amalgam of indiscriminate Irish-interest reading material, which did much to motivate its audience, and which played an important role in the development of nationalist enthusiasm.[230]

But what, if any, is the difference between history and storytelling? In his inaugural lecture at Oxford, Roy Foster has addressed this question against the background of the gap between history-as-past-events and history-as-description-of-past-events.[231] Story, in Foster's exposé, is essentially a narrative ordering of diverse and equivocal facts and materials, rendering the past coherent by fitting it into the schemata and motifs of beginning and end, heroes and villains, quest and obstacle, helpers and opponents.

Such historical narrativism can be very illuminating, as Foster demonstrates, when applied to Irish historiographical practice. Irish authors were particularly keen to impose some discursive organity or organization on a past which to them appeared traumatically disjointed and random, and they were at the same time keenly aware of the extent to which that past failed to conform to the sense of order and closure which a narration or history would imply. However, that awareness is not limited to Ireland or to the nineteenth century, and there are added connotations in the pursuit of history as story which I would like to put forward in addition to Foster's analysis.

A scientific world-view, unlike a magical or mythical one, *progresses*: new generations are not content to follow in the footsteps of earlier masters and to emulate their example, but attempt to improve upon what they see as the shortcomings of earlier practice. This notion comes close to what Karl Popper sees as a central defining characteristic of scientific discovery: falsification, the exposure of insufficiencies in previous models to accurately account for the processes of empirical reality. Although history-writing is not a technical, empirical science, it is certainly a scientific endeavour to the extent that its academic praxis follows this pattern of falsification-driven progress. Ann Rigney analysed a generic tendency towards intertextual antagonism, the 'agonistic drive' in historians' relations with their forerunners and rivals: unlike fiction-writers and storytellers, historians are in a position to express this agonistic drive by way of mutual falsification, i.e., proving that another's version of historical events is inadequate or deficient.[232]

The popular, often illustrated stories/histories of Ireland which were published in great number in the closing decades of the nineteenth century, were, by this definition, all of them stories and none of them histories proper. In contrast to professional debates like the one between Lecky and Froude, Sullivan-style popular histories are not concerned with correcting the shortcomings or blind spots of other histories; they echo them, even recycle them, taking up Keating's myth as much as eighteenth-century historians such as Sylvester O'Halloran's or abbé MacGeoghegan's (continued in sequel by, respectively, Sullivan and John Mitchel). Each of them, time after time, sets out again to tell, once more, in fresh words, the Story of Ireland, her glorious antiquity and manifold wrongs. It is like the obsessive workings and reworkings of the Deirdre story: each sets forth the same familiar tale in different words. And much of this was done, Griffin-style, in a sub-Walter-Scott register of historical romance, often aimed at juvenile audiences, crammed with historical detail and driven by an educational, nationalist purpose.[233]

Standish O'Grady's various historical-cum-literary-cum-mythological works show the close interaction between these discursive fields: his *Story of Ireland* (London, 1894), reaches from the Milesians to Parnell, and, going by its simple language, is apparently aimed at a juvenile readership; his *History of Ireland* of 1878–1880 is a reworking of native saga, universally recognized as providing the Yeatsian movement with its main fund of imaginative material, whereas his later *History of Ireland: Critical and philosophical* sets out to be, 'not constructive or imaginative',[234] but a critical, scholarly investigation with accurate source reliability; but even though O'Grady himself is at pains to distinguish these two different forms of 'historical composition' which led to such similarly-titled books, the two *Histories of Ireland* share the same opening chapter, describing the early history of Ireland from the Pleistocene onwards.

In other words, O'Grady appears to run squarely into the intractable confusion between Irish myth and Irish historical fact. Accordingly, the last chapter of the *History of Ireland: Critical and philosophical* must come to terms with the vexed problem of the historical reliability of native mythical sources. The source-critical chapter is entitled 'Verification of the Irish bardic history, how far reliable, doubtful, and mythical' (425–464); but in the final analysis, the factual and the fanciful, the truthful and the poetic, the *vero* and the *ben trovato* are not so much distinguished as reconciled: both provide a 'rattling good read'. Even if O'Grady's bardic-based recounting of ancient native history were to prove 'mere cloud-land, the enchanted world of poetic tradition' (425), it can still be read 'as a sketch by me of a great imagined history of our ancestors [. . .] a creation of the bardic or bardic-Christian genius'. 'Read even in this light', O'Grady concludes, such a story 'cannot fail to be interesting' (463).

And that, after all, was what Davis had wanted from history: something that could thrill and energize the readership with a mixture of factual accuracy and poetical colour. O'Grady had set academic, factualist history aside as mere 'archaeology', and aims to find a middle ground between the 'archaeologian' and the 'novelist and romancer'.[235] Thus, the Irish literary imagination makes itself at home, not in the realm of the realistic novel, but in the realm of the colourful past. Popular, illustrated histories of Ireland, from Milesian antiquity to the present day, are for the Irish reading public what George Eliot and Thomas Hardy are in England, and the *imaginaire* of the Irish literary renaissance of the 1890s and 1900s is steeped in mythological lore and historical fact: in Keating and Cuchulain rather than in Flaubert or Fontane, with their fictional narratives of contemporary life, their interest in the psychology and social interaction of the contemporary individual.

Such history-writing, which is part of imaginative literature rather than of an academic, scholarly endeavour, does not *progress*. Older histories have no obsolescence. Eighteenth-century historians like MacGeoghegan and O'Halloran speak as immediately to a nineteenth-century Irish readership as Swift or Goldsmith. Characteristically, when O'Grady evokes how his youthful ardour had been fired by O'Halloran's *History of Ireland*, he misdates that book in a bizarre, multiple anachronism. 'He wrote, I think, in the second decade of the century, and before the rise of the Vallency [sic] school'.[236] The only datability or obsolescence of older historical texts lies, not in the progress of historical knowledge, but in the cut-off point of the terminus *ad quem*, the chronological meaning of the phrase 'until the present day'. Sullivan ends his *Story of Ireland* with an '*Unfinished* chapter of eighteen hundred and sixty-seven', and a similar pattern is noticeable in many historians: that they take their narrative up to the present, and leave it to a future sequel to give a verdict and finish the story (which implicitly tends towards the revindication of Irish independence). Emmet's statement that his epitaph is not to be written, that his biography is to remain open-ended, until the day of Ireland's independence, is implicitly echoed by all these open-ended histories with their Fenian or Parnellite sympathies.[237]

Accordingly, we see how historians concatenate, take up older historians and continue their narratives. John Mitchel takes abbé MacGeoghegan's history of Ireland (of which an English translation by Patrick O'Kelly had appeared in 1844), and brings its narrative up to date in a continuation;[238] Sullivan does something similar to O'Halloran's *History of Ireland* (Boston, 1884). Indeed, that book's title deserves to be quoted in full:

> The pictorial history of Ireland, from the landing of the Milesians to the present time; detailing, in chronological order, all the important events of the reigns of the kings and chieftains, and embracing authentic accounts of their several wars with the Romans, Britons, Danes and Normans; with graphic descriptions of the battle of Clontarf; Strongbow's invasion; the death of king Roderick O'Connor; crowning of Edward Bruce king of Ireland; war of the O'Neills and O'Donnells against England; confiscation of Ulster; Cromwell's invasion; persecution of the Catholics; war between king James and William of Orange; siege of Derry and battle of the Boyne; siege of Athlone; battle of Aughrim; siege and treaty of Limerick; penal laws; the Volunteers; the United Irishmen; rebellion of '98; the Union; Catholic Emancipation and Repeal; the Young Irelanders; the Fenian insurrection; the Land League, etc. etc.

The very title of this 'pictorial history' sums up an entire historical attitude. Not only does it trace the (by now familiar) course from Milesians to the present, but it does so in an enumeration of famous and already known picturesque high points, a potted conspectus amounting almost to that gallery of events which Davis had suggested to be enshrined in national paintings. What is more, an obvious break in the title occurs around Brian Ború: first, there were the reigns and battles of Milesian kings and chieftains, then follow the crises and catastrophes which puncture the course of time, from the battle of Clontarf to the Land League. (The reader is left wondering what the final 'etc. etc.' may refer to.) This break is highly significant (and heralded on the title page by a change of typeface). Generally speaking, the description of history by reign of succeeding monarchs allows for a traditional, sedate and well-ordered mode of reign-by-reign historiography; this was the mode adopted by Moore and Haverty.[239] For historians like Sullivan, this reign-by-reign organization can only be followed for the Gaelic, pre-invasion part of Irish history. Irish history after Henry II can be described only in the succession of repeted catastrophes, wars and insurrections, and its narrative cannot fit the organizational stability of succeeding monarchs and the implicit notion of 'the king is dead, long live the king'. James and Freeman Wills's *The Irish nation: its history and its biography* stated the same awareness at the beginning of its 'historical introduction':

> The history of Ireland is marked by peculiarities which do not affect that of any other country. It comprises the remotest extremes of the social state; and sets at nought the ordinary laws of social transition and progress, during the long intervals between them. Operated on by a succession of *external* shocks, the internal advances, which form some part of all other history, have been wanting; and her broken and interrupted career, presents a dream-like succession of capricious and seemingly unconnected changes, without order or progress.[240]

That echoes Griffin's nightmarish view of the Irish past (above, p. 51) and anticipates Stephen Dedalus's sentiment, in *Ulysses*, that history is a nightmare from which he is trying to awake. But the notion of Irish history as intractable chaos was perhaps most trenchantly stated by the Fenian sympathizer Dion Boucicault, in a twenty-four-page pamphlet entitled *The fireside story of Ireland*. It begins:

> Let me tell you the story of Ireland. It is not a history. When we speak of the history of a nation, we mean the biographies of its kings: the line of monarchs forming a spinal colum from which historical events seem to spring laterally. The history of Ireland is invertebrate. It has no such royal backbone. [. . .] The efforts of the Irish race to regain their country present a monotonous record of bloodshed extending over seven centuries, even to our own day: the last of these massacres occurred eighty-three years ago. These convulsions are the only reigns into which the story of Ireland can be perspicuously divided. They might be called Reigns of Terror.[241]

This is almost worthy of Michelet. The clever and highly apposite use of the vertebrate metaphor makes it possible to link the chaos of Irish history to the country's oppression under foreign rule and loss of nationhood, and to see the opposing principles of independence and bloody oppression, not only as a matter of historical fact, but also as a problem for Irish people to comprehend their own past. Under foreign dominance, even Irish history has fallen apart and loosed mere anarchy upon the historical record. Thus historical consciousness truly becomes a nationalist enterprise, and sorting out the past becomes a necessary step in the reconstitution of national independence.

And so, history was revived to inspire the present. Not only that, but the reviving of history was performed time and again, by writer after writer, each of them telling the old story afresh, like a needle stuck in the groove, in an uncanny, obsessive recycling process of the past, of the old familiar, oft-told story of the past. If history, from Griffin to Wills to Boucicault to Stephen Dedalus, is a nightmare, it is particularly so because of its *uncanniness*, which, following Freud's intriguing essay on that subject, is characterized by a combination of familiarity, incomprehensibility and insistent recurrence.[242] Irish history is familiar, it is incomprehensible, and it re-occurs again and again, as in a nightmare or a neurosis. If extended to the adjoining sphere of the literary imagination, this would imply that it might be rewarding to see the *imaginaire* of nineteenth-century Irish fiction (especially Irish Gothic), not just against the background of the post-Burkean Sublime, but rather against the background of the Uncanny as typified by Freud. Nineteenth-century Irish history appears to shift from *das Erhabene* to *das Unheimliche*.

THE PRESENCE OF THE PAST:
Peasantry, Community and Tradition

Beyond politics? Irish culture and the Irish language

The development of cultural nationalism, in which historical debates and historical literature played such an important role, was also deeply influenced by an interest in living Irish culture, traced in the Gaelic language, folklore and song. It should be remembered that, although these cultural concerns span most of the century, they were, until the 1870s, marginal to parliamentary politics and to great national questions: the constitutional status of Ireland, the ascendancy of the Church of Ireland, landlordism. There was a wide gap between political and romantic nationalism, between the tendency to defend Ireland's right to self-government from arguments of political economy and constitutional principle (as O'Connell and Parnell did) or the tendency to claim Irish right to self-government from arguments of linguistic, ethnic and cultural identity (as the Young Irelanders and the later nationalists were to do). Much has been made by earlier historians of the fact that Daniel O'Connell, himself from a prestigious native family with Gaelic roots, showed little interest in the preservation of the Irish language. But as I have argued in the introduction, the link between nationalistic politics and linguistic revivalism only came after O'Connell. It was simply non-existent for a political nationalist like O'Connell, who argued from religious and constitutional elements rather than from the Herderian-Hegelian point so fundamental to post-Romantic nationalists: that *cultural* identity should be the main authenticating principle for *national* identity.

Accordingly, politics in this context meant primarily the tension between Whig and Tory, or between religious denominations; the very word was synonymous with party factionalism and religious sectarianism. Accordingly, the pursuit of cultural projects like the cultivation of the Irish past or of the Irish language – something which is so very obviously political to a latter-day observer – was considered apolitical at the time. Indeed the notion of nationality and of a national culture was (or at least could be) considered as a transcendence of merely political pursuits – much as if a Whig and a Tory would meet in the concert-hall to enjoy an opera together. Charles Gavan Duffy himself felt that 'on the neutral ground of "ancient history and native art", Unionist and nationalist would meet without alarm'.[1]

We must, therefore, come to terms with the fact that movements which we see primarily as instances of cultural nationalism were considered, by the people involved, to be apolitical, and that the pursuit of Irish culture and Irish antiquity was considered a sanctuary where men of different religious or political persuasions could meet. In all the succession of antiquarian and revivalist Gaelic initiatives in the course of the nineteenth century the common injunction is always that 'politics is to be kept out of our business'.

This is all the more understandable as, for most of the century, learned societies (which formed the most important institutional filiation of cultural interest between Vallancey and Hyde) were constituted largely of an élite membership. Unlike the members of O'Flanagan's Gaelic Society, who had published cheap grammars and primers of Irish with one foot in the hedge-school, the later societies were composed of peers, baronets, the liberal professions and gentlemen scholars, with a sprinkling of some native-speaking interest embodied in names such as O'Donovan, O'Curry and Archbishop MacHale. Witness, not only O'Reilly's Iberno-Celtic Society of 1818, but also the Irish Archaeological Society, established in 1840 for the scholarly publication of ancient manuscript material. Its membership included, under the patronage of the prince consort, two archbishops, eight bishops, three dukes and thirty other peers, as well as O'Curry, O'Donovan, Petrie, Hardiman, Thomas Moore, Daniel O'Connell, William Smith O'Brien, Charles Gavan Duffy, Sir Robert Peel, and four peerage-endorsed clan chiefs with 'The' before their name. Drawing as they did on such a high-powered mix of public personalities, it becomes easy to see why these societies should wish to keep political debate at bay.[2] The Gaelic Society and the Iberno-Celtic Society, founded in the bitterly antagonistic pre-Emancipation years, set the tone with this identical formula:

> No religious or political debates whatsoever shall be permitted at any of the meetings of the Society; such objects being foreign to the objects of the institution.[3]

The formula became *de rigueur*, and was couched in its most revealing phraseology when the Kilkenny Archaeological Society was established in 1849. Its rules stated that all matters 'connected with the religious and political differences which exist in our country' are not only 'foreign to the objects of this society', but also 'calculated to disturb the harmony which is essential to its success'. The same studiously apolitical attitude was observed in the short-lived Irish language journals that were established from time to time. Philip Barron's *Ancient Ireland* resolved from the outset that it 'should be totally unconnected with Politics'.[4]

Again, when John Fleming began his long career as a language revivalist by starting the Society for the Preservation of the Irish Language in 1877, the same note of respectability was sounded; tellingly, this society brought together men from opposite political camps like Archbishop MacHale (the Society's patron) and Samuel Ferguson (a Council member). It was this initiative which was to lead ultimately to Hyde's Gaelic League: a more activist segment of the Society for the Preservation of the Irish Language seceded in 1880 as the Gaelic Union (with Hyde among the members), and transformed itself in due course, under the presidency of Eugene O'Growney, into the Gaelic League.[5] The Gaelic Union, again, repeated the old pious transpartisan formula, but with some tell-tale qualifications:

> While the Council of the Gaelic Union is thoroughly Irish, there is nothing sectarian or political in its aims – its members, while retaining their own private religious and political opinions, do not obtrude them on others; and they stretch out the hand of fellowship to their Celtic kinsmen of Scotland, Wales, the Isle of Man, and Brittany. Their only opponents are the Philistines and Vandals, who would annihilate the Irish language, regardless of its antiquity, beauty and literature, and because of its close connection with Irish nationality.[6]

Irish nationality is here beginning to slide from a transpolitical to a political category; and the pan-Celtic ethnicism is likewise a new development.

In this light, it becomes understandable both why Douglas Hyde should have been so emphatic in his refusal to see language revival as a political issue, and why his refusal should have been so singularly out of touch. He was echoing a hallowed stance in Irish cultural pursuit, but the stance had become untenable by 1890, when living Irish culture was becoming the badge of nationality and nationalism. Hyde's anti-political disclaimers in *On the necessity for de-Anglicising Ireland* appear either naive or disingenuous; but Hyde stood by them, to the point of stepping down as president of the Gaelic League when it became clear that he could not stem the tide of politicization.[7] Pearse's comment (characteristically citing, and applying to himself, words spoken by Christ) is apt indeed:

> Whenever Dr. Hyde, at a meeting at which I had a chance of speaking after him, has produced his dove of peace, I have always been careful to produce my sword; and to tantalize him by saying that the Gaelic League has brought into Ireland 'not Peace but a Sword'.[8]

But that was in 1913. In the course of the nineteenth century, statements of apolitical intent had been made, not only in linguistics but also in folklore, in an attempt to define a neutral common ground for all sections of Irish society, untroubled by history or politics. In the event, these attempts turned into a debate over the 'middle ground' of Ireland's popular tradition, and over the right to speak on behalf of the illiterate peasantry of the country. Who is to be the spokesman for the Plain People of Ireland, and who can authenticate his Irish cultural nationality by a recourse to a demotic constituency of unquestioned Irishness?

Popular culture and the fairies: Croker and Allingham

Popular tradition becomes, next to a quest for the authentic past, the main ideal of Irish cultural pursuits and debates. It is defined by its orality and performance, in contrast to literature proper, which is defined by its written character. That basic distinction between low oral culture and high written culture feeds into a whole set of similarly aligned oppositions: between spontaneous effusion and polished reflection, between transience and permanence, between the emotional and the cerebral, between the timelessness of primitive customs and the historicity of developing civility, between the Celt and the Saxon. Popular, native culture is one of remains and relics; it is yet another mode of establishing a filiation between the post-Union, indeed post-Famine present and the ancient roots of Irishness. It is also a reservoir of raw material to be mined and cultivated: to be retrieved from its illiterate repository, the peasantry, who hoard this cultural heritage with spontaneous and unreflective naivety, without the necessary intellectual refinement to appreciate its higher interest.

Many aspects of nineteenth-century cultural history in Europe have been studied by social historians in terms of a civilizing offensive. There is very little of that sort of thing happening in Ireland; there was very little caring, paternalistic improvement attempted apart from the quixotic Bible missions and the interesting case of the National School system, which was treated with some mistrust in the very quarters it was supposed to benefit.[9] Rather, what is much more prominent in nineteenth-century cultural relations is quite the opposite of a top-down civilizing offensive: the high culture of the Anglo-Irish elite seeks to rejuvenate and energize itself through an osmosis with the unspoilt, primitive energy and ebullience of native low culture.

The Anglo-Irish cultivation of popular tradition takes on three forms: that of song and verse, of folklore and of the Gaelic language. Much of it starts off as an attempt to avoid the pitfalls of political-historical research, as we can gather from the trail-blazing worker in this field, Thomas Crofton Croker.

Croker was born in Cork in the fateful year 1798 and later became a civil servant of unionist persuasion, eventually settling in England. It was Croker who collected the important *Fairy legends and traditions in the south of Ireland*, which appeared in 1825 and immediately met with enormous success, both in the British Isles and on the Continent. The collection was translated by the Grimm brothers, who were among Croker's correspondents, in the very year of its appearance; and the book became the fountainhead for folklore interest in Ireland in the nineteenth century. Pookahs, leprechauns *et hoc genus omne* were introduced to the non-Gaelic reading public by this man, who may safely be called the Irish Grimm.

It is important to see Croker's activity in the context of the mid-1820s: the dark years before the Clare by-election, the time of Moore's *Captain Rock*, the time when Catholic agitation and agrarian unrest heightened the tension in a stagnated polity, when sectarian history-writing seemed to have taken over historiographical practice for good, and when no revival of history-writing or of antiquarianism was yet in sight. The *Fairy legends and traditions of the south of Ireland* was preceded one year previously (in 1824) by Croker's other main claim to fame, a book whose title is worth quoting in full: *Researches in the south of Ireland, illustrative of the scenery, architectural remains, and the manners and superstitions of the peasantry. With an appendix containing a private narrative of the rebellion of 1798.* If the appended narrative of '98 places the book in the context of the sectarian evaluations of that traumatic event, so widespread in the decades between Union and Emancipation, a fresh departure is indicated by the title's novel reference to 'manners and superstitions of the peasantry'. That unusual departure is elaborated in the book's chapter on 'Fairies and supernatural agency' – the topic to which Croker in the next year was to devote the *Fairy legends and traditions*. In the *Researches*, the chapter sits oddly, and marks a shift in the book's more straightforward antiquarian-cum-geographical interest (i.e. scenery, remains). Again, I think that this shift, coming as it does at this time, is not merely Croker's idiosyncrasy, but that it marks a wider change in the general scholarly preoccupation with Ireland.

Croker's forerunners in this vein of learning are the antiquarians of the late eighteenth and early nineteenth century – men like Vallancey, O'Conor, O'Halloran, Walker, Ledwich, Campbell and O'Flanagan, who, whatever their scholarly and political differences, were united in their belief that Ireland's Gaelic antiquity was a treasure-house of historical or anthropological interest. The first half of Croker's title follows in the footsteps of these his predecessors, the older generation of scholars, amateurs, enthusiasts and autodidacts (it recalls, for example, Thomas Campbell's *Philosophical survey of the south of Ireland* of 1777), and also follows the contemporary trend towards a regional interest. Indeed, Croker himself became a member of the Society of Antiquaries, of the Camden Society and the Percy Society; his role in English antiquarianism was a prominent one.[10] But the odd phraseological shift in the title, from 'architectural remains' to the 'manners and superstitions of the peasantry' indicates a deliberate break away from received practice; in his first chapter, the author states in effect that he has no time for the bygone glories of Gaelic antiquity and instead has chosen to investigate the surviving traditions of the peasantry. In a way, then, Croker's book signposts an alternative interest in the cultural study of Ireland, alongside the vexed terrain of history and antiquity; interestingly, Croker was to become an antiquarian in England and a folklorist in Ireland.

What is more, the appearance of Croker's *Researches* pretty neatly coincides with another major shift in Irish cultural history: the death of Gaelic as a living written tradition. By the early 1820s, the last traditional poet/scribes such as the Ó Longáins and Tadhg Gaelach had just laid down the quill, and little poetry was composed or copied through the medium of writing; indeed, the last vestiges of literacy in Gaelic, and of written literary activity in that language, were moving from the rural peasant communities into the scientific and professionally academic sphere of the scholarly societies, the Ordnance Survey and the university, just as Croker published his book of folklore. Croker, a middle-class Protestant from a provincial town, abandoned Gaelic culture and antiquity, leaving the field to philologists proper like O'Reilly, O'Curry and O'Donovan.

The net result: Croker begins to deal with Gaelic culture as a predominantly oral and contemporary one rather than as a written and historical one. This coincides, fairly precisely again, with the point in history when that culture has lost everything except its orality, when that culture is not just oral, but downright illiterate. In fact, it so happens that the *Researches* contain a remarkable post-mortem on the death of Gaelic literature: Croker describes (with some outrage) his discovery in 1821, of a sheaf of 'about four hundred popular ballads (chiefly printed in Limerick),' more than one-third of which 'were of a rebellious tendency'. As Georges-Denis Zimmermann's survey of such political broadsheets illustrates,[11] these were the last medium in which *aisling* poetry, in English, Irish or a mixture of the two, could be divulged in a written rather than an oral form. Interestingly enough, both Allingham and Yeats, Croker's foremost successors in the fairy vein, later on revived the folksy potential of the broadsheet tradition for their own purposes – Yeats with his bibliophile Cuala prints, and Allingham because he thought the folksongs sung around his native town of Ballyshannon were indecent, and wanted to counter-act their immoral tendencies by having bowdlerized, sentimental pseudo-folksongs distributed in broadsheet format.[12] In all these instances there is an attempt by Protestant writers to tap into the living vein of popular tradition.

The Irish peasantry, until then seen as the pauperized, brutish and sullen dregs of a dead old culture, full of disaffection and hatred for their new rulers, gain cultural interest. They come to be seen, in Romantic, Grimm-like fashion, as the repository of quaint superstition and primordial folk and fairy tales. That folklore interest is already operative in full force in the questionnaire for the Ordnance Survey fieldworkers (quoted here, p. 257, n. 102). Throughout the century, collections like Croker's were published: by Charles Lover (*Legends and stories of Ireland*, 1831) or Mrs S.C. Hall (*Stories of the Irish peasantry*, 1850). Indeed, much of Carleton's work in the *Traits and stories of the Irish peasantry* should be seen in this context, in that Carleton, who claimed to give an almost anthro-pological record of daily life and culture of low Gaelic life, aimed for a similar combination of description and amusement, and included much detail on superstitions, story-telling and pastimes. Witness how Carleton (who invokes the character of the folklorist by the old-fashioned appellation of 'social anti-quary') authenticates his literary work as an intelligent and informed folkore record of living culture:

> [. . .] the subject is one which I ought well to understand, not only from my humble position in early life, and my uninterrupted intercourse with the people as one of themselves, until I had reached the age of twenty-two years, but from the fact of having bestowed upon it my undivided and most earnest attention ever since I left the dark mountains and green vales of my native Tyrone, and began to examine human life and manners as a citizen of the world. [. . .] My father, indeed, was a very humble man [. . .] When the state of education in Ireland during his youth and that of my mother is considered, it will not be a matter of surprise that what they did receive was very limited. It would be difficult, however, if not impossible to find two persons in their lowly station so highly and singularly gifted. My father possessed a memory not merely great or surprising, but absolutely astonishing. [. . .] My native place is a spot rife with old legends, tales, traditions, customs, and superstititons [. . .] It was [. . .] from my father's lips in particular, that they were perpetually sounding in my ears. *In fact his*

memory was a perfect storehouse, and a rich one, of all that the social antiquary, the man of letters, the poet, or the musician, would consider valuable [my emphasis, JL]. As a teller of old tales, legends, and historical anecdotes he was unrivalled, and his stock of them was inexhaustible. [. . .] With all kinds of charms, old ranns, or poems, old prophecies, religious superstitions, tales of pilgrims, miracles, and pilgrimages, anecdotes of blessed priests and friars, revelations from ghosts and fairies, was he thoroughly acquainted. [. . .] My mother, whose name was Kelly – Mary Kelly – possessed the sweetest and most exquisite of human voices. [. . .] she had several old songs [in Irish] which at that time, – I believe too I may add at this,- had never been translated; and I very much fear that some valuable ones, both as to words and airs, have perished with her.[13]

Carleton thus hallmarks the value and authenticity of his tales by way of stressing the native, untutored authenticity of his family background, in the process setting up his parents as the very prototypes of ideal folklore subjects.

Folklore was to become a major industry for Irish writers after Croker. Croker's antiquarian-cum-anthropological enterprise was to lead ultimately to the scholarly collections of 'proper' folklorists like Jeremiah Curtin, Patrick Kennedy, Joseph Jacobs, William Larminie and Douglas Hyde.[14] Meanwhile, however, the popular and entertaining versions of folk and fairy stories occupied a niche in the interstice between fact and fiction, amusing a middle-class readership with something that was both entertaining and instructive, a window on the exotic folk-life of the Irish peasantry. It is in this light that we should see, for instance, Samuel Lover's *Legends and stories of Ireland* (1831, with fresh editions in 1832, 1834 and 1899) and *Popular tales and legends of the Irish peasantry* (1834), Denis Florence MacCarthy's *Irish legends and lyrics, with poems of the imagination and fancy* (1858), Edmund Leamy's *Irish fairy tales* (1890, second edition 1894) or even Speranza Wilde's collections (*Ancient legends, mystic charms and superstitions of Ireland*, 1887; *Ancient cures, charms and usages of Ireland. Contributions to Irish lore*, 1890).[15]

These tomes of tales bring oral and written culture together, merge anonymous peasants with Lover and MacCarthy (with Carleton as go-between): witness *Irish pleasantry and fun: A selection of the best humourous tales by Carleton, Lover, Lever and other popular writers* (1882). Moreover, the penchant for tales and stories did much to de-historicize and de-politicize the image of the Irish peasantry. The peasantry is not a social group whose lives and actions, sympathies and aspirations take shape in a politically or historically distinct moment, but rather the timeless repository of a primeval, timeless life, primitive in the root sense of that term, aboriginal and untouched by modernizing influences from outside. The peasant's way of reflecting on life is not by way of discursive reference but by the rehearsing of old stories; his intelligence is not that of analysis but of intuitive insight, soothsayings and proverbs. It is no surprise to find the commonplace that this peasantry-as-folklore-reservoir is always on the verge of diminution or extinction (witness the fact that Carleton's mother Mary Kelly has taken valuable [!] old songs into the grave with her); this puts the folklore researcher into what has aptly been termed a 'salvage paradigm'.[16] Raymond Williams has famously pointed out, in the opening pages of *The country and the city*, that each generation believes it witnesses the final disso- lution of traditional country life, until then apparently unspoilt and pristine; a commonplace[17] evidently inspired by the notion that country, the peasantry, extra-historical as it is, has no regenerative or expansive energy and, passively retentive as it is confined to be, can only lose, never regain, in the changes of historical time. The peasantry for Irish folklorists is taken out of the realm of political conflict, and translated into the realm of the timeless superstitition, the folktale, the otherworld and the living past. It is a striking fact that of all the elements in Irish popular culture, the notion of fairies and leprechauns came to dominate everything else; and that this 'fairification' of Irish popular culture was cultivated most assiduously by Protestant, conservative, unionist writers. Fairies are not found in *The nation*, whose frame of cultural reference is historical and ancient-Gaelic; the fairy-stuff of popular culture is found in the *Dublin University magazine* and similar conservative reviews, and tends to be penned by authors such as Croker, Maginn, Carleton, Lover, and later Allingham, the early pre- Maud Gonne Yeats, Larminie and Alfred Perceval Graves.

The attitude as outlined here is *idyllic*; and the idyllic imagination of country life was widespread all over Europe in the mid-century. We find it in the rural novels of Mrs Gaskell and George Eliot (specifically in the quaint characters who make up the background), in the rustic novels of George Sand, and in Germany in the widespread Biedermeier genre of the *Dorfsidylle* or *Dorfgeschichte* (village idyll). This mode of imagining traditional country life is usually, and plausibly, interpreted as a nostalgic reaction against the technological modernization brought by steam engines, railways and mass production. The readership catered for by such nostalgic tales were usually middle-class, second- or third- generation city-dwellers. What is more, there is in such idylls a radical division between the subject-matter and the intended readership: such idylls are *about* country folk but rarely intended to be read *by* them.[18] The German case offers also the best theoretical reflection upon this social opposition: Ferdinand Tönnies' classic sociological treatise *Gemeinschaft und Gesellschaft* ('Community and Society'), which defined two types of social structure, one, the *community*, traditional, with ingrained hierarchical bonds, exerting social control through familial and peer-group pressure, with intense mutual solidarity but little individual freedom; the other, *society*, loose-knit, modern, with social control effected through a professional apparatus of administration and law enforce- ment, with more individual freedom but less solidarity and greater anonymity. Tönnies' analysis is redolent with a nostalgia for a pre-Bismarck, pre-industrial Germany of romantic villages and traditional harmony; his contradistinction between the idyllic community and the faceless, modern society captured more than any other work a mood that in similar nostalgic vein was operative all over Europe; including Ireland. In Ireland, however, there was an additional, cultural factor playing into the opposition between society and community: the former was Anglo-Irish, the latter Gaelic-Irish, and more than in other countries, the opposition between high and low society still echoed an originary contrast between conquerors and conquered, colonizers and colonized. In the case of Ireland, the idyllic sociological view of community was in fact closer to the stance taken by Sir Henry Sumner Maine, whose lectures on *Village-communities in the east and west* (1871) were inspired by his imperial experiences as an Indian official (where his foremost assistant had been Whitley Stokes). Maine stated the tension between tradition and progress, exoticism and supremacism, nostalgia and hegemony, succinctly:

> It is by its indirect and for the most part unintended influence that the British power metamorphoses and dissolves the ideas and social forms underneath it; nor is there any expedient by which it can escape the duty of rebuilding upon its own principles that which it unwillingly destroys.[19]

Such overtones make the idyllic appreciation of the rustic community in Ireland particularly resonant. The habitual way of seeing the Irish cultural landscape was one of layers of conquests, beginning with the Firbolg and ending with the English presence; even the fairies themselves were representative of earlier strata in Ireland's settlement, in that they were seen as the remnants of the Tuatha Dé Danann. Fairies in Ireland appealed to the imagination for more reasons than were immediately obvious; they were representatives of a golden Otherworld for which the Irish peasantry was the privileged intermediary, having been half-ousted themselves from the quotidian reality of the here and now.

The best case to illustrate this is provided by the famous and indeed quintessential fairy poem, William Allingham's 'The fairies'. The opening and closing stanzas are identical and run as follows:

> Up the airy mountain,
> Down the rushy glen,
> We daren't go a-hunting
> For fear of little men.
> Wee folk, good folk,
> Trooping all together,
> Green jacket, red cap
> And white owl's feather!

These twee Victorian leprechauns, not unlike the plaster gnomes that push wheelbarrows in suburban gardens, are the descendants of the Tuatha Dé Danann. This is the story: When the Gaels conquered Ireland, that country was ruled by the Tuatha Dé Danann. The Gaels defeated the Tuatha in battle, and a rather unfair arbitration was imposed by the poet Amergin. Amergin divided Ireland in two, giving the part above ground to the Gaels and the subterranean half to the Tuatha Dé Danann. Accordingly, the Tuatha withdrew into the hollow hills, the fairy-forts, and merged with the chthonic spirits of Ireland, the fairies or *síde*.

That traditional story, while explaining the presence of fairies in Ireland, ends with the comment that the Tuatha, for each province of Ireland, left five of their number behind, who increased battles, struggles, strife and conflict among the Gaels. Accordingly, the fairies in Allingham's poem steal a human child and indeed inspire enough unease to keep people from going a-hunting in their domain. That domain ('airy mountains', 'rushy glen') is precisely the wilder part of the landscape, away from the settled fields and villages whence the ousted race would have been driven; consider the saying attributed to Catholic Ulster peasants, that after the Plantations 'the Protestants took the land and left us the views'. Allingham is not only echoing a popular superstition at this point, he follows the centuries-old discourse of the master race as it exorcizes some twinges of uneasiness in its ascendancy, by associating subdued aboriginals with imaginary fantasy-beings – both of them marginalized beyond the pale of normal, well-ordered life, beyond the pale of reality.

There seems to be something peculiarly interesting in the image of that ousted race, banished from the normalcy of daytime civilization, withdrawing into the nether fringes and the upper fringes of existence, *under*ground and into the *super*natural. From the wild and uncivilized parts of the landscape they threaten the settled order and rational plausibility of the victors' existence: changing babies in the cradle, luring people away from hearth, home and family. So powerful is this theme that we recognize its parallels even in the fictions of the modern, urban imagination – witness the Morlocks in Wells's *The time machine*, or the lurid crime-infested slums of Eugène Sue, Charles Dickens and Arthur Conan Doyle. An ordered social surface is threatened, here as in the Gaelic imagination, by an underground or underworld, a dark threat of dispossessed outcasts. Vico's notion that social inequality had its origin in an original conquest and ousting of the aboriginal inhabitants was spreading in the course of the nineteenth century,[20] and was present in poems like Michael Tormey's 'The ancient race', originally published in *The nation*. It was written in support of the Land League and in order to combat the drain of emigration:

> What shall become of the ancient race,
> The noble Celtic island race?
> Like cloud on cloud o'er the azure sky,
> When winter storms are loud and high,
> Their dark ships shadow the ocean's face –
> What shall become of the Celtic race?
>
> . . .
>
> They shall not go, the ancient race –
> They must not go, the ancient race!
> Come, gallant Celts, and take your stand –
> The League – the League will save the land;
> The land of faith – the land of grace,
> The land of Erin's ancient race![21]

Allingham's fairies are like Whiteboys or ousted Celts translated into dream-terms. The turn-of-the-century critic George Saintsbury was more insightful than he realized when he detected a Scots-Jacobite subtext in Allingham's poem: there is indeed an analogously phrased Scottish ballad which tauntingly states that the obedient citizens dare not go into mountain or glen for fear of encountering the unreformed Stuart faithful.[22] The analogy helps to draw our attention to the centre-periphery tensions within Allingham's poem, between social order and threatening wilderness where the ousted ones lurk. Samuel Ferguson's early fairy poems, 'The fairy thorn' and 'The fairy well' (though they are as close to Christina Rossetti's *Goblin market* as they are to Allingham) follow the same spatial distribution of an *Unheimlichkeit* at the picturesque margins of ordered society.[23] Again, the child-stealing fairies are dealt with in a Gothic manner in Le Fanu's chilling story, 'The child that went with the fairies' (which, by Le Fanu's standards, has an unusually high degree of Irish peasant local colour), and leads ultimately to Yeats's fairy poems.

The notion of ousted folk living at the fringes of society provides, I suggest, an imaginative link between fairy fashions and the Ascendancy's attitudes *vis-à-vis* the peasantry. Fairies have for their sounding board the theme of emigration, addressed by the *Nation* poet: the aboriginal Irish, having once wrested the land from the Tuatha Dé Danann, are in their turn being driven out, leaving trouble and strife behind in their passing. Ousted, like the Tuatha Dé Danann, the remaining Irish peasantry inhabit the infertile wild areas of the country, the airy mountains and the rushy glens where 'we daren't go a-hunting'.[24] Allingham thus sentimentalizes an idyllic version of the Irish popular tradition with its superstititons, while at the same time informing it with enough of an inkling of *Unheimlichkeit* or uncanniness to make it memorable and particularly effective; a similar evocation of the *unheimliche Heimat*, the vaguely uncanny community and its fairy superstitions, was to be made by Ferguson and the early Yeats in his fairy poems. Indeed, Allingham's poem was hugely successful and reverberated throughout the century, and triggered a Victorian mania for Fairies. An indication is given by the picture-book by Richard Doyle, *In Fairyland. A series of pictures from the Elf-World*,[25] which contained a dramatic poem by Allingham called 'A forest in Fairyland'. In this manner, the political tensions of Irish life are obscured, placed in the realm of fantasy and made subservient to an idyllic celebration of community and tradition.[26]

For that is what Allingham, like Croker, set out to do; his evocation of Ireland sees it exclusively as a community, as a *Gemeinschaft*, to the extent of denying the fact that Ireland was also a *Gesellschaft* or society. Allingham, as an Irishman, has no country; he only has a region, a homeland, a place of origin – in his case, the town of Ballyshannon. As he himself whimsically put it:

> An Englishman has a country
> A Scotchman has two
> An Irishman has none at all
> And doesn't know what to do.[27]

Again, when Allingham wrote an obituary on George Petrie, he defended Ireland on the grounds that it was fundamentally apolitical in that Irishmen 'had no country':

> These Irishmen, the salt of the country, have no sympathy with Fenianism or any other revolutionary scheme; but they know that in their fathers' or grandfathers' time Dublin was really a capital – Dublin was a centre. It is such no longer, and they have neither the wish nor the power to make London *their* centre. They are included, and glad to be included, in the circle of English laws; but they feel that intellectually, and also as a matter of sentiment, *they have no country*. Ireland has ceased to be a country, and England is not theirs.[28]

This is insightful indeed, and phrases from a unionist point of view precisely the opposition that Davis made repeatedly between a nation and a province;[29] Allingham turns Ireland into a region rather than a polity, a community rather than a society, an idyll rather than a problem. Accordingly, Ireland is a place without centre, without capital or political arena, and the quintessential Irish place is his native small town of Ballyshannon. Of this place he says, at the outset of his diary:

> No outrage at all, I believe, was done by the 'Whiteboys', or whatever they were; and in fact I have never, since I was born, known or heard of any political or secret society offence in our Town or its district. Ballyshannon was a sort of island of peace in my day, as it had been for generations, and I hope is carrying on the good tradition. We were far from centres of excitement and agitation; Dublin remote, the nearest considerable towns some twenty-five and thirty miles distant, and the scene of our county elections to Parliament (very seldom contested) still further away (17).

This idyllic celebration of Ballyshannon was to suffuse Allingham's Irishness, and was kept alive by the fact that Ballyshannon became, indeed, an Elsewhere, a distant mirage, as Allingham settled in London. Allingham shared with the peasantry at least the emotional pangs of emigration: he sighed for Ballyshannon when he was in London, and sighed for London when he was in Ballyshannon.[30] In the event he became a minor luminary in London literary life, a faithful hanger-on with Tennyson. Though he met Froude and Lecky, and their table-talk was occasionally of matters Irish, their is very little mention of Ireland, Irish history, or Irish politics in his diary; neither the Famine nor O'Connell rate as much as a mention, and the topic of emigration is merely treated in sentimental, quasi-folksy ballads where young men must leave their native – no, not their native land, but their native townland:

> Adieu to Belashanny! where I was bred and born;
> Go where I may, I'll think of you, as sure as night and morn
> [etc.]

This was based on the reality of the Famine and its aftermath, but sanitized into what was to become a favourite sentimental topic, the emigrant's farewell. Lady Dufferin had trail-blazed the genre ('Lament of the Irish emigrant', 'Terence's farewell'). Frequently such poems adopt the speaking voice of an artless, untaught but honest and endearing Irish persona, with whom the author sentimentally identifies.

There is a danger at this point of becoming one-sided. Allingham's relations with Ireland went beyond the mere sentimental evocation, though sentimental evocation was the most obvious aspect of it. He had a genuine paternalist concern for the idyll he loved, and defended it against the Saxonist dismissiveness of the Carlyles and Tennysons whom he admired. He even dared to stand up, albeit ever so diffidently, against his great model Tennyson; witness the following dialogue as represented in his diary

> T.   'Couldn't they blow up that horrible island with dynamite and carry it off in pieces – a long way off?'
> W.A.   'Why did the English go there?'
> T.   'Why did the Normans come to England? The Normans came over here and seized the country, and in a hundred years the English had forgotten all about it, and they were all living together on good terms.'
> (I demurred. T. went on, raising his voice). 'The same Normans went to Ireland, and the Irish with their damned unreasonableness are raging and foaming to this hour!'
> W.A.   'The Norman Duke had a claim on the crown of England.'
> T.   'No rightful claim.'
> W.A.   'But suppose all these to be bygones. You speak of a century, a short time in history – think of what Ireland had to complain of only in the last century – the penal laws, and the deliberate destruction of their growing industry by the English government: what do you say to that?'
> T.   'That was brutal! Our ancestors *were* horrible brutes! And the Kelts are very charming and sweet and poetic. I love their Ossians and their Finns and so forth – but they are most damnably unreasonable!'[31]

Damnably unreasonable, indeed. It must have taken courage, and some patriotism, to demur when Mr T. was on his high horse. Allingham also testified to his practical patriotism when he wrote a long didactic poem on agricultural unrest and its possible solutions, *Laurence Bloomfield in Ireland*. It was based on paternalist benevolence, full of sympathy for the disaffected natives but at the same time convinced that they must be guided by their betters, the upper classes. The system of landlordism is to be tempered by equity and honesty, but to remain intact. As the poet phrases it,

> I would that Irishmen could Ireland rule;
> They cannot, Irishmen are still at school.

Accordingly, the civilizing mission of the title hero, Laurence Bloomfield, consists in giving his violent and disaffected tenants, Ribbonmen one and all, a moral education, improving their lot with practical advice and the milk of human kindness. He gets them interested in the improvement of their character and of their lands, roads and waterways,

> And humbler Keltic genius gladly caught
> At every hint, and better'd what he taught.

Laurence Bloomfield was quoted by Gladstone in the House of Commons, and earned Allingham a civil list pension. Obviously the notion of pacifying Ireland into bucolic placidity, community-style, appealed to enlightened English policy-makers as a possible alternative to Tennysonian dynamite. After all, as Tönnies pointed out, power relations in a *community* are stable and go unquestioned; authority rests on the charisma acquired by that tradition of institutional stability which was already defended by Burke in his *Reflections on the revolution in France*. It is not for nothing that the invocation of an idyllic, rustic, traditional countryside as the backbone of the country's identity and stability belongs properly at the conservative end of the political spectrum; in that respect the notorious 'comely maidens' of de Valera are close analogues of the Georgians' celebration of 'England, my England'. Both derive political cohesion from a notion of the community, Tönnies-style, with its implied Burkean institutional stability.

The pleasant peasant

Rustic, ahistorical and apolitical community life, the idyllic view of Ireland as a mere province or backwater where timeless quaint characters go about their humble and picturesque ways, is obviously a conservative, unionist mode of idealizing Ireland, and as such squarely opposed to the glorification of ancient culture as performed in and around *The nation*. This idyllic trend tended to set up quaint characters ranging from Lover's 'Mother Machree' and Charles Lever's 'The Widow Malone' to Yeats's 'Moll Magee' and Alfred Perceval Graves's 'Father O'Flynn'. The machree and mavourneen register of mid-century peasant evocations continues well into the Celtic Twilight: witness Nora Hopper's poem 'A ghost', which begins 'Ochone, astore, and it's strange you've grown'.[32] The use of Kiltartanese or Hiberno-English as a literary medium, so prominent in Synge and Lady Gregory, is often traced back to Douglas Hyde's work; but Hyde himself continues an earlier vein of folklorism and ballad-collection, and the literary use of hibernicisms likewise goes back into the mid-century. The genre of peasant evocation begins at least as early as Lady Morgan, with her poem on 'Kate Kearney', whose name is still perpetuated by the Killarney tourist trade ('O, did you not hear of Kate Kearney? She lives on the banks of Killarney', etc.). A sample of the style may be given by the idyllic poem 'Rory O'More', by Lover.

> Young Rory O'More courted Kathleen bawn,
> He was bold as a hawk, and she soft as the dawn;

> He wish'd in his heart pretty Kathleen to please,
> And he thought the best way to do that was to tease.
> 'Now Rory, be aisy,' sweet Kathleen would cry,
> Reproof on her lips, but a smile in her eye;
> 'With your tricks I don't know, in troth, what I'm about;
> Faith, you've teased till I've put on my cloak inside out.'
> 'Oh! jewel,' says Rory, 'that same is the way
> You've thrated my heart for this many a day,
> And 'tis plaz'd that I am, and why not, to be sure?
> For 'tis all for good luck,' says bold Rory O'More.

I trust the reader will forgive me for not including the other two, equally excruciating stanzas. The type is obvious and well known from a multitude of more-or-less sentimental Victorian and post-Victorian sources, reaching as far as Percy French. It is the humorous invocation of a spalpeenish Irish character: likeable, unruly, cute; unpolished but charming, slightly mischievous but fundamentally un-threatening, exemplified by Dion Boucicault's Myles na Gopaleen or Somerville and Ross's Flurry Knox. Such a bit-of-a-lad aims to elicit the indulgent smile; his impish failure to conform to middle-class Victorian standards may be occasionally troublesome but never ill-intentioned, and can be paternalistically humoured on the grounds that such a character knows no better and is not bad at heart; in other words, child-like, boyish.

As many critics in recent years have pointed out, the British-Irish stereotyped opposition is genderized in that the Irish character is seen as fundamentally feminine, as opposed to the masculine qualities of England. But the notion of manhood, which England predicates to itself, has more antonyms than female alone: the opposite number of man can take the form 'beast' (and accordingly the Irish were made out as bestial subhumans in English representations from Giraldus to Fynes Moryson[33]), or it can take the form 'child' or 'boy'. Kipling's attitude to India and Indian natives, for instance, is crucially concerned with the combined values of masculinity and mature adulthood; and similarly, the sentimental Victorian evocation of colourful Irish characters appears to be constructed along an adult–juvenile axis – witness the paternalism of Allingham's *Laurence Bloomfield*. As we shall see, Irish nationalists were later to turn this polarity to rhetorical advantage, imputing the decrepitude of a Spenglerian old age to Britain and claiming for Ireland all the vigour of youth.

Many critics, again, have debated the question whether such colourful spalpeen characters were, or were not, Stage Irish. The term has been generally used in a loose, vaguely rhetorical sense in order to take certain authors, like Somerville and Ross, to task for supercilious stereotyping; those who would come to the defence of such authors would usually plead that their use of Irish characters was good-natured, positive, appreciative and therefore free from the taint of Stage-Irishness.

To use the term in such a loose way (as a Mark of the Beast, an anathema assigning a fatal flaw in a text's literary integrity) is unhelpful. It seems to presuppose that the prototype of the Stage Irishman is a malicious and unflattering, slanderous caricature, like the cartoons of gorilla-shaped Irish brutes in *Punch*.[34] Such usage is rhetorical rather than critical, and, as it happens, misplaced. For the Stage Irishman, if we mean by that term the stereotyped, Irish stock character as deployed in the English theatre, has since the mid-eighteenth century been represented in quite amiable, sentimental terms – a far cry from *Punch's* neanderthals. In fact, although some seventeenth- and early eighteenth-century plays deploy dim-witted, inferior, violent and detestable Irish characters, the typology seems to have been fixed rather by the far more numerous Stage Irish characters from the second half of the eighteenth century, when, in the context of the Sentimental Comedy, Irish characters were uniformly presented as rustic provincials or trusted servants, with little education but much honest and instinctively upright good sense. A favourite theatrical device was to contrast their bumbling manner and brogue-and-bull-ridden comic speech with their artless, naive honesty and goodness – usually in a context where other characters' polished manners and glib speech would indicate a duplicitous or foppish nature.[35]

In other words, the artless, honest, rustic Stage Irishman of sentimental comedy follows exactly the same typology as the pleasant peasant of the Anglo-Irish nineteenth century. There is a deep structure in his stereotyped characterization from which there is almost no escape. If, firstly, an Irishman is to be characterized in positive terms; and if, secondly, he is to be characterized in terms that oppose him to the polished middle-class values of genteel urban English society, then the result will be to forcibly gravitate towards a specific register. That register is shared by Macklin, Foote, Colman and other sentimental comedy-writers of the eighteenth century, by Morgan, Edgeworth, and Anglo-Irish novelists with their incidental Oirish background characters, up to and including Charles Kickham (witness Matt the Thrasher, in *Knocknagow*); it is shared by the humorous-sentimental Anglo-Irish Victorian versifiers from Charles Lover to A.P. Graves, shared by a nationalist playwright like Dion Boucicault or by Anglo-Irish gentry authors like the early Yeats and Somerville and Ross, and it is shared to no small extent by the Abbey Theatre's kitchen comedies. It seems spurious to exonerate some of those authors from the charge of Stage Irishism while damning others by it, since the distinction usually involves a vague sense as to whether or not one chooses to find a given author offensive or insufficiently sympathetic in his/her treatment of the Irish character. With the exception of playwrights like Synge or Shaw, who look the stereotype in the face and deliberately subvert it in their characterizations, all the authors above-mentioned use stereotyped Stage Irish characters, almost as automatically and unthinkingly as they used a twenty-six-letter alphabet. The stereotype governed their outlook and literary praxis as a self-evident part of the literary conventions within which they worked. Lover and Allingham are not the egregious perpetrators of sentimental Stage Irishism merely because they did so from a conservative, unionist perspective, as opposed to Kickham or Boucicault;

the point seems rather that with a nationalistically sympathetic audience, the stereotyped characters of nationalist authors like Kickham and Boucicault seem to have caused less offense. What makes a character Stage Irish is not the degree to which its characterization is stereotyped (for that is a constant from Macklin to Somerville and Ross), but the variable degree to which a changeable audience choses to accept the stereotype as sympathetic or obnoxious.

Ballads, verse, music

The folk element in Irish culture had by definition an important oral component, not only in the matter of prose tales but also in the realm of poetry and music. A very important part of Anglo-Irish poetry in the early to mid-century authenticates itself as Irish by insisting on a musical, or at least oral quality, as a melody, song or ballad. In part, this was more than a mere invocation: songs and balladry constituted, in fact, one of the most important cultural expressions of the Irish peasantry, and testifies to their uncertain position between two languages, English and Irish, and between the registers of orality and literacy. Many of the more important eighteenth-century poems and aislingí were, quite literally, *amhráin* (songs) rather than *dánta* (poems); there was a stock of favourite airs which would serve even for new texts as these were being composed by poems such as Seán Clárach Mac Domhnaill or Seán Ó Tuama an Ghrinn; many poems were glossed in manuscript as being 'to the air of' 'Caitlín Tirial', 'Eibhlín a Rún', 'An Cnóta Bán', or other evergreens. In such cases, poems as written texts should be seen as mere transcripts of performed song-lyrics, almost like the sleeve notes on records and discs. What is more, there was a lively trade in broadsheet ballads, where the words and possibly music of a newly-composed song would be sold to the appreciative audience, either as an aid to performance or as an *aide-mémoire* in learning it off by heart. Such broadsheets are among the more valuable remains of popular Irish literature of the early nineteenth century, and accordingly they figured largely in Croker's folklore interests.

But such printed manifestations of a living folk tradition were only the tip of the iceberg. The assumption was, that in daily life and domestic practice there was a wealth of performed, oral, non-recorded music and song which accordingly was vulnerable, subject to erosion and gradual disappearance; as a result, a harvesting instinct set at work (much as in the above-noted recording of folk- and fairy tales), and performers were invited to have their songs and music recorded.

The most important work in this field was done, of course, by Edward Bunting; his career is so well known that it scarcely needs elaborate treatment here. It originates in the patriotic climate of the 1780s and 1790s when harpers were invited at festivals to display their skill and repertoire. The famous harpers' festival in Belfast in 1792 took place partly under United Irish auspices; Bunting was present to transcribe the airs into musical notation. His first collection of

Irish music was published in 1796, in a venture which at the time must have seemed like a musical parallel to the literary antiquarianism of Charlotte Brooke and the *Reliques of ancient Irish poetry*.

But Bunting's career and influence outlasted the patriotic and United Irish enthusiasm of the 1790s. He continued his collection and investigation of Irish music until the mid-nineteenth century, publishing a second collection of Irish airs in 1809, and a third one, dedicated with permission to Queen Victoria, in 1840. That last collection incorporated, in its learned introduction, work by Samuel Ferguson and George Petrie, who himself was a good amateur musician and a great lover of Irish music. Alongside all his other accomplishments in the fields of landscape painting and archaeology, Petrie continued the collection work of Bunting and published his own *Collection of the ancient music of Ireland* in 1855.

Nor is that just of musicological importance. Bunting's first collection also had the important side effect of triggering the work of Thomas Moore on his *Irish melodies*. It may even be said that Moore's *Melodies* were an application, in the field of poetry, of Bunting's musical collection. As I have pointed out earlier, Moore was to present his *Melodies* as in part a project in musical antiquarianism, recording and preserving beautiful airs by cloaking them in his verse. For that reason also, it has become a commonplace in Moore criticism that the *Melodies* cannot be appreciated if the words only are read off the printed page – they need the vocalization and their musical setting to stand out in their true colours; even the metre and the scanning of many *Melodies* would be wrong if one weren't given the melodic metre and rhythm.

Bunting, for one, was less impressed with Moore's strong claim to orality, and his way of grafting Regency verse onto the oral music tradition of native Ireland. He felt that Moore had ransacked his work for his own purposes (of the sixteen first numbers of Moore's *Melodies*, eleven were taken from Bunting), and that indeed Moore was unfaithful to the musical character of the original airs. In Bunting's view, Moore had tampered with them and submitted them to the uncongenial demands of verbal elegance. This he set forth with barely-contained animus in his introduction to the third collection of ancient music, which appeared in 1840; reminiscing about his first, 1796 volume, he reflected:

> The Editor was gratified to find out that the tunes which had thus for the first time been brought before the public, were soon adopted as vehicles for the most beautiful popular songs that have perhaps ever been composed by any lyric poet. [However, many airs] now assumed a new dress – one, indeed, in point of poetic diction and classical ornament infinitely more elegant than they had ever worn before – under the hands of Mr. Moore; but the Editor saw with pain, and still deplores the fact, that [. . .] instead of the words being adapted to the tune, the tune was too often adapted to the words, a solecism which could never have happened had the reputation of the writer not been so great as at once to carry the tunes he deigned to make use of altogether out of their old sphere among the simple and tradition-loving people of the country.

Not only does it cause Bunting some 'chagrin' to see 'the old national music' 'thus unworthily handled and sent abroad throughout the whole world in a dress so unlike its native garb' – there is also a strong endorsement of authenticity over refinement. Traditional music, in its authentic, demotic setting, may not be as refined as Moore's polished treatment, but it deserves preference because it is a truer record of the Irish people's cultural achievement in this field. Bunting, in other words, defends anthropological purism against commercial adaptation; he and Moore are engaged in contention for the laurels of authentic Irishness, Moore having (in Bunting's view, spuriously) cashed in on the Irishness of the *Melodies*. In other words, the contested aim is to establish a genuine Irish authentication of one's cultural pursuits.[36] Accordingly, Bunting is at pains to establish both his acquaintance with the demotic, popular tradition of music performance, from which he has gleaned his material, and the ancient roots of that material itself. What is more, Bunting tried to protect his melodies from what he saw as Moore's hijacks by supplying words to them and not leaving that field open to the competition; the second volume of 1809 contains versifications with twenty melodies, and Bunting was especially proud to have enlisted the services of the (then famous, now forgotten) poet Thomas Campbell in four instances. Nine other melodies had words by one Miss Balfour, and the collection also included Swift's version of *Pléaráca na Ruarcach*. The claim to authenticity was bolstered by the (somewhat doubtful) assertion that these versifications were based on literal translations of the original Irish.[37]

Irish music was to remain an important cultural pursuit. It had from early days onwards been highly appreciated, even among those who were unsympathetic to Ireland in general, it combined native particularism with apolitical present-day appeal and frequently invoked the affecting and titillating notion that a great tradition was lingering in neglect, like an old manuscript in a forgotten attic, half-forgotten but still there to be salvaged. The figure of Carolan had begun to acquire mythical proportions in the second half of the eighteenth century, and was indeed the spiritually presiding genius over the harp festivals of Granard and Belfast, as well as occupying a centrally important place in Joseph Cooper Walker's *Historical memoir of the Irish bards*. Carolan was a symbolically cardinal figure, mediating between the pauperized native culture of Penal Ireland and the great aristocratic clan society of the Middle Ages; in that respect he was a close parallel to that other towering figure of native culture struggling against decline, Charles O'Conor of Belanagar (who had been a frequent host to Carolan). The figure of Carolan was to be assiduously cultivated in the decades before and after the Union, by Bunting and others, and became the prototype for the romantic image of the Gaelic artist, up to and including Raftery. Popular ballads refer to 'Old Carolan with his golden harp',[38] Lady Morgan had put up a plaque to his memory in St. Patrick's Cathedral, and a large part of Hardiman's *Irish minstrelsy* was taken up with Carolan material. What is more, although the harp was to be revived as a traditional instrument in various Celtic countries, Wales foremost among them, it was an instrument which was somehow specifically predicated to Ireland.[39] An instrument spuriously known as 'Brian Ború's harp' was (and still is) carefully kept in the collection of Trinity College Dublin, while Carolan's harp was a prized heirloom of the Roscommon O'Conors (the instrument is still kept in Clonalis House, Castlerea). We have seen how 'the voice of Ireland' was constantly couched in terms of harpistry in Moore's *Melodies*; the United Irishmen made use of the emblem of the harp, and there is even the heraldic canonicity of the harp as the kingdom of Ireland's emblem (still present in the coat of arms of the British monarch). The harp as an icon counterbalanced the denigration of Ireland as a land of Paddies and potatoes, and testified to a cultural heritage that dovetailed with the antiquity of Apollo's lyre and the biblical King David. The harp is the one nineteenth-century national symbol which has maintained widespread currency in official twentieth-century iconography, on coins and other state emblems.

Throughout the nineteenth century, the collection of folk music occupies an important place in the cultivation of Ireland's heritage. Such musical interest reinforced the emphasis on orality and performance among editors and writers of Irish materials, which tended to gravitate to the register of songs and ballads rather than poetry. The poets of *The nation* fully shared in this tendency, in that most of their nationalistic poems were more properly songs, set to a melody and intended to be sung as such.

I have indicated how, in the second half of the century, popular histories and folktale collections became an intense field of publishing activity, dipping again and again into the Danaids' Vat of the Irish past and the Irish peasantry to tell the ancient myth, the history and the stories of Ireland over and over again, with new versions, and re-editions, or sequels and continuations, of earlier versions. A similar activity is noticeable with regard to the reservoirs of Irish poetry and balladry. These fields (history, balladry, and folklore) have some overlap, of course: the tale of Fionn Mac Cumhaill can be told in a book on Irish history, a book of Irish folk and fairy tales, or (in verse form) in a book of Irish ballads. We have already seen how Davis wanted to create a 'ballad history of Ireland' so as to capitalize on the appeal of rousing verse (the phenomenal success of Gavan Duffy's *Ballad poetry of Ireland*, 1845, proving his point); in the event, balladry was to become a publishing obsession no less intense than the one with histories or folk- and fairytales. Crofton Croker himself published *Popular songs of Ireland* (1839), and, for the antiquarian Percy Society, *Historical songs of Ireland illustrative of the revolutionary struggle between James II and William III* (1840) as well as a four-part collection of *Popular songs illustrative of the French invasions of Ireland* (1845–1847). The bookseller John O'Daly published *The Irish language miscellany: being a selection of poems by the Munster bards of the last century* in 1876; more famously, the selfsame O'Daly had earlier collaborated with Edward Walsh on *Reliques of Irish Jacobite poetry, with biographical sketches of the authors, interlinear literal translations, and historical notes* (1844, 2nd ed. 1866), and with Charles Mangan on *The poets and poetry of Munster: A selection of Irish songs by the poets of the last century* (1849, 2nd ed. 1850, 3rd ed. 1883; a second series, by

George Sigerson under the pseudonym Erionnach, appeared in 1860). Edward Walsh, a *Nation* poet, collected *Irish popular songs with English metrical translations and introductory remarks* (1847, 2nd. 1883). M.J. Barry's *The songs of Ireland* knew three editions (1845, 1846, 1869), and Denis Florence MacCarthy tried the market with his *Book of Irish ballads* (1846). Samuel Lover chimed in with *The lyrics of Ireland* and *Poems of Ireland* (1858), and a selection of Hardiman, Lover and MacCarthy was brought out in New York in 1868 (*The poets and poetry of Ireland*).[40]

Ultimately, these ballad books were to become an important influence on the literary revival of the end of the century: witness, not only Ferguson's *Lays of the western Gael* (1865), but also Douglas Hyde's *Abhráin grádh Chúige Chonnacht, or the love songs of Connacht* (1893) and his *Abhráin Dhiadha Chúige Chonnacht, or the religious songs of Connacht* (initially serialized in the *New Ireland Review*, 1895–97).

As in the case of Glorvina's songs in *The wild Irish girl*, such balladry transcends the oppositions between orality and literacy, and brings the literate culture of the ancient Gaels and the Dublin book trade together with the oral folk culture of the contemporary peasantry. It propagates, through the medium of printed books, the communitarian echoes of an earlier, oral Ireland, which is accordingly lyrical and emotionally direct.[41] The ongoing presence of Irish verse and song as a performed, oral medium is still a powerful factor in the work of Joyce – witness 'The lass of Aughrim' in 'The dead',[42] or the snippets of lyrics floating through *Ulysses* and *Finnegans Wake*. But in order to establish the political charge of these exercises in ballad collection, it is relevant first of all to return to the memorable case of one of the genre's prototypes: James Hardiman's *Irish minstrelsy* (1831), which was to provoke Ferguson's counter-versions ultimately published in *Lays of the western Gael* (1865).

Hardiman, Ferguson and the Gaels

We have already come across the name of James Hardiman as the historian of Galway and as the contributor on cartographical and other MS material in the Royal Irish Academy (above, p. 107). Hardiman's interests took him to literary history and balladry, of which he prepared an important anthology; it was an eloquent stance against the folklorism of Crofton Croker, in that it brought out the fact that Ireland's oral, traditional culture was not exclusively the province of a quaintly naive, superstititous peasantry. The material that Hardiman brought together, for all that it was oral and hailed from the non-canonical outer margins of what was considered high culture, was at the same time refined, subtle, and civilized – anything but folksy. Oral culture was in Hardiman's collection[43] presented as 'Bardic remains' and thus derived from a Gaelic-aristocratic background; the introduction, which relied heavily on the work of O'Conor of Stowe, emphasized the ancient establishment of *belles lettres* in Ireland. The lyrics were presented in the original Irish (where Hardiman had received help from James Scurry as well as an ex-Professor of Irish at Maynooth, Martin Loftus, and a priest from Bandon, Daniel O'Sullivan). Among the translators who provided English versified versions accompanying the Gaelic originals was none other than John D'Alton, as well as Thomas Furlong, Henry Grattan Curran, William Hamilton Drummond and Edward Lawson.

Hardiman's *Irish minstrelsy* was doubtless the most important collection of Irish original literature since the days of Charlotte Brooke; but whereas Brooke's concern had been antiquarian, with a strong emphasis on older, mythical (Ossianic) material, Hardiman dealt with remains from the historical period, largely the eighteenth century. It stands, as such, at the beginning of a supremely important tradition in Irish letters where the living or recent native tradition is collected and edited so as to provide inspiration and a better cultural self-awareness to the Irish public at large. Hardiman's *Irish minstrelsy* is followed up and echoed in this respect by Mangan and O'Daly's *Poets and poetry of Munster* (1849), Ferguson's *Lays of the western Gael* (1865), Douglas Hyde's *Abhráin grádh Chúige Chonnacht*, 1893), up to and including Seán Ó Tuama's and Thomas Kinsella's *An Duanaire: Poems of the dispossessed* (1981).

The collection consists of four parts. Material by Carolan is given pride of place as part one, sentimental song makes up part two, and a selection of 'odes and elegies' closes the anthology. The most explosive portion was doubtless the third part, which contained 'Jacobite relics' – the sort of material which fomented rebellion and resistance, which fed into the subversive broadsheet tradition disapprovingly registered by Crofton Croker; the sort of thing which Allingham tried to palliate by providing harmless alternatives. The anti-English *aislingí* of penal times were now reproduced in full, and the Hidden Ireland was finally allowed to reach the ears of the Irish public-at-large in its own voice. Coming, as it did, hot on the heels of Catholic Emancipation and amidst still-continuing agrarian unrest, it conjured up a most threatening picture: that of a peasantry which was vocal, politically informed and conscious, disaffected and anything but naive, anything but satisfied with their humble lot in life. It showed that the current stereotypes were all wrong: neither were the Whiteboys, Rockites and rebels mere violent, uneducated brutes, nor were the singsonging and story-telling peasantry as harmlessly picturesque and politically naive, as Croker, Allingham and Lover would have it. The folk tradition of the peasantry turned out to be a tradition, not just of stories and soothsayings, pookahs and leprechauns, but a tradition of resistance, an eloquent voice against English and Protestant domination.

Nor did Hardiman bother to disguise that aspect of his anthology. His introduction to the anthology as a whole opposed native literacy to English oppression and ruination, celebrating 'the ancient bards of Ireland' as being champions 'deserving of national honour'; and the introduction to the section containing the Jacobite material reviewed Irish history since Henry II in a scathing manner, denouncing English duplicity and cruelty. In short, Hardiman's anti-English stance fully shared the outlook of the poems themselves.[44] What was more explosive still, the tradition of popular resistance was explicitly extended to the present day, and Hardiman stated in so many words that he placed his enterprise in the context of the romantic revival of folk poetry and its attendant growth of national awareness. In other words, Hardiman invoked Jacobite auspices to formulate a programme of Romantic nationalism; he did so by citing the example of the Greek fight against Turkish oppression, which had interested Europeans deeply for the past decade (witness Byron's help and that of the Philhellenes) and which had been bolstered by the publication in Paris, in 1824, of a collection entitled *Chants populaires de la Grèce moderne*. It was this collection that Hardiman invoked as an example for his own enterprise, going as far as to draw parallels between Greek-Turkish and Irish-English relations:

> The political situation of the Irish with respect to England, has been frequently compared with that of the Greeks in their relation to Turkey. [. . .] The bards of these devoted nations have nearly in the same manner embodied in their songs the feelings of the conquered and oppressed people of both countries; but the cry of suffering humanity is the same in every age and clime. [. . .] The former were oppressed by the Turks, the latter by Christians, and to the shame of these English Christians be it recorded, that in the exercise of their tyrannic sway of Ireland, they have excelled the most furious followers of Mahomet in Greece (2: 3–5).

There is, then, no other way of seeing Hardiman's enterprise than as a nationalist one; indeed, in its combination of oral material and a historical interest, in its reliance on the demotic mass of the people as the true cultural representatives of the nation, in its invocation of the right to self-determination, and in its tendency to draw international parallels between European patterns of oppression, Hardiman's book seems the very prototype of romantic nationalism in Ireland. It predates the outlook of *The nation* by more than a decade, comes precisely at the moment when O'Connell was transforming his agitation for Catholic Emancipation into a movement for Repeal of the Union, and is the cultural-historical counterpart to O'Connell's constitutional-political enterprise. The violent anger which penal oppression had instilled into Hardiman's glosses and explanatory footnotes was only nominally assuaged by the passing of Catholic Emancipation, and there is something disingenuous about the final footnote:

> Ungrateful, indeed, must have been the task [i.e., of adding these explanatory notes, JL], to turn over the crimsoned annals of a people, whose calamities have classed them amongst the most persecuted of mankind. One great consolation, however, was afforded, by the reflection that the day of persecution has passed away; that the children of the tyrant and the slave, the oppressor and the oppressed, now mingle, without distinction, in the great mass of society; and that the angry passions which formerly raged with violence, are generally and rapidly declining. May no untoward circumstance occur to interrupt this happy procedure; and, in the language of one of out modern bards,

'May Erin's sons, of every caste,
Be Irishmen, from first to last,
Nor name or creed divide them' (2:168–169).

What we see at work here is precisely the mechanism which Oliver MacDonagh has outlined so deftly as 'the Irish habit of historical thought', which was to suffuse the doctrine of Irish nationalism throughout the nineteenth and twentieth centuries.[45] The importance of remembrancing, so eloquently stated by Moore's melodies, means that the past, whenever it is contemplated in all its injustice and brutality, inspires fresh generations with renewed rancour and indignation, and that the improvements of the present are at best but fragile ways of glossing over the deep-seated traumas, constantly threatened by the continuing legacy of remembered hostility and violence. In this outlook, the past is by no means a foreign country; the past is unfinished business, neither forgiven nor forgotten.

This is not just an Irish problem, of course. When Renan, in 1881, offered his valuable thoughts on what constitutes a nation (to wit, the implicit voluntary willingness of the people concerned to endorse and accept a shared identity), he pointed out that the shared sense of identity might always hide ancient divisions and oppressions at its historical roots; that the national idea is a master-plot dispensed by an élite. Renan concludes that a shared national sense of identity must ignore these cracks, that it can only exist on the basis of a modicum of 'historical ignorance and even historical error' (see motto at the beginning of this book); and indeed he has been proved right in his misgivings about the growth of historical discovery in that the development of historical awareness since 1881 has given strong arguments to various minorities across Europe to start taking exception to their national position. Conservative politics, so deeply concerned with a harmonic, communitarian model of society, have always stressed the importance of letting bygones be bygones. The most powerful expression of this principle had come from none other than Edmund Burke, who, in the *Reflections on the revolution in France*, had criticized the revolution's tendency to settle old scores, to bring the nobility and the church finally to task for the past centuries of exploitation. In Burke's view, such a cult of collective responsibility directly threatened the cohesion of the social fabric, and he memorably laid down the distinction between personal and collective accountability. Collective guilt cannot, in Burke's view, outlast the lifetime of the individuals concerned. That was the conservative attitude underlying *Punch's* humorous rejoinder to Thomas Moore: 'Let Erin forget'.[46]

In Hardiman's case, that view is emphatically set aside. Collective guilt is remembered, shared oppression held up as an example, and an ethical debit-credit relation is used to establish continuity between past and present. This tendency was to be an indispensable ingredient in Irish nationalism, right down to the invocation of the dead generations, quoted, under God, as the most important legitimizing authority in Pearse's 1916 Proclamation of the Irish Republic.

It was precisely this aspect of Hardiman's work which conservative, unionist opinion took its most violent exception to. In his famous four-part review of Hardiman's collection for the *Dublin University magazine*,[47] Samuel Ferguson engaged in a strenuous and brilliantly-argued contest for the question as to who could claim to be the natural heir and spokesman for the dead generations and ancient Ireland in general. What gives Hardiman, of all people, the right to impose on 'Erin's sons', from first to last, a standard as to what it takes to be 'Irishmen'? What gives Hardiman, of all people, the right to claim for his own (to the exclusion of other persuasions in Irish society) the heritage of ancient Gaelic culture? Why should Irish Catholic nationalism be exclusively allowed to trace its parentage back to the native tradition, condemning all other persuasions in Irish society to a hateful lineage of foreigners and alien oppressors? The review flings down a proud challenge at anyone presuming to interpose himself between the Protestant Anglo-Irish intellectual Ferguson, and that Irish past which he, Ferguson, chooses to affiliate to. And there was nothing which angered Ferguson so much as Hardiman's half-hearted acknowledgement of Catholic Emancipation:

> [Hardiman] had written the greater portion of his notes and comments previous to Catholic emancipation; and, in them, had freely indulged in what those who would agree with Mr Moore would denominate natural indignation against England and the English. [. . .] [But even now, Hardiman] does not expunge an expression of inveterate and unchangeable hatred of Clan Luther, and the Saxon, but disfigures his book, and disgraces himself by flinging in the teeth of his manumission, the whole miserly hoardings of his hatred when a slave (p. 464).

Ferguson's review (each of its four parts dealing with one of the sections in Hardiman's anthology) accordingly follows a dual track: one, to congratulate Hardiman and to celebrate his way of making the native Irish tradition available to a latter-day reading public; the other, to challenge the Catholic, nationalist complexion that the Irish native tradition acquires in Hardiman's presentation, and to advance an alternative mode of coming to terms with this heritage from the past. The review is one of Ferguson's masterpieces (though overly florid and pugnacious in places; it is eighty-four pages long and was written when the author was twenty-four years old). In order to demonstrate his right to participate in the cultivation and appropriation of the native tradition, Ferguson adds a number of translations of his own, as opposed to the ones contained in Hardiman's anthology which he dismisses as deficient in 'poetical art', though not in 'poetical feeling'. These translations are the first efforts at what Ferguson was to publish much later as *Lays of the western Gael* (1865).[48] In order to recuperate a stake in the national, native tradition, Hardiman praises the selection of ancient material throughout while reserving his opprobrium for the translations. These are called 'spurious, puerile, unclassical – lamentably bad' and are blamed for attempting 'to elevate the tone of the original to a pitch of refined poetic art altogether foreign from the whole genius and *rationale* of its composition'

(p. 454n., p. 455n.). In other words, whereas Hardiman's translators had rendered the material according to contemporary taste, Ferguson sees this as a betrayal of the primitive, artless and spontaneous vigour of the originals. To that extent he follows Bunting's preference of genuineness over contemporary appeal.[49] That is as may be; indeed Ferguson's translations read better nowadays, to this author at least, than the ones he chided; but a political *parti-pris* in this criticism comes out when he exempts Drummond, among the translators, from his wrath. 'Perhaps we are prejudiced in Dr. Drummond's favour, in consequence of the absence of anything like political hatred or sectarian malignity in his contributions.'[50] Accordingly, also, Ferguson refuses to see Roisín Dubh as a national allegory, choosing instead to take a provocatively Orangist view: it is a poem describing the plight of a love-stricken priest, who is caught between his tender passion and his vow of celibacy. Ferguson concludes with harsh, sectarian humour:

> We sympathize with the priest's passion, we pity his predicament; but we despise his dispensatory expedients, and give him one parting advice, to pitch his vows to the Pope, the Pope to purgatory, marry his black rose-bud, and take a curacy from the next Protestant rector.[51]

Such occasional slips into bigotry fundamentally invalidate Ferguson's criticism of Hardiman. Hardiman is blamed for sectarianism and 'a spirit of petty anti-Anglicanism' (p. 515); yet what Ferguson offers instead is not some sense of trans-sectarian national harmony, but rather an alternative, aristocratic-sectarian partiality. True, there is some justification in his complaint that 'Mr Hardiman has interposed between us and our countrymen at large' (p. 516), and that 'he certainly holds out no very alluring prospect of reconciliation' (p. 515); and Ferguson hits the nail on the head when he points out that Hardiman, in alienating non-Catholics, perpetuates the very divisions he denounces:

> Such, at least, is our impression of Mr. Hardiman's feeling towards that portion of his countrymen [the Protestants], with whom we join in preferring things as they are, to things as we apprehend his party's design would make them. It has ever been the policy of that party to affect the monopoly of native Irish sympathies, and, standing between the aristocracy and the people, to intercept the best charities of society (p. 516).

– but what does Ferguson offer by way of an alternative? In voicing the attitude of the 'aristocracy', he speaks, not of 'fellow-countrymen', but of 'natives' and 'peasantry', as a charming but backward primitive society swayed by ingrained papist loyalty; he invariably uses the third person, and describes native Ireland as something to be *led* and *improved* (Ferguson calls for 'Education based upon the only true basis – Scriptural education', 448). Surely he cannot presume to blame nationalists for not entertaining a similar sense of superiority, for engaging in a closer identification with the peasant portion of society; nor is it fair on

Ferguson's part to speak of 'interposing' when nationalists choose not to share his aloofness.

There is also some disingenuousness in Ferguson's anger at Hardiman's denunications of penal oppression, charging him with 'fretful, querulous, undignified malice' and 'rancorous and puerile malignity' (p. 515). Ferguson is particularly outraged, as we have seen, at the fact that Hardiman did not mitigate his aggressive anti-English glosses after the enactment of Catholic Emancipation. But does he mean to imply that historians may no longer indict the eighteenth-century penal laws, since these laws are now revoked? Is Catholic Emancipation to be seen as a retroactive cancelling of all past sectarian injustice, which should therefore henceforth remain unmentionable, smothered under the cover of historical oblivion in the name of reconciliation?

Part of the animus is undoubtedly inspired by Ferguson's refusal to be shut out from the solidarity between Hardiman and the native tradition. Ferguson was deeply and sympathetically interested in the Irish past, and felt alienated from his own loyalty by Hardiman's enterprise. Witness the florid closing paragraph of his review, in which Ferguson triumphantly congratulates himself in almost duelistic terms at having savaged Hardiman, at having driven him from the field, and having uprooted his presumptions. The fierce and feverish rhetoric bespeaks an eagerness to claim his title to a shared Irish culture and Irish history:

> Still great as is our remorse for Mr. Hardiman at death's door [i.e., so severely battered by the hammering Ferguson has given him], greater, we confess, would have been our chagrin had he, in spite of us, remained the mote in Ireland's eye. [. . .] and therefore, while weeping Mr. Hardiman's misfortune, we smile to behold our successful dislodgment of so formidable an eyesore, and take leave of our companion through some months, with a sincere hope that we may meet him again in his walk of native literature, even though he should sow his path with brambles as thorny as those which we have been trying to weed away from about the Irish Minstrelsy.[52]

But how, precisely, does Ferguson himself see the native tradition and its verse remains? In Ferguson's appreciation of Irish popular poetry, there is a good deal of patronizing primitivism. The rapturous lyricism of the love poems is linked to the habit of the peasantry of marrying early, undaunted by the material inexpedience of such rashness: the young couples may not be able to live decently, but Irish swains and maidens are 'unconscious of the shame of poverty'.[53] There is room for a condescending smile at this reckless charm-in-rags: 'If he but justify his imprudence in such songs as Mary Chuisle and Ellen a Roon, we could forgive him' (p. 167).

This attitude of paternalist sympathy towards a charming but untrustworthy populace leads to a very complex stance when Ferguson has to face the fact that much Irish poetry, regardless of the way Hardiman chooses to gloss or translate it, is rebellious or seditious in nature. Ferguson, in trying to account for the enduring loyalty to native traditions and to the Stuart cause, again marshalls some condescending national psychology to his aid: the Irish character is marked by a tendency towards blind loyalty, as opposed to the more feudal, English type; 'In fact, this self-encumbering excess of devotion characterizes every operation of Irish loyalty'. It means that, unlike England, Ireland never developed a parliamentary check on monarchical power; instead there was the abject celebration of the chief's supremacy in bardic poetry. It accounts for the stubborn Catholicism of the country.

> On concluding such a record of misplaced and insulated loyalty, obstructing its own exercise by its own excess, and pressing that valour and fortitude which should have been applied to the preservation of the country, into the vexatious service of petty feuds and self-consuming factions, who can avoid lamenting the perversion of so noble, but so dangerous, a quality of the Irish heart? Had it centered on a monarch, it would have given the means of a vigorous and healthy government; but it never centered on a monarch; nothing but the tremendous engine of Roman Catholicism could ever collect or fire it (p. 463).

This attitude is very close to the bigotry of someone like Tennyson ('The Kelts are so utterly unreasonable! The stupid clumsy Englishman – knock him down, kick him under the tail, kick him under the chin, do anything to him, he gets on his legs again and goes on; the Kelt rages and shrieks and tears everything to pieces!'[54]) Given such a sense of radical difference, why should Ferguson wish to identify with native Ireland at all?

Yet the need for a national, and *Irish*, identification is there. At the very outset of the review, it is stated that 'We will not suffer two of the finest races of men in the world, the Catholic and Protestant, or the Milesian and Anglo-Irish, to be duped into mutual hatred by the tale-bearing go-betweens [. . .]' (p. 457); and remarkably, in the very year that Ferguson savaged Hardiman, he himself began a series of historical tales in the selfsame *Dublin University magazine* under the title *Hibernian nights' entertainments*,[55] evoking the courage and derring-do of Red Hugh O'Donnell in his brave fight against English oppression, and lovingly adding a wealth of mythological and antiquarian detail, interpolating digressive myths and tales. The *Hibernian nights' entertainments* are a remarkable effort at that almost-impossible genre, an Irish historical novel; Ferguson as much as announces this project in the first part of the Hardiman review, when he recounts the story of Red Hugh (pp. 158–9). What is more, he tends to conclude the various instalments of that review with poignant celebrations of Ireland and his loyalty to that country. The first installment ends on an elegiac appreciation of Carolan ('the last flicker of the expiring light, and all has been darkness since'), followed by a quotation of Moore's 'The harp that once' (p. 477); the third part ends with his translation of Mac Conmara's *Ban-chnoic Éireann óigh* ('The fair hills of Holy Ireland'), concluding this homage with the addition *ERIN GO BRAGH!* (p. 467), and the same poem in a slightly different translation also concludes his final selection of translated specimens (p. 542).

The reiterated choice of 'The fair hills of holy Ireland' as Ferguson's own focus of Irish identity and Irish loyalty is significant. It is already present in the review's opening sentence, which pre-echoes its closure and announces its main theme: 'O ye fair hills of holy Ireland, who is he who ventures to stand between us and your Catholic sons' goodwill?' (p. 465). This bespeaks a sense of Ireland which is in the first place territorial: Ireland is a *country*. It is this sense of place which unites the loyalties of Milesian and Anglo-Irish:

> This sacred loyalty [the native love of the country] we have reserved for our con-
> clusion, as a green spot of neutral ground, where all parties may meet in kindness,
> and part in peace. We have prosecuted our inquiry after the nature of Irish senti-
> ment through many a perplexing and many dangerous topic, 'per ignes suppositos
> cineri doloso'. Grateful to our parched feet is the dewy sward of shamrocks; and
> here, standing on the firm ground of love for our country, we call for a chorus of
> Irishmen of all denominations to 'The Fair Hills of Holy Ireland' (p. 467).

Sentiment like this makes it clear why the topographical labour of love that was undertaken by the Ordnance Survey should have been invested with so much hope and enthusiasm, not in the last place by Ferguson himself.[56] Indeed, given the political, religious and even ethnic dividedness of Irish society, the shared sense of place is one of the few neutral points of non-contentious loyalty left, and it is no coincidence that the great career of Petrie should have begun in landscape painting.

Ferguson's political attitude emphatically endorsed, as we have seen, the Protestant Ascendancy. It appears that he would ideally like to see Ireland as another Scotland, Dublin as another Edinburgh: both countries led by a British-oriented, loyalist and English-speaking elite centered, next to London, on their own metropolis, loyal to their British status but proud of their non-English heritage, bound in benevolent paternalism to their hinterland of highland peasantry. As an Ulsterman, Ferguson seems to have been more open to the notion of Ireland and Scotland as sister kingdoms, rather than seeing the relations with Britain purely as Irish-English ones.[57] He was a committed Protestant and a firm aristocrat, i.e., a believer in the justness of hierarchical divisions of society. What is more, he endorses the post-Romantic belief in ethnic, inborn national character in racial-essentialist terms:

> we believe that great proportion of the characteristics of a people are [sic] inherent,
> not fictitious; and that there are as essential differences between the genius's as
> between the physical appearances of nations. We believe that no dissipating
> continuance of defeat, danger, famine, or misgovernment, could ever, without the
> absolute infusion of Milesian blood, Hibernicize the English peasant; and that no
> stultifying operation of mere security, plenty, or laborious regularity could ever,
> without actual physical transsubstantiation, reduce the native Irishman to the
> stolid standard of the sober Saxon (p. 154–5).

Indeed, Ferguson's attitude in the growing debate between Saxonists and Celticists is quite remarkable, and, again, bespeaks his desire of the right to identify with Ireland. In an (anonymous) article in the *Dublin University magazine* in 1852, Ferguson argues the astounding case that it is wrong to call the Milesian population of Ireland Celtic. In fact, the Irish Milesians, so far from being the opposites of the English Saxons, are themselves of Gothic (i.e., Germanic) descent! The true Celts of Ireland were a bronze age culture of megalith-builders (so Ferguson's case goes), who were ousted by the iron-age Gothic Milesians, their inferiors in civility but more efficient at warfare. This idiosyncratic juggling of ethnic terminology effectively muddles the terms of the racist Irish-English opposition as it was conducted at the time; it allows Ferguson to celebrate the greatness of the ancient Celts without having to kowtow to Ireland's latter-day, boorish Milesians, and it means that ethnically speaking, Milesians and Anglo-Irish are both representative of the same category, neither having a superior title to the other in claiming right of presence. In the racial layering of the often-captured territory of Ireland, the older layers have become mere story: Tuatha Dé Danann have become Allingham's fairies, the Celts have become Ferguson's gold-working dolmen-builders, and the Anglo-Irish are no less legitimate a presence than the Gaelic-speaking peasantry themselves; Ferguson's implicit parallel is the Saxon conquest of Celtic Britain, which was being glorified in the neighbouring isle by Kemble, Froude, Freeman and Green. Ferguson's model divorces the present-day peasantry from Ireland's ancient civilization and gives both 'races' of modern Ireland (Milesian and Anglo-Irish, Gothic one and all) an equal footing in their Irishness.[58]

This is very much Ferguson's idiosyncrasy, his attempt to establish his own national footing in Irish-cum-Protestant terms; but even in its very idiosyncrasy, it formulates a sense of contradiction which was to haunt the Irish national awareness through the next half-century. Essential Irishness should be contra-dictorily manifested in the two idealized but irreconcilable notions of *past and peasant*: the ancient, aristocratic society of pre-Norman Ireland, and the present-day, demotic community of the peasantry.

Idyll and inspiration: Allingham, Yeats and the escape from history

William Allingham's Ballyshannon regionalism preferred to look at Ireland as a province rather than as a nation. The difference between a regional and a national consciousness can be neatly encapsulated in the double criterion that a region has no centre and no history. A nation is focused on its own metropolis, whence power emanates and whither the energies of the country gravitate; a nation also invokes its individual identity in part through its historical con-sciousness, in that it sees history as a locally generated process, a pattern of growth and decline, crisis and resolution, development and maturity. History is seen as an accretion of diachronic experience, shaping a nation's collective values and attitudes, much as the faculty of memory holds the experiences and growth of an individual character together.

By contrast, these presuppositions are largely absent in the notion of a region or a province. A region is centered on, dependent upon, a metropolis elsewhere, to which it is subordinate and which it cannot claim for its own. Also, a region's sense of history is secondary and incidental to the historical patterns of the nation-at-large; indeed, in many cases the region is seen as somehow a-historical, a place where metropolitan historical developments were passively registered (rarely shaped or influenced), a place where life follows the slow patterns of unchanging tradition or cyclical nature, a place where the capital's fashions penetrate after a time-lag, where the modernizations and changes of modernization penetrate only in weakened or blunted form. Regions often count as backwaters, as places where time has stood still or which have been bypassed by history. Throughout Europe, the nineteenth-century literary imagination of the countryside is one where peasants are ignorant of metro-politan topicality and speak the language of unchanging proverb and slowly-accumulated natural wisdom.

This attitude was to remain influential in Yeats, who in many respects is a straightforward continuation of Allingham. Allingham himself had freely moved in the Pre-Raphaelite circles of London which Yeats tried to gain access to; his verse had been illustrated by Rossetti and Millais. Allingham's evocation of the Irish countryside as an idyllic, timeless, traditional community with a hint of faery uncanniness was followed by young Yeats in poems like 'The stolen child' and 'The man who dreamed of Fairyland'. True, Allingham's was an influence which Yeats attempted to shed, for it ran counter both to his desire of becoming a nationalist and to his idea of being a serious, philosophical poet; in a way, Yeats's immersion in Blake was in part his exorcism of Allingham. But if Yeats, in 'To Ireland in the coming times', acknowledges only the names of 'Davis, Mangan, Ferguson' as his Anglo-Irish forerunners, then he is doctoring the record, and the presence of an unacknowledged Allingham comes out towards the end of the selfsame stanza: 'Ah, faeries dancing under the moon / A Druid land, a Druid tune!'

In fact, young Yeats was structurally in the same position as Allingham, working towards an artist's career in the empire's capital. The nostalgic home-sickness expressed in 'The lake isle of Innisfree' evokes a sunny, rural, timeless image which works on the very same opposition between the London metropolis and an Irish countryside as that which is so important in Allingham. It is no surprise, then, to see that Yeats anthologized Allingham's verse in 1892 under the telling title 'Irish poems and flower fancies', and paid homage to Allingham's

> curious devotion of the people for the earth under their feet, a devotion that is not national, but local, a thing at once more narrow and more idyllic. He sang Ballyshannon and not Ireland.

Yeats's distinction between Ballyshannon and Ireland is perceptive, and based, I think, on a shared outlook and on the obvious parallel between Allingham's Ballyshannon and Yeats's own nearby Sligo. Yeats goes on:

> Here he grew up, filling his mind with all the quaint legends and fancies that linger still in such odd corners of the world, and with that devotion to the place where he was born, felt by few people so intensely as by the Irish.

And the parallel with Yeats's devotion to Sligo is made explicit when Yeats remarks that

> To feel the entire fascination of his poetry, it is perhaps necessary to have spent one's childhood, like the present writer, in one of those seaboard Connaught towns.[59]

What we see at work here is a tendency to canonize the westernmost fringes as the true, authentic Ireland, the eternal Ireland whose primal essence is not obscured by the fuzz and incidents of the modern world. Allingham had evoked precisely such a timeless western coast in his diary, when he attempted to capture his sense of homesickness in London:

> This home-love is strongest in her [Ireland's] wild and barren places, rock-strewn mountain glens and windy sea-shores, notwithstanding the chronic poverty in which so many of them live. In these remote and wild parts Erin is most characteristically herself, and the most unlike to Saxon England. Her strange antiquities, visible in gray mouldering fragments; her ancient language, still spoken by some, and everywhere present in place-names, as well as phrases and turns of speech; her native genius for music; her character – reckless, variable, pertinacious, enthusiastic; her manners – reconciling delicate respect with easy familiarity; her mental movements – quick, humorous, imaginative, impassioned; her habits of thought as to property, social intercourse, happiness; her religious awe and reverence; all these, surviving to the present day, under whatever difficulties, have come down from times long before any England existed, and cling to their refuge of the Old World, among lonely green hills, purple mountains, and rocky bays, bemurmured day and night by the Western Ocean.[60]

Such descriptions might have been penned by Lady Morgan. It is important to emphasize Allingham's conflation between peripherality and timelessness, as it is one of the dominant modes of nineteenth-century Celticism. The evocation of the Celtic temperament as being curiously otherworldy, shadowy, liminal and remote from the practicalities of the real world and real time, likewise dovetails geographical peripherality with ahistoricity. The Celts have, as it were, dropped out of the march of history. The two key texts in formulating this idea are, of course, the opening paragraphs of Ernest Renan's *La poésie des races celtiques* (1859) and Matthew Arnold's *On the study of Celtic literature* (1867): Renan describes the transition into Brittany as a change from the material interests of

France proper into a progressively more bare and timeless, dreamy landscape, leading towards the ultimate emptiness of the sea at Finistère;[61] Arnold describes how, at Llandudno, the east means Liverpool, Birkenhead, boats, traffic and tourism, bustle, business and material progress, whereas the west means nature, the mountains, mystical Wales where the past still lives and the people still commune with the past, until one's gaze meets the empty sea disappearing 'one knows not whither'.[62] Arnold and Renan, though they were supremely important for the dreamy mysticism of the Celtic Twilight,[63] have not invented this commonplace, they were merely among the most important critics to give it a succinct and influential formulation. Allingham's evocation of the rocky, timeless, Atlantic shore predates Arnold, as Balzac's evocation of Brittany predates Renan, when, in *Les Chouans*, he describes a difficult penetration into Brittany almost as having to hew your way through the thornbushes surrounding the castle of Sleeping Beauty:

> La Bretagne est, de toute la France, le pays où les moeurs gauloises ont laissé les plus fortes empreintes. [. . .] Là, les coutumes féodales sont encore respectées. Là, les antiquaires retrouvent debout les monuments des Druides. Là, le génie de la civilisation s'effraye de pénétrer à travers d'immenses forêts primordiales.[64]

It may be useful to draw attention to the extraordinary tenacity and persistence of such anachronistic imaginative schemata: the Celtic-Gaulish isolation and extra-historicity of Brittany (embracing megalith-builders, Gauls and Bretons) is a continuing chronotopical commonplace up to, and including, the contemporary comic strip 'Astérix'. In practically each Astérix album, the title page is accompanied by a map of France. A huge Roman aquila is planted in the heart of France, or 'Gavle' as it is described on the map (the nomenclature and typography explained by the addition *50 avant J.-Chr.*). The symbolism is further clarified by the historical explanation 'Conqvête Romaine'. This straightforward rendering of historical reality is broken by an anachronistic magnifying glass which hovers over Brittany, in the extreme northwestern tip. The Breton coastline, thus magnified, shows a tiny village surrounded by palisades and a cordon of Roman camps; this is the fictional and comic universe of Astérix le Gaulois, where history-as-we-know-it is suspended. Here, owing to a magic potion, Gaul resists the course of history and the Roman conquest, and generates hilarious adventures and rampant anachronistic jokes, already heralded in the place-names of the Roman camps (Babaorvm, Petitbonvm). Set apart from the real world and from actual history, the Gaul of Astérix resists 'encore et toujours', as the accompanying text has it, and in order to do so is located precisely on the Breton coastline. Breton local colour is further enhanced by the fact that the comic-book's strongman, Obélix, is in the menhir trade.

In thus choosing a Breton location for the unconquered, truly Celtic part of Gaul, Uderzo and Goscinny follow a long-standing tradition (witness Balzac's evocation of 'les monuments des Druides'): one which identifies Brittany with ancient Gaul on the basis of their shared Celtic nature, one which sees Brittany as the locus of ancient autochthonous French culture, with menhirs and all, and cordoned off from the metropolitan centre. Like Allingham's Atlantic seaboard, Astérix's Brittany lies in a liminal position on the very edge of the national landmass and at the very edge of history. Accordingly, the timeless image of the West is no less tenacious in Ireland, where the Arnoldian commonplace was taken up with gusto by the Dublin nationalists. One language revivalist traced a penetration into Connemara (in typical telescoping, stage-by-stage fashion[65]) as if it were a journey back in time and back into the days of myth; ultimately, a veritable revivalist Tír-na-nÓg is reached, where Douglas Hyde's desideratum for de-anglicization is pre-empted because Connemara was never anglicized in the first place:

> No greater treat can be in store for the Gaedhilgeoir, than to travel from Galway west through Bearna, Spiddal, and Cashla to Connemara, to hear the Gaelic growing in volume and richness as he proceeds, till at last the English language is as unknown as it was in the days of Maev.[66]

And that selfsame Connemara was evoked as an extratemporal sanctuary by E.W. Lynam in 1914, again in a reiterated telescoping style, describing the place as the periphery of a periphery: the most western tract of the westernmost province of a country on the northwestern edge of Europe, and accordingly 'remote from the highroad of progress and civilization':

> The island called Ireland lies away on the north-west verge of Europe, remote from the highroad of progress and civilization. Iar-Connaught is the most western tract of the western province of Ireland, [. . .] Iar-Connaught is not a historic country, for the great events of history have passed it by; its barren mountains and sedge-lands have never tempted commercial speculators, nor its fiery people invited feudal lords. [. . .] It is a land of wind and rock and water [. . .] a land given up to dreamers and outlaws, despots and fairies, to ancient feuds and the treacherous will of the sea.[67]

Once identified, this chronotope appears to be operative in almost all descriptions of outlying Celtic-language districts during the nineteenth and twentieth centuries, even in twentieth-century cinema – witness the prototypical *Brigadoon* (about a Scottish valley, Shangri-La-style, where time has literally stood still), or Powell and Pressburger's *I know where I'm going* (set in the extratemporal dreamscape of a Hebridean island) or the more recent *Local hero*. As regards Ireland, the treatment such as we have encountered it in Lynam's commonplace sketch is practically standard over the last two centuries, from the novels of Lady Morgan until films like *Un taxi mauve*.

The commonplace has been long been recognized as such and has received critical treatment at the hands of various scholars, from Francis Shaw to Malcolm Chapman and George Watson.[68] Here a chronotope or representational sphere is created where time it seen to pass at a different rate than elsewhere. The Celtic Fringe is a place of stasis, a place where time moves slowly or stands still. It is also a place at the very edge of the real world, usually glimpsed dimly in the distance, a place with a somewhat ambiguous ontological status, liminal, half-ghostly. It is for that reason, also, that such places tend to be distant destinations, to be approached in an asymptotic deferral, like Achilles chasing the tortoise: glimpsed on an ever-retreating horizon, sought in an ever emptier landscape, approached stage by stage by stage, never reached or occupied but only beheld as an Outside, an ectopia.

In other words, Ireland (and particularly the west), becomes an alternative to everything that modern, urban civilization stands for; and this precisely at the moment that, in the wake of Crofton Croker, folkore studies begin to emerge as a cultural and scholarly concern.[69] As we have seen, collections of folktales, in the course of the century, become a third bonanza for Irish publishing, alongside popular history and ballad collections. Folklore was a major influence in the revival's literary activities of the turn of the century; indeed, Yeats himself began his career principally as a folklore adept.[70]

With Yeats, the commonplace of an Irish folk community, preserved in a time-warp outside history, obtains its most powerful literary treatment. Yeats (like others before him) made grateful use of the Victorian stereotypes concerning the Celts and distant, rustic communities – indeed, it would have been more remarkable if he had *not* partaken of that ubiquitous commonplace. More than that, Yeats had a specific way of linking those stereotypes to his symbolist, *fin-de-siècle* sensibility and merging the two into a highly effective literary programme. There is, to begin with, the fact that Yeats, as a would-be mystic, sees the Irish west as a congenial *ambiance*. The congeniality is nothing less than overdetermined: Yeats was born there, had invested the place with pre-lapsarian childhood memories (much as Bretagne connoted, to the older, agnostic Renan, the days of his Catholic, pious youth), and its widespread reputation as an otherwordly place matched his occult, symbolist interests and quests for an extramaterial, platonic, higher reality. It is on this basis that his invocation of the folk community living in the west, and his usage of the fantasies and fables with which this community has filled the landscape, transcends the straightforward treatment at the hands of someone like Allingham. For Yeats, the Irish peasantry is the repository of an ahistorical, pre-Christian faith and wisdom, which may redeem modern readers from the banality of contemporary values. The dehistoricizing phraseology in his 1888 introduction to *Fairy and folk tales of the Irish peasantry* adapts the commonplace to his specific interests:

> These folk-tales are full of simplicity and musical occurrences, for they are the literature of a class for whom every incident in the old rut of birth, love, pain, and death has cropped up unchanged for centuries: who have steeped everything in the heart: to whom everything is a symbol. They have the spade over whom man has leant from the beginning. The people of the cities have the machine,

which is prose and a parvenu. They have few events. They can turn over the incidents of a long life as they sit by the fire. With us nothing has time to gather meaning, and too many things are occurring for even a big heart to hold.[71]

Yeats's invocation of the peasantry crucially relies on their ahistoricity and otherworldliness. The story 'Village ghosts', in *The Celtic twilight*, opens with a typical sense of chronotopical remoteness:

> The ancient map-makers wrote across unexplored regions, 'Here are lions.' Across the villages of fishermen and turners of the earth, so different are these from us, we can write but one line that is certain, 'Here are ghosts.'[72]

That, then, is the combination: distant in space, distant in time, distant in ontology; this enables Yeats to follow his anti-realist, anti-naturalist literary programme (which was deeply influenced by French symbolism and its London *fin-de-siècle* adepts) with a degree of local, Irish reference. Yeats did not feel at home in the London of Kipling and of Gilbert and Sullivan; and it is significant that he can present his Irish literary nationalism as part of the anti-realist trend in Europe at large:

> [The Celtic Movement] comes at a time when the imagination of the world is as ready as it was at the coming of the tales of Arthur and of the Grail for a new intoxication. The reaction against the rationalism of the eighteenth century has mingled with a reaction against the materialism of the nineteenth, and the symbolical movement, which has come to perfection in Germany in Wagner, in England in the Pre-Raphaelites, in France in Villiers de l'Isle-Adam and Mallarmé, and in Belgium in Maeterlinck, and has stirred the imagination of Ibsen and D'Annunzio, is certainly the only movement that is saying new things.[73]

Thus Yeats's negative motivation of being against the dominant, realist/materialist taste of the times can lead him into multiple alliances: with the élitist and even snobbish notions of symbolism (according to whom, only the elect and the noble could truly appreciate beauty), and with the simple country folk of rural Ireland. This duality is to suffuse Yeats's poetry, which celebrates princes and beggars, horsemen and vagrants, the élite and the demotic,[74] and reserves its harshest dislike for the middle classes with their vulgar, materialist stolidity. His penchant for gyrating, oscillating dialectics, as expressed in *A vision*, with the implicit celebration of extremes over the lukewarm middle ground in-between, even penetrates into Yeats's attitude towards age: he celebrates youthful vigour and ageing wisdom, but middle age hardly seems to exist for him. He is the poet of 'a man young and old'; one would almost think, judging by his poems, that he passed straight from his thirtieth birthday to his sixtieth.

In the passage of time, too, the peasantry and the heathenish primitivism of the Irish countryside appear like a redemption. The folk are childlike and timeless, ancient and innocent at the same time; much as Yeats's fairies 'are old, old and gay', they 'chase frothy bubbles' as well as 'weaving olden dances'. Folk superstition is, quite literally, timeless and offers an escape out of the dreary predictability of normal chronology and history. *The Celtic twilight* ends with a poem, 'Into the twilight', which expresses precisely this idea. It addresses the poet's 'Out-worn heart, in a time out-worn' urging it to seek comfort in the grey twilight, where 'time and the world are ever in flight', and stating in so many words that 'Your mother Eire is always young'. Roy Foster's insightful comment is worth quoting:

> It was necessary for Yeats passionately to adhere to the idea that Sligo people did believe in fairies and talked about them all the time. So they did, of course – to *children*, as Lily Yeats remembered. The difference was that her brother expected to go on being talked to about them. This tendency is powerfully connected with laying claim to the lost domain of childhood.[75]

The notion of an Ireland that is always young, and unchangingly so (almost like Keats's Grecian urn), like a sanctuary against the 'filthy modern tide', could lead to a simple regionalism, an idyllic notion Allingham-style. Yeats's progress beyond Allingham is precisely that he refuses to acquiesce in regionalism, and that he tries to incorporate into his celebration of Irish timelessness (or at least allochrony) a national commitment. As I have pointed out before, the notion of nationality seems to presuppose a historical rather than a timeless-idyllic awareness, and accordingly Yeats attempts to square his recourse to a timeless, primitive peasantry with a historical assessment of his own situation as a symbolist European writer. The result is laid down in a vaguely Vicoesque model argued in 1893, in an essay significantly entitled 'Nationality and literature'.

Again, Yeats expresses an overriding sense that he is caught in the wrong historical period. European culture at the turn of the century is flawed and in decline. A literary tradition grows, Yeats argues, like a tree, 'through a constant subdivision of the constituent cells'; accordingly, a historical model of a literary tradition is invoked through the simile of a tree, growing from the central unity of the trunk into the branchings and dividing ultimately into boughs and twigs.

> In youth it is simple, and in mid-period it grows in compexity, as does the tree when it puts forth many branches, and in mature age it is covered by an innumerable variety of fruits and flowers and leaves of thought and experience.[76]

The illustration of this model is twofold, and draws on the cases of Greek and English. Greek literature starts with the central preoccupation of describing 'great racial or national movements or events', such as the siege of Troy in the Iliad. Then, the Attic tragedies

> subdivide these great movements and events into the chararacters who lived and wrought in them. The Siege of Troy is no longer the theme, for Agamemnon and Clytemnestra and Oedipus dominate the stage.

Then comes the last, refined but decadent period: that of the *Anthology*, which deals with abstract, disembodied complexities and emotions.

The other example is closer to the bone: English literature. It begins with Beowulf and Malory; Shakespeare individuates national history into the various history plays; and the last stage is heralded by Shelley and Keats, who deal with the complexities of emotion and experience.

So far, Yeats's historical vision is straightforward *fin-de-siècle* decadence: it exemplifies the idea, shared by the French decadents, of living and working belatedly, after the moment for literary glory and originality has passed and when all that is left is the refined cultivation of precious abstractions, complexities and ambiguities. That notion remains important. A similar model is expressed years later, *c.* 1930, in the three-line verse 'Three movements':

> Shakespearean fish swam in the sea, far away from land;
> Romantic fish swam in nets coming to the hand;
> What are all those fish that lie gasping on the strand?[77]

It is in this respect that Yeats's invocation of Irishness allows him to break out of this historical cul-de-sac. He argues that his imagination is not part of English decrepitude since it has been fed on the still-unused, fresh and pristine material of Irish myth and Irish folklore. The fact that Ireland is backward, outside the pale of English historicity and English modernity, becomes a rejuvenation formula – much as in later life, monkey hormones were to be his answer to the march of time within his own metabolism.

> are we not, perhaps, merely a little eddy cast up by the advancing tide of English literature and are we not doomed, perhaps, to its old age and coming decline? On the contrary, I affirm we are a young nation with unexpected material lying within us in our still unexpressed national character, about us in our scenery, and in the clearly marked outlines of our life, and behind us in our multitude of legends.

Thus, Ireland is not only old and timeless, but also young. The falling out between O'Connell and Young Ireland, when O'Connell said that he was for Old Ireland, is here short-circuited in a highly effective formula,[78] where Ireland can simultaneously benefit from the virtues of youth and old age.[79]

The feeling is not wholly new. When the *Freeman's journal* wrote in support of Barron's *Ancient Ireland* in 1835, it already used revivalist language:

> This appears to us a very proper time for the revival of Irish literature. Now that the golden age of English literature seems passing away, disfigured and corrupted as it daily is becoming, by French tinsel and technicalities, let us hope that the time is not remote when writing to a literary friend, we will be enabled to say, as Horace said to his patron: 'Docte utriusque linguae / Learned in both languages'. Thereby meaning the English and the Irish tongue.[80]

But such feelings did not truly come into their own until the *fin-de-siècle*. As is well known, the later nineteenth century, the decades of Nordau and Lombroso, became obsessed with the notions of decadence and degeneracy. A nationalistic recourse to the unspoilt freshness of ancient Ireland could signal an escape out of the seemingly inevitable process of decay, decrepitude and cultural entropy. The most expressive encapsulation of this mood was the notion of a *revival*, or rebirth: youth rising from the ashes, a bright future rising from a crumbling past. The notion of a sudden reversal of the natural process of decay is all-pervasive in Irish cultural nationalism of the turn of the century: in the language movement (the *athbheochán*, re-vivification, revival in the root sense of the term), where Gaelic was, on the very brink of becoming a dead or extinct tongue, to be rescued and to be brought around to a fresh lease of life, and in the literary movement, which was to rescue Ireland from provincialism and stagnation in what was almost immediately seen as a renaissance. Indeed, it was this sense of a national rebirth which constituted perhaps the most important influence exerted by cultural nationalism on political separatism. This was no longer the nostalgic, Moore-style model of undoing the past, or to Repeal the Union: the programme now became to revive the nation and to redeem it from western decay. William O'Brien, in a political speech, put it as follows:

> The world is a-weary with pessimism. It has lost its innocence. It is losing its faith in most things here or hereafter. [. . .] For this poison of moral and intellectual despair which is creeping through a sad world's veins, what cheerier antidote is within reach than the living tide of health, and hope, and simplicity and hilarity, the breezy objectiveness and stoutness of muscle, and ardour of emotion which flows full and warm through the heroic myths of the men of Erin?[81]

The phoenix became a potent separatist icon (as it still is for present-day Sinn Féin). Kathleen Ní Houlihan became, famously, in Yeats's play an old woman rejuvenated; the similes invoked withered rose-bushes brought to fresh bloom by the blood sacrifice of young men; and the symbolism was summed up in the notion of a Rising (*éirí amach*) upwards from the sloth of a death-like sleep, staged on the feast day of Easter, commemorating Christ's rising from the dead. The idea went back at least as far as Davis's 'The west's awake'; and even Yeats's idyllic nostalgia for the Lake Isle of Inisfree invoked, unlike anything in Allingham, the opening assertion that 'I shall arise and go now', with its implication of breaking free from the burden of ingrained acquiescence and trudging normalcy.

History, peasantry and revival

Two, contradictory modes of national consciousness-raising are, then, at work. One, to tap into old springs of inspiration and to escape from contemporary drabness, the other to borrow energy and youth from them. One harks back to the past, the other remains in the present; one goes for high culture of yore and ancient important figures, the other emphasizes the Plain People now living in their rustic cottages; one tends to opt for the literary prestige of a high tragic mode (the melancholy Celticism common to Macpherson and young Yeats), the other is more comic and vitalistic to the point of rubbing shoulders with Stage Irishness. There is, then, a dual, indeed contradictory, way for Anglo-Irish authors and nationalists to place their endeavours under Irish auspices: the antiquarian and the folkish. One mode of authentication is by turning to the genuine past, the sort of past which was being elucidated by scholars in the wake of Petrie, O'Donovan and O'Curry, and to graft a nineteenth-century present onto the old roots and trunk of the native, pre-anglicized culture of Ireland; that was the endeavour of Ferguson and Standish O'Grady. The other mode was to draw legitimacy from a contemporary constituency of unquestioned, genuine Irishness, the peasantry with their still-living, spontaneous Gaelic speech and traditions.

The language revival of the nineteenth century faced precisely this dilemmatic choice between the return to the pristine example of antiquity, or the vigour of the living demotic tradition. In this context, the debate concentrated around the question as to what sort of Irish should be cultivated: the correct, literary (though pedantic and complex) standard language of the eighteenth century (when Irish was still a vehicle for written cultural activities), or the living, actual speech as it still clung to existence in present-day Irish, though diffracted into various dialects and corrupt or debased from a prescriptive point of view. Was the prime objective to link back to the great national past, or to link up with the native-speaking peasant? The debates around this question, and the underlying attitudes, have been very well charted by Philip O'Leary in his excellent book on the language movement.[82] In the event, it was *cainnt na ndaoine*, 'popular speech', which carried the day. The ideal was to cultivate living Irish and to base one's revivalism on the practice of the Native Speaker.

In the light of earlier developments, this emphasis on contemporary rather than historical links, on synchronic rather than diachronic relations, need not surprise us. The nativist recourse to the folk portion was preferable to a historical recourse to the past, in that it served a double function: not only did it provide language revivalism with a set of bearings and a course of action, it also helped to bring two separate parts of society together under national auspices. The cultivation of history, with its emphasis on the noble, aristocratic achievements of ancient Gaelic society, had been pursued by societies of gentlemen intellectuals, far removed from populism, and counting among their ranks even unionists such as Ferguson or O'Grady. Such scholarly societies had functioned, as we have seen, in the uneasy awareness that their activities might fuel political ends, and had always tried to keep that genie bottled up by insisting on the apolitical nature of their scholarly and cultural endeavours.

As far as the revivalist end of that spectrum was concerned, the rejection of the encroaching dominance of the English language was on the whole undertaken by educated, city-based men, who accordingly needed some form of authentication. Urban and middle-class (or upper-middle-class), it constantly seeks to validate its pursuit by invoking the *Idealtypus* of an authentic Ireland, the Ireland of the placenames, of the Native Speaker, the *Gaeilgeoir*. Hence the great symbolical emphasis placed on the existence of the *Gaeltacht*, the areas where Irish is still the community's native, first language. The symbolical importance of the Native Speaker is not so much that he should speak Irish, but rather that he speaks no English. The ignorance of English is idealized as a lost state of pristine purity, virgin, unsullied authenticity. The title of Hyde's trail-blazing lecture, which sparked off the Gaelic League, betrays much: 'The necessity for de-anglicising Ireland'. English cultural influence should be washed away like an unsightly stain, so as to return to a pristine state of unadulterated Gaelophone purity.[83]

That such a programme should be conceived and propagated by an English-speaking middle class is, in an ironically twisted form, a re-enactment of earlier forms of hegemonism. The issue of Gaelic culture is conjured up in a deliberately, strenuously depoliticized form so as to screen the possibility that social and economic tensions might be lurking behind Ireland's diglossia. The tension is glimpsed in this exercise dialogue from *An Fíor-Éironnach* (1862) between 'An old gentleman and a labourer':[84]

> G. –   I know there is great distress among the labourers and small farmers
> L. –   We must all leave old Ireland
> G. –   Ireland for ever Paddy.
> L. –   We'll go where the rich man does not reap what the poor man sow's [sic]
> G. –   Ireland for ever Paddy.
> L. –   Bread for ever for me, sir.
> G. –   Well, bread for ever for me, too; come with me and I'll give you work.
> L. –   Long life to your honour, and Ireland for ever.

The Gaelic peasant is enlisted for nationalist purposes, as a symbolically important but hierarchically subordinate partner in the scheme. The peasant is to provide symbolical goods rather than rent, tithes, produce or cheap labour: he is asked to furnish a native knowledge of the language and a correspondingly picturesque lifestyle; he is asked to provide that authenticity and that unbroken link with past traditions which the revivalists by definition do not have, and cannot do without. Occasionally, his stories or poems are written down and published (usually in bowdlerized form); and he can win medals and diplomas by dancing and playing and reciting at *Oireachtas* or *Feis*; but that is all he gets out of the bargain.[85]

While language revivalism defines itself as a transpolitically national concern, it follows the generally current, romantic image of Ireland as a country split along class and regional lines. The rural peasant is held to embody authentic, Gaelic Ireland, but his role in national developments and politics is a passive, submissive one; the urban bourgeoisie holds an active, leading position in the socio-economic and political sphere but by the same token lacks cultural authenticity. It is in these terms that a pattern of cultural trade-off emerges which serves to establish a national unity and community of interests under Gaelic auspices; and such a practical effect would render a populist model of language revivalism preferable to a historicist one, which has only linguistic and scholarly purity to recommend it.

But the choice between classical Irish and living Irish was, as Philip O'Leary's book has shown, not a straightforward one and was not easily resolved; it engendered much, often acrimonious debate; and in the case of the literary renaissance, too, the separate and to some extent dilemmatic possibilities of tuning into vitalistic folk practice or into the august past generated contradictions. While Yeats, for instance, may have relied on folk and folklore for much of his early work,[86] the ancient tradition of heroic Gaeldom, the aristocratic warrior-like Cuchulain and Fergus, were no less powerful sources of inspiration. Likewise, Lady Gregory, who wrote folksy 'kitchen comedies' for the Abbey Theatre, and who worked to establish a linguistic identity by cultivating English-style *cainnt na ndaoine*, Kiltartanese, turned the peasants' Hiberno-English dialect into a medium of literary expression and was as preoccupied with myth and saga as she was with folklore. Her re-tellings of the legendary material which had been made available by the previous generation of scholars is noteworthy in this respect, especially her seminal re-telling of the *Táin* – that text which, since O'Flanagan, Ferguson and, especially, Standish O'Grady, had come to be venerated as Ireland's oldest and most authentic native epic.

Lady Gregory's *Táin*: between Kiltartan and Muirthemhne

In analysing Lady Gregory's appropriation of the *Táin* and her image of the native material, it is difficult not to let our own image of Lady Gregory get in the way. There is reason, first and foremost, to speak a word in vindication of her achievement in making the entire Ulster cycle available to a wide audience, practically for the first time, and in retrieving the Ulster cycle from the idiosyncrasy of O'Grady's heroic-aristocratic *machismo*. Although nowadays one might be tempted to think that she did so in an anodyne, Victorian, bowdlerized way, that may be partly a facile anti-Victorian imputation on our part. Between us and Lady Gregory stands, of course, Thomas Kinsella, whose version of the *Táin* (so different from Lady Gregory's) has been as influential for the later twentieth century as Gregory's was for the later nineteenth. If we read Gregory's *Cuchulain of Muirthemne* side by side, not only with Kinsella, but also with its original (as edited and translated by Cecile O'Rahilly), we cannot but be struck with the deftness, completeness, elegance and fidelity of Gregory's translation; and it is in such a doubled juxtaposition (with Kinsella and with the original as made available by O'Rahilly) that we must try and calibrate our assessment of Lady Gregory's fidelity or distortiveness, and to see to what extent she tried to assimilate and incorporate this ancient source for her revivalist purposes.

Of course (and this will surprise no-one) there was the unavoidable Victorianization, which is implicit almost in the very fabric of the discourse and the period English she uses. It reminds us of Salvador Dalí's dictum that it is senseless to try and be deliberately modern – since it would be impossible in the first place not to be modern. We are always our own contemporaries. In practice, that means that a mere word like 'queen' must mean an altogether different thing for Gregory than in the original, as different as words in *Don Quixote* were for Cervantes and for Pierre Menard. To call Maeve a queen means to associate her phraseologically with Queen Victoria and Maud Gonne in the role of Kathleen Ní Houlihan; it instills the word 'queen' with a Pre-Raphaelite or *fin-de-siècle* ideal of noble, exalted and portly womanhood, spiced up possibly with a dash of the *femme fatale*. And such, indeed, are the women characters in *Cuchulain of Muirthemne*: Deirdre, Maeve or Findabair are proud, admirable superwomen whose beauty subdues heroes; but they are also somehow disembodied, statuesque, as if they (like Gregory herself) wear stays.

It is precisely this genteel sexlessness of *Cuchulain of Muirthemne* and its respectable, gentleman- and ladylike protagonists, which has been sniggeringly pointed out as a typical instance of Victorian bowdlerization. This, I think, is not wholly warranted.

The one instance where Gregory admits as much, is when the original lets Cuchulain be confronted (and stared down) by the Ulster women 'exposing all their nakedness and shame to him'.[87] In the translation, they are merely topless, and Gregory goes as far as excusing what she herself considered an infidelity, by explaining it from her audience's (rather than her own) prudery:

> It was to shock Cuchulain's modesty it was done, as we know by his hiding his face, & the partial undressing was enough for that. Priests might legitimately say the other called up an indecent picture.[88]

The suppression of other 'indecencies' – references to urine, excrement, menstruation and copulation – should be seen in the context of a more general tendency to accommodate the *Táin* and its wild stalwart heroines to nineteenth-century taste. Not only the sexual references, but also the grotesque hyperbole of the original is toned down: e.g. Cuchulain's heroic beauty consisting in the fact that he has three (or elsewhere, seven) pupils in each eye; or his capacity of stripping the bark off trees between his bare fingers. Such hyperbolical details are suppressed by Gregory as much as she suppressed the references to bodily functions. Again, Cuchulain's odd 'warp-spasm', a convulsion which seizes the hero in moments of battle frenzy and which is described in grotesquely heightened terms, is reduced by Gregory to a mere 'hero's halo' which fetchingly shines around his head, Arthur Rackham-style. Such de-barbarizations are part of a Victorian reading which attempts to make sense of a difficult and disturbing original, and which sees the Irish past through sentimentally sympathetic eyes; it should not be seen as a neurotically prudish phobia of sexuality, which is perhaps our present-day stereotype of Victorianism. Indeed, Gregory is frank enough by nineteenth-century standards: she is quite straightforward, for instance, when describing Cuchulain's admiration for the swell of Emer's breasts.

Another aspect of Lady Gregory's adaptation of the Táin to a latter-day set of values lies in the fact that she presents 'the Gaels' as a unitary, albeit feud-ridden nation, comprising all the inhabitants of Ireland. This fully fits the nationalist views of the time, which saw the country's radical un-Englishness in terms of a 'real', originally Gaelic Ireland overlaid by foreign, Norman and English intrusions. What Gregory's outlook could not accommodate (indeed, archaeologists and philologists had not yet developed the insight) was the fact that the Táin testifies to a period in Irish history when there was no such thing as a homogeneously Gaelic population either in fact or in outlook; the Ireland as described in the Táin is inhabited by a number of ethnically distinct and mutually inimical tribes; the Ulaid or Ulstermen are a different tribe from the fir Hérend or 'men of Éire' [meaning, in the root sense of the terms, 'men who have the goddess Ériu for their tribal deity']; and the Gaileóin or Leinstermen are wary, ill-accommodated strangers within Maeve's and Ailill's army. These deep ethnic divisions are not recognized as such by a translator for whom 'the Gaels' are the homogeneous ethnic unity of all authentic native Irish people.

Again, it would be unhelpful to smugly denounce such adaptive accommodations merely to flatter our own superior insight. Indeed, our late-twentieth-century heightened awareness of the alienness of the Táin may be as much an attempt to adapt and to accommodate it into our own modernist or postmodernist worldview. In order to illustrate this, it is useful to turn to the version which appears to have been most formative in our present-day understanding, that of Thomas Kinsella. Kinsella's tendency is certainly to valorize and foreground the coarse, primitive and grotesque elements; thus, the version of the Deirdre story (which has come down in various MS variants) which appeals most to him is the oldest one, and he criticizes Lady Gregory's translation mainly on the grounds that she had '[refined] away the coarse elements and [rationalized] the monstrous and gigantesque'.[89] No attempt here to smooth things down and to rationalize. The illustrator, Louis Le Brocquy, gives Rorschach-style ink blots, evocative rather than representational, trying to keep them as 'impersonal as possible' since they are about 'the memory and concern of a people over some twelve hundred years'.[90] What is stressed is the historical and cultural distance, rather than the recognizability or contemporary appeal. Indeed, this deliberate emphasis on alienness and impersonality fits Kinsella's own outlook and his poetics. Yet, a dilemma lurks here, and we can trace its repercussions throughout Kinsella's version of the Táin: the conscious maintaining of unrefinement is a contradiction in terms and turns the primitive into primitivism; and the very act of translating the Táin is an act of appropriation which stands at odds with the emphasis on difference and alienness, tuning the exotic into exoticism. The brutality of the original, in the process, is updated and adapted to the cruelty of Kinsella's A technical supplement; the savage warrior ethos of the Táin becomes a reflection on human existence in a hostile universe. Significantly, the Kinsella who criticizes Lady Gregory for rationalizing the Táin, criticizies a scholarly, faithful translation (by Winifred Faraday) on the completely opposite score that it is 'difficult to read with any pleasure, partly because it transmits the flaws of the text so accurately' (x); indeed, Kinsella himself admits that he has intervened to correct the obscurity and incomprehensibility of the original: 'As far as possible, the story has been freed of inconsistencies and repetitions. Obscurities have been cleared up and missing parts supplied from other sources' (xi).

The dilemma between alienation and appropriation surfaces most obviously in the use of proper names. These are all given in the original's Old Irish form: Medb rather than Maeve, Derdriu rather than Deirdre. This is to some extent a matter of consistency and of fidelity to the original; it is also a signal that Kinsella, unlike earlier translators, chooses to leave things alien. However, when territorial and geographical names are given in their Old Irish form, the mechanism becomes ensnared in contradiction. The Shannon (modern Irish: Sionann) is named as the Sinann, Teltown or Tailte as Tailtiu, and when the Connacht army is camped in Cúil Sibrille, the name is glossed as 'Cenannos, as it is now called' (72). It is now called Kells, or in Irish Ceanannas; certainly not Cenannos. So far, so good; but while the names are distanced from the reader's frame of reference by this historical alienation, they are at the same time brought closer to home by means of a spatial, geographical explanation in the very tradition of the Ordnance Survey's Historical Memoir: maps are supplied showing the geography of Ireland and indicating the location of Cúil Sibrille and Tailtiu. Territorial, spatial approximation goes together with temporal, historical alienation.

In my opinion, this contrasting motivation is a late-twentieth-century example of that mechanism which we have already seen at work in Lady Morgan, in the Irish spelling and typography of proper names in The nation, and in the excessive encumbrance of footnotes to Griffin's The invasion. There is at the same time a national sense of familiarity and an exoticist sense of difference at work: an ancient culture is mediated to a modern readership with an emphasis on shared identity (e.g., in that the locale of the Táin is shown to be the selfsame Irish territory as Kinsella's own modern Ireland), and a link of filiation is thus established between modern, English-speaking Ireland and its Gaelic roots;[91] but at the same time there is an exoticizing element, in that the names are kept deliberately alien, and Kinsella's translation emphasizes the unfamiliar ethos of an iron-age warrior society, with its grotesque descriptions of battle frenzy, its cold, matter-of-fact brutality, its enigmatic feats of prowess, its casual, off-hand honesty in matters of sex and excretion.

Just how deliberately these alien, exotic aspects are emphasized, transpires from a juxtaposition with, again, Lady Gregory's translation and the original(s). There is some sense that Kinsella bends over backwards to strip the Táin of the Tennysonian register which Lady Gregory's translation had imposed. Thus, successive translations of a single source texts are linked in a dialectics of mutual antagonism, each translation claiming its raison d'être by impugning (and improving upon) the inadequacy of earlier ones. (Jorge Luis Borges, in discussing the various translations of the Arabian Nights, called them 'a dynasty of enemies'.) If Lady Gregory suppresses the monstrous, rationalizes the bizarre, and in some cases tones down the sexuality of the original, Kinsella goes to town on precisely these aspects. If Lady Gregory's women heroes are dignified noblewomen, with a hint of Lady Bracknell, Kinsella (in accordance with late-twentieth-century fashions) sees them as wild, strong earth goddesses:

> Probably the greatest achievement of the *Táin* and the Ulster cycle is the series of women, some in full scale and some in miniature, on whose strong and diverse personalities the action continually turns: Medb, Derdriu, Macha, Nes, Aife. It may be as goddess-figures, ultimately, that these women have their power; it is certainly they, under all the violence, who remain most real in the memory (p. xiv–xv).

In Kinsella's endeavour to render the text in what he sees as its proper roughness, he relies on an older source text. Whereas Gregory had used the more polished, unified narrative contained in the Book of Leinster, Kinsella turns to the more fragmented, earlier, and less polished version as written down in the Yellow Book of Lecan. But not all differences between Gregory and Kinsella can be explained from these different source texts. Kinsella himself is often forced to turn to the Book of Leinster version in order to make sense of the fragments related in his main source, the Yellow Book of Lecan.

Just how deliberate Kinsella's de-Gregorification is, may appear from a few examples. To begin with, there is the matter of Fergus and his sword. At some point, Fergus has sex with Medb; and while he is thus engaged, Medb's cuckolded husband Ailill has Fergus's sword stolen. At the end of the tryst, Fergus finds himself swordless, with an empty scabbard. He does not get his sword back until the final battle, and meanwhile has to make do with a wooden imitation sword. Kinsella glosses the episode in Freudian terms:

> Their [Fergus's and Medb's] encounter in the wood, where Fergus (clearly not up to Medb's demands) loses his sword, is the source of continual phallic joking in the Táin until the sword is restored [. . .] (p. xiv).

There is little textual evidence to bear out this genital symbolism in the matter of the lost sword, and there is (*pace* Kinsella) no suggestion of sexual shortcomings on Fergus's part. Matters are more complex; for in the Book of Leinster version as translated by Lady Gregory, the tryst in the wood is described, the stealing of Fergus's sword and the wooden replica figure likewise, but Fergus is never really swordless: his weapon lies in all its redoubtable length across his thighs when he goes in his chariot to parley with Cuchulain.[92] What is more, the wooden sword takes on a completely different role, and becomes the envoy's white wooden wand, which (like a modern white flag) is a sign for Cuchulain that Fergus comes, not as a challenger, but as an emissary.

Thus Kinsella's re-sexualization of the Táin should be seen, not as a greater fidelity to 'the' source, but as exploiting the fact of contradictions within the variant sources so as to project a more modernist sensibility. The following synoptic scheme may illustrate this. It gives three differences between Kinsella's and Gregory's translations, and places these differences side by side with the different manuscript versions used by them: the Book of Leinster in the case of Lady Gregory, the Yellow Book of Lecan in the case of Kinsella. The 'primmer' impression conveyed by Gregory as opposed to the 'rougher' impression conveyed by Kinsella (as in the central two columns, below), turns out, thus contextualized, to be caused by the greater fidelity of Lady Gregory to her source and the greater tendency of Kinsella to 'spice up' his version, against straight-forward source fidelity. In the first example, it turns out that Gregory has used a less sexually explicit original; in the third example, Kinsella does supply a detail suppressed by Gregory, but he has to go out of his way to glean it; the second (middle) example is a combination of Gregory's source fidelity and Kinsella's wayward quest for the more explicit and rough elements.[93]

Gregory's source (Book of Leinster)	Gregory's version	Kinsella's version	Kinsella's source (Yellow Book of Lecan)
Medb offers golden brooch	Medb offers golden brooch	Medb offers friendly thighs	Medb offers friendly thighs
Medb offers close friendship	Medb offers close friendship	Medb offers friendly thighs	(EPISODE IS ABSENT)
Medb menstruates and urinates	(EPISODE IS SUPPRESSED)	Medb menstruates and urinates	(EPISODE IS ABSENT)

The moral of this source-critical comparison is not to be too easily dismissive of the Victorian or *fin-de-siècle* appropriation of the native past. Accusations of distortion or even invention of tradition are easily provoked by the historical distance between us and the nineteenth century; but every century looks at the past though its own glasses, and even the naked eye includes a lens which bends the light to our convenience. More importantly perhaps, the relevance of this comparison is that it illustrates the curious bi-directional notion of tradition. On the one hand, a tradition is chronological, passing material downstream on the river of time, handing on the baton in a relay race from generation to generation. Thus, the *Táin*, and the mythical Gaelic past generally, constitute a tradition in that the material is transcribed from scribe to scribe, from MS to MS, is printed and translated (as in the case of the Deirdre story) from O'Flanagan to Moore to Ferguson, to O'Grady, and into the Irish Literary Renaissance. On the other hand a tradition is retroactive, in that each generation turns towards the past and searches it for one's own antecedents, selects some and disregards others, adapts them to one's immediate concerns as much as adapting oneself to the lessons learned from history: tradition in such terms is an excavation, digging around in the past for ore or for treasure.

In both cases, what really matters is the motivating desire; and in both cases, the motivating desire appears to involve a notion of the value of *authenticity* and of the *original*. The irony of my chosen example is precisely that the *Táin*, of all texts, has no unified, homogenous original – despite its symbolic status as the bedrock and mainspring of Irish literary culture. The differences between Gregory and Kinsella are not just divergent adaptations fanning out from a common point of departure; that common point of departure, the 'original', turns out on closer scrutiny to be no less diverse and contradictory, incorporating conflicting MS redactions and, even within these redactions, offering a plurality of possible ways of how the tale might be told. Even for the medieval redactions, the *Táin* was an old, almost lost textual heirloom, and there is one ancillary story (*réamhscéal*) which describes how the sages of Ireland had to reconstitute an almost-lost original. The story, *Dofallsigud Tána Bó Cuailnge* ('The retrieval of the Táin Bó Cuailnge') relates how each poet of Ireland remembered only a small portion of the complete narrative, and how Senchán Torpéist sent his son and his pupil on a quest to find the complete story. Eventually, the ghost of Fergus himself recites the full tale in a type of *aisling* vision.

The fact that such a story is prefixed to the medieval corpus of the *Táin* text already indicates that its availability and its verbal substance were by no means obvious or straightforward; worse, even this story in itself partakes, at one remove, of the contradictory and fragmentary nature of knowledge of the *Táin*, since it equivocates between two different versions as to how the *Táin* was retrieved: it concludes with suggesting an alternative version to the effect that 'there are some who say that the story was told to Senchán himself after he had gone on a fast to certain sons of the seeds of Fergus. This seems reasonable'.[94]

The Táin itself is full of such alternative possible versions as to how things might have happened differently accordingly to some. The operative verb in this case, indicating a hypothetical mode closely attendant on the register of fiction, is *asberat*, 'it is said' – the Latin *dicitur* or the French *on-dit*, which testifies to the tenuous nature of knowledge-by-hearsay. Given the fact that the *Táin* was for centuries transmitted orally, the notion of hearsay and of different possibilities of putting things is a central element; the text is riddled with suggestions of possible alternative versions, and the 'original' which was later to be cultivated as providing a basis and starting point to a national literary imagination is in itself a fragmented and contradictory complex of remembrances and variants. Thus, the Book of Leinster scribe who compiled a unified text ends his work with a *ne varietur* which reads almost like a sigh of relief at having brought the volatile source material into one organized whole:

> A blessing on every one who shall faithfully memorise the Táin as it is written here and shall not add any other form to it.[95]

The moral of the story? Tradition is one long, ongoing, never-resolved and never-abandoned attempt to impose an imaginative unity on the contradictions of the past. That is the common concern of Senchán Torpéist, the scribe of the Book of Leinster, Lady Gregory and Thomas Kinsella. Tradition is not the pious passing on of a discrete heirloom, but the ever-renewed and never-completed attempt to bring order to a vast and chaotic curiosity shop. As Camus said, *il faut imaginer Sisyphe comme heureux*.

Each new translation of the *Táin* is an act of appropriation, an attempt to bring a distant text closer to home. That is foregroundedly the case in that the obscure and incomprehensible language of the original is replaced by standard English; it is more subtly present in other strategies which explain or mediate in the cultural distance between original and intended audience. One of the strategies is, interestingly, the use of paratext: explanatory footnotes, asides in which the (usually self-effacing) translator becomes momentarily a helpful commentator. The use of paratext has been a constant presence in the nineteenth-century material dealt with in this book, from Lady Morgan's novels to the poems of *The nation* and the corrections added by Eugene O'Curry to Griffin's *The invasion*. Here, again, the footnotes, prefaces and other additions seem to fulfil a similar, auto-exoticist function: they occupy a shadow zone alongside the text, accompanying it, yet not intruding upon it, leaving the unfamiliar original intact yet palliating its strangeness and helping to mediate in making it comprehensible to an exoteric, uninitiated audience. Paratextual coatings become necessary when there is a radical difference between the frame of reference of the audience and the frame of reference in the text. Exotic Ireland as decribed and evoked in all its pristine, unadulterated authenticity in Morgan's and Griffin's novels and *The nation*'s poems, is explained and made accessible and comprehensible in the footnotes to those novels and poems. The paratext around the *Táin* has a similar function. In Kinsella's translation, there are the illustrations, themselves accompanied by the illustrator's explanatory note; there are Kinsella's footnotes, the maps, prefatory note and acknowledgements, introduction, a list of further reading on the subject, and a glossary on the pronunciation of Irish words and names (those Irish words which Kinsella, as we have seen, decided to keep in their most off-putting orthography, much like the poets of *The nation* giving Irish names in their most authentic and least familiar typeface). As the above analysis has made clear, it is often in the tension between text and paratext that we can register the workings of auto-exoticism and the way in which the appropriation of nationality takes place.

That applies equally to Lady Gregory's version. Specifically the dedication becomes highly suggestive, for this book is dedicated, curiously, 'To the people of Kiltartan'; the 'ingratiating and patronizing dedicatory letter'[96] begins:

> My Dear Friends: – When I began to gather these stories together, it is of you I was thinking, that you would like to have them and be reading them. For although you have not to go far to get stories of Finn and Goll and Oisin from any old person in the place, there is very little of the history of Cuchulain and his friends left in the memory of the people, but only that they were brave men and good fighters, and that Deirdre was beautiful (p. 5).

It is remarkable: the translation of an archaic, epic text on cattle raids in an aristocratic warrior society is described here as if it had been a pursuit in folklore, as if Gregory had been engaged in 'gathering stories together'. (In part this was perhaps Gregory's overreaction against *her* predecessor, the macho primitivist Standish O'Grady with his all-action-hero Cuchulain.) Not only is the written epic turned into the homely, oral register of 'stories' to be collected, the natural environment for the *Táin* is thereby located in the oral, storytelling peasantry. It is of these Gregory was thinking, and it is to the peasantry she would like to offer these 'stories', so as to enrich their stock of narrative material. The dedication is, quite literally, an offering. The élite culture of two thousand years ago is to be ploughed back into the soil, into the contemporary demotic culture of the peasantry, who 'would like to have' the 'stories'.

The most charitable way of looking at this is that Gregory is paying a debt. Together with Yeats she had collected stories around her Coole estate, had gathered pearls of wit and imagination, and had imbued the peasants' diction of quaint, Hiberno-English dialect, all of which was to stand her in good stead in her work for the Abbey Theatre. Hence her desire to give something to the peasantry who had given so much to her; a sympathetic gesture, and doubtless part of her intention. Accordingly, Gregory collapses the distinction between past and peasant, brings the two together: the brutal and lofty heroism of the *Táin* is related in the relaxed, homely diction of an oral tale, and in the style of the rustic Hiberno-English peasant dialect. In other words, the *Táin* goes native, and the two mainsprings of literary imagination in Anglo-Irish national literature, the ancient Gaels and the contemporary folk community, are reconciled. It is this that makes Gregory's retellings of the ancient myths and sagas of Ireland so seminally important. The peasantry are elevated to a dignity beyond the register of the picturesque Myles na Gopaleens, Matt the Thrashers or Father O'Flynns; they can henceforth aspire to the status of tragic dignity in Synge's *Riders to the sea*, and the Abbey Theatre's anti-comic invocation of a native folk community characteristically vests them with more than mere picturesque background interest. This status of the peasantry needs a sense of historical depth and must redeem them from the one-dimensional timelessness in which Allingham and other earlier Victorians have seen them: the contemporary Real Ireland of the peasant folk community is given the sounding board of a historical Real Ireland of the ancient Gaels; the notion of the 'story', and the resonance of myth and symbol being the point of intersection between the two.

But Lady Gregory's gesture of symbolical reimbursement is, precisely, a gesture, and a pretty empty one at that. The word 'friends' occurs twice in the dedication's above-quoted fragment, and in both cases seems misplaced. 'Cuchulain and his friends' sounds like Enid Blyton rather than the Ulster Cycle, and the opening words are a condescending courtesy for a landowner who cannot bring herself to address the tenant peasantry as 'ladies' or 'gentlemen'. *Friends* here means something like 'good, worthy people'; the patronizing tone becomes more obvious later on, when the translator tells her 'friends' that she has decided to shield them from objectionable things which might spoil the lovely effect of the fact that 'Deirdre was beautiful': she left out 'a good deal I thought you would not care about for one reason or another'. On closer scrutiny, we must ask ourselves who *really* benefits from this friendly offering, this dedicatory gesture? Surely not the peasant dedicatees. Unless we are to believe that Lady Gregory had free copies of the book distributed around Coole, her *Cuchulain of Muirthemne*, published in London by John Murray of Albemarle Street, would not have been affordable or even available to the peasant dedicatees, who, in fact, have just provided Lady Gregory with a good excuse for her occasional infidelities towards the original. Just as it was priests who might complain at the full frontal nudity of the women of Ulster, so it is the pretended peasant audience which must be protected against the untamed wildness of the original. In other words, Gregory is invoking her audience by way of legitimation, and little else. Despite the posturing of the dedication, this book is not intended for the people of Kiltartan to whom it is dedicated; it is by no means a cheap, popular publication, and the introduction by Yeats obviously appeals to a wholly different market. I, for one, cannot see how Yeats thought he was benefiting the people of Kiltartan by explaining to them that poetry is 'a habit of mind caught as in the beryl stone of a Wizard' (p. 266).

In fact, the dedication makes this clear; that the people of Kiltartan are Lady Gregory's legitimizing constituency. This purported pseudo-audience authenticates the translator's endeavour by linking it back to that native Ireland of which Gregory herself forms no part. By invoking her Kiltartan connections, the Anglo-Irish landowner Gregory appropriates Gaelic antecedents as if they were her own. The invocation of the peasantry as a virtual constituency is necessary if the Anglo-Irish gentry claims to represent Ireland or Irish nationality.[97]

The double issue as to who should represent the True Ireland, and in what terms; and indeed, what representation could or could not claim to be; that was to come to a head when the finest writer of the Irish Literary Renaissance, Synge, was to produce dramas with folk settings for the Abbey Theatre which failed to conform to the inherited conventions and wrong-footed the audience's prior expectations.

Irish nationality, literary revival

Roy Foster has argued that the death of Parnell, Hyde's lecture 'On the necessity for de-Anglicising Ireland', and the beginnings of the Irish Literary Society, which coincided in 1891–1892, should not be seen as a radical break in Irish political life – although that is how Yeats and his contemporaries would have liked to look at it.[98] Certainly, Foster's point has been amply borne out in the preceding pages. The traditions of folklore, language revivalism, historical and mythological interest and political imagination show an unbroken development from the mid-century into the 1890s; what changed was perhaps that, after the dismantling of landlordism and the death of Parnell, the cultural aspects of Irish nationalism were no longer condemned to the margins of the great political debates.

The various initiatives in cultural nationalism of the 1890s were nothing if not diverse, involving literary, dramatic, linguistic, sporting, and journalistic elements with different sympathies, different social roots and different gradations of separatism. Even within the dramatic movement (on which I shall concentrate in the next few pages), a snobbish, patrician element existed alongside a more populist wing, much as the Gaelic League itself was divided between nativist and progressive elements.[99]

In the light of all this complexity, my aim here is not so much to establish who the nationalist factions were and what changeable relations of rivalry and collaboration existed between them, but rather to trace what ideas concerning Irish nationality were invoked in these shifting alliances and conflicts. In this respect it is illuminating to look at some of the developments surrounding the dramatic movements and the Abbey Theatre – not in terms of the development of stagecraft in Ireland, but in terms of the way cultural debates and contradictory patterns of national self-identification were sparked off by one of the more prestigious and long-lived initiatives in Irish cultural nationalism.[100]

The launching of the Irish Literary Theatre in 1899 was characterized by a polarity which was to remain operative and divisive throughout the following years: one between cosmopolitanism and nationalism. On the one hand, Yeats, as a *fin-de-siècle* artist, was keenly aware of the literary climate in other European countries and explicitly wanted his Irish venture to be a part of this. There are frequent references in his writings of these years to the art theatres of Paris, the Norwegian renaissance around Ibsen, the work of Maeterlinck and other contemporaries. The use of the word 'literary' was to reflect precisely these artistic, aesthetic (rather than spectacular) notions of *fin-de-siècle* stagecraft.

On the other hand, the theatre was to be Irish as well as literary, and it was here that the shoe rubbed. Yeats attempted to steer a political course through dangerous terrain. He conceded that the Irishness of the venture was to be cultivated deliberately by selecting 'plays about Irish subjects',

> about legends associated with the rivers and mountains of Ireland, or about Irish historic personages or events, or about modern Irish life[101]

But that was only a concession on his part. Ideally, for him, Irishness should be part of the natural, self-evident fibre of the literature he hoped to create, something that needed no special elaboration:

> Although we have for the moment decided to produce no plays not upon Irish subjects, we know that when Irish literature is more developed Irishmen will utter the personality of their country, no matter what subjects they write about. When they have learned their lesson, when they have come to understand the country they live in, they will write admirably about other countries. All literature and all art is national. The Eastern poets, Homer and the Greek dramatists, the writers of

the Icelandic sagas, Dante, Shakespeare in 'King Lear' and in the historical plays, Goethe in 'Faust' [. . .] and Ibsen at almost all times, have written about the history and legends of their own countries. Shakespeare, Calderon, Milton, in writing of the history and legends of other countries, have written out of emotions and thought that came to them because of their profound sympathy with the life about them. Egyptian art differs from Greek, Dutch art differs from Italian, French art differs from English, because they have come out of different nationalities.[102]

This was confusing and it was to vex Yeats's enterprise. If nationality is so spontaneous, so implicit and so self-evident, it cannot be made the basis of a programmatic agenda; and if the Irishness of Yeats's Literary Theatre is to form an explicit part of a nationalist movement, it cannot be comparable to the implicit Englishness of Shakespeare or the Greekness of Homer. In other occasional writings of these years, Yeats was to put down far more muscular principles of national or even racial identity: he extolled the uniqueness of an inter-Celtic contribution to the European imagination, and hailed the Gaelic League as a great initiative and as a valuable asset in the struggle to recapture the national spirit. In 1892 he had stated that 'no man who deserts his own literature for another's can hope for the highest rank. The cradles of the greatest writers are rocked among the scenes they are to celebrate. [. . .] there is no nationality without literature, no literature without nationality.' In the same year he predicted that a Celtic, national school of Irish writing might deliver 'that new great utterance for which the world is waiting', but only on condition that 'we study all things Irish, until we know the particular glamour that belongs to this nation, and how to distinguish it from the glamour of other countries and other races'. In celebrating the poetry of Fiona MacLeod, Yeats had dived even further into ethnic essentialism and stated his hope to create

> l'union de sentiment [. . .] entre les Celtes irlandais et écossais, en leur rappelant tout à la fois leurs origines semblables et ces trésors d'héroïques légendes. Une communité de sentiments, non seulement entre ces deux peuples, mais encore avec les Celtes gallois, sera peut-être l'un des résultats décisifs du 'Mouvement Celtique' et bien des évènements sociaux, politiques aussi bien que littéraires, en peuvent dériver.[103]

Yeats was trying to chart a course between cosmopolitanism and nationalism; but in his eagerness for support he appears to have adapted his message to whatever audience he happened to be addressing himself to. The uncharacteristically strenuous nationalism of the American lecture tour is an example.[104] Such occasional waving of the green flag could always cause embarrassment later on. Thus, Griffith quoted Yeats à l'Américaine damningly on the front page of the United Irishman, 11 February 1905, at the height of a controversy, when Yeats had come to defend artistic freedom against the dictates of nationalist propaganda and was deeply embattled by outraged theatre audiences. The statement which Griffith now quoted back at Yeats must have read as a mendacious chutzpah:

> Our dramatists now study what the people want, and then we give it to them in
> such form that thirty or forty police must often be stationed inside the theatre to
> prevent riots. You can do something with people like that (MID 3: 15).

On the whole, however, there is an unmistakable honeymoon period in the
early years of the century between Yeats and populist nationalism, specifically as
regards relations with the Gaelic League. The revised version of an 1899 lecture
on 'The literary movement in Ireland' in 1901 shows changes which turn
qualified, hesitant approval of the Gaelic League into whole-hearted support.[105]
We even see Yeats contribute to D.P. Moran's fiercely nationalistic *The leader* in
1900, echoing Gaelic League truisms to the effect that the Gaelic language will
save Ireland from vulgarity and atheism.[106] The result of this love affair with the
language movement was that Irish plays began to be staged by the Irish Literary
Theatre with actors drawn from the League's Keating branch. Douglas Hyde's
Casadh an tsúgáin[107] was billed together with *Dairmuid and Gráinne*, jointly written by George Moore and Yeats. Whereas Hyde's short sketch in Irish attracted
universal benevolence, reactions to *Diarmuid and Gráinne* were more mixed. The
Freeman's journal sounded a note which was to prove portentous in the light of
later developments:

> There is one particular proposition concerning women which, however archaic in
> form, is an unmistakable echo of the Paris boulevards. It comes with a shock on
> the audience and it is an offence from which even the most audacious of latter-day
> problem playwrights would shrink.[108]

Relations with the nationalist audience were by no means as easy-going and
straightforward as Yeats's ingratiating stance would make it seem. The Irish
Literary Theatre had got off to a very bad start indeed with the scandal surrounding Yeats's *The Countess Cathleen*, a play written some years earlier and intended
for production in 1899. The play, as is well known, was somewhat suspect on
the point of Catholic doctrine, and coming as it did from a Protestant, Anglo-
Irish playwright it caused umbrage with the middle-class, Catholic nationalist
audience. The whistle was blown by the veteran nationalist and ex-Parnellite
MP, Frank Hugh O'Donnell, who, in a train of thought which was to set a
pattern for later conflicts, argued that such a morally equivocal play had no right
to call itself Irish or Celtic.

> In this 'Celtic Drama' I saw at once many reasons why it continues to be unrepre-
> sented, but not a single reason why it should be called Celtic. Let it suffice to say,
> Mr. W.B. Yeats's notion of what is Celtic is everywhere illustrated by his harpings
> on his pet 'Celtic idea', that the Gaels of Erin have and had only the thinnest
> veneer of Christian religion and civilization, and really reserve their deepest beliefs
> for demons, fairies, leprachauns, sowlths, thivishes, etc., whom he loves to
> describe in the stilted occultism of a Mrs. Besant or a Madama Blavatsky, and that
> 'Catholic shrines', 'Catholic priests' and Catholic prayers and places are little more
> than sport for the pranks of the devil's own.[109]

This was barbed indeed. O'Donnell, like Griffith later on, had the knack of quoting Yeats back at himself – for Yeats had in fact argued much the same thing as O'Donell here paraphrases in his *The Celtic twilight*, which had appeared one year before O'Donnell's pamphlet.[110] The fact that Yeats, with his complex cultural attitude, voiced different emphases and different aspects at different times and for different audiences, made him particularly vulnerable to being confronted with his own words.[111] O'Donnell not only accuses Yeats of occultist tendencies (and, hence, of a set of beliefs condemned by the Catholic Church, which *ispo facto* bars him from modelling a play on the Catholic doctrine of sin, indulgence and redemption); what is worse, the scornful enumeration of demons, fairies and leprechauns damningly places his symbolist belief in folk superstition in the context of Crofton Croker's and Allingham's fairy folklorism – not the sort of thing which a national theatre should rely on for the vindication of the nation's constitutional rights.

The type of attack instigated by O'Donnell, with its defence of Catholic doctrine and seemliness, might easily be taken for bigotry; and indeed the agitation usually took the form of redneck intolerance. This may lead latter-day critics to the view that here as in later, similar instances, Yeats's theatre was at a cutting edge which the 'hyper-sensitive, hyper-puritanical public morality' of turn-of-the-century Ireland was not yet ready for.[112] But there is more at stake than just a standard literary tension between convention and innovation.[113] What was sensed by men like Frank Hugh O'Donnell was also that Yeats represented country life, as Croker and Allingham, Lover and A.P. Graves had done, 'from above', and wrote about rural Ireland in a benevolent but slightly condescending third person, in terms of quaintness, exoticism and otherness. This is how the *Gaelic journal* in 1901 criticized an article by Synge on the Aran islands:

> Mr. J.M. Synge, whoever he be, appears to be inclined to look down at the natives of Arann from a very high eminence indeed. He discourses of them in a quasi-learned style, as if they were some tribe of Central Africa, instead of Irish Irelanders of simple and unaffected manners. We beg to inform the writer that the type is *not* disappearing from Ireland.[114]

Any sense of Ascendancy snobbery was resented, for the rural folk had a completely different symbolical function for the urban, Catholic nationalists: they were the last remains of the real, oppressed Ireland that had remained faithful to the old language and the old religion, in the teeth of the oppression imposed by the forebears of Yeats and Synge who now presumed to hijack them for their aesthetic ends.

It is for that reason that so much of the protest claimed to be in the name of Irish nationality; this is, I think, the subtext to the *Daily express's* criticism, in its review of *The Countess Cathleen*, that Yeats was ignorant of the ways and thoughts of the Irish peasantry (MID 1: 42). It was because of such reservations that the simplistic playlets in Gaelic which were staged side by side with Yeats's plays were received which such indulgent benevolence: if they were inferior in point of stagecraft, they were certainly based on a complete and unreserved sense of identification with their topic, and a great degree of authentic folk credibility. It must have been a bit of a climbdown for Yeats, who had so emphatically put forward his intention of staging Irish plays on Irish subjects, to defend himself against this criticism in the following terms:

> The chief endeavour with [*The Countess Cathleen*] has been to get it spoken with some sense of rhythm. [. . .] The play is not historic, but symbolic, and has as little to do with any definite place and time as an *auto* by Calderon.[115]

The years 1899 to 1904, after the contretemps about *The Countess Cathleen*, were a period of conciliation between the dramatic movement and the cultural nationalists around D.P. Moran and Arthur Griffith. The tendency remained, to be sure, to express a certain wariness *vis-à-vis* the more aestheticizing plays: thus the *Freeman's journal* wrote, when reviewing AE's *Deirdre* in 1902: 'The name Literary Theatre has fortunately been got rid of, but the thing remains. *Deirdre* was a literary play in the worst sense of the word.'[116] But Yeats prudently emphasized his national commitment rather than his aesthetic principles, staged a few plays in Gaelic, and in most cases the productions were unobjectionable: witness Alice Milligan's *The last feast of the Fianna* or Edward Martyn's *Maeve*, in which a modern Irishwoman hesitates to accept the marriage proposal of an Anglo-Norman, Fitzwalter, because she senses the radical lack of kinship between them; as a reward for this spontaneous sense of racial purity she is taken by her mythical namesake, Queen Maeve, to Tír na nÓg. The height of this conciliation between Yeats and the nationalists was, of course, Yeats's own *Kathleen Ní Houlihan*, with Maud Gonne in the title role.

Kathleen Ní Houlihan was an uncharacteristic exception and marked the transitory zenith of Yeats's involvement with populist nationalism ('our movement is a return to the people'[117]); once this moment had passed, the painful discovery of internal difference set the tone for the next years. Maud Gonne's involvement with the dramatic movement ended shortly afterwards (amidst some acrimony over Synge's *In the shadow of the glen*), and Annie Horniman, with her relentless élitist aestheticism, took over where the political activist Gonne had left off.[118] The 1903 season opened with a highly successful national play, James Cousins's *The sword of Dermot*; but Padraic Colum's *The Saxon shillin'*, already published in Griffith's *United Irishman*, was rejected on the pretext of 'dramatic problems'.

Even as Synge's *In the shadow of the glen* went into rehearsal, stalwart nationalistic members such as Dudley Digges and Máire Quinn resigned. The premiere of that play, in late 1903, was to mark a fatal rift between the theatre and the nationalists. In a later clash in 1905–1906, the fact that *In the shadow of the glen* was maintained on the repertoire alongside *The well of the saints* caused a further rift, when the last representatives of the nationalist ideal (Máire and Frank Walker, Pádraic Colum as well as Stephen Gwynn and George Russell) left the company and Annie Horniman's influence increased (much to Synge's dismay). The final straw came when the Irish National Theatre Society dropped the word 'Irish' from its name and incorporated itself into a limited liability company, the 'National Theatre Company, Ltd.' – a move which turned former fellow-workers into employees and vested all power in a board of directors.[119] When a successful and profitable tour of England was undertaken in November/ December 1905, *The nationalist* commented sarcastically that this was par for the course, since 'the Abbey Theatre, in which the Irish National Theatre Company had been located and, we may add, lost, owes its establishment to British money'. It went on to ask various uncomfortable questions as to the change from national idealism to business-style pragmatism and 'what connection, if any' there was with 'the old *Irish* National Theatre Company' –

> We ask these questions so that we may know how far this venture is a National Theatre and how far it is a speculation run for the aesthetic benefit of some members who have plays to produce (MID 3: 41).

The intensifying conflict between art and nationalist activism culminated in 1907 with the notorious case of Synge's *The playboy of the western world*. The famous riots surrounding that play were sparked off by a reference to female underwear and by the fact that the male lead in the play, Christy Mahon, could unrepentingly present himself as a father-murderer; could derive as a consequence a degree of popularity in the small Irish village where he shows up; and could, in particular, derive a certain amount of glamorous sex appeal from his notoriety with the women of the village, especially young Pegeen.

Synge's play is, like any comedy worthy of the name, an accumulation of multiple ironies which ultimately target the audience as much as the characters. Its main achievement is perhaps the exploitation of Oedipal tension as a comic topic; and there are excellent *coups de théâtre* such as the repeated resuscitation of Mahon *père*, who at every turn outlives his son's ambitions towards parricide. But the audience's reactions were oblivious to such theatrical feats; indeed, the staging of the *Playboy* was hardly allowed to get as far as the revivification of Christy's father. Earlier on in the action, when Pegeen does an unmentionable thing like naming an undergarment or flirting with the professed father-murderer, the Abbey Theatre was already resounding to the cries of 'Irishmen do not harbour murderers' and 'we respect Irish virtue'. The reviewers likewise denounced 'Mr. Synge's preposterous theory that Irish peasant girls fall in love at first sight with the worst type of murderers'. They called the *Playboy* an 'unmitigated, protracted libel upon Irish peasant men and, worse still, upon Irish peasant girlhood'.[120] Given all this furious outrage, the Abbey refrained from staging Synge's *The tinker's wedding* altogether; but even in its printed unperformed form the anticlerical elements in that play caused offence (MID, 3: 243).

To discard these reactions as mere bigotry is unhelpful; not does it suffice to state, in Jauss's terms, that Synge's nonconformism and innovations had given a painful jolt to the audience's 'horizon of expectation' (cf. here, pp. 283–4, n. 113). The mixture of outraged literary taste and outraged national feeling requires a deeper analysis, and might more fruitfully be seen in the poetical terms as outlined by Gérard Genette, who uses the twin concept of *vraisemblance* and *bienséance* (drawn from neo-Aristotelian poetics) to pinpoint the audience's ambivalent set of values in coming to terms with fictional narrative. Genette has studied earlier scandals in French literature to point out that the audience applies the double norm of *plausibility* and *seemliness*: a fictional story, and the actions and motivations of its characters, should be *plausible*, and should, in order to convince, correspond to real life – or at least to the real-world experiences and expectations of the audience. Moreover, the actions and motivations of the characters should be *seemly* in that they should correspond, if not to how people behave in reality, then at least to the way which the audience would expect them to behave.

What makes these obervations interesting is Genette's point that the two norms operate in tandem. If a fictional text actually incenses the public, it is not just because it is poorly constructed or because it is ethically flawed: each of those two strictures by itself would account for disappointment or disappreciation, not for anger. In the case of a literary scandal, the indictment is based on a combination of both elements: the text is both unrealistic and morally reprehensible. This is what Genette's chosen examples show, and it also obtains in the case of the *Playboy*.[121] Pegeen's behaviour is both unconvincing (*no Irish girl would behave like that*) and infamous (*no Irish girl should be made out to behave like that*). The fact that Synge makes Pegeen's behaviour out as he does is both unrealistic and immoral: it is an outrage both to plausibility and to seemliness, *vraisemblance* and *bienséance*. The reviewer in the *Evening mail* states that he left the theatre 'entirely unconvinced that such a thing could have happened' and resents the fact that Synge 'deliberately assails our ears with coarse or blasphemous language'.[122]

According to Genette's analysis, literary and social attitudes intersect at such points: the patterns of audience expectations (the horizon of expectation) are ideological both in a literary and in a social sense.

> Seemliness and plausibility merge into a joint criterion: 'everything that conforms to the taste of the public'. That 'taste', be it actual or imputed, may in modern terms fairly adequately be called an *ideology*: a set of tenets and prejudices constituting both a world-view and a system of values.[123]

Genette's use of the term *ideology* is highly apt in the case of the *Playboy* riots. Not only do the slogans shouted in the Abbey Theatre denounce the play's lack of fidelity to the real Ireland which it is supposed to represent ('That is not life in the West!'), but overtly political voices are heard as well. 'Sinn féin, sinn féin amháin, sinn féin for ever'; nationalist songs were sung like 'The west's awake' or 'A nation once again': the audience reacts to poor realism by vindication of the independence of the fatherland.

As we have seen, Yeats's theatrical initiative attempted to merge, or at least to reconcile, cosmopolitan taste and national energy. As a result, the repertoire of his dramatic movement can be roughly divided into two types: the category which was to become known as the kitchen comedy, and the category of the national allegory. The kitchen comedy was represented by Hyde's Irish-language sketches and the short pieces such as Yeats's *The pot of broth* or Lady Gregory's one-acters. They relied on good-humoured fun and invoked the Gaelic, rustic character of the pleasant peasant, already made popular by Dion Boucicault: uneducated but canny Irish peasants with homely speech and impish wit. These benevolent comic pieces were naturalistic in their setting and in their storyline, and invoked, not Gaelic, but the dialectal speech patterns of Hiberno-English or Kiltartanese.

On the other hand, the more serious plays relied on mythical material or on older Gaelic history: Alice Milligan's *The last feast of the Fianna*, James Cousins's *The sword of Dermot*, Yeats's *Kathleen Ní Houlihan*. There were characters like Cuchulain, Deirdre or Queen Maeve; the diction was elevated, the technique was inspired by the continental art theatre (e.g. lines were chanted), and there was often a political, allegorical meaning attached. Frequently, female characters are made to represent an abstract principle like Ireland or Irish values – witness Yeats's *Kathleen Ní Houlihan* or the symbolism in Martyn's *Maeve*.[124]

This may already go some way to explain the shock effect of the *Playboy*. People expected, from the realistic setting and the rustic speech, a comedy; indeed the play was billed as such. They must soon have found the grotesque and cynical aspects of Synge's play too uncomfortable to be accommodated in the same category as the anodyne pieces that the Abbey Theatre had previously staged as comedies. The *Freeman's journal* in its initial review grumbled that 'This squalid, offensive production is incongruously styled a comedy.'[125] So what was the alternative? The Abbey audience had been trained to see comedies as based on the traditional type of the pleasant peasant, and serious theatre in somehow allegorical terms. Yet if Christy and Pegeen are allegories (default value: 'Irish manhood', 'Irish girlhood'), they are indeed highly unflattering reflections of what they were supposed to stand for.

In short: the *Playboy* was caught between stools in the theatrical conventions that had been established in previous years. We can infer as much from the review in the *Evening mail*, which begins by pointing out that the story is far too grotesque to make a convincing comedy, and goes on to surmise

> or, perhaps, it is an allegory, and the parricide represents some kind of nation-killer, whom Irishmen and Irishwomen hasten to lionise. If it is an allegory it is too obscure for me.[126]

But the question as to what Pegeen was supposed to stand for was not a new one; it carried with it the burden of a literary–political debate which had been fought over an earlier female character in a Synge play: Norah Burke in *In the shadow of the glen*. Indeed, the Playboy riots need to be seen against the backdrop of controversies surrounding Synge's and Yeats's earlier plays. The riots of 1907 are, in their confusion between aesthetic and political critique, a mingled, cacophonous, indistinct uproar. To add subtitles to the audience's whistles and catcalls, and to the heated exchanges and passion-choked reproaches bandied back and forth, it is useful to look at the terms of the conflict as they had already been established earlier on; and therefore it is useful to move back in time to late 1903, when controversy arose over *In the shadow of the glen*.

Synge's women, Boccaccio and the Irish folk

The conflict of 1903–1904 is less notorious than the *Playboy* riots; it was strenuous but still sedately argued, and clarifies more about the contentions and conflicting ideals than the riots of 1907. In turn, the terms of the conflict in 1903 had already been in the air when people had taken objection to *The Countess Cathleen* in 1899. Thus, Frank Hugh O'Donnell rode again in early 1904 as he had done in 1899, this time with a pamphlet entitled *The Stage Irishman of the pseudo-Celtic drama*:

> [Yeats's] occult mission, it seemed, was to celebrate the wedding of Madame Blavatsky and Finn MacCumhail. A sort of witch's cauldron of aboriginal super-stition and Ibsenite neo-paganism was declared to be the permanent spring of Celtic genius and Celtic religion. [. . .] When you pretend to be Irish and Celtic, you must follow, not outrage, Irish and Celtic sentiment (quoted MID, 2: 95–97).

This time, O'Donnell's reproaches found widespread endorsement. Even the *Irish times* wrote in August 1904:

> In the main we find ourselves in agreement with Mr. O'Donnell's contention that whatever Mr. Yeats's work may be it has little claims to be considered Celtic. No doubt Celtic legend supplies the motive of much of it, but that alone is not sufficient to make it Celtic (quoted MID 2: 98).

But although the debate by mid-1904 had begun to centre around Yeats, the cause of outrage this time was Synge, not Yeats; what was it in this brief sketch that outraged Irish and Celtic sentiment?

When *In the shadow of the glen* was produced in late 1903, the audience, Griffith foremost among them, found it an insult to the Irish peasantry. It must be admitted that the Irish peasantry is not presented in a very flattering light: an old peasant pretends to be dead in order to test the fidelity of his young wife; a neighbour is willing to console the pretty widow with her inheritance, but cynically sides with the old husband when that quasi-corpse rises from under his shroud and expels his wife from the house. Worse than that, Synge evokes domestic life in the Irish countryside as a stifling prison, where material pro-tection comes at the cost of a loveless marriage and emotional starvation.

But that was not the immediate cause of the audience's outrage at *In the shadow of the glen*. Their ire was provoked, not by the cruel experiment performed by the old peasant upon his wife's emotions, nor by the neighbour's cowardly egotism. What outraged the audience was, ironically, the figure of Norah Burke and her frank avowal of the frustrations of her married life. Again, as in the later case of the *Playboy*, we can see that Norah Burke is automatically interpreted as an *Idealtypus*, a personification of Irish womanhood and of all the nationalistic ideals that the nostalgic Dublin audiences projected into Irish womanhood. As such, the audience's sense of *vraisemblance* and *bienséance* was bitterly disappointed, and Norah Burke was considered an insult. Thus, Griffith wrote in his review:

> Mr Synge – or else his play has no meaning – places Norah Burke before us as a type – 'a personification of an average' – and Norah Burke is a lie.[127]

Accordingly, Griffith, like O'Donnell, declares that the Abbey Theatre has forsaken 'National' values for the sake of 'Literary' aestheticism. An Irish, National Theatre (the company at the time was called the Irish National Theatre Society) should celebrate, not slander, the Irish peasantry and its domestic family values. Synge's play is un-Irish and even anti-Irish to the extent that it does not do so. 'The play has an Irish name, but it is no more Irish than the Decameron.'

The *Decameron*? Griffith develops a thematic filiation in which he traces the theme of the 'consolable widow' back from Synge to a story in Boccaccio's *Decameron*, and from there to the classical Latin novel *Satyricon* by Petronius Arbiter. In fact, Griffith demonstrates, Synge has done little else than to rehash the old and unedifying theme of the Widow of Ephesus.[128]

That is in itself an interesting observation. But Griffith does not intend it as a compliment to place Synge under the auspices of Boccaccio and Petronius. On the contrary: not only does a borrowing of metropolitan themes flaw the originality and authenticity which is required to create a new, national art,[129] there is also the moralistic objection that such decadent Continental ribaldry should be kept out of Ireland. The theme, 'a stock one in the Quartier Latin', which could be 'purchased in the Palais Royal', was 'invented by the wits of decadent Greece and introduced, with amendments, into Latin literature by the most infamous of Roman writers, Petronius Arbiter, the pander of Nero'. Accordingly, Synge's work 'is not a work of genius – Irish or otherwise – it is a foul echo from degenerate Greece' (MID 3: 11–12). That nativist attitude is, again, in tune with the general pattern of Griffith's nationalism: one of autarky, of political and cultural self-sufficiency, aloofness from nefarious foreign (especially English) influences. Griffith's inward-looking 'ourselves alone' is thus applied to cultural politics as well. If Irish art takes part in international cultural intercourse, it will be tainted by the decay and decadence of Europe. Hence, if Yeats's literary ambitions are cosmopolitan, if they invoke the examples of Mallarmé, Maeterlinck, Ibsen and D'Annunzio, then that is a fatal threat to the national integrity and viability of an *Irish* theatre. A similar point was made by Frank Hugh O'Donnell in his 1904 pamphlet:

> Mr Yeats writes a sort of Maeterlinckish-Ibsenitish-Baudelairean drama, or what he calls a drama, and labels his characters Maive, and Cathleen, and Oona, and Grania, and Diarmuid, and Conan, and Shemus, and Maureen (quoted MID 2: 95–96).

Thus, the nationalists point out the incompatibility of Yeats's stance (and the 1904–1905 debate around Synge very quickly became a debate around Yeats). On the one hand, Yeats takes recourse to an Irish *imaginaire* so as to invigorate his creativity and to escape from the decline of mainstream English literature; on the other hand, he instills this Irish enterprise with all the self-professed drooping decadence of Continental symbolism, and complicates the simple truths of Irish peasant life with the moral dilemmas and perplexities of the contemporary metropolis. In the atmosphere of the growing conflict between art and propaganda, Yeats had written that

> beauty and truth are always justified to themselves, and [. . .] their creation is a greater service to our country than writing that compromises either in the seeming service of a cause.[130]

Griffith now pointed out that Yeats could not have it both ways:

> Mr Yeats writes that the Irish National Theatre Society has no propaganda but that of good art. If so, the Society is no more Irish and National than the Elizabethan Stage Society. [. . .] When it ceases to be national, it will also cease to be artistic, for nationality is the breath of art.

Again, this was awkward in that it echoed Yeats's own arguments, made at a time when his nationalist enthusiasm had been more in the ascendant ('there is no nationality without literature, no literature without nationality').

Thus, Griffith turns Yeats's attempt to merge aestheticism and Irishness into a dilemma. Yeats, however, had pre-empted this charge by attacking Griffith's conflation between art and propaganda, his confusion between nationality and nationalism. Good nationalist propaganda did not necessarily make good art; the sort of positive treatment that Griffith wished to see meted out to Irish peasant characters reduced them to the one-dimensional Pleasant Peasants of Victorian vintage. In a letter to the *United Irishman* in October 1903, Yeats spoke scathingly of 'the hatred of ideas of the more ignorant sort of Gaelic propagandist, who would have nothing said or thought that is not in country Gaelic', and of the intolerant politician 'who would reject every idea which is not of immediate service to his cause'.

> It will be safer to go on, one says, thinking about the Irish country people, as if they were 'picturesque objects', 'typical peasants', as the phrase is, in the foreground of a young lady's water-colour.[131]

In the same debate, sparked off by Synge's blighted *In the shadow of the glen* with
its decadent, degenerate roots, Jack Yeats (senior) emphasized the distinction
between nationality and nationalism, and reiterated his son's dictum that art is
art because it is not nature, nor politics.[132] It was argued that the Abbey could be
Irish and national without necessarily becoming a platform for Sinn Féin or
Gaelic League propaganda, that it could be Irish and national 'as the Shannon
and the Wicklow mountains and the Lakes of Killarney are national, because it
has grown up on Irish soil and out of it.' That echoed W.B. Yeats's earlier notions,
advanced in 1899, about the spontaneous, unpremeditated nationality of his
enterprise (above, pp. 208–9); but the way things had been put left a fatal
opening for Griffith to deal a devastating riposte. With a sidelong pointer to the
fact that Synge 'spends most of his time away from Ireland, and under the
operation of foreign influences', Griffith stated that *In the shadow of the glen*, with
its Greek-Latin-Italian-French background, failed to answer Yeats's own criteri-
um of nationality.

> Art is truth, and Mr. Synge's play is not truth. It did not grow up on Irish soil and
> out of it (MID 2: 82).

This remarkable and scintillating debate clarifies much. Not only is it a necessary background against which to understand the intensity of the later *Playboy*
riots; not only does it illustrate a fascinating interaction between realism and
symbolism; it also brings out the opposing notions of Irish nationality that were
being invoked at the time. For Griffith and his nativist *Sinn Féin* attitude,
national was the opposite of *foreign*; for Yeats and his group, it was the opposite
of *provincial*. For Griffith and like-minded nationalists, to be a national theatre
meant to cultivate homegrown, folk-steeped literature without foreign contamination; accordingly, to allow a foreign influence in the Abbey meant to abandon
homegrown, domestic values for foreign frippery and to expose Ireland to the
European blight of decadence.[133] On the other hand, for Yeats and his circle,
national meant to transcend the provincialism and shallowness of the sentimental Allingham school. Their aim was to take Ireland out of the backwater of
Victorian regionalism, to elevate it to a mature standard where it could rank
with other European nationalities; and for that purpose it was quite acceptable
to emulate the example of Boccaccio and other luminaries in the European
tradition.[134]

This pattern of conflicting ideas, the clash between national exclusivism and
national enrichment, is of momentous importance in Irish developments. It was
widespread at the time (e.g. in the Gaelic League's relations between nativists
and progressives as charted by Philip O'Leary), and it kept its hold over Irish
cultural debate long after Griffith had become acting head of state in 1920 or
Yeats had become a senator in 1922. Much of twentieth-century Irish history is
dominated by the question of whether Ireland should seek its identity in an
introspective or an extroverted mode, whether or not it should quarantine

itself from the vexations of modern life. Ultimately that choice boils down to the question whether or not Irish nationality is to be defined specifically by its differences from the rest of the world, by its particular otherness.

Ironically, that choice, which was perhaps most trenchantly argued by the opposing camps in the debates here paraphrased, was based on a false opposition: that between folk culture and European literature. Both sides in the debate shared an *a priori* idea as to the relation between those two narrative traditions: one spontaneous and artless, the other refined; one strong on invention, the other on artifice; one *substance*, remarkable mainly in its thematics, the other *form*, remarkable mainly in its manner of handling the material.

Griffith impugned the Irishness of Synge's *In the shadow of the glen* because, despite its setting, it lacked folk authenticity and was tainted by a literary, European provenance. Yeats and Synge argued against this that Synge's theme was a widespread one in oral folk culture and that Synge had heard it told by an old man on the Aran Islands. That became the main focus of the debate as it flared up again in 1905, when *In the shadow of the glen* was revived, and with it the vexed question of Norah Burke's morality and/or Irishness. Synge demanded that the *United Irishman* authenticate his play by printing the folktale as he had transcribed it; Griffith extricated himself by pointing out that the folktale was 'essentially different to the play he insolently calls *In a Wicklow glen*. In the Aran islands story the wife appears as a callous woman – in Mr. Synge's play the wife is a strumpet'; in any case, the story was, as Griffith put it, 'of insufficient merit to entitle it to a place in our columns'. The original transcript of the story as told to Synge by Pat Dirane is extant. It has been included in Ann Saddlemyer's edition and has been used fruitfully by Synge scholars; Éilís Ní Dhuibhne-Almqvist has traced the story's background in Irish folklore, and its relation to Synge's dramatic treatment, in her investigation of 'Synge's use of popular material in *The Shadow of the Glen*'.[135] Her conclusion is that the selfsame 'mixture of the burlesque and the tragic' (165–166) which the Abbey audience found so baffling and irritating, and which triggered their rejection of Synge as being 'absurd and un-Irish', was taken by Synge precisely from the oral tradition whence he had obtained the storyline. In fact, then, the irony of the matter is that Synge, so far from being insufficiently attuned to the real peasantry or with true life in the west, failed to make the peasantry's oral narrative sufficiently palatable to the Dublin theatregoers and their metropolitan, middle-brow demands of *vraisemblance* and *bienséance*. It is not decadent European literature which has an exclusive monopoly on equivocal morality and a sense of the perplexities of life, nor is the folk tradition innocent and simplistic in its world-view.

What is more, there is no necessary, let alone absolute, contradiction between European literature and the Irish folk tradition. A storyline used by Petronius or Boccaccio may also be found in folktales widely across the globe. Yeats, of course, was alert to this idea that high literature and folklore shared a common profound reservoir of imagination, and he pointed out as much in a few letters to the *United Irishman*.[136] There is, however, a further irony. Only a few years after the Synge controversies, tales were recorded in Irish Ireland, in the pure, unsullied, Gaelic-speaking, innocent Ireland which Griffith championed against Synge's slanders – tales which derived obviously from no other source than, precisely, Boccaccio's *Decameron*. These tales comprised precisely that sort of stuff which Griffith wanted to keep out of Ireland. More or less under Griffith's nose, an English translation of that repugnant *Decameron* found its way into the Blasket Islands, where the honest rustics liked it so much that Gaelic versions of some episodes found their way into the repertoire of storytellers.[137] The confusion this has occasioned among folklore scholars is due in no small part to the old-fashioned assumption, which lies at the root of nineteenth-century folklore as it had been instigated by the Grimms, that *orality* on the part of their sources equals naïve pre-literacy, that the folk's orality is the orality of children or of primitive societies who have not yet learned to read and write. Tales that were passed on by word of mouth, the assumption used to be, must have been first obtained by word of mouth. The relationship between spoken and written culture has long been assumed to be a one-way process: writing is a secondary activity, transcribing the primary activity of speaking, and occurring at a later, more advanced stage of a society's development. The idea that things could go the other way around, and that written and oral narrative culture exist side-by-side in a two-way-permeable continuum, is a more recent insight and has necessitated the revision of some romantic, nineteenth-century, Crofton-Croker-style cliché's about the peasantry. It shows that the stock character of the aboriginal peasant, the timeless Ireland, is flawed precisely in its dehistoricizing reflex, its tendency to see the Irish peasantry as uninvolved in a historical dynamics.[138]

Conclusion: history revived, or, the nightmare of anachronism

Time for a summing-up. The turn-of-the-century initiatives in an imaginative, literary recuperation and celebration of Ireland's nationality were unavoidably constructed on an auto-exoticist self-image. Irish individuality and Irish identity were sought in those aspects in which Ireland was most distinctively un-English; as a result, the privileged areas of Irish culture in the literary imagination were the distant, pre-Norman or mythical past and the contemporary native, as yet un-anglicized, peasantry. This double focus on past and peasant coincided with an attempt to extricate the ideal of Irishness from a prevailing, Europe-wide sense of decadence and degeneracy – after all, we are in the decades of Max Nordau and Oswald Spengler. Metropolitan history is considered to be in its afterdays, freewheeling from a great past into a future of cultural attrition and decay; an escape from that decline might be found in the freshness of the folk tradition or the unspoilt resources of ancient myth.

The tendency to invoke past and peasant, not just for exoticist or picturesque purposes, but towards a *revival*, makes the case of Ireland special. There have been other moments in European history when the demotic backbone of national culture was invoked as a counter-measure against foreign adulteration and sterile, slavish imitation of a mightier neighbour;[139] but in turn-of-the-century Ireland, such a literary 'back to our own roots' call was made with a revivalist, rejuvenating resonance. History had been a series of defeats and misadventures, the agenda was to return to a pristine *status quo ante*, to de-anglicize, to undo the Conquest. If, then, a reviewer in the *Evening mail* calls the *Playboy* 'absurd and un-Irish' because 'it smacks of the decadent ideas of the literary flaneurs of Paris rather than of simple Connaught',[140] we see how in the opposition between young, innocent Ireland and old, decadent Europe, an important temporal connotation is at work, alongside the social folk-élite polarity between flaneurs and simple folk. Placing a theme from Boccaccio and Petronius in a western Irish setting is almost tantamount to a dirty old man importuning an innocent young girl.

This brings me to one final ingredient in the Synge controversies, and perhaps the one which, for all that it was rarely stated outright, was perhaps the deeper cause for the rifts which Synge's plays occasioned in the nationalist camp: his use of the vocabulary of old versus young, decrepitude versus freshness, decadence versus revival.

The horizon of expectation of the Abbey audiences was habituated, through a thousand turns of phrase and metaphor, to see Irish cultural nationalism as aiming at a *revival*, a *rejuvenation*, turning Kathleen Ní Houlihan from an old hag into a young queen. It is precisely in this respect that Synge's plays most specif-ically went against the grain. Synge's treatment of the revival or rejuvenation theme insistently tended the other way. When old, 'dead' Burke arises from under his shroud, in *In the shadow of the glen*; when old 'dead' Mahon shows up alive in the village where he son is now living like a playboy; then these revivals are by no means the escapes from history, the glorious phoenix-like rebirths that the audience were used to. On the contrary, revivals in Synge are not rejuvena-tions but a reassertion of the power of the old over the young.[141] These revivals thwart the future prospects of Norah Burke, of Christy and Pegeen: the younger characters, who struggle to get out from under the shadow of a burdensome and insistent past.

Synge's handling of the terms of youth, old age and revival goes squarely against standard patterns at the time. Therein lies what we may call his original-ity, or his creative genius; therein lies certainly the deeper reason why he outraged his audience.[142] It is in this respect, also, that his cardinal position in the thematic development of Anglo-Irish literature becomes apparent.

The recurrence of the dead past, bursting into the living present; the aware-ness of buried, unfinished business yet awaiting definitive settlement – all this has important antecedents and begins perhaps with the cult of remembrancing initiated by Moore and the anti-Unionists. It fuels the 'Irish habit of historical thought'; it is present in much of the tradition of the Irish Gothic, starting with Maturin and his lurid *Milesian chief* (a book which Mangan called 'the most intensely Irish story he knew of'[143]). It is no surprise that the figure of the aristocratic vampire, undead remnant of a feudal past battening on the vitality of the living, is an appealing one for Irish authors from Boucicault (who used the topic for a play) to Le Fanu to Stoker, and even for Yeats.[144] The *frisson* of Irish Gothic (from Melmoth to Dracula) and the appeal of the Big House theme (including Yeats's own *Words upon the window pane* and *Purgatory*[145]) lay partly in the fact that 'the lively expectations of the young' tended to be 'devoured by the guilt and errors of their elders'.[146] The theme reverberates with worried reservations as to the straightforwardness of time, with an uncanny sense that Irish history, the sheer weight and bloodiness and persistence of it, will trouble the present's course towards the future.

This cultivation of an undead past, which provides the blueprint and the ideals for future resuscitation, gives a morbid hue to the pretended vitalism of the Gaelic Revival and the Irish Renaissance. It was, of all authors, Synge, with his quick corpses, who brought out the uncanny and sinister undertones of such revivals. This, I submit, it what constitutes his originality, his greatness, and (at the time) his controversial position. It is also what makes him, in my view, the great forerunner of Joyce. If Joyce's Stephen Dedalus defines history as 'a nightmare from which I am trying to awake'; if one of the main themes in *Ulysses* is that of Hamlet, where the ghost of the dead father comes to trouble the son; and if Joyce's cyclical, Vicoesque view of history invokes yet another Irish undead hero rising up on his own wake (the ballad's rollicking stonemason Tim Finnegan), then we see in such aspects the echoes of a preoccupation which Synge, of all earlier Irish writers, did most to come to grips with.[147]

Which brings us to 16 June, 1904; the day when James Joyce brought the Irish nineteenth century to a close.

CONCLUSION:
How Time Passes in Joyce's Dublin

The permanence of matter through time is one of our fundamental *a priori* assumptions about the world. Berkeley (coincidentally an Irishman) had played devil's advocate in this respect by arguing a counter-intuitive, yet almost-watertight case for 'immaterialism'. If we lose a coin one day, and the next day we find a coin, who is to tell whether this is one and the same coin? If we look at a tree, then close our eyes, and then look again, who is to tell that this is one and the same tree? What objective proof can be given for the fact that this tree continued to exist at all while we weren't looking? Berkeley argued that existence is tantamount to being perceived; that the world consists of our perceptions rather than of objects; and that the 'permanence of matter through time', between moments of being perceived, is merely a facilitating psychological assumption on our part, not an objective condition of empirical reality.

When Kant disproved Berkeley, he argued categorically that the permanence of matter through time is an analytical and therefore unprovable, but *a priori* valid, tenet. In time-hallowed fashion Kant distinguished between the substance of things and their incidental qualities (their location, aspect, temperature, movement etc.). The incidental qualities of a given object are changeable through time; its substance is what remains if you discount all incidental qualities, i.e. the substance of an object is by definition that which is not changeable through time; *quod erat demonstrandum.*[1]

In all the multifarious developments I have charted in the foregoing pages, we can register variations on one basic theme: attempts to see through the mutability, the changes and the incidental qualities of Irish history with all its disruptions, and to distill a core, a *substance*. There is a constant search for some permanent principle which would define the essence, the transhistorical formula, of Irishness. That project was by no means unique to Ireland; it was central to all nationalisms in Europe, in a century when each state and each nation sought to define itself by cultivating its essential and individual character as it had been postulated by Herder and, after him, by Hegel.

But in Ireland the project was much more fraught and complex than elsewhere, because Ireland, perhaps more than any other European nation, had undergone a particularly violent and disruptive historical development over long centuries of never-resolved conflict, and had (unlike Germany) for most of its recorded history been subject to foreign control. The closest European parallel to the Irish case in this respect is possibly Poland. Irish history seemed to be all incident and no permanence.

Imagining Ireland in the nineteenth century involves, in true Romantic fashion, an ongoing attempt to see through the vicissitudes of political incident and historical confusion. The literary or historical imagination and representation of Ireland tries to redeem a True Ireland from the violent mutability of history and political divisions – and in the result, a Romantic literary agenda becomes also a national project of finding, defining and formulating an ideal Irish identity. Many European nationalities in the wake of Romanticism are preoccupied with identity construction; in the case of Ireland, that project is grafted onto a long-standing confrontation with the neighbouring isle, takes place in a climate of barely-contained hostile divisions, carries a burdensome political heritage and is invested with great, contentious political urgency.

The self-image that takes shape in nineteenth-century Ireland is heavily invested with politics and provides important rhetorical ammunition in the social and ideological conflicts of the time – between Morgan and English indifference, between Moore and Protestant unionists, between Hardiman and Ferguson, between Griffith and Yeats. But its built-in idealist, Romantic character (the search for a transcending, true identity) often moves it into a non-political direction, and the True Ireland is piously sought in a non-contentious register: the past (that is, those less violent portions of the past, which are not so wild and bloody as to forbid representation altogether) or the idyllic parts of Irish society (the peasantry with their rustic folkways).

Both mechanisms follow an exoticist impetus in that both try to characterize a True Ireland in those aspects which are different, un-mundane, other: 'when Malachi wore the collar of gold', or where timeless picturesque custom is enacted in quaint language. Hence, one of the deep-seated motifs of nineteenth-century cultural reflection in Ireland is that which I have termed *auto-exoticism*: to look for one's own identity in the unusual, the extraordinary, the exotic aspects of experience, to conflate the notions of one's distinctness and one's distinctiveness. Irish history, as a result, tends to be inevitably traced back to mythical, fictional but colourful roots; Irish life tends to be reduced to its un-English aspects. The cultivation of the ancient, pre-Norman past, with its aristocratic society and refined culture, intersects throughout the century in numerous interesting ways with the cultivation of the contemporary peasant, with his homely humours and artless charm. Despite their great differences, these two elements, past and peasant, become linked and even conflated because both represent a radically un-anglicized, ideal Ireland – witness the overlap between popular history, mythography and folklore in the later century; witness Lady Gregory's Cuchulain, who speaks with a Kiltartanese brogue. Past and peasant also meet because both are imagined as situated outside factual history: the one in a mythical prelapsarian past, the other in a de-historicized chronotope situated on the margins of the world as we know it.

Also, the attempt to create ideal Irelands as a response to a less than ideal political predicament involves a number of imaginative and discursive strategies of anachronism. As we have seen, such strategies of unifying history and transcending mutability often involve the substitution of the historical *Nacheinander* by a spectacular *Nebeneinander*. The mutability of history, with its shifting and multifarious warring parties, is reduced to a conspectus of scenes on the invariant formula of English misrule and Irish resistance (always the same England, the same Ireland, from Red Hugh O'Donnell to Robert Emmet). The past, in its physical monuments or in its *lieux de mémoire* such as Round Towers, in its literary or poetical or musical remains or in its ossified, unchanging, continuously repeated historical narrative, has direct symbolical significance for a present-day sense of identity. Voices from the past are put before an audience by the retrieval of old manuscripts (be it in the fictional pages of Morgan and Maturin, or in the real-world endeavours of O'Donovan and O'Curry). Supernatural characters stalk the literary imagination, who in their trans-individual or trans-historical identity preside over historical change and fleeting centuries: Captain Rock, Melmoth, Dark Rosaleen in all her different renderings, Kathleen Ní Houlihan. They are personifications of the act of remembrance, walking and living (or at least undead) memories that haunt successive generations from century to century. Remembrance from Moore to Davis becomes a cardinal element in the unification of history; towards the end of the century it becomes institutionalized in the penchant for centenary commemorations (of Moore, of O'Connell, of Tone) and in the cult of funerals, which appears simultaneously with the growing belief in a revival of dead ideals and a redemption for Ireland from the historical entropy of Europe.

As a result of all these varied responses and variations on the one underlying theme, the cultural history of Ireland offers an excellent example of the various modalities of turning history either into myth or into spectacle. The borders between history and story are thin: history tends to be told in a 'once upon a time' mode, emphasizing the enduring presence of the same old masterplot, while literary stories tend to clutter their narratives with factual asides, footnotes, pieces of background information. Ireland becomes everything that is excluded by the bald statement of what is the case: Ireland is couched in terms of what used to be, what failed to be, what might have been, what must become. Thus, ironically, the desire to retrieve a sense of permanence conspired in the end to exoticize Ireland and to remove it from mundane reality.

Ireland as chronotope: a place with an uneven distribution of time-passage, where time is apt to slow down and come to a standstill at the periphery: that emerges, from the foregoing pages, as one of the formative notions in the literary and historical imagination of Ireland. However, the very notions of what is a centre and what is a periphery are of course fluid, and depend on the perspective of the beholder. Islington might be a suburban periphery from the point of view of Sloane Square or Chelsea, but it counts as part of the metropolis for someone from Lincolnshire, whilst Lincolnshire in turn is the Tennysonian heartland of England for someone from the Hebrides, Canada or Fiji. One and the same place can variously be seen as peripheral or central; the best case being, perhaps, Dublin.

Part of the trauma of the Union was, precisely, a sense of marginalization and rustication now that Dublin ceased to be home to a parliament, ceased to be the central capital of a nation. When Yeats, Moore, Martyn and Gregory started their literary and dramatic movement, they did so with a sense that they were going to launch their renewal of dramatic practice from a peripheral vantage point, similar to Ibsen in Norway, Maeterlinck in Flanders, Chekhov in Russia. Accordingly, their movement, launched from the fringes, was to have all the timeless, slow-moving qualities of the periphery: a liminal shadow-zone between life and dream, reality and myth, where lines were to be chanted, and plot or action were secondary to the slow, still spectacle of successive *tableaux* on stage.

To construct a given place as peripheral or central moves an entire apparatus of signalling devices, signs and standard attributes into place. Places and locations are given central status by being given the attributes of development, a linear, forward-moving progression from past into present into future: time in the centre introduces constant innovation, and history progresses (for better or worse: into growth or into decay). The modernist dynamic treatment of the metropolis (New York in Dos Passos, Berlin in Döblin) is the outstanding example. Conversely, the periphery stands still, or lags behind, has an intact link with the past (tradition). Witness the archaic countryside of Thomas Hardy's Wessex, the provincial second-rate boredom of Dublin in George Moore' *Muslin*, the Provence of Pagnol, the dormant and stagnant Flemish towns of Rodenbach's *Bruges la morte*, the treatment of the Irish countryside in almost all of nineteenth- century Anglo-Irish literature.

In the case of Dublin, the work of James Joyce offers an interesting example how one and the same place can be seen as peripheral at one moment, central at the next, and how the attendant registers of description match that contradictory construction. The Dublin of *Dubliners*, with its contant emphasis on stagnation and paralysis, is a provincial town, stifling individual initiative under a smothering blanket. The movements of the characters trail as aimlessly as their lives and experiences. Life in Dublin is a process of stagnation and attrition, and vain hopes for a more exciting life are fixed on an elsewhere, an escape: the exotically named bazaar in 'Araby', Buenos Aires for Eveline, the cultural wealth of continental Europe for Gabriel Conroy in 'The dead'. There is good cause to see this atmosphere, where Dublin becomes (as Joyce famously called it) 'that hemiplegia or paralysis which many consider a city', as a lack of true metropolitanism. The 'parochial, colonized' and colonially disinherited Dublin of *Dubliners* lacks the vitality and energy of a proper city: Dublin is 'falling deeper into provincialism and [is represented] in the decaying and constraining middle-class streets'.[2]

It is against this background that we should see the well-known opposition between the Irish west and the European continent in 'The dead'. Although the west may be held out as a place for revivalist journeys by the Gaelic Leaguer Miss Ivors, it is also the place from which yet another unquiet shade comes to haunt the present (yet another representative of that class, alongside Tim Finnegan, the Burke and Mahon characters in Synge's plays, and Count Dracula). The spectre of long-dead Michael Furey, buried at Oughterard, is conjured up out of the past to trouble the present, to spoil Gabriel's complacent fondness and his hopes for a new stage in his marriage and his cultural development by going to the Continent.[3] The power of the dead over the living, in *Dubliners*, is precisely that of old Burke over Norah, in *In the shadow of the glen*. History thus dominated by an undead past is a nightmare from which it is impossible to escape, and it is significant that so much time and space in *A portrait* is given, not only to the dead weight of post-Parnellite recrimination, but also to the sermon with its infernal vision insisting so very heavily on the idea of eternity.

There can be no stronger contrast than between the stagnant Dublin of *Dubliners* and the vibrant Dublin of *Ulysses*. Joyce himself appears to revel in the depiction of a Newtonian Dublin, where time and space coexist in a physical, dynamic relationship, dominated by movement and crisscrossing trajectories through space and time, where space divided by time equals speed. This Dublin he constructed with the quintessential organizing tools of space and time: a map and a watch, dovetailing *Nebeneinander* and *Nacheinander* in what is fittingly the book's central episode: The Wandering Rocks.[4] That episode, set squarely in the middle of Bloomsday and of *Ulysses*, opens with, precisely, a Jesuit, the superior, the very reverend John Conmee, S.J., resetting his smooth watch – one of the central images in the entire work. If the description of Dublin is fragmented and cubistically broken up (Luke Gibbons speaks quite rightly of a 'montage' technique[5]), the effect is not so much to represent an alienated, fractured state of affairs or state of mind, but rather to celebrate the multifarious and complex ways in which the various elements of this Newtonian universe interact, cross paths, gravitate, attract and repel each other.

It is in this sense of dynamism and movement, and the insistent use of physical clock-time, that Dublin is rendered a metropolis, an omphalos indeed, the quintessenial twentieth-century city: a centre rather than a periphery, and quite redeemed from its stagnation and paralysis as described in *Dubliners*. If *Ulysses* signals the triumph of modernism, it is marked, not only by its verbal ingenuity, its redefinition of the relationship between content and form, and its irreverent play on conventions, but also because it is placed in direct proximity to the rest of the world-at-large, and abandons, with a palpable sense of release, the ingrained nineteenth-century patterns of the realist, allochronic representation of Ireland.

It will be obvious that this interpretation stands at odds with the one advanced by Udaya Kumar in his fine book *The Joycean Labyrinth*. Kumar argues that *Ulysses*'s textual coherence is based on fugatic echoes, cross-allusions and repetitions rather than on a 'narrative deep structure'. His point is valuable particularly in that it highlights a corresponding attitude to history, which, nightmarish as it is, lacks internal order and exhibits only a superficial repetitiveness close to the Freudian notion of the uncanny; Kumar thus places *Ulysses* on the interesting point of intersection between Berkeley's theory of perception and ontology, and a modernist theory of time and history. Nevertheless, this argument holds only for *Ulysses* as *sjužet* (the textual surface arranged into discontinuous and manipulated episodes, ranging from the opening word 'Stately' to the closing word 'Yes'). The *fabula* of Ulysses (its underlying subject-matter, the manifold events taking place, or remembered, in Dublin on 16 June 1904) is by no means chaotic; on the contrary, it is carefully organized and orchestrated. All parallaxes, echoes, repetitions, analeptic and proleptic cross-references, neatly converge into a consistent and non-contradictory set of events which take place in a precise and tidy choreography. It is indicative that Kumar finds it difficult to come to terms with the episode which is most explicitly constructed on the parallax as organizing principle and on the interplay between *Nebeneinander* and *Nacheinander*, 'The wandering rocks'.[6]

It is precisely in the centre of Dublin, at Nelson's Pillar, that the dynamic vortex of movement swirls to its greatest intensity. The breathless, frenetic, breezy Aeolus episode opens:

> IN THE HEART OF THE HIBERNIAN METROPOLIS
> Before Nelson's pillar trams slowed, shunted, changed trolley, started for Blackrock, Kingstown and Dalkey, Clonskea, Rathgar and Terenure, Palmerston Park and upper Rathmines, Sandymount Green, Rathmines, Ringsend and Sandymount Tower, Harold's Cross. The hoarse Dublin United Tramway Company's timekeeper bawled them off:
> – Rathgar and Terenure!
> – Come on, Sandymount Green!
> Right and left parallel clanging ringing a doubledecker and a singledeck moved from their railheads, swerved to the down line, glided parallel.
> – Start, Palmerston Park![7]

This Dublin is indeed a place built on the coordinates of *Nebeneinander* and *Nacheinander*.[8] It is a clockwork city for plotting movement, a grid on which location and moment provide the precise coordinates for the action. The vice-regal procession as traced through 'The wandering rocks' is prefigured in the viceregicidal plotting explained in 'Aeolus':

> B. is parkgate [. . .] T is viceregal lodge. C is where the murder took place. K is Knockmaroon gate. [. . .] F to P is the route Skin-the-Goat drove the car for an alibi, Inchicore, Roundtown, Windy Arbour, Palmerston Park, Ranelagh. F.A.B.P. Got that? X is Davy's publichouse in upper Leeson street (112).

W.J. Mc Cormack has spotted this element in *Ulysses* with his usual acumen, and points out that the *Nebeneinander* might evoke 'the simultaneity of all events in the "nightmare of history"', adding that 'In colonial Ireland sequence and simultaneity are rival experiences of history.'[9] But it should be added that all the above-cited instances of the dovetailing of space and time represent so many refusals to follow the standard allochrony, the 'times passes slowly, history has passed overhead' patterns which had dominated almost the entire representation of Ireland in the previous century (including *Dubliners*, although the movements of the Two Gallants give an inkling of Joyce's new, urban approach).

The metropolitan centrality of Dublin is stressed at a multitude of different levels – even in the free indirect discourse that ironically impersonates Father Conmee's urbane complacency:

> Moored under the trees of Charleville Mall Father Conmee saw a turfbarge, a towhorse with pendent head, a bargeman with a hat of dirty straw seated amidships, smoking and staring at a branch of poplar above him. It was idyllic: and Father Conmee reflected on the providence of the Creator who had made turf to be in bogs whence men might dig it out and bring it to town and hamlet to make fires in the houses of poor people (p. 182).

This metropolitan notion of a surrounding country serving the needs of the centre is later echoed in the apotheosis of Leopold Bloom, in the 'Ithaca' episode, when the entire universe and the engineering skills of the empire concur in providing water for him to make cocoa:

> What did Bloom do at the range?
> He removed the saucepan to the left hob, rose and carried the iron kettle to the sink in order to tap the current by turning the faucet to let it flow.
> Did it flow?
> Yes. From Roundwood reservoir in county Wicklow of a cubic capacity of 2400 million gallons, percolating through a subterranean aqueduct of filter mains of single and double pipeage constructed at an initial plant cost of £5 per linear yard by way of Dargle, Rathdown, Glen of the Downs and Callowhill to the 26 acre reservoir at Stillorgan, a distance of 22 statute miles, and thence, through a system of retrieving tanks, by a gradient of 250 feet to the city boundary at Eustace bridge, upper Leeson street [etc.] (p. 548)

Thus, *Ulysses*, as well as being so many other things, becomes an immense effort at normalizing and calibrating the position of Dublin in space and time, at showing how much part of the world it is, how it is synchronized with, and in proximity to, the rest of the world. This concern is never abandoned throughout the book and indeed is present in its very closing words.

For the final words of *Ulysses* are not the famous 'yes I said yes I will Yes'; they are not some Everlasting Yea ventriloquized through Molly as the fleshy incorporation of *Das ewig Weibliche*. The last words of *Ulysses*, the ones that provide the true closure, are (and it is proper and fitting in an Irish novel that they should be) paratextual: an annotation made in the author's own voice, and situating the book deliberately and precisely in real space and in real time. 'Trieste-Zürich-Paris 1914–1921'. That is not just a modernist variation on the scribal signing-off flourish: it brings to Joyce's celebration of Ireland precisely that geographical and historical context from which Ireland had been so often removed by the earlier literary imagination. Joyce carefully situates the fictional universe of Dublin, 16 June 1904, not in a Celtic never-never-land or in a stagnated out-of-the-way backwater, but squarely in the space-time of the Joyce family and its vagaries across Europe.

The great originality of Joyce is that he dared to describe an Irish setting in terms of its *normalcy* – for that was precisely the quality which all earlier authors, whatever their persuasions and sympathies, had denied Ireland. It took, then, one of the greatest innovatory geniuses in European literature to break through the mould of the ingrained discourse of marginality and allochrony which had dominated and suffused the representation of Ireland. In retrospect, that fact makes clear how very protean and all-pervasive that mode of imagining Ireland had been in the nineteenth century; and even today its abiding influence remains noticeable. The acknowledgement of normalcy is still very rare in Ireland-related discourse.

Of course, anyone is free to imagine one's nation, its cultural profile and its status in the world and in history, as one sees fit. But our freedom of imagination does not exempt us from the necessity of sober reason and critical judgement. No loyalty should exist by virtue of going unquestioned. It is important to look at the ramifications, connotations and presuppositions of our modes of cultural and political identification; and one underlying question must be faced, and must be faced seriously. Should any nation really wish to restrict its self-definition, its sense of 'what we are', to the exclusivist, particularist and exoticist terms of 'the way in which we differ from the rest of humanity'? Joyce's *Ulysses*, in rejecting the poetics of anachronism, also rejects such nineteenth-century particularism, and gives eloquent proof of a truth which had become obscured in the preceding century: that Ireland, like any nation, is part of the world at large, and that Irish nationality, like any nationality, is to be defined as part of, and not in contradistinction to, the world as a whole.

NOTES

Introduction

1 Declan Kiberd has drawn my attention to the telling fact that the Fenians, the first nationalist movement to give themselves a Gaelic name (derived from Fionn Mac Cumhaill's warrior band, *na Fianna*), were known in Gaelic, not as *na Fianna*, but by the neologism *na Féiníní* – the nativist invocation of Gaelic antiquity was lost, ironically, on the native-speakers.

2 M.R., 'James Duffy the publisher', *Irish monthly*, 23 (1895): 596–602.

3 'How James Duffy rose to fame', *Irish book lover*, 18 (1930): 168–69.

4 Joseph Guinan, *The soggarth aroon* (Dublin: Duffy, 1905) contains appended an 84-page 'Classified list of books suitable for parochial libraries' (bound into the copy at the National Library, Dublin).

5 C.f. Hugo Dyserinck, 'Komparatistische Imagologie: Zur politischen Tragweite einer europäischen Wissenschaft von der Literatur', in *Europa und das nationale Selbstverständnis. Imagologische Probleme in Literatur, Kunst und Kultur des 18. und 19. Jahrhunderts*, ed. H. Dyserinck and K.U. Syndram (Bonn: Bouvier, 1988), pp. 13–37, and the sources cited there; my own 'Echoes and images: Reflections upon foreign space', in *Alterity, identity, image. Selves and others in scholarship and society*, ed. R. Corbey and J. Leerssen (Amsterdam: Rodopi, 1991), pp. 123–38, and cited sources. I am, moreover, indebted to the work of Edward Said for its demonstration of the way in which such image formations interact with political and inter-ethnic power relations. See *Orientalism* (London: Routledge and Kegan Paul, 1978); *Culture and imperialism* (New York: Knopff, 1993).

6 Paul Ricoeur, *Soi-même comme un autre* (Paris: Seuil, 1990).

7 *The invention of tradition*, ed. E. Hobsbawm and T. Ranger (Cambridge University Press, 1992), is justly famous. I have found great inspiration in Piet Blaas's book *Anachronisme en historisch besef: Momenten uit de ontwikkeling van het Europees historisch bewustzijn* (The Hague: Nijgh & Van Ditmar, 1988) and in Pierre Nora's monumental project *Les lieux de mémoire* (3 vols. in 5; Paris: Gallimard, 1988–93).

8 Luke Gibbons has recently made interesting and inspiring use of the *Nebeneinander/Nacheinander* distiction in aesthetics.

9 Edward Shils, *Center and periphery. Essays in macrosociology* (University of Chicago Press, 1975). It is worth pointing out that Shils has also given an extremely valuable, if not sufficiently well-known, contribution to the investigation of historical consciousness: his excellent *Tradition* (University of Chicago Press, 1981). An interesting extension of centre-periphery systemics has been elaborated in literary studies by Itamar Even-Zohar: 'Polysystem theory', *Poetics today*, 1 (1979): 287–310.

10 Gérard Genette, *Seuils* (Paris: Seuil, 1987). Mikhail Bakhtin, 'Forms of time and of the chronotope in the novel', in id., *The dialogic imagination*, ed. M. Holquist (University of Texas Press, 1981), pp. 84–258.

Around the Union

1   W.J. Mc Cormack, *Ascendancy and tradition in Anglo-Irish literary history from 1789 to 1939* (Oxford: Clarendon Press, 1985), p. 123.

2   Maria Edgeworth, *Castle Rackrent*, ed. George Watson (Oxford University Press, 1964), pp. 4–5.

3   Oliver MacDonagh, *States of mind. A study of Anglo-Irish conflict 1780–1980* (London: George Allen and Unwin, 1983).

4   Mathew Carey, *Vindiciae Hibernicae* (Philadelphia, 1819), p. [iii]. C.f. also here, p. 271, n. 226. On Carey, c.f. Martin J. Burke, 'The politics and poetics of nationalist historiography: Mathew Carey and the *Vindiciae Hibernicae*', in *Forging in the smithy: National identity and representation in Anglo-Irish literary history*, ed. J. Leerssen, A.H. v.d. Weel and B. Westerweel (Amsterdam: Rodopi, 1995), pp. 183–94.

5   Roy Foster, *Paddy and Mr. Punch: Connections in Irish and English history* (London: Penguin, 1993), p. 2.

6   For an analysis of Michelet's history of the French revolution in these terms, see Ann Rigney, *The rhetoric of historical representation: Three nineteenth-century histories of the French revolution* (Cambridge University Press, 1991).

7   Raoul Girardet, *Mythes et mythologies politiques* (Paris: Seuil, 1986), p. 13.

8   Boris Reizov, *L'historiographie romantique française, 1815–1830* (Moscow: Editions en langues étrangères, n.d. [1962]); Rigney, *Rhetoric of historical representation*.

9   As Malcolm Brown has pointed out, Davis 'read and emulated [Michelet] as a matter of course. Those stiff saffron-robed pre-Conquest Gaels with their charming barbarisms of *geasa* and fosterage, stock figures in the future Irish literary movement, came ultimately through Davis out of Michelet's medieval pageantry. Passing beyond Michelet, Davis found his true guiding star in [. . .] Augustin Thierry, whom he repeatedly exalted above "any other historian that ever lived"' (*The politics of Irish literature: From Thomas Davis to W.B. Yeats* (London: George Allen and Unwin, 1972), p. 46. Similarly, Gavan Duffy was highly appreciative of Thierry (Roy Foster, *Paddy and Mr. Punch*, p. 8).

10   Lady Morgan, *Patriotic sketches written in Connaught* (2 vols.; Dublin, 1807), 2: 18–9.

11   Edward Snyder, *The Celtic revival in English literature, 1760–1800* (Harvard University Press, 1923); Jeanne Sheehy, *The rediscovery of Ireland's past: The Celtic revival, 1800–1830* (London: Thames and Hudson, 1980); Hobsbawm and Ranger, *The invention of tradition*.

12   MIFG chapter 5, 6, and S.J. Connolly, *Religion, law and power: The making of protestant Ireland, 1660–1760* (Oxford: Clarendon Press, 1992), pp. 120–122.

13   The trend in recent studies has been to abandon the year 1800 as a terminus *ad quem* or *a quo*: witness the work of scholars such as MacDonagh, Mc Cormack and Connolly. The main factor of continuity across the Union was, of course, the ongoing restiveness of an exploited peasant underclass.

14   This ambiguity is addressed by Maurizio Viroli in his *For love of country: An essay on Patriotism and nationalism* (Clarendon Press, 1995), and in the collection *Patriotisms: The making and unmaking of British national identity*, ed. Raphael Samuels (3 vols.; London: Routledge, 1989), esp. vol. 1, *History and politics*.

15   It is thus with (often differing) assessments of the position of Molyneux and his pamphlet; of Swift with his Drapier's letters; of Flood, Grattan and even Burke. These

'Anglo-Irish' men are assessed within an a-priori polarity of mutually antagonistic, indeed manichean, English and Irish interests, and their 'Patriotism' is explained within a national paradigm. In its crudest form, such a view can boil down to a debate as to whether these men were, or were not, 'good Irishmen'. Their vindicators would stress their love of their country and their battle against English oppression, their critics would point out that they were implicated in a colonialist, Penal system imposed by English conquerors and ruthlessly intolerant of the rights of the majority of the population. I refer not only to the outdated arguments of men like Corkery and De Blácam, though these still crop up nowadays in the more populist histories of Ireland; national parameters also continue to circumscribe more cautious assessments like those of, for example, J.G. Simms and Owen Dudley Edwards. The description of the Patriot outlook as 'colonial nationalism' has been rightly denounced by S.J. Connolly as 'another of the unexamined terms that litter modern writing on the period' (*Religion, Law and Power*, p. 123); it is analeptical and anachronistic, tethering one ideology to the terms, values and aspirations of a different, later one.

16 Indeed most of the various examples given here of early occurrences of the term 'Patriot' and its derivations have been quoted from their citations in these dictionaries, or else been recapitulated from the discussion of the term in MIFG, pp. 300–15. Only references which do not come from any of these cumulative sources have been given separate source-references.

17 C.f. generally R.R. Palmer, *The age of the democratic revolution: A political history of Europe and America, 1760–1800.* 1: *The challenge* (Princeton University Press, 1959), p. 224 (which outlines the early American usage of the term 'citizen', also Palmer's footnote, ibid.), and pp. 317–20 (where an account is given of the way British Dissenters aimed for emancipation and full civil rights by invoking 'the usual privileges and general benefits of citizenship').

18 The portraits on the frontispiece of John Toland's edition of Harrington's *Oceana* (1700) show Brutus, William III, Moses, Solon, Confucius, Lycurgus and Numa. C.f. the list of names mentioned by Mathew Carey as quoted above, p. 9, and Franco Venturi, *Utopia and reform in the Enlightenment* (Cambridge University Press, 1971), pp. 59–60.

19 According to the OED, the divine use of the word philanthropy as God's love for man falls out of use after 1711, whereas the word 'philanthropist' makes its first appearance in 1730.

20 The standard work on Molesworth and the 'commonwealthmen' who came after him, is Caroline Robbins' *The eighteenth-century commonwealthman. Studies in the transmission, development and circumstance of English liberal thought from the restoration of Charles II until the war with the Thirteen Colonies* (Harvard University Press, 1959). Further interesting comments on Molesworth and the commonwealthmen (especially, among these, on Toland and on Shaftesbury) are given by Franco Venturi, 'English commonwealthmen', in his *Utopia and reform in the Enlightenment*, pp. 47–69. Their later influence is charted in Albert Goodwin's *The Friends of liberty: The English democratic movement in the age of the French revolution* (London: Hutchinson, 1979), and in John Sainsbury, *Disaffected Patriots: London supporters of revolutionary America, 1769–1782* (McGill-Queen's University Press, 1987).

21 C.f. Christine Gerrard, *The Patriot opposition to Walpole: Politics, poetry and national myth, 1725–1742* (Oxford: Clarendon Press, 1995).

22 Venturi, *Utopia and reform*, p. 45.

23 Thus, during riots in Nîmes in 1790, royalist counter-revolutionaries shouted 'à bas la Nation!' Conversely, when Drouet rallied the inhabitants of Varennes to arrest the fleeing Louis XVI in 1791, he asked the locals if they were 'bons patriotes'. The king of France was then apprehended by the community which *en masse* had replied 'nous sommes tous des patriotes!' The king's coach was accordingly ordered to halt 'au nom de la Nation'. Jules Michelet, *Histoire de la Révolution française*, ed. G. Walter (2 vols; Paris: Pléiade, 1952), 1: 380, 597–607.

24 A Sheffield radical newspaper of around 1792 was called *The Patriot*; an important radical club around 1795 was the 'Norwich Patriotic Society'; c.f. generally Goodwin, *The friends of liberty*, p. 223, pp. 377–8, and Linda Colley, 'Radical Patriotism in eighteenth-century England', in R. Samuels (ed.), *Patriotisms*, 1: 169–87. In the concept of 'political philanthropy', a shift towards the revolutionary end of the political spectrum can likewise be noticed: the United Irish corresponded with a Hamburg-based Jacobin club known, ominously, as the 'Philanthropic Society', 'devoted to the spreading of republican principles throughout Europe' (Goodwin, *The friends of liberty*, p. 453). This semantic field in the *Begriffsgeschichte* around Patriotism might be extended further by exploring the overtones of a word like 'philadelphia', the 'brotherly love' which gave its name to an American city and foreshadowed the *fraternité* which came second only to *liberté* in the Revolutionary Trinity, and well ahead of the *égalité*, which was only added later. (A great-aunt of Jane Austen was given the Christian name of Philadelphia.)

25 Quoted from I. Leonard Leeb, *The ideological origins of the Batavian revolution. History and politics in the Dutch republic 1747–1800* (The Hague: Martinus Nijhoff, 1973), p. 78.

26 Witness also the role played in both countries by public societies of a philanthropic or scholarly nature, or by efforts (partly channelled through these societies) to improve the national economy. As regards the Dutch situation in this respect, c.f. Leeb's chapter on 'New organizations and economic Patriotism', in *Ideological origins*, pp. 104 ff. Leeb overlooks, however, the most important of these improving societies, the *Maatschappij tot Nut van 't Algemeen* (Society for General Benefit), founded in 1784 by a Baptist minister and recalling, in its aims, those of the Dublin Society.

27 C.f. Palmer, *Democratic revolution*, 1: 88 (where he quotes private remarks to this effect by the Marquis d'Argenson), and generally pp. 88 ff., describing the opposition of the various *parlements* against court policy.

28 A telling example of the double-think which resulted from this was Sir Hercules Langrishe's attitude to Catholic emancipation. Though, as a Patriot, he recognized the iniquity of the Penal Code and its exclusion of the majority of the Irish people from civil rights, he shrank back, as an Ascendancy man, from the implications of that realization, and shilly-shallied his way out of the resulting dilemma by contending 'that the Roman Catholics should enjoy everything *under* the State, but should not be *the State itself*'. This point was taken up devastatingly by Burke in his *Letter to Sir Hercules Langrishe*.

29 C.f. Zera S. Fink, *The classical republicans. An essay in the recovery of a pattern of thought in seventeenth-century England* (second ed. Northwestern University, 1962), esp. pp. 170–92.

30 Leeb, *Ideological origins*, 158; and generally, pp. 136 ff. and 156, the chapter on 'J.D. van der Capellen, "Born Regent" and Patriot par excellence'. Also, Palmer, *Democratic revolution*, 1: 329.

31 C.f. generally *Remous révolutionnaires. Armée française, république batave*, ed. A. Jourdan and J.Th. Leerssen (Amsterdam University Press, 1996). In the light of these developments, nineteenth-century Dutch historians, usually Orangist in tone, tended to see the Patriots as Quislings, traitors to their native soil and to the national dynasty, and henchmen to the French oppressors. (The French set up, first a puppet republic, then a puppet kingdom, and ended up by annexing Holland altogether into Napoleon's empire.) Hence, though this dim view of the Patriots has been changed in recent decades, the name of 'Patriots' still lacks, to a Dutch ear, that aprioristical nationalist connotation which it carries in English-speaking countries. As regards the assessment of the Patriots in Dutch historiography, see E.O.G. Haitsma Mulier's 'De geschiedschrijving over de Patriottentijd en de Bataafse Tijd', in *Kantelend geschiedbeeld. Nederlandse historiografie sinds 1945*, ed. W.W. Mijnhardt (Utrecht/Antwerpen: Spectrum, 1983), pp. 206–27 and pp. 352–5. Also, G.J. Schutte, 'Van verguizing naar eerherstel. Het beeld van de Patriotten in de negentiende en twintigste eeuw', in *Voor vaderland en vrijheid. De revolutie van de Patriotten*, ed. F. Grijzenhout et al. (Amsterdam: De Bataafsche Leeuw, 1987), pp. 177–92.

32 Witness Sir William Temple's celebration of the federalist and heteronomic structure of the United Provinces; the widespread admiration for the similarly constituted Swiss confederacy; the federal nature of the American republic; the original Girondist agenda for a France of *fédérations* (scotched by the Jacobin ideal of a *république une et indivisible*); the various attempts in Germany to have a *Bund* rather than a *Reich*; the ideal for a future united Europe on a federal or confederate basis.

33 C.f. also Seamus Deane, 'Edmund Burke and the ideology of Irish liberalism', in *The Irish mind: Exploring intellectual traditions*, ed. R. Kearney (Dublin: Wolfhound Press, 1985), pp. 141–56.

34 Mary Helen Thuente, *The harp re-strung. The United Irishmen and the rise of Irish literary nationalism* (Syracuse University Press, 1994), pp. 171–92. And see here, pp. 79–81.

35 Some important titles are: Benedict Anderson, *Imagined communities: Reflections on the origin and spread of nationalism* (London: Verso, 1983); Peter Alter, *Nationalismus* (Frankfurt/Main: Suhrkamp, 1985); Ernest Gellner, *Nations and Nationalism* (Oxford; Blackwell, 1983); E.J. Hobsbawm, *Nations and Nationalism since 1780. Programme, myth, reality* (Cambridge U.P., new ed. 1992); Otto Dann, *Nation und Nationalismus in Deutschland, 1770–1990* (München: Beck, 1993).

36 C.f. Fichte's *Reden an die deutsche Nation* of 1810. On the role of Hegel, C.f. Karl Popper, *The open society and its enemies* (2 vols.; London: Routledge and Kegan Paul, 1945), especially the chapter on 'Hegel and the new tribalism'.

37 Thomas Crofton Croker, *Researches in the south of Ireland, illustrative of the scenery, architectural remains, and the manners and superstitions of the peasantry. With an appendix containing a private narrative of the rebellion of 1798* (London, 1824), pp. 12–3. For a good theoretical background to such a typology, c.f. Seamus Deane, 'Irish national character 1790–1900', in *The writer as witness: Literature as historical evidence*, ed. T. Dunne (Cork University Press, 1987), pp. 90–113. Earlier English estimates of the Irish character, to which Croker is obviously indebted (witness the standard imputation of childish, un-adult attributes which are implicitly silhouetted against the Irish' counterpart, England), form the substance of MIFG, chapters 2 and 3.

38 There is no example in nineteenth- and twentieth-century European history where such attempts at territorial compartmentalization have succeeded in obviating cultural-political tensions. Cultural population patterns are so fuzzy and complex that the neat linearity of political borders cannot do justice to them; redrawing political borders in order to suit cultural aspirations will inevitably create as many minority problems as one might wish to solve. C.f. my 'Europe as a set of borders', *Yearbook of European studies*, 6 (1993): 1–14.

39 Nationalism in the looser sense denotes the vindication of the Irish right to self-determination against English or British domination. A good example of an analysis in these terms is D.G. Boyce, *Nationalism in Ireland* (3rd ed.; London: Routledge, 1995).

40 Roy Foster, *Paddy and Mr Punch*, p. 78.

41 MacDonagh sees this as a result of 'The Germanic [sic] type of idealism and romanticism'. Oliver MacDonagh, *O'Connell. The life of Daniel O'Connell, 1775–1847* (London: Weidenfeld & Nicolson, 1991), p. 310.

42 Charles Gavan Duffy, *Young Ireland: A fragment of Irish history, 1840–1850* (London, 1880), p. 161.

43 P.N., 'Our national language', *The Celt*, August 1858, pp. 259–61. The reference to Tyre and Sidon implies that the author subscribed to the theory that Gaelic descends from Phoenician (see here, pp. 72–4). Articles on race included: 'The Celtic race' (September 1857), 'Saxon and Celtic criminals' (November-December 1857) and 'An Irish mother' (October 1859). On Körner: September 1857. Roy Foster rightly points to *The Celt* as one of the true beginnings of Irish cultural revivalism (*Paddy and Mr. Punch*, p. 272).

44 'Mr. William O'Brien on the national language', *Irisleabhar na Gaedhilge / Gaelic Journal*, 4, 42 (July 1892): 157–160 (157).

45 For a more extensive discussion of mid-century Saxonism and Celticism, see here, pp. 91–100.

46 F.S.L. Lyons, *Ireland since the Famine* (London: Fontana/Collins, 1973), p. 84.

47 *Gaelic Journal*, 18, 3 (March 1980): 141.

48 In his chapter 'The American revolution: The people as constituent power', *Democratic Revolution*, 1: 213 ff.

49 C.f. MIFG, chapter I ('The idea of nationality: Terminology and historical background'), pp. 15–31.

50 The link is explored, in the British context, in Linda Colley's *Britons: Forging the nation, 1707–1837* (Yale University Press, 1992).

51 Venturi, *Utopia and reform*, p. 72.

52 Larousse's *Grand dictionnaire du XIXe siècle* gives a good survey, s.v. 'Nation' and 'Patrie'. C.f. also Viroli, *For love of country*.

53 Leeb very rightly points out that Orangist authors in Holland were jealous of the 'virtuous' connotations which inhered in the word Patriot, and which accordingly were being annexed into the Patriot stance; and there were, as a result, Orangists in the Dutch Republic (e.g. Adriaan Kluit) who attempted to apply to their stance the honourable name of Patriot, 'to deprive the name of its exclusively anti-Stadhouderly connotations' (*Ideological origins*, p. 251–3).

54 A Patriot example: the poetry of Jacobus Bellamy (1757–86), e.g. his *Vaderlandsche gezangen*, influenced by Rousseau. An Orangist example: Onno Zwier van Haren and his epic *Aan het vaderland* (1769).

55   *Von dem Nationalstolze*, 1st ed. 1758, revised ed. 1760, 1768; English trans. 1771. Lady Morgan mentions him in her *Patriotic sketches* as a household name, 1:55.

56   A good description of the position of Price, and of the radical English Patriots of the late eighteenth century, is given by Goodwin, *Friends of liberty*, esp. pp. 106–12.

57   Goodwin, *Friends of liberty*, p. 111. The use of the word *nationale* by that *assemblée* of commoners was carefully chosen after much deliberation, and advanced by Sieyès. It is pregnant with the connotations which I have pointed out in the foregoing pages, and was intended to be so. C.f. Michelet, *Histoire de la Révolution française*, 1: 101–2.

58   For a parallel development in England, c.f. Hugh Cunningham, 'The language of Patriotism', in Samuels (ed.), *Patriotisms*, 1:57–89.

59   An excellent Europe-wide survey is given by Léon Poliakov, *Le mythe aryen: Essai sur les sources du racisme et des nationalismes* (new ed. Bruxelles: Complexe, 1987). As regards The Netherlands, see Hooft's play *Baeto, oft oorsprong der Hollanderen* (Bato, or the origins of the Hollanders). On the Batavian ancestry myth in post-1600 Holland, c.f. Auke van der Woud. *De Bataafse hut: Verschuivingen in het beeld van de geschiedenis (1750–1850)* (Amsterdam: Meulenhoff, 1990). As regards England: Samuel Kliger, *The Goths in England: A study in seventeenth and eighteenth century thought* (Harvard University Press, 1952). As regards Germany: M.A. Wes, 'Van Hermann tot Hitler', in id., *Verslagen verleden: Over geschiedenis en oudheid* (Amsterdam: Wetenschappelijke uitgeverij, 1980), pp. 124–208. As regards France: *Nos ancêtres les Gaulois*, ed. P. Viallaneix and P. Ehrard (University of Clermont-Ferrand, 1982), and, for the pre-Revolution period, *Primitivisme et mythes des origines dans la France des Lumières*, ed. Ch. Grell and Chr. Michel (Université de Paris-Sorbonne, 1989). As regards Belgium: H. v.d. Linden, 'Histoire de notre nom national', *Académie royale de Belgique, Bulletin de la classe des lettres*, 5e série, 16 (1930): 27–40. As regards Switzerland: Ulrich Im Hof, *Mythos Schweiz: Identität, Nation, Geschichte, 1291–1991* (Zürich: Neue Zürcher Zeitung, 1991).

60   I have described its meanderings in greater detail in MIFG, pp. 294–376.

61   C.f. MIFG, pp. 296–300, on the contradiction in Molyneux's *Case*, which took care to distinguish historically between the loyal Anglo-Irish and the rest of Ireland. The anonymous *Answer to Mr. Molyneux* of 1698 argued, astutely enough, that, going by Molyneux's own arguments, the Irish parliament whose legislative rights Molyneux advocated was the exclusive platform of that part of Ireland to which the Anglo-Irish did *not* belong: the renegade, Jacobite Old English.

62   C.f. Norman Vance, 'Celts, Carthaginians and constitutions: Anglo-Irish literary relations, 1780–1820', *Irish historical studies*, 22, 87 (March, 1981): 216–38.

63   Paul Hiffernan had, in his *The Hiberniad* of 1754, proclaimed a programme for a regionally distinct Anglo-Irish literature; Charlotte Brooke, besides translating from Gaelic originals, also wrote her own poems on Gaelic themes. And as early as 1716, a Mrs Sarah Butler, of whom we know little, had published a volume of *Irish tales* based on old Gaelic history and myth.

64   Despite such omissions, the *Field Day anthology* allows for a fresh look at the literary record in that it sidesteps, to a large extent, the problems of using the year 1800 as a cut-off date, and in that it uses the neutral concept of *writing* for the canonical and author-bound notion of *literature*.

65   As regards the plays by Dobbs and Howard which are discussed here, see MIFG, pp. 368–72.

66 An indication of the extent to which this represented an ideological shift is provided by looking at two earlier plays on Irish antiquity (likewise absent from the FDA): Charles Shadwell's *Rotherick O'Connor* of 1720 and William Phillips's *Hibernia freed* of 1722. Although their Gaelic characters (or at least some of them) are treated with a certain amount of sympathy, and are sometimes even given lofty speeches indicating their love of their country and its independence (*Hibernia freed* even gives a sympathetic account of Brian Ború's struggle against the Danes) both plays still support the view that the English (Anglo-Norman) conquest was a 'Good Thing', necessary to import virtue and liberty into a benighted, uncivilized and despotically ruled country. I have dealt with these plays, practically the first to use a setting in Gaelic antiquity, in somewhat greater detail in MIFG, pp. 326–29.

The Burden of the Past

1 *The Irish novelists 1800–1850* (Columbia University Press, 1959), p. 36.
2 Quoted in Barry Sloan, *The pioneers of Anglo-Irish fiction, 1800–1850* (Gerrards Cross: Colin Smythe; Totowa, N.J.; Barnes & Noble, 1986), p. 138.
3 Quoted Sloan, *Pioneers of Anglo-Irish fiction*, p. 142. On the extent to which these explanations of Ireland to a British audience obtained their intended effect, see Barbara Hayley, '"The Eeerishers are marchin' in leeterature": British critical reception of nineteenth-century Anglo-Irish fiction', in *Literary interrelations: Ireland, England and the world*, ed. W. Zach and H. Kosok (3 vols.; Tübingen: Narr, 1987), 1: 39–50.
4 Sloan, *Pioneers of Anglo-Irish fiction*, 41–2. Sloan is here discussing the formulaic pattern of Morgan's and Maturin's Irish novels, but recognizes a similar pattern in novels like *The absentee*, *Ennui* and Banim's *The Anglo-Irish of the nineteenth century* (98); indeed, in that last-mentioned novel, the hero, Gerald Blount, only sets foot in Ireland halfway through vol. 2 and for a further twenty pages believes himself to be in Wales. A coach-journey into the west throws him together with a garrulous interlocutor (his future father-in-law), who, though a landlord and a Protestant, plays devil's advocate in the debate by posing as a fiery Irish nationalist (3: 114– 135); and the two debate matters Irish during the journey. (*The Anglo-Irish of the nineteenth century. A novel* (3 vols.; London, 1828). Only in the last half of the third volume is there anything like a love interest. The novel should be read as a political tract in story-form, on the pattern of the 1825 'Captain Rock' exchange between Thomas Moore and Mortimer O'Sullivan, and breathes the same bitterly antagonistic political spirit of the years immediately preceding Catholic emancipation (c.f. here, pp. 76–79).
5 Flanagan, *Irish novelists 1800–1850*, p. 133.
6 Eileen Kane, 'Stereotypes and Irish identity: Mental illness as a cultural frame', *Studies*, 75 (1986): 539–51 (549).
7 I may add that it is no less remarkable to me to see how such national soul-searchings allow for the most dexterous and logic-defying manipulations of the first-person 'we'. That collective subject can with impunity be kneaded, stretched and shrunk into whatever shape or size suits the argument from moment to moment.
8 'Essay on romance', in Scott's *Essays on chivalry, romance and the drama* (Chandos classics; London, n.d.), pp. 226–69.
9 For famous generic distinctions between romantic and novelistic prose fiction (e.g. Johnson in *The rambler*, Hawthorne in the preface to his *The house of the*

seven gables, spanning a century bisected by Scott), see Gillian Beer's brief but useful *The romance* (London: Methuen, 1969).

10 Walter Scott, *Waverley, or 'tis sixty years since*, ed. Clare Lamont (Oxford: Clarendon Press, 1981), pp. 103–7. Also, here, pp. 188–90.

11 Letter from Edgeworth to James Ballantyne, quoted in *Scott, the critical heritage*, ed. John O. Hayden (London: Routledge and Kegan Paul, 1970), p. 78. C.f. also John Leycester Adolphus's anonymous *Letters to Richard Heber* (London 1821), pp. vii, 125. See my 'Over de ontologische status en tekstuele situering van imagotypen: Exotisme en Walter Scotts *Waverley*', in *Deugdelijk vermaak. Opstellen over literatuur en filosofie in de negentiende eeuw*, ed. E. Eweg (Amsterdam: Huis aan de Drie Grachten, 1987). Also, more generally, Herbert Grierson, 'History and the novel', in Herbert Grierson et al., *Sir Walter Scott lectures 1940–1948* (Edinburgh: At the University Press, 1950), pp. 31–51.

12 Mikhail Bakhtin, 'Forms of time and the chronotope in the novel'; and c.f. here, pp. 49–50.

13 That polarization has been traced in the field of history-writing and historical consciousness by Donald MacCartney's important essay 'The writing of history in Ireland, 1800–1830', *Irish historical studies*, 10, 40 (Sept. 1957): 347–62; and c.f. here, p. 75.

14 Dennis Jasper Murphy (i.e. Charles Maturin), *The wild Irish boy*, 2 vols. (New York, 1808), 1:5.

15 Lady Morgan, *O'Donnel: A national tale*, 3 vols. (London: printed for Henry Colburn, 1814), 1:x–xi.

16 Niilo Idman, *Charles Robert Maturin: His life and works* (Helsingfors: Centraltryckeri, 1923) p. 70. Much the same point was made by Sloan, *Pioneers of Anglo-Irish fiction*, pp. 41–2 (see here, p. 36).

17 Charles Robert Maturin, *The Milesian chief* (4 vols.; London, 1812), 1: 63–4.

18 For the more paranoid aspects of the Irish Protestants' historical awareness at the time (exemplified in Sir Richard Musgrave, among others), see MacCartney, 'The writing of history in Ireland, 1800–1830'; on the ongoing remembrancing of the 1641 rebellion as the violent paradigm of anti-Protestant hatred, see Jacqueline Hill, '1641 and the quest for Catholic emancipation', in *Ulster 1641: Aspects of the rising*, ed. B. Mac Cuarta (Queen's University, Belfast, 1993), pp. 159–71.

19 Lady Morgan, *The O'Briens and the O'Flahertys: A national tale*, 4 vols. (London: Henry Colburn, 1827) 2:147. Such dark hints at plots by Jesuits, and evocations of the cloistered and mysterious life of monasticism add up to a sub-theme in this novel invoking an eminently Gothic topic, so luridly described in Lewis's *The monk*, Radcliffe's *The Italian* and Maturin's *Melmoth the wanderer*.

20 Scott does something like that in the 'Flora's waterfall' passage from *Waverley*, which contemporaries criticized for being contrived and implausible: he added a footnote to a later edition vindicating his description and its impeached *vraisemblance*.

21 On *The wild Irish girl* and its footnotes, see here, pp. 56–60; as regards Maturin, see, for example, *The Milesian chief* 1:127 and 4:204, ascertaining a description of Irish dress by referring to a scholarly source; or *The wild Irish boy*, 1:104 and note. It may be added that even in the comparatively mundane tale of *Castle Rackrent*, Edgeworth finds herself compelled to throw her personal credit behind some of the descriptions, and states in footnotes that she has herself witnessed some of the scenes which might strain her readers' credulity.

22 *The Milesian chief*, 1: 20. Also quoted in Julian Moynahan, *Anglo-Irish: The literary imagination in a hyphenated culure* (Princeton University Press, 1995), p. 111.

23 Originally in *Foreign quarterly*, here quoted from *Essays on chivalry, romance, and the drama*, pp. 431–68.

24 Johannes Fabian, *Time and the Other: How anthropology makes its object* (Columbia University Press, 1983).

25 Sloan, *Pioneers of Anglo-Irish fiction*, p. 49, p. 181, p. 195.

26 Roy Foster, *Paddy and Mr. Punch*, p. 7; Tom Dunne, 'Haunted by history: Irish romantic writing, 1800–1850', in *Romanticism in national context*, eds., R. Porter and M. Teich (Cambridge University Press, 1988), pp. 68–91 (69).

27 Terry Eagleton, *Heathcliff and the Great Hunger. Studies in Irish culture* (London: Verso, 1995), p. 179.

28 Luke Gibbons, *Transformations in Irish Culture* (Cork University Press, 1996), pp. 149–163.

29 The above-noted strictures by Maria Edgeworth on *Waverley's* chapter 22 denounce the *staginess* of Scotts description ('a scene', 'stage effect') and thus seem to criticize, not only the fact that Scott had strayed into the register of Romance, but also his proneness to the register of drama: sentimental comedy or melodrama.

30 Lady Morgan, *The wild Irish girl* (London and New York: Pandora, 1986), p. 44. Page references are to this Pandora paperback edition, which has been collated with the first edition: *The wild Irish girl: A national tale*. By Miss Owenson (3 vols.; London, 1806).

31 The pattern is almost always that a love affair develops between an English boy meeting an Irish girl. A direct reversal of that role distribution (Irish boy meets English girl) is almost nowhere to be found: even in Maturin's *The Milesian chief*, though the male protagonist is Irish, the female (Armida) is Continental with an Italian upbringing; and Neil Jordan's film *The Crying Game* likewise avoids a straightforward reversal of the stereotype pattern. That pattern is reinforced by the fact that, traditionally, mobility is a masculine attribute: a traveller who arrives in Ireland and explores that country is therefore more easily conceived of as male. When a gender-reversed pattern does occur, it is usually in the earlier, eighteenth-century anti-Irish stereotype of the 'fortune hunter' (a late revival of that type being Thackeray's *Barry Lyndon*): the male Irish character being a picaresque, penniless adventurer, marrying the English girl for her greater wealth. (A fuller narrative treatment is given to Trollope's Phineas Finn.) C.f. generally Roy Foster, *Paddy and Mr. Punch*, pp. 139–70 and pp. 281–305.

32 This satirical allegory was inspired by disappointed Unionist feelings among the Anglo-Irish in 1707, when the parliamentary union between England and Scotland (rather than between England and Ireland) was concluded. England is seen as a faithless swain who abandons his first and most steadfast love (Ireland) for the attractions of a rival (Scotland).

33 Mikhail Bakhtin, 'Discourse in the novel', in *The dialogic imagination*, pp. 259–422.

34 I use the term 'paratext' in the sense coined by Gérard Genette, as all typographical material which, while not forming part of a text, surrounds it: title, page numbers, chapter headings, blurb, illustrations, footnotes, etc. etc. C.f. Genette, *Seuils*, and Shari Benstock, 'At the margin of discourse: Footnotes in the fictional text', *PMLA*, 98 (1983): 204–25.

35 For a somewhat fuller discussion, see my 'Echoes and images'.

36 Eagleton, *Heathcliff and the Great Hunger*, p. 171.

37 Such a scene is, by the way, 'too good to be true', a contrivance which blithely sacrifices veracity for anecdotal charm. For although *amo, amas, amat* may be a handy paradigm for the conjugation of Latin verbs, the Gaelic for 'to love' is a prepositional circumlocution unsuitable for such grammatical exercises as described here: the expression in its usual form takes the form *tá grá agam (duit)*, 'there is love with me (for you)'. There is nothing of the kind in 'Vallancey's grammar', of course (presumably Charles Vallancey's *Grammar of the Iberno-Celtic or Irish language* of 1782).

There is more to this point than trivial pedantry; for it illustrates, once again, the difficulty of reconciling the registers of truthful explanation and romantic narrative. A parallel latter-day example is provided by Brian Friel's play *Translations*, which contains linguistic exercises (e.g. etymologies of latinate words) purportedly conducted in Gaelic, but which in Gaelic would in fact be impossible to conduct in that form. Thus the representation, through English, of verbal activity in Gaelic, though intended as a gesture of rendering the other language present, tends to presents a generic 'other speech', modelled on English. The representation mimics, not the Irish language, but its being the vehicle of difference; and we slide back into exoticist projections and schemata. More importantly, the turbulent interference between wooing and linguistic parroting in Morgan's cited passage foreshadows directly the bilingual (or rather sesquilingual) place-naming love scenes in *Translations*.

38 See the analysis by Thuente, *The harp re-strung*, esp. pp. 171–92; and here, pp. 81–2.

39 *The lay of an Irish harp, by Miss Owenson* (London, 1807), pp. 1–7.

40 C.f. Mary Campbell, *Lady Morgan. The life and times of Sydney Owenson* (London: Pandora, 1988), pp. 18–22, p. 77.

41 MIFG, pp. 113–42.

42 Campbell, *Lady Morgan*, p. 77.

43 'Maria Edgeworth and Lady Morgan: Legality versus legitimacy', *Nineteenth-century fiction*, 40 (1985–6): 1–22. On symbolic marriages in Morgan, see also Eagleton, *Heathcliff and the Great Hunger*, pp. 180–1.

44 Bakhtin, 'Forms of time and of the chronotope in the novel', p. 95.

45 C.f. Dale Spender, 'Lady Morgan and political fiction', chapter 17 in her *Mothers of the novel: 100 good women writers before Jane Austen*, London and New York, 1986, pp. 301–14. There are many instances on record of Moore's and Edgeworth's snobbish disdain for Morgan; these and other examples of the reservations she inspired in many contemporaries – including, of course, the violent attacks by John Wilson Croker – are given by Lionel Stevenson, *The wild Irish girl: The life of Sydney Owenson, Lady Morgan (1776–1859)* (London: Chapman and Hall, 1936), as well as in Campbell, *Lady Morgan*.

46 Flanagan, *Irish novelists*, p. 120.

47 Tom Dunne, 'The best history of nations: Lady Morgan's Irish novels', *Historical studies*, 16 (1987): 133–59.

48 Dunne, 'Haunted by history', p. 76.

49 Peter Brooks, *The melodramatic imagination: Balzac, Henry James, melodrama and the mode of excess* (Columbia University Press, 1984).

The Challenge of the Past

1   C.f. the acts 25 Henry IV c.4 (1447), 5 Edward IV c.3 (1465), 28 Henry VIII (1543). *The statutes at large passed in the parliaments held in Ireland* (13 vols.; Dublin, 1786).

2   C.f. Arnaldo Momigliano, 'Ancient history and the antiquarian', in id., *Contributo alla storia degli studi classici* (Roma: Edizioni de Storia e Letteratura, 1955), 67–106 (69). Momigliano comments: 'I suggest that to many of us the word "antiquary" suggests the notion of a student of the past who is not quite a historian because: (1) historians write in a chronological order, antiquaries write in a systematic order; (2) historians produce those facts which serve to illustrate or explain a certain situation; antiquaries collect all the items that are connected with a certain subject, whether they help to solve a problem or not. The subject-matter contributes to the distinction between historians and antiquaries only in so far as certain subjects (such as political institutions, religion, private life) have traditionally been considered more suitable for systematic description than for a chronological account.'

3   The relationship between antiquarianism, archaeology and history in England in the mid-nineteenth century has been sketched admirably by Philippa Levine, *The amateur and the professional. Antiquarians, historians and archaeologists in Victorian England, 1838–1886* (Cambridge University Press, 1986). In Levine's treatment, archaeology refers specifically to the excavation of pre-medieval (often non-European) artefacts from their covered deposits; an emphasis on the 'dig' which she describes in its incipient development (pp. 31–5). My own treatment will concentrate rather on its role as a scientific, later development of antiquarianism which eventually came to supplant its forerunner.

4   The British-Israelite theory attracted a considerable number of followers and published widely, especially in the decades around the last turn of the century. A contemporary manifestation of its tenets (partly incorporated also into the beliefs of Mormonism) is found in the theories of the American Donald W. Armstrong, founder of the *Plain Truth* magazine. Theories about the symbolic significance of the dimensions of the Great Pyramid were propounded in the later half of the nineteenth century by Piazzi Smyth; such speculations still do the rounds in occultist or New Age circles (Rosicrucianism, anthroposophy). An interesting survival of the pre-scientific paradigm is Robert Graves' book *The white goddess* (1948).

5   C.f. geneally Dáire Keogh, *The French Disease: The Catholic church and Irish radicalism, 1790–1800* (Blackrock: Four Courts Press, 1993).

6   For an excellent survey, see Clare O'Halloran, 'Golden ages and barbarous nations: Antiquarian debate on the Celtic past in Ireland and Scotland in the eighteenth century' (Ph.D. thesis, Cambridge, 1991).

7   Vallancey, 'The tree the symbol of knowledge', *Collectanea de rebus Hibernicis*, 5 (1790), pp. 105–46.

8   The system goes back to early-modern scholars and Bible commentators, for whose influence on seventeenth- and eighteenth-century linguistics, see Daniel Droixhe, *La linguistique et l'appel de l'histoire, 1600–1800. Rationalisme et révolutions positivistes* (Genève: Droz, 1978). A typical exponent of the Japhetic model was James Parsons with his *Remains of Japhet: Being historical enquiries into the affinity and origin of the European languages* (London, 1767).

9   Donald MacCartney, 'The writing of history in Ireland, 1800–1830', emphasizes Ledwich's critical sense as an Enlightenment historian in the Mabillon tradition,

but does so on the basis of downplaying Ledwich's own speculative *parti-pris* (pp. 348–9). This somewhat one-sided estimate is echoed by Roy Foster, *Paddy and Mr. Punch*, p. 5.

10 Walker to Pinkerton, 31 October 1798, in John Pinkerton, *Literary correspondence* (2 vols.; London, 1830), 2: 37. Walker did concede in the next sentence that 'Latterly, indeed, the Milesians have rallied around the standard of rebellion.'

11 A favourite stratagem with which to bring out this parallel was by hunting for similarities between ancient Carthaginian language and Gaelic – the best available sample being a macaronic speech spoken by a Carthaginian soldier in Plautus' comedy *Poenulus*. This speech was drawn on by the French antiquarian Samuel Bochart in the mid-seventeenth century, by the native Irish scholar Seán Ó Neachtain in the early eighteenth century, by Vallancey in his *Essay on the antiquity of the Irish language, being a collation of the Irish with the Punic language* (1772) and by John D'Alton in his 'Essay on the ancient history, religion, learning, arts and government of Ireland' of 1828 (*Transactions RIA* 16: 1–380, esp. pp. 12–14). Less fanciful attempts to make sense of this fragment (with reference to its Semitic structures rather than through contrived parallels with Irish) were offered by James Hamilton in the 1830s (*Transactions RIA*, 10: 3–64) and, most recently, by Maurice Sznycer, *Les passages puniques en transcription latine dans le 'Poenulus' de Plaute* (Paris: Klincksieck, 1967).

12 Vallancey, *Essay on the antiquity of the Irish language*, p. 3.

13 For a good survey, see MacCartney, 'The writing of history in Ireland, 1800–1830'. Patriots were vindicated by men like Barrington; Carey and Taaffe vindicated the United Irishmen, and the anti-papist stance was voiced most vehemently by Sir Richard Musgrave. The most interesting text to come out of this welter of partisan historiography was doubtless Thomas Moore's *Memoirs of Captain Rock* (1824), concerning which, see here, pp. 85–7.

14 *Transactions RIA*, 13 (1818), section 'Antiquities', pp. 3–80.

15 Essay read 10 June 1805, published in *Transactions RIA*, 10 (1808), section 'Antiquities', p. 21.

16 *Transactions RIA*, 15 (1828), section 'Polite literature', pp. 1–86, esp. pp. 10–11. The author, *gadelice* Séamas Ó Scoireadh, was a native speaker and scribe from Co. Kilkenny.

17 Thus 'An essay on the nature and influence of the ancient Irish institutes, commonly called the Brehon Laws, and of the number and authenticity of the documents whence information concerning them may be derived; accompanied by specimens and translations from some of their most interesting parts; with an appendix, containing a catalogue of the principal ancient Irish Laws, to be found in the MSS library of Trinity College, and other libraries', *Transactions RIA* 14 (1825): 141–223; also, his 'Chronological account of Irish writers, and descriptive catalogue of such of their works, as are still extant in verse or prose', in *Transactions of the Iberno-Celtic Society*, 1 (1820): xi–ccxxxvii; and also, his *Sanas Gaoidhilge-Sags-Bhéarla. An Irish-English Dictionary with numerous comparisons of Irish words with those of a similar orthography, sense or sound in the Welsh and Hebrew languages, to which is annexed a compendious Irish grammar* (Dublin, 1817; 2nd. ed. 1821).

18 Founded in 1806; its sole volume of *Transactions* appeared in 1808. Its establishment had been assisted by Dr. Lanigan, the erstwhile Professor of Hebrew at Pavia University now returned to Ireland, but its membership was in the main

comprised of 'a number of variously gifted individuals in the middle state of life, some endued with talents superior to their pecuniary means'. Membership fees were kept low so as 'to ensure the co-operation of talents and genius in the humble walks of life. In this rank, in Ireland particularly, many are found who are most conversant in their native language' (J. Warburton, J. Whitelaw and R. Walsh, *History of the city of Dublin* (2 vols.; London, 1818), 2: 930–931). Among the members were O'Reilly himself, the radical United Irishman and defrocked priest Dennis Taaffe, and scholars (ranging from hedge-schoolmasters to Maynooth lecturers) like Patrick Lynch, William Halliday, William Neilson and Paul O'Brien. With the figure of its instigator and editor of its transactions, Theophilus O'Flanagan, the Gaelic Society's roots reach back into pre-Union antiquarianism: O'Flanagan had worked for the libraries of Trinity College (where he had obtained a BA in 1789) and the Royal Irish Academy, had assisted Vallancey, Walker and Charlotte Brooke, and had published an account of an Ogham inscription in the *Transactions RIA*, 1 (1787): 3–16, which, though it had come under suspicion of falsification, was vindicated by Samuel Ferguson (*Proceedings RIA*, second series, vol. 1 (1872–77), 160–168; 265–271; 315– 322). O'Flanagan, whose career was repeatedly thwarted by 'an unfortunate propensity for intemperance and irregular habits' (*History of the city of Dublin*, 2: 931–2n.) moved out of Dublin, first to Birr, then to Kerry and ultimately (in 1812) to Limerick, where he died in 1814 at the age of 52. It is not clear what became of the Gaelic Society after the publication of its sole volume of *Transactions* in 1808. The *History of the city of Dublin* (pub. 1818) speaks of it as a functioning body, and mentions that as of 1815 it was under the secretariat of Patrick Lynch (c.f. also the title page to Lynch's *For-Oidheas ghnaith-Ghaoighilge* of 1815; concerning Lynch, see *Catalogue of Irish MSS in the British Museum*, 2: 326). The Gaelic Society seems to have merged into the new Iberno-Celtic Society, for the table of contents to the *History of the City of Dublin* refers to the chapter on the Gaelic Society as 'Gaelic, or Hiberno-Celtic Society'; Philip Barron in his review *Ancient Ireland*, 4 (1835): 52, likewise referred to a conjoint 'Gaelic or Hiberno-Celtic Society'. The continuity is also attested by C. Anderson in his *Historical sketches of the native Irish and their descendants* (2nd ed. Dublin, 1821), 100. For further notices of individual members of the Gaelic Society, see the gossipy footnotes to *History of the city of Dublin*, pp. 930 ff., and P.J. Dowling, 'Patrick Lynch, schoolmaster, 1754–1818', *Studies*, 20 (1931), pp. 461–71; Séamus Ua Casaide, 'Richard McElligott, Honorary Member of the Gaelic Society', *Journal of the North Munster Archaeological Society*, 3 (1913–15), pp. 362–70.

19 Witness the failure of Peter O'Connell to get his magnificent dictionary published (c.f. Dermot F. Gleeson, 'Peter O'Connell, scholar and scribe', *Studies*, 33 (1944): 342–348). The dismissive attitude of his namesake Daniel O'Connell, when asked for support in the year of Peter O'Connell's death (1824) is well known; c.f. Oliver MacDonagh, *O'Connell*, 11. Daniel O'Connell was, however, among the subscribers to Edward O'Reilly's *Sanas Gaoidhilge-Sags-Bhéarla* of 1817 (c.f. 2nd ed. of 1821, pp. v–vi).

20 O'Reilly annexed an Irish grammar to his *Sanas Gaoidhilge-Sags-Bhéarla*; William Haliday, *Úraicecht na Gaedhilge. A grammar of the Gaelic language* (Dublin, 1808); William Neilson, *An introduction to the Irish language* (Dublin, 1808); Paul O'Brien, *A practical grammar of the Irish language* (Dublin, 1809). Patrick Lynch appended

'An abstract of Irish grammar' to his *Life of St. Patrick* (Dublin, 1810) and published *For-Oideas ghnaith-Ghaoighilge na h-Eireand. Introduction to the knowledge of the Irish language as now spoken* in 1815, with a motto taken from Francis O'Molloy's Irish grammar of 1677. All these grammatical ventures are discussed in, and superseded by, the 'definitive' Irish grammar: John O'Donovan's *A grammar of the Irish language, published for the use of the senior classes of the College of St. Columba* (Dublin, 1845), pp. liv–lxiv.

21 This O'Conor was librarian to the Duke of Buckingham and based his con-spectus on the Stowe MSS in that nobleman's possession. (I shall refer to him as 'O'Conor of Stowe', so as to distinguish him from his grandfather, Charles O'Conor of Belanagar). His impressive inventory was sumptuously published on the Duke's account; the Stowe MSS later became the backbone of the British Museum's holdings in ancient Irish material.

22 C.f. Peter Denman, *Samuel Ferguson: The literary achievement* (Gerrards Cross: Colin Smythe, 1990), p. 36.

23 It was marked by an unseemly public washing of dirty linen as he attempted to divorce his wife, the arrogant but deeply unfortunate hobbledehoy, Queen Caroline. The pompous and much-orchestrated coronation finally took place on 19 July 1821; George was crowned in Westminster Abbey, where Grattan had been buried one year previously, and as the ceremony unrolled in solemn state, and behind closed doors, there were brawls outside as the estranged queen fruitlessly attempted to effect an entrance.

24 The *New Edinburgh review* interpreted the visit as a dignified and unrepentant transcendence of ancient enmities, almost like the reconciliation pattern of Walter Scott's national novels, and used the occasion to dismiss, in a balanced and measured summing-up, the bitter memories of 1745 (see the interesting review of *Letters to Sir Walter Scott, bart. on the moral and political character and effects of the visit, in August 1822, of his majesty king George the fourth to Scotland*, in the *New Edinburgh review*, 3 (1822): 568–581).

25 Anon [i.e. W.R. MacDonald], *The Dublin mail; or, intercepted correspondence* (4th ed. London, 1822), 16. Justin McCarthy and Justin Huntly McCarthy's *A history of the four Georges* (4 vols.; London: Chatto & Windus, 1901), a text which is by no means sympathetic to George, fails to find any comparable dissonances in the Edin-burgh visit. The authors are reluctantly compelled to conclude that the visit to the Scottish capital, as opposed to the Irish one, passed more harmoniously and with a more positive spin-off (pp. 41–2). Thomas Carlyle is on record, to be sure, as having been disgusted at the visit; but then he was disgusted at very many things.

26 *Personal recollections of the life and times, with extracts from the correspondence, of Valentine Lord Cloncurry* (Dublin, 1849), 277. A fund was established for a com-memorative monument; grandiose plans were elaborated (John Banim called for the establishment of an Academy of Arts) but all that materialized was King's Bridge (now Heuston Bridge) and the pathetic obelisk, still to be seen at Dun Laoghaire harbour, marking the spot where the monarch left.

27 RIA, 23N4 and 23B37: 'P. Ua Conaill *cc* ag fáilteaghadh Rígh Seoirse go hÉirinn'. It may suffice here to quote the English translation as given by a Mr O'Flaherty: 'A hundred thousand welcomes to Ireland, to the King of the United Empire of England, Ireland & Scotland. Long may your Royal Majesty wear the Crown, with success, health & contentment, as it is thou thyself who came among us in

peace & love, a new & heavenly conqueror, coming as none of thy Royal predecessors came for Centuries before. We think thou art the person foretold by our Saints & Bards, by our Prophets, & Righteous, sent to redress the grievances of the Irish people [orig. *leathtrom Gaoidheal Éireann*, J.L.], to remove their jealousies, their fears, and their feuds!' (23B37)

28 Thaddeus Connellan, *The king's letter, in Irish and in English; with an introduction to the Irish language, and reading lessons for the use of his majesty's Irish subjects* (Dublin, 1822). Thaddeus Connellan (Tadhg Ó Coinnialáin) was an Irish scholar in the employ of the Irish Society (c.f. Pádraig De Brún, 'The Irish Society's bible teachers, 1818–27', *Éigse*, 19, no. 2 (1983)). On this type of evangelization through Irish – later to take the objectionable form of 'souperism' – see Desmond Bowen, *The Protestant crusade in Ireland, 1800–1870: A study of Protestant-Catholic relations between the Act of Union and Disestablishment* (Dublin: Gill & Macmillan, 1978). The Irish Society for Promoting the Education of the Native Irish through the Medium of their Own Language had been sparked off by the educationalist Christopher Anderson and his *Brief sketch of various attempts which have been made to diffuse a knowledge of the Holy Scriptures through the medium of the Irish language* (Dublin, 1818). It relied largely on native scholars such as the prolific Thaddeus Connellan, or else on a small band of Tory Churchmen clustered around the tiny Irish department at Trinity College: tracts and primers were published initially by Henry Monck Mason and Charles Edward Orpen, and, in the later 1840s and 1850s, by men like the Rev. Daniel Foley, Thomas De Vere Coneys and Charles H.H. Wright.

29 C.f. MacDonagh, *O'Connell*, pp. 175–77. George himself voiced the pious hope that his visit should lead to the end of faction and the beginning of Catholic equality (p. 177).

30 William Henry Curran had published in 1819 a biography of his father, *The Life of the Right Honourable John Philpot Curran*, of which a second edition appeared hot on the heels of George's Dublin visit (2 vols.; Edinburgh, 1822); it was scathingly anti-unionist. ('In whatever light the act of Union be viewed in its ultimate consequences to the empire, the assembly which perpetrated it must be considered as having reached the farthest limits of degeneracy', 1: 162.)

31 *The Dublin mail*, 98; McCarthy, *History of the four Georges*, 36; Thomas Moore, *Journal*, ed. W.S. Dowden (6 vols.; University of Delaware Press, 1983–1991), 2: 485.

32 C.f. *Personal recollections of Cloncurry*, p. 277.

33 Some of these, of course, are unspecific celebrations of valour and freedom, part of the generally prevailing climate of the anti-Napoleonic wars. Among the explicitly Irish poems, it should be noted, there are some apolitical celebrations of the Shamrock or of 'Sweet Innisfallen', of locations like the Vale of Avoca or the Isle of Arranmore, or amusing legendary anecdotes like 'St. Senanus and the lady' or the 'Origin of the harp'. One poem transmutes Irish grievances into a celebration of Ireland's love of George IV ('Though dark are our sorrows'). The fact that some *Melodies* are sentimental and others are nationalistic has seduced later critics, who viewed them as a whole, into thinking that they were 'sentimentally nationalistic'.

34 Moore himself saw the ambiguity of his verses, which tried to combine entertaining performance with discursive statement. Thus, his elegy on Henry Grattan 'Shall the harp then be silent' consists of eleven stanzas praising the great Patriot and the brief heyday of national liberty in the 1780s; of these, as a footnote notes, 'only the first two verses are either fitted or intended to be sung'.

35 It would, I believe, be highly rewarding to undertake a comparative history of the reception, reputation and canonicity of Moore in Ireland and Britain, respectively. Whereas, in Ireland, he appears primarily as the poet of the *Melodies*, he seems to be known among British critics as a minor Romantic: the friend and biographer of Byron, the Regency satirist and the author of *Lalla Rookh*. For the theoretical importance of such a reception-oriented comparison between the canons of Anglo-Irish and mainstream English literature, c.f. my 'Literatuur op de landkaart: Taal, territorium en culturele identiteit', *Forum der letteren*, 34 (1993): 16–28.

36 It was only in his *Life and death of Lord Edward Fitzgerald* (2 vols.; London, 1831), that Moore explicitly acknowledged that 'O breathe not his name' was an elegy on Emmet, who had been a close friend of Moore's in their student days (1:303n.). Moore's continuing radicalism can be gleaned from his remembrances of 1798 as written in that book, more than thirty years later: 'Though then but a youth in college, and so many years have since gone by, the impression of horror and indignation which the acts of the government of that day left upon my mind is, I confess, at this moment, far too freshly alive to allow me the due calmness of a historian in speaking of them. Not only had I myself, from early childhood, taken a passionate interest in that struggle which, however darkly it ended, began under the bright auspices of a Grattan, but among these young men whom, after my entrance into college, I looked up to with admiration and regard, the same enthusiasm of national feeling prevailed' (1: 300). For Moore's continuing radicalism in 1832, c.f. here, p. 87.

37 'Oh blame not the bard', 'The minstrel boy', 'Dear harp of my country', ''twas one of those dreams', 'There are sounds of mirth', 'The wandering bard' etc. Some of these poems explicitly address his own ambivalent position, torn between socialite light verse and stern national commitment.

38 'The harp that once' (on the bygone glories of the Gael), 'Shall the harp then be silent' (elegy on Grattan), 'My gentle harp once more I waken' (on the continuing misfortunes of Ireland); 'Sing, sweet harp' (ditto); 'Dear harp of my country'; 'Origin of the harp'. C.f. also Dunne, 'Haunted by history', p. 87.

39 Thuente, *The harp re-strung*, p. 139, p. 150, p. 169.

40 It should be realized that Moore did not so much set verses to music as compose words to accompany airs: the *Melodies* are, first and foremost, precisely that: melodies. Repeatedly there are footnotes stating that a given song is included in the collection because the melody deserved being recorded. There are repeated references to other musical collections such as those of Edward Bunting or one entitled *The Hibernian muse* (see notes to 'When first I met thee', 'Desmond's song', 'When cold in the earth', 'The young May moon', 'Oh! Where's the slave'). On Moore and Bunting, see also here, pp. 174–5.

41 MacCartney, 'The writing of history in Ireland, 1800–1830', p. 360. Yet MacCartney, even while registering the contemporary political effect of the *Melodies*, pointing out Moore's way of linking 'romantic nostalgia with impassioned contemporary politics', and drawing attention to the radicalism of *Memoirs of Captain Rock*, feels that 'The dapper little poet [. . .] remained pathetically unaware of the part he played in the development of Irish nationalism' (pp. 360–1).

42 Quoted in Moore, *Journal*, 5: 2040. Thierry also wrote an essay on the *Irish melodies* in his *Dix ans d'études historiques*. This Augustin Thierry and his brother Amédée (author of the *Histoire des Gaulois*) greatly popularized the view that nationality and national (or even ethnic) conflict were the foremost mainspring

of all historical movement (a view shared by English historians of the Froude and Freeman school, and still endorsed by anti-revisionist Irish historians today). Moore, however, was unimpressed when he consulted the *Histoire de la conquête de l'Angleterre* in 1834; in his *Journal* he wrote that he found it 'a showy, superficial book – built upon a theory, too, which though imposing & perhaps borne out at the commencement of the history, becomes ridiculous, from its forced application, as he goes on' (4: 1622). On Thierry and Ireland, see also Malcolm Brown, *The politics of Irish literature*, pp. 46–7.

43   For a 'Memoir of Roger O'Connor, Esq.', see R.R. Madden, *The United Irishmen, their lives and times with several additional memoirs, and authentic documents, heretofore unpublished; the whole matter newly arranged and revised* (2 vols.; Dublin, 1858), 2: 590–612. O'Connor was the father of Feargus O'Connor, the chartist leader.

44   Anon [i.e. Thomas Moore], *Memoirs of Captain Rock, the celebrated Irish chieftain, with some account of his ancestors. Written by himself* (London, 1824), p. 6.

45   *Proceedings RIA*, 1 (1836–1840): 20, 47–48. W. Obermüller, *Die gaelischen Annalen, nach der Übertragung O'Connor's* (Vienna: Historisch-ethnologische Gesellschaft, 1879); L. Albert [i.e. L. Herrmann], ed./trl. *Die Urbibel der Ario-Germanen* (Berlin: Otto Dreyer, 1921); id., *Six thousand years of Gaelic grandeur unearthed. The most ancient and truthful chronicles of the Gael, vol. 1: 5357 to 1004 BC, with a preface, containing history of the discovery, and a dissertation presenting numerous proofs of authenticity and antiquity* (London, Foyle, n.d. [1936]); id., *The buried-alive chronicles of Ireland. An open challenge to the Celtic scholars of Breo-tan and Er-i* (London: Foyle, 1938) – both these brochures printed at Berlin. Also, F.T. Perry, *The chronicles of Eri, or the ancient Irish, who they were, and their connections with the Coronation Stone* (London: Stockwell, n.d. [1939]).

46   These processes have some importance for our understanding of the history of science and scientific progress. The Kuhnian model of fresh 'paradigms' ousting and replacing older, outworn ones is perhaps too lapidary, and should rather be re-considered in terms of a steady marginalization of older paradigms into pro-gressively more peripheral circles and towards a 'lunatic fringe' and away from the central institutions of scholarly learning; so that 'outdated' paradigms may still influence and inform ideological and cultural attitudes long after they have lost currency in serious scholarship. (The creationist vs. evolutionary debate in present-day American education is an example.) This process was pointed out astutely by Samuel Ferguson when he reviewed Sir William Betham's *Etruria Celtica* in *Blackwood's Edinburgh magazine*, 57 nr. 354 (April, 1845): 474–88: 'But follies are like fashions, which, having once prevailed in the metropolis, usually run the round of the provinces. And so this fantastic trick of interpreting the names of antiquity by modern equivalents [i.e., historical argument based on ungrammatical etymological analogies, as practised by seventeenth-century Flemish linguistic antiquarians] spreading from the schools of Antwerp and Ypres, still shows itself occasionally in the outskirts of the republic of letters' (p. 479).

47   C.f. for a survey of such fabrications, c.f. Wim Zaal, *De verlakkers: Literaire vervalsin-gen en mystificaties* (Amsterdam: Amber, 1991), and Z.R. Dittrich et al., *Knoeien met het verleden* (Utrecht & Antwerpen: Spectrum, 1984). Also, David Greene, *Makers and Forgers* (G.J. Williams Memorial lecture; University of Wales Press, 1975).

48   Such satire is not too far off the mark. C.E.H. Orpen's *The claim of millions of our fellow-countrymen of present and future generations, to be taught in their own and*

only language: the Irish. Addressed to the upper classes in Ireland and Great Britain (Dublin, 1829) was published for the Ladies' Auxiliary Committee of the Irish Society for Promoting the Education of the Native Irish through the Medium of their Own Language.

49 *Memoirs of Captain Rock*, ix–x.

50 Moore has various jibes at the staunchly Protestant convert, Mortimer O'Sullivan (a 'Reverend Pamphleteer', author of *The case of the Church of Ireland stated*). O'Sullivan (1791–1851) was practically the Protestants' anti-Moore. He wrote a counterpiece, *Captain Rock detected: or, the origin and character of the recent disturbances, the causes, both moral and political, of the present alarming condition of the South and West of Ireland, fully and fairly considered and exposed by a Munster farmer* (London, 1824), which blamed grasping landlords rather than churchmen for Irish disaffection. O'Sullivan was also to write a counterpiece to Moore's *Travels of an Irish gentleman in search of religion*. O'Sullivan's main platform was the *Dublin University magazine*, largely run by his brother Samuel O'Sullivan; c.f. Charles Gavan Duffy in *A short life of Thomas Davis* (London, 1895), pp. 42–3. See also FDA, 1: 1135–8.

51 C.f. Ann Rigney, 'Relevance, revision and the fear of long books', in *A new philosophy of history*, eds. F. Ankersmit and H. Kellner (London: Reaktion, 1995), pp. 127–47.

52 MacDonagh, *O'Connell*, p. 299; *Insurrections irlandaises, depuis Henri II jusqu'à l'Union, ou mémoires du Capitaine Rock, le fameux chef irlandais, précédés de quelques détails sur ses ancêtres* trans. I. Nachet (Paris, 1829).

53 *Life of Curran*, 1: 138–9.

54 *Journal*, 4:1501–2.

55 'When I committed to your hands my Memoirs, embracing some small portion of the story of our land, I thought you would have given them to the world in the garb wherewith I had invested them; how great then was my surprise, on my arrival here, to find them decked in an elegance of style, and a delicacy of taste, of the display of which I was incapable!' (pp. 1–2).

56 There is a corrigendum on p. 374, correcting 'Erin' into 'Eri' – a name for Ireland not found outside O'Connor's *Chronicles*. Also, the author of the *Letters to George IV* gives extensive details concerning the vicissitudes of Roger O'Connor during the 1798 rebellion, adding at one point: 'With this anecdote I was favoured by O'Connor himself; its claims to authenticity, therefore, are indisputable' (p. 209). Indeed. Just how 'indisputable' the authority of O'Connor 'himself' is, may appear from the list of the main instigators of the 1798 rebellion as given on pp. 202–3, which begins with the three most important ones:

> 'And first, O'Connor, who is supposed to have been the prime mover and the life of the conspiracy: – a man of the blood-royal of Ireland.
> 'Next, Arthur O'Connor, who signed the treaty of alliance with France
> 'Lord Edward Fitzgerald, the illustrious Geraldine.'

Then follow the other, lesser United Irishman, a list featuring both Wolfe Tone and Castlereagh . . .

57 The reviewer of the *Dublin University magazine*, 5, 20 (June, 1835): 613–629, gave a savage reception to the first volume of Moore's *History of Ireland* for precisely the same reason: 'he reiterates the mischievous fable of papal supremacy' (p. 621). But there was also, as we have seen, a long-standing feud between Moore and the *Dublin University magazine*.

58 Georges-Denis Zimmermann, *Songs of Irish rebellion: Political street ballads and rebel songs 1780–1900* (Hatboro, Pa.: Folklore Associates, 1967), pp. 29–31, and DNB *s.v.* Walmesley. Charles Walmesley, titular bishop of Rama and fellow of the Royal Society (1722–1797) had written a book in 1771 under the pseudonym 'Signor Pastorini', entitled *The general history of the Christian church, from her birth to her final triumphant state in heaven, chiefly deduced from the Apocalypse of St. John the apostle* (reprinted in Dublin in 1790). This book contained a prediction that Protestantism would be wiped out in 1825. That prophecy became widespread in Ireland in the 1820s, where excerpts were circulated in broadsheet form, feeding into the Rockite disturbances. On the sectarian dimension in peasant unrest during these years, see James S. Donnelly, 'Pastorini and Captain Rock: Millenarianism and sectarianism in the Rockite movement of 1821–4', in *Irish Peasants: Violence and political unrest, 1780–1914*, eds. S. Clark and J.S. Donnelly (Manchester University Press, 1983), pp. 102–39.

59 Latham, in J.C. Prichard, *The eastern origin of the Celtic nations proved by a comparison of their dialects with the Sanskrit, Latin, and Teutonic languages: forming a supplement to researches into the physical history of mankind*, ed. R.G. Latham (London, 1857), p. 376.

60 Prichard's *Eastern origin of the Celtic nations*, 1857 ed. The title is vague and ambiguous in its use of 'eastern'. Prichard as an ethnographer was a firm defender of the monogenist tenet that all nations shared a common descent, and indeed his firm Christian belief meant that he would look for that common point of origin somewhere in the Middle East. In his early work, Prichard had been influenced by Bryant, and although later on he came to profit from the insights of the German comparatist school (*Eastern origins* is dedicated to Jacob Grimm), he never wholly abandoned his Biblical frame of reference. In that respect, Prichard as an ethnographer took up a lone stance against the growing polygenist tide of nineteenth-century anthropology, which stressed radical interracial differences. For Prichard as a key figure in early anthropology, see George W. Stocking's introduction to Prichard's *Researches into the pysical history of man* (University of Chicago Press, 1973). Prichard's status in the early history of comparative linguistics is asssessed by R.G. Latham's 'Supplementary chapter' to his 1857 edition of Prichard's *Eastern origin of the Celtic nations*, pp. 354–87.

61 Adolphe Pictet, *De l'affinité des langues celtiques avec le sanscrit. Mémoire couronné par l'Institut/Académie royale des inscriptions et belles-lettres* (Paris, 1837). Pictet gives an interesting assessment of the *status quaestionis* as he sees it: 'Le groupe des langues celtiques, après avoir servi pendant quelque temps à étayer d'absurdes systèmes, est tombé, par un effet de réaction, dans un oubli très peu mérité. Les savants linguistes allemands, Grimm, Bopp et Schlegel, qui ont les plus contribué à l'avancement de la philologie comparée, les ont laissées entièrement en dehors du cercle de leurs travaux. M. Schlegel même a énoncé des doutes sur la parenté des langues celtiques avec la famille indo-européenne' (VI). Pictet offers, by way of an appendix, a copy of his letter to Schlegel urging the importance of Celtic for Indo-European studies (pp. 172–6).

62 Franz Bopp, 'Über die celtischen Sprachen vom Gesichtspunkte der vergleichenden Sprachforschung', in id., *Kleine Schriften zur vergleichenden Sprachwissenschaft. Gesammelte Berliner Akademieabhandlungen 1824–1854* (Leipzig: Zentralantiquariat der DDR, 1972), pp. 149–234: c.f. pp. 214–25 and 233n. Bopp's lecture is largely a review and elaboration of Pictet's essay.

63 Nicholas Wiseman, *Twelve lectures on the connexion between science and revealed religion, delivered in Rome* (New ed.; Dublin, 1866), pp. 34–9. Wiseman's strong endorsement of Prichard may have had something to do with the fact that both men, as devout believers attempting to square biblical models and ethnographical data, held monogenist views as to the origins of humanity.

64 *Proceedings RIA*, 1 (1836–1840): 142; session 28 February 1838; and see here, pp. 128–132.

65 Hugh MacCurtin, *The elements of the Irish language, grammatically explained in English* (Louvain, 1728); Conchobhar Ó Beaglaoich and Aodh Mac Cruitín, *The Irish–English dictionary* (Paris, 1732). On Mac Curtin, see MIFG, pp. 316–18.

66 Pictet's letter to O'Reilly, dated 24 January 1835, is quoted in O'Donovan, *Grammar of the Irish language*, pp. liii–iv(n).

67 O'Donovan, *Grammar*. Zeuss further uses older textual material gleaned from O'Flanagan's version of the Deirdre story, in the *Transactions of the Gaelic Society* of 1808.

68 Sir William Betham, *Etruria Celtica. Etruscan literature and antiquities investigated; or, the language of that ancient and illustrious people compared and identified with the Iberno-Celtic, and both shown to be Phoenician* (2 vols.; Dublin, 1842), pp. 305, 312.

69 Ferguson, in his review of Betham's work, singles out the same passage and comments that Betham's Irish roots, as adduced by him, 'have neither grammatical relation to one another, nor any other coherent meaning in their united senses' (*Blackwood's Edinburgh magazine*, 57, 354 (April, 1845): 474–488; for Ferguson's authorship, see the checklist in Denman, *Samuel Ferguson*, pp. 195 ff.)

70 Ferguson, op. cit., p. 481. Ferguson's review is devastating and qualifies Betham's work as 'fatuity and presumption' and 'mere lunacy' (p. 483, p. 484). Betham's book was also savaged in the *Quarterly review*, 76 (1845): 45–49.

71 For monogenism and polygenism in nineteenth-century anthropology, see Nancy Stepan, *The idea of race in science: Great Britain, 1800–1960* (London: Macmillan, in association with St Antony's College, Oxford, 1982).

72 Wiseman, *Twelve lectures*, pp. 34–9.

73 Thus the Taylorian professor at Oxford, Max Müller, great popularizer of the Indo-European model, in 1888: 'To me an ethnologist who speaks of Aryan race, Aryan blood, Aryan eyes and hair, is as great a sinner as a linguist who speaks of a dolichocephalic dictionary or a brachycephalic grammar. It is worse than a Babylonian confusion of tongues – it is downright theft. We have made our own terminology for the classification of languages; let ethnologists make their own for the classification of skulls, and hair, and blood.' Quoted in Hugh A. Mac Dougall, *Racial myth in English history: Trojans, Teutons, and Anglo-Saxons* (University Press of New England, 1982), 121. Müller's 'keep off the terminological grass' is disingenuous: the nomenclature he claims as having been copyrighted by linguistics was, as we have seen, disseminated by a scholarly proto-discipline which involved the joint presence of linguistic and ethnological interests, and the confusion he denounces was a pre-inscribed part of the situation.

74 Beddoe received a prize of 100 guineas from the Welsh National Eisteddfod in 1867 (the year of Arnold's *On the study of Celtic literature*) for the best essay on the origin of the English nation; this work was subsequently embodied in *The races of Britain*. Beddoe became a Fellow of the Royal Society in 1873, received an honorary LL.D. from the university of Edinburgh in 1891 and numerous

other honours. See, for a recent general survey, Michael Banton, *Racial theories* (Cambridge University Press, 1987), esp. pp. 52–60.

75 Matthew Arnold, *On the study of Celtic literature* (Everyman ed.; London: Dent 1910), p. 26; paraphrased also in Frederic E. Faverty, *Matthew Arnold the ethnologist* (Northwestern University, 1951), pp. 163–4. For a wider background to Humboldt's Aryanism, and a similar *exposé* of Schleiermacher, Bunsen and Feuerbach, see the rest of Faverty's chapter (on 'The Semitic vs. the Indo-European genius'), pp. 162–85. Faverty wrote under the very shadow of the Holocaust; his tendency to expose and denounce the parallels between Arnold's Victorian racialism and the Nazi ideology is sometimes too inculpatory *ex posteriori*, and heedless of the historical differences between Victorian England and Nazi Germany; but although the historical development has been better studied by Poliakov, *Le mythe aryen*, Faverty's groundwork in bringing to light the (as yet 'respectable') antecedents of twentieth-century racism remains valuable.

76 C.f. Levine, *The amateur and the professional*, pp. 79–80. As these examples illustrate, Teutonism could silhouette the 'Saxon' English identity against a variety of possible counterparts: Romance/Latin Continental culture, Jews, or Celts. It is this last polarity with which I am concerned here.

77 Faverty, *Matthew Arnold the ethnologist*; Stepan, *The idea of race in science*; MacDougall, *Racial myth in English history*; L.P. Curtis, *Anglo-Saxons and Celts: A study of Anglo-Irish prejudice in Victorian England* (University of Bridgeport, CT: Conference on British Studies, 1968), esp. the chapters 'Anglo-Saxonist ethnology' and 'Anglo-Saxonist historiography', pp. 66–89.

78 C.f. Kliger, *The Goths in England*.

79 C.f. Curtis, *Anglo-Saxons and Celts*, pp. 82–6. It should be added that there was, besides the patriarchal influence of Carlyle, also the echo of French romantic historiography. Especially the historical works of the Thierry brothers tended to see national developments in terms of the various racial substrata subsisting within the nation and still vying for dominance; thus Amédée Thierry's view of Gaulish-Frankish conflicts actuating French history (taken over in Henri Martin's *Histoire de France*), or Augustin Thierry's view of Norman-Saxon enmity in Britain (*Histoire de la conquête de l'Angleterre*). The French-English physician W.F. Edwards, author of a volume of *Recherches sur les langues celtiques* and member of the Société ethnologique de Paris, performed cranial measurements in France and found two skull-types territorially distributed. This result, which appeared to confirm Amédée Thierry's racial view of French history, he published in an open letter to Thierry, *Des caractères physiologiques des races humaines considérés dans leurs rapports avec l'histoire* (Paris 1829; c.f. Faverty, *Matthew Arnold the ethnologist*, p. 36). Cranial measurement and ethnology thenceforth gained scholarly status in the study of cultural and political history. Arnold engaged with Edwards in *On the study of Celtic literature* (pp. 75–7); and Edwards's inspiration is behind Beddoe's *The races of Britain* of 1885.

80 Quoted in Faverty, *Matthew Arnold the ethnologist*, pp. 19, 195. Green's *Short history of the English people* (1874) begins with the sentence 'For the fatherland of the English race we must look far away from England itself' – that is, Schleswig on what is now the German-Danish border – and opens with the consideration that 'their political and social organization must have been that of the German race to which they belonged'. The history opens with the fifth-century conquest of Britain by 'the English'; any information concerning Celtic or Roman Britain

prior to 449 AD is given only incidentally by way of analeptic flashbacks, 'background' information, 'pre'-history.

81 Luke Owen Pike as quoted in MacDougall, *Racial myth in English history*, p. 91.

82 William Allingham, *Diary*, ed. G. Grigson (Fontwell, Sussex: Centaur, 1967).

83 Thomas Carlyle, 'Repeal of the Union', in id., *Rescued essays*, ed. P. Newberry (London, 1892), pp. 17–52.

84 The racial view of political and cultural history, thinking as it does in the horse- or dog-breeding terms of ethnic bloodlines, inheritance and native disposition, sooner or later blurs the distinction between race and species and excludes certain groups of humanity altogether from the ranks of true *homo sapiens*. The Spanish *conquistadores* had doubted whether American natives had souls at all; Carlyle links Irish Celts and American Indians to wolves; Hitler was later to liken the Jewish presence in the German body politic to that of rats and other parasitical vermin; and in the last two centuries there has been a broad tendency to see African races as somehow close to simian primates rather than as part of humanity. Similarly, the well-known work of L. Perry Curtis has shown how cranial indices and other ethnological concepts helped Lavaterian physiognomy to create, among British cartoonists, a type of Irish caricature that was highly ape-like in appearance. Stephen Jay Gould, *The mismeasure of man* (New York: Norton, 1981); Jan Nederveen Pieterse, *White on black: Images of Africa and blacks in western popular culture* (Yale University Press, 1992); L.P. Curtis, *Apes and angels: The Irishman in Victorian caricature* (Washington: Smithsonian Institution, 1971).

85 Douglas Bush, *Matthew Arnold: A survey of his poetry and prose* (London: Macmillan, 1971), p. 109; A.L. Rowse, *Matthew Arnold: poet and prophet* (London: Thames & Hudson, 1976), p. 108.

86 C.f. the interesting analysis in David Cairns & Shaun Richards, *Writing Ireland* (Manchester University Press, 1988), 42–57. Curtis, *Anglo-Saxons and Celts*, already points out that the stereotype of the Celt is characterized in all its aspects by being opposite to the ideal of the self-possessed Victorian gentleman.

87 Arnold's Celtic interest dates back to 1859, when he had visited Brittany and met Ernest Renan. On that occasion, he had become aware of his connection, through his mother, with a Cornwall which he now realized was part of the Celtic world. Poetry in 1859 included 'Saint Brandan' and 'Stanzas Composed at Carnac'. When writing to his sister Jane, in a letter praising Renan's *La poésie des races celtiques*, Arnold stated his preference for 'the Celtic races' as against 'the somewhat coarse Germanic intelligence'. In the same letter, he congratulated himself 'at our own semi-Celtic origin, which, as I fancy, gives us the power, if we will use of it, of comprehending the nature of both races' – a stance which applies equally to Arnold's familial background and to the ethnic background of the English nation as a whole. C.f. Rowse, *Matthew Arnold*, pp. 108–9.

88 C.f. his essay 'On the Social Progress of States', originally appended to his edition of Thucydides, 1830; in Thomas Arnold, *Miscellaneous works* (London, 1845), pp. 79–111. Here, Arnold pays homage to the *Scienza nuova* of Giambattista Vico, one of whose very first adepts in Britain he was, and to Thierry. Accordingly, Arnold explains social inequality as resulting from ancient differences between conquering and conquered races, and argues that history exhibits a general tendency towards gradual progressing emancipation and equality, threatened by the dangers of despotism and warfare.

89 'The Christian duty of conceding the claims of the Roman Catholics' (1829), in *Miscellaneous works*, pp. 1–78 (34).

90 Letter to Archbishop Whately, 4 May 1836; in A.P. Stanley, *The life and correspondence of Thomas Arnold, DD* (2 vols.; London, 1881), 2: 30.

91 Hippolyte Taine's enumeration of three determinants of national identity, *race*, *milieu* and *moment* (in the Preface to his *Histoire de la littérature anglaise*, 1864) is famous. Similarly, Thomas Arnold, in his 'On the Social Progress on States' (see p. 255, n. 88), mentions two history-governing determinants: inherited national character and climatological environment. 'It is vain to deny that differences of national character apparently constitutional, and belonging to distinct families of the human race, have immensely influenced the greatness and happiness of each; it is equally clear, that the physical geography of the several parts of the earth has advanced or prevented the moral or intellectual progress of their respective inhabitants' (*Miscellaneous Works*, p. 110).

92 There is a risk of exaggerating this rosy view. No sooner was Emancipation enacted, than the sectarian conflict over primary education (National Schools versus Christian Brothers) broke loose, in 1831. This sowed the seeds of a denominalization of Irish national politics later in the century (see here, pp. 150–51). And even in his 1830s Repeal agitation, O'Connell drew his strength exclusively from, and saw his consituency exclusively in, the Gaelic, Catholic part of the population; witness the terms of his *Memoir on Ireland native and Saxon* (Dublin, 1843).

93 A thorough factual history is given by John Andrews, *A paper landscape. The Ordnance Survey in nineteenth-century Ireland* (Oxford: Clarendon Press, 1975). On the Gaelic dimension, see the various studies by Art Ó Maolfabhail: 'An tSuirbhéireacht Ordanáis agus logainmneacha na hÉireann, 1824–34', *Procceedings RIA*, C series, 89 (1989); 'Eadbhéard Ó Raghallaigh, Seán Ó Donnabháin agus an tSuirbhéireacht Ordanáis', *Proceedings RIA*, C series, 91 (1991); 'Eoghan Ó Comhraí agus an tSuirbhéireacht Ordanáis', in *Ómós do Eoghan Ó Comhraí*, ed. P. Ó Fiannachta (An Daingean: An Sagart, 1995), pp. 145–84. For earlier reactions and estimates of the enterprise, see DNB *s.n.* Larcom; anon. [i.e. J.T. Gilbert], *On the life and labours of John O'Donovan, LL.D.* (London, 1862); anon. [i.e. Samuel Ferguson?], 'Ordnance Survey in Ireland', *Dublin University magazine*, 23 (1844): 494–500 (the identification of Ferguson as the author of that article is put into doubt by Denman, *Samuel Ferguson*, pp. 212–3).

94 Lady Ferguson, in her biography of her late husband, *Sir Samuel Ferguson in the Ireland of his day* (2 vols.; London/Edinburgh, 1896), cites oral information from Larcom to the effect that O'Donovan was initially recommended in 1828 by the Irish Society – an evangelist, proselytizing body that made much use of native teachers (1: 62–63; and c.f. above, note 28). See also the letter quoted by Ó Maolfabhail, 'Eoghan Ó Comhraí agus an tSuirbhéireacht Ordanáis', p. 147.

95 The notion, so prevalent in *Translations*, that the travesty of authentic placenames formed part of the cultural estrangement inflicted by colonial rule derives probably from remarks to that effect in Douglas Hyde, *On the necessity for de-anglicizing Ireland* (1892; new ed. Leiden: Academic Pess, 1994). See also the exchange between Brian Friel and John Andrews ('*Translations* and *A paper landscape*. Between fiction and history', *The crane bag*, 7, 2 (1983): 118–124), which took place on the premissed admission that 'Friel's text made some play, both in the

events it represents and in its *dramatis personae*, with Andrews' scrupulous *A paper landscape*' (p. 118). Andrews might have pointed out that Friel's play, far from 'making play with his book', gave a serious and unironic distortion of the historical reality which it implicitly claimed to represent and to adhere to. But he was too courteous to go that far and instead chose graciously to excuse Friel's play on the ground of its very failure to be realistic, allowing that it did not deal, did not even claim to deal, with historical reality at all and instead constructed its own projection of an imagined Ordnance Survey as 'only a dramatic convenience' (p. 121).

96 For that reason, some later critics of an a-critically nationalist persuasion have hinted that the Ordnance Survey was halted by the British Government for ideological reasons. Andrews describes the extent to which 'the suspension of the Ordnance Survey' came to be added to a list of national Irish grievances at the hands of a repressive British government, 'a deliberate act of cultural warfare, on a par with the Statutes of Kilkenny or Cromwell's act of satisfaction' (Andrews, *A paper landscape*, p. 174); the view was probably first brought into currency by Stokes' life of Petrie, and voiced at its most strident by Alice Stopford Green and the Rev. P.M. MacSweeney (whose *A group of nation builders: O'Donovan, O'Curry, Petrie* was published in 1913 for the Catholic Truth Society).

97 William Stokes, *The life and labours in art and archaeology of George Petrie, LL.D.* (London, 1868), p. 95.

98 Quoted Stokes, *Life and labours of Petrie*, p. 97.

99 Levine, *The amateur and the professional*, p. 61, p. 71, p. 60.

100 The raw material collected by the Historical Department concerning topography, language, history and antiquities alone amounted to 468 large quarto volumes; a library of Borgesian uncanniness. C.f. Stokes, *Life and labours of Petrie*, pp. 401–2.

101 Andrews, *A paper landscape*, pp. 157–8.

102 Quoted by Ferguson [?], 'Ordnance Survey in Ireland', p. 498. How detailed the cultural and social information was, is illustrated by the relevant 'Heads of Inquiry' in Larcom's instructions to his field-workers. Apart from registering geographical and geological data, fieldworkers were to look into matters such as – 'Habits of the people. Note the general style of cottage, as stone, mud, slated, glass windows, one story or two, number of rooms, comfort and cleanliness. Food; fuel; dress; longevity; usual number in a family; early marriages; any remarkable instance of either on these heads? What are their amusements and recreations? Patrons and patrons' days; any traditions respecting them? What local customs prevail, as Beal tinne, or fire on St. John's Eve? Driving the cattle through fire, and through water? Peculiar games? Any legendary tales or poems recited around the fireside? Any ancient music, as clan marches or funeral cries? They differ in different districts, collect them if you can. Any peculiarity of costume? Nothing more indicates the state of civilisation and intercourse.' (Quoted Andrews, *A Paper Landscape*, p. 148; also in *The Crane Bag*, 7, 2 (1983): 119).

103 Quoted Andrews, *A paper landscape*, pp. 160–1.

104 Andrews, *A paper landscape*, pp. 168–9; see also the letter quoted by Ó Maolfabhail, 'Eoghan Ó Comhraí agus an tSuirbéireacht Ordanáis', pp. 173–4.

105 Gilbert, *Life and labours of John O'Donovan*, p. 11.

106 It may be mentioned, in addition, that Larcom edited Sir William Petty's *Down Survey* (the great precursor of his own Ordnance Survey project) for the Irish Archaeological Society in 1851.

107 Thus, the author of the article 'Ordnance survey in Ireland' in the *Dublin University magazine* (who, if he was not Ferguson – c.f. p. 273, note 93 – certainly voiced a Fergusonian attitude) concluded his comments on the following optimistic note: '[. . .] is it not a delightful spectacle, now perhaps for the first time exhibited in Ireland, to see Irishmen of all parties and creeds, the most illustrious in rank and the most eminent in talent, combining zealously for an object of good to their common country? and may we not take it as an auspicious omen of the happiness and peace yet in store for us, and which must follow as an inevitable result of the continuance of a unity thus happily begun?' (p. 500). Also, Andrews, *A paper landscape*, p. 175, points out that 'In the spring of 1844 the Irish press broke out with a display of interest and enthusiasm seldom seen outside party politics and with a unanimity that must have been without precedent.'

108 Quoted DNB *s.n.* Larcom.

109 *Life and labours of John O'Donovan*, p. 9.

110 Sir William Wilde, 'Irish popular supersititions', *Dublin University magazine*, 33 (May 1849): 544; quoted by Alf MacLochlainn, 'Gael and peasant – a case of mistaken identity?', in *Views of the Irish peasantry, 1800–1916*, ed. D.J. Casey & R.E. Rhodes (Hamden, CT: Archon, 1977), pp. 17–36 (32–33).

111 I here follow the established view, voiced as early as 1868 by Stokes in his *Life and labours of Petrie* (London, 1868), 73–74; there is no reason to believe that the established view should be incorrect, and at any rate it echoes the feeling of contemporaries like Hamilton himself; c.f. Hamilton's speech of 24 June 1839, on presenting Petrie with the Cunningham medal (*Proceedings RIA*, 1 (1836–1840): 350–4).

112 The museum took shape when the Academy, through a public subscription fund, acquired the collection of antiquities of the late dean of St. Patrick's, Dawson, who had died in 1840. Throughout the 1840s, further artefacts and collections were bought. (RIA, Council minutes)

113 Betham in 1837 concluded one of his lectures 'On the affinity between the Hiberno-Celtic and Phoenician languages' by observing 'that such members of the Academy as were Freemasons must be struck by analogies which he could not more clearly explain' (*Proceedings RIA*, 1 (1836–1840): 36).

114 Richard D'Alton, *The history of Ireland, from the earliest period to the year 1245, when the Annals of Boyle, which are adapted and embodied as the running text authority, terminate; with a brief essay on the native annalists, and other sources for illustrating Ireland, and full statistical and historical notices of the barony of Boyle* (2 vols.; Dublin, 1845). On D'Alton and Hardiman's archive-based investigation of local history, see MacCartney, 'The writing of history in Ireland, 1800–1830', pp. 350–1; for a wider context and a startling English parallel to this double trend in the joint activities of Reprint Societies and County Histories, see Levine, *The Amateur and the Professional*.

115 D'Alton, 'Essay on the ancient history of Ireland': *Poenulus*, pp. 12–4; Round Towers, pp. 134–44.

116 Margaret Stokes, *Early Christian architecture in Ireland* (London, 1878), pp. 53–90; also George Lennox Barrow, *The Round Towers of Ireland* (Dublin: Academy Press, 1979).

117 *Blackwood's Edinburgh magazine*, 57, 354 (April 1845): 487.

118 A spoof on the convoluted controversy took place in early 1843, in which one John Flanagan satirically argued that Round Towers did not exist at all and were

in themselves mere figments of the imagination. His 'opponent' Matthew Delany argued that he had verified the existence of the Clondalkin Round Tower with the aid of all the five senses: sight, hearing (there is an echo inside), touch, smell (a bit musty) and even taste (slightly soapy, from which the author infers that Round Towers were originally cyclopean greased maypoles which contenders had to scale in order to win a prize hat or bandana, dangled from the topmost window by a venerable druid). This is all in jest, of course, lampooning the increasingly bizarre theories that were doing the rounds at the time. But the emphasis on sensual evidence is nevertheless indicative: the physical, kickable presence of the Round Towers was the most arresting thing about them. The skit in question consists of three pamphlets: John Flanagan, *A discourse of the Round Towers of Ireland; in which the errors of the various writers on that subject are detected and confuted, and the true cause of so many differences among the learned, and the question of their use and history, is assigned and demonstrated* (Kilkenny, 1843); Matthew Delany, *An answer to Mr. Flanagan's extravagant assertions respecting the Round Towers of Ireland; with some original views as to their real origin and uses, and certain singular particulars on the one at Clondalkin, worthy the attention of the curious* (Carlow, 1843); John Flanagan, *Delany confuted; or, an exposure of the flagitious frauds of the writer of that name in forging evidence to prove the existence of a Round Tower at Clondalkin, in the county of Dublin. With some further observations on the ancient Phoenician smelting furnace in Sancanathice, in Kilkenny* (Kilkenny, 1843).

119 Nora, *Les lieux de mémoire*; Shils, *Tradition.*

120 Originally in *The nation* and *The spirit of the nation*; FDA 2: 59–60. There was also a famous reference to Round Towers in one of Moore's Irish Melodies, 'Let Erin Remember'. The passage was usually quoted to illustrate the persistence of a figment of Giraldus Cambrensis's imagination. 'On Lough-Neagh's bank, as the fisherman strays / [. . .] / He sees the round towers of other days / In the wave beneath him shining!' The Giraldean source apart, however, it is interesting how Moore like MacCarthy uses the Towers, dimly seen submerged under water, as metaphors for the persistence of historical memory through the passage of time. In other words: as cyphers for historical permanence. 'Thus shall Memory often, in dreams sublime, / Catch a glimpse of the days that are over; / Thus, sighing, look through the waves of Time / For the long-faded glories they cover!'

121 It is quite possible, as later historians have hinted, that this highly popular poem materially contributed to the tenacity of the 'Phoenician' or pre-Christian hypotheses as to the Round Towers' origins. See here, pp. 143–4 and 267, n. 190.

122 There are shades of Roger O'Connor in this character. The Morres or Mountmorres family, landed gentry, claimed to descend from one of the Anglo-Norman barons of 1169, one Monte-marisco or Montmorency. The present tract on the Round Towers includes various digressions aimed at proving the author's claims to that august name and baronial title (c.f. pp. 17–8); he also published various genealogical tracts to bolster this claim (*Genealogical memoir of the family of Montmorency de Marisco or Morres*, Paris 1817; *Les Montmorency de France et les Montmorency d'Irlande*, Paris 1827). Indeed various branches of the family Morres / Mountmorres had their name changed by royal warrant to 'assume', as Debrett's Peerage politely phrases it, 'the old name of Montmorency'. However, the claim leaves room for considerable doubt. Hervey Morres/Montmorency, a former United Irishman now in the French military service, had his case judged (with positive result) by the credulous Ulster King of

Arms, Sir William Betham, resulting in a name-change by royal warrant in 1815; the copy of the *Historical and critical enquiry into . . . the Irish pillar-tower* in the National Library, Ireland, is inscribed to Betham (c.f. Debrett's *Peerage s.n.* Montmorency; DNB *s.n.* Morres; S.H. Fitzmaurice, 'Hervey de Montmorency', *Journal of the old Wexford society*, 2 (1969): 19–25. Obviously, the re-invention of the past was something that went on, not only in national but also in familial-genealogical terms.

123   The main argument usually works on the basis of similarity in appearance. This has led to multifarious conjectures, unsurprisingly so in view of the fact that tower-shaped buildings are found in most civilizations. Thus, pagodas, minarets and Sardinian *nuraghe* have all been cited as 'meaningful' analogues to Round Towers, indicating common origins, while the 'beacon' theory was obviously inspired by the Round Towers' similarity to lighthouses. Here as in pre-scientific etymology, the same fallacy obtains: that argument is derived from mere incidental similarity in appearance (between a Round Tower and a pagoda, between the name 'Erin' and the name 'Iran'), without structural contextualization.

124   It is true that Round Towers do not resemble the other known types of defensive fortification. However, the other known types of fortification are inherited either from Roman prototypes or from Norman and Crusaders' forts, which would not have been known prototypes in pre-Norman Ireland. Unfortunately, one major effort to clarify the history of military architecture in Ireland, Petrie's prize essay of 1837 for which he received a gold medal from the Royal Irish Academy, has not been printed and remains in manuscript; there is, however, a synopsis in Stokes, *Life and labours of Petrie.*

125   *Transactions RIA*, 14 (1825).

126   *Transactions RIA*, 15 (1828): 101–241; esp. 182–220. Beauford cites the similar placenames 'Iran' and 'Erin'.

127   *Transactions RIA*, 16 (1829): 1–380, esp. pp. 134–44.

128   Stokes, *Life and labours of Petrie*, p. 146.

129   Stokes, *Life and labours of Petrie*, p. 147 states that there were three entries. D'Alton, who was on the Council at the time, says there were five (*History of Ireland*, 2:32–3). RIA, Council minutes 4 (March 1822 – January 1837), which are not comprehensive in this respect, mentions three submissions. There is some reason to suspect that the third, unsuccessful entry was by the Blarney parish priest Fr Matthew Horgan: in the Academy's Windele papers (23G15) there is, among other writings by Horgan from the 1830s, an essay on the Round Towers.

130   This much is intimated in D'Alton, *History of Ireland*, 2: 32–4. Similarly, the reviewer in the *Dublin penny journal* says that, while the Council of the Royal Irish Academy wished O'Brien to purge his essay of its more 'outré' and 'objectionable' passages, the work in book form 'is not only very different from that sent into the Academy, but all the objectionable passages are still retained' (2, 98 (17 May 1834): 364).

131   C.f. George Petrie, *Letter to Sir William Hamilton, LL.D., in reply to certain charges made against the author by Sir William Betham* (Dublin, 1840), p. 3, p. 8.

132   *Dublin penny journal*, 1, 2 (7 July 1832): 9.

133   C.f. the Introduction to O'Brien's *The Round Towers of Ireland, or the history of the Tuath-De-Danaans for the first time unveiled* (1834; new ed. London, 1898), p. lxxi.

134   Thus, in describing the Round Tower at Aghadoe, 13 October 1832: 'I could say a great deal about round towers, and would do so now, having my own opinion as well as others on this disputed subject, only that I understand there is a premium

now afforded for the best essay on the subject, by the Royal Irish Academy' (p. 126); again, in describing the Round Tower at Swords, 1 December 1832: 'Respecting the uses of those singular ancient buildings, we deem it improper to express any opinion, till the Royal Irish Academy shall have announced its decision of the prize essays on this subject, now under its consideration' (p. 177).

135 *Dublin University magazine*, 1, 1 (January 1833): 104.

136 Thus, the *Dublin penny journal* for 8 November 1834 (vol. 3): 'A recent antiquarian appears to have thrown the light of historical evidence upon this *vexata questio* of the learned brotherhood. His essay, which was honoured with a prize and a medal by the unanimous [*sic*] decision of the Royal Irish Academy, is not yet before the public. [. . .] His arguments, it is generally said, are free from conjecture, and founded on authentic history [. . .]' (p. 150 n.)

137 RIA, Council minutes, 4 (March 1822–January 1837): 182–3.

138 Among the subscribers were John D'Alton, Lady Morgan, Daniel O'Connell, Caesar Otway, and Henry O'Brien himself. The book is dedicated to the Royal Irish Academy, thanking that learned body for the hospitality of its library now that the author himself had been deprived of his own books. Villanueva (1757–1836; he lies buried at Glasnevin) is a highly interesting figure. Erstwhile house chaplain to the Spanish king, member of the Royal Spanish Academy, and representative in the Cortes of Cadiz, he had played an important role in the intellectual and political life of his own country before, during and after the French occupation; his career in ecclesiastical politics was wrecked by the slanderous imputation of Jansenist sympathies and he spent the remainder of his days in Dublin under the protection of Archbishop Murray, to whom he dedicated his edition of the writings and textual fragments attributed to St. Patrick (*Sancti Patricii, Ibernorum apostoli, synodi, canones, opuscula et scriptorum quae supersunt, fragmenta scholiis illustrata a Joachimo Laurentio Villanueva presbytero*, Dublin 1835). An interesting volume of poetry in his native Spanish was also published in Dublin, with subscriptions from William Drennan, John D'Alton, Lady Morgan, Thomas Moore and Daniel O'Connell: *Poesias escogidas del dr. D. Joaquín Lorenzo Villanueva*. Some of these poems are on Irish themes: 'Glendalogh', 'Devil's Glen', 'Black Rock', 'Ballyshannon', 'El vaquero de Irlanda', 'El cabrero de Gurlough'. On Villanueva, see the entry under his name in the *Enciclopedia universal ilustrada europeo-americana*, 68: 1463–1646. He became an honorary member of the Royal Irish Academy in 1833.

139 *Gentlemen's magazine*, 103, no. 2 (October, 1833): 340–342.

140 'Viderint eruditi Iberni num idoli *Astoreth* sapiat originem jocunda amatoria cantilena, Moly-Astore, quae a vetustissimis temporibus in ore est Iberniae ruricolarum et civium' (*Ibernia Phoenicia*, p. 144n.) Such solecisms, derived from Vallancey, were taken up by later speculative antiquarians: I. Webber Smith, O'Brien himself and Keane all adduce 'Molly Astore' as evidence of Astarte-worship; conversely, such practice illustrates the magnitude of the task of Petrie, O'Donovan, O'Curry and their factualist and critical method.

141 'To the learned of Europe, to the heads of its several universities, to the teachers of religion and the lovers of history, more especially to the Alibenistic Order of Freemasons, to the fellows of the Royal Society, to the Members of the Royal Asiatic Society, to the fellows of the Society of Antiquaries, to the editors of the Archaeologia Scotica, to the committees of the Societies for the Propagation of the Gospel and the Diffusion of Useful Knowledge, and to the Court of the Honourable the East India Company'.

142 Accordingly, Thomas Moore, in the *Edinburgh review*, suspected 'that Mr. O'Brien's engraver has been induced to accommodate the Tower of Clondalkin to his learned employer's theory' (April 1834: 149). Thomas Davis stated that 'the phallic theory never had any support but poor Henry O'Brien's enthusiastic ignorance and the caricaturing pen of his illustrator' ('The Round Towers of Ireland', in *Prose writings: Essays on Ireland* (London, 1889), pp. 90–103).

143 Serpent worship had been described as a primordial pagan religion by Bryant in his *Analysis of antient mythology* (1775, reprint ed. 1806).

144 For an example, see the epistemological relativism of Kevin Barry's palliative treatment of historical errors in Brian Friel's play *Translations*, *The crane bag*, 7, 2 (1983): 118–120 (c.f. p. 256, n. 95).

145 C.f. Rigney, 'Time for visions and revisions'.

146 O'Brien cites Heeren's reflections on the possible links between Old Iranian and Sanskrit, and hypothesizes a link between those Oriental languages and Irish, going as far as to state: '[. . .] until the *Irish Language* can be raked from its ashes, no accuracy can ever be obtained either in the Zend, Pahlavi or Sanscrit *dialects* [. . .]' (p. 183). The insight was true, the correlation meaningful, albeit based on the flawed premise that Gaelic was the mother tongue of all these.

147 Payne Knight's work was taken up by the French authors Jacques Antoine Dulaure and Charles Dupuis in the early nineteenth century. For a good analysis, see G.S. Rousseau, 'The Sorrows of Priapus', in id., *Perilous enlightenment. Pre- and post-modern discourse: Sexual, historical* (Manchester University Press, 1991), pp. 65–108; kindly brought to my attention by Luke Gibbons. Payne Knight's treatise does not refer to Irish material, only to a Celtic fort excavated in The Netherlands. How Payne Knight's phallic-religious theory may have reached O'Brien is not quite clear, but there was one adept at least in Irish intellectual circles. James Wills, in his review in the *Dublin University magazine* (3, 16; April, 1834; for the identification of the reviewer's identity, c.f. *Wellesley index*, p. 4), gives a hint which I have not been able to substantiate further: 'It was known to all who took any interest in the subject what his [O'Brien's] theory was [when he submitted his essay]: and to many how he came by it. The occasion of his writing was, in fact, the accidental discovery of the opinion of another person – the most unprincipled piracy of an essay not his own. It matters not how worthless was the theft; the dupe may by consistently combined with the name: he thought the mare's nest of poor Mr. R—n to be a treasure, and stole it accordingly' (p. 378). A trawl through the DNB yielded as the most likely candidate the Orientalist Frederick August Rosen, born in 1805 in Hanover, erstwhile student of Bopp, and from 1826 until 1830 professor of Sanskrit at University College London. Rosen had written for the Penny Cyclopaedia, and had published a volume on 'The Hindoos' for the Library of Entertaining Knowledge. He was also the first English-based scholar to give an edition and translation of the Rig-Veda. The reviewer of the *Dublin penny journal* hints in a different direction (D'Alton?): 'We have heard it asserted that a large proportion of the precious compound was furnished by a ci-devant member of the Council of the Academy. This, however, we can scarcely credit; for however the opinions in the essay appear to correspond with some others that learned gentleman put forward in his Penny magazine, while it was in existence, we still think he has more [. . .] common sense, than to perpetrate such a hoax on an individual he calls his friend, and for whom he was the chief means of obtaining the twenty pounds [i.e. the consolation prize]' (2, 98 (17 May 1834): 364).

148   Godfrey Higgins, *Anacalypsis, an attempt to draw the veil of the Satic Isis; or, an inquiry into the origin of languages, nations, and religions* (2 vols.; London, 1836) contains specific references, not only to Vallancey, but also to Payne Knight (1: 339 and n.). While Higgins was a strenuously low-church anti-papist, his books are full of masonic references.

149   Godfrey Higgins, *The Celtic druids; or, an attempt to shew that the druids were the priests or Oriental colonies who emigrated from India, and were the introducers of the first or Cadmean system of letters, and the builders of Stonehenge, of Carnac, and of other Cyclopean works, in Asia and Europe* (London, 1829), pp. 150–1 and n.

150   Reprinted together with Payne Knight's *Discourse on the worship of Priapus* (New York: Dorset Press, 1992); Sheela-na-Gig material discussed pp. 33–41.

151   Thus the anonymous author of *Phallic objects, monuments and remains, illustrations of the rise and development of the phallic idea (sex worship) and its embodiment in works of nature and art* (privately printed, 1889); the copy in the Librarian's Office, National Library of Ireland, carries advertisements for other works by the same author, likewise privately printed in apparently limited editions: *Phallicism, a description of the worship of lingam-yoni in various parts of the world; Ophiolatreia, an account of serpent worship; Cultus arborum, a descriptive account of phallic tree worship* and *Fishes, flowers and fire as phallic symbols*. This book relies, not only on O'Brien, but also on Betham and on Bryant's Cuthite hypothesis as taken up by Marcus Keane.

152   One reprint was made in London 1898, the other, more recent, under anthroposophical auspices under the New Age title (inappropriate but doubtless commercial) *Atlantis in Ireland* (New York: Steinerbooks, 1976, reprint ed. 1992). The masonic interest is vouchsafed by the fact that O'Brien devotes much space to the mythical figure of the *Goban Saer* or 'arch-builder', a primordial architect in Irish myth obviously suited to Masonic beliefs. One of the only positive reviews of O'Brien's book appeared in the *Freemasons' quarterly review*, quoted by O'Brien in *Gentleman's magazine*, N.S. 2 (1834): 366–7. Similarly, we also see that the Round Towers as evidence of an early architectural 'craft', are given much positive attention in the professional journal, *The Irish builder*, in the years 1867–1886 (see below, note 197). The anthroposophical reprint (with an introduction by Paul M. Allen) makes much of the transatlantic parallels drawn occasionally by O'Brien, and sees the book as a forerunner of Ignatius Donnelly's theories concerning the lost civilization of Atlantis. For the ritualistic use of Round Towers in the masonically-inspired initiation rites of the Ancient Order of Hibernians, see here, pp. 143–4.

153   *Dublin University magazine*, 3, 16 (April, 1834): 375–86 (380).

154   *Gentleman's magazine*, N.S.1 (1834): 299.

155   *Dublin penny journal*, 2, 98 (17 May 1834): 361); 3, 156 (27 June 1835): 410–1.

156   *Journal*, 4: 1611, entry for July 1834.

157   *Journal*, 4: 1537, entry for 27 May 1833. An ironic letter to an unknown addressee, dated 23 April 1833, declining the pleasure of having the secret of the Round Towers divulged to him, is in *The letters of Thomas Moore*, ed. W.S. Dowden (Oxford: Clarendon, 1964), 2: 763; evidently in answer to the letter(s) mentioned belatedly in the Journal. It is possible that this unknown 1833 correspondent was none other than O'Brien, who, after the disappointment of the Academy adjudication, sought to sell the fruits of his labour to the national poet, known at that time

to be preparing his *History of Ireland*. That suspicion is strengthened by the fact that Francis Mahony, in a satire against Moore, twice mentions private correspondence between Moore and O'Brien prior to Moore's hostile review of the *Round Towers*. Mahony accuses Moore of ridiculing O'Brien's book 'having first negotiated by letter with him to extract his brains, and make use of him for his meditated "History of Ireland" – (the correspondence lies before me)'; again, it was unworthy of Moore to attack O'Brien 'after the intimacy of private correspondence' ('The rogueries of Tom Moore', orig. in *Fraser's magazine*, 1835; in *Reliques of Father Prout*, London, 1859, p. 145, p. 162.).

158 *Letters*, 2: 783–784; *Journal*, 4: 1603; 5: 2227.

159 *Reliques of Father Prout*, pp. 141–2. Contemporary audiences frequently read nationally Irish, allegorical meanings into *Lalla Rookh*. 'Who [. . .] did not know that the oppressed *Iran* was Erin, Ireland? that the heroic *Gheber* was the Catholic Celt? that the moslem maid, "Araby's daughter", typified the generous soul of England, awakening to the merits and unmerited misfortunes of a race so long oppressed?', Bernard O'Reilly. *John MacHale, Archbishop of Tuam. His life, times, and correspondence* (2 vols.; New York & Cincinnati, 1890), 1: 74. See also Thuente, *The harp re-strung*, pp. 188–90.

160 'The bells of Shandon' is in the style of Richard Milliken's famous 'The groves of Blarney' (FDA 1: 1101–2), of which Prout gave French, Italian, Latin and Greek versions. A similar case is that of William Maginn, Mahony's counterpart in these jokey but recondite wordplays – witness his bilingual English-Latin 'The wine-bibber's glory' / 'Toporis gloria' (FDA 2: 18–9).

161 Moore was deeply irritated by this satire and could not bring himself to acknowledge its brilliance. The only mention of Father Prout in his *Journal* is towards the end of 1840 when he peevishly mentions Mahony as 'a clever *Vaurien*' (5: 2172).

162 Father Prout can therefore freely adopt the discourse of visionary antiquarianism in his satirical 'A plea for pilgrimages'. The Blarney Stone, 'the palladium of our country' and main resource of great Irishmen like Dan O'Connell, 'was brought hither originally by the Phoenician colony that peopled Ireland, and is the best proof of our eastern parentage.' That even the Balearic Islands are named after the Blarney Stone 'will appear at once to any person accustomed to trace Celtic derivations: the Ulster King of Arms, Sir William Betham, has shown it by the following scale [. . .] BaLeARes iNsulAE = Blarnae!' (*Reliques*, p. 52).

163 'His book on "the Round Towers" has thrown more light on the early history of Ireland, and on the freemasonry of these gigantic puzzles, than will ever shine from the cracked pitchers of the "Royal Irish Academy" or the farthing candle of Tommy Moore. And it was quite natural that he should have received from them, during his lifetime, such tokens of malignant hostility as might sufficiently "tell how they hated his beams". The "Royal Irish" twaddlers must surely feel some compunction now [after his death], when they look back on their paltry transactions in the matter of the "prize essay"; and though we do not expect much from "Tom Brown the younger" or "Tom Little" [both of them pseudonyms used by Moore] [. . .] still it would not surprise us if he now felt the necessity of atoning for his individual misconduct [. . .]' (p. 163). In such passages, the satirical, anti-Moorean intent overshadows the irony *vis-à-vis* O'Brien; and it become understandable why this piece was frequently seen as an unreserved endorsement of O'Brien's theories.

164   Eugene O'Curry, *On the manners and customs of the ancient Irish*, ed. W.K. O'Sullivan (3 vols.; London, Dublin, New York, 1873), 3: 52.

165   *Dublin penny journal*, 2, 98 (17 May 1834): 364.

166   Betham did, however, state unreservedly in 1842 that 'poor O'Brien was mad' (*Etruria Celtica*, 2: 31).

167   *Dublin University magazine*, 3, 16 (April 1834): 378–9.

168   'On the history and antiquities of Tara Hill', *Transactions RIA*, 18 (1839), pt. 2.

169   *Proceedings RIA*, 1 (1836–1840): 142.

170   Moore, *Journal*, 5: 1997; 4 September 1838.

171   *Lectures on the manuscript materials of ancient Irish history* (Dublin, 1861), p. 154.

172   The letter, on the occasion of receiving Petrie's essay on the antiquities of Tara (published 1839), is quoted in Stokes, *Life and labours of Petrie*: 'I believe I have already told you that I mean, in a preface to the fourth volume of my "Ireland", to take a retrospect of my whole work, notice criticisms, correct errors, and avail myself of any new lights that may have been struck out, by myself or others, since the time when I commenced the work. Then I hope to do you justice [. . .]' (p. 121).

173   There are hints that within the Ordnance Survey, Petrie was sometimes too tardy in producing needed information (Andrews, *A paper landscape*, pp. 161–2).

174   Petrie, 'On the history and antiquities of Tara Hill', p. 104.

175   *Proceedings RIA*, 1 (1836–1840): 350–4; Stokes, *Life and labours of Petrie*, p. 109.

176   RIA Council minutes, 5 (January 1837 – July 1840): 278–80; RIA minutes, 2 (January 1827 – March 1849): 196.

177   Sir William Betham, *Letter to Sir William Rowan Hamilton, President of the Royal Irish Academy* (Dublin, 1840), p. 16.

178   Petrie, *Letter to Sir Willam R. Hamilton*, pp. 17–25.

179   RIA 12 G 15 (Horgan/Windele papers), III item 4; c.f. catalogue p. 3462.

180   Quoted Stokes, *Life and labours of Petrie*, pp. 133–5.

181   *Proceedings RIA*, 2: 372 (Betham); 563–7 (Clibborn).

182   RIA, Council minutes, 6 (September 1840 – April 1845): 277–307; RIA minutes, 2 (January 1827 – March 1849): 334–49. The Academy endorsed the Council's stance and ordered the entire sordid correspondence, to Betham's shame, to be made public by having it printed: *Proceedings RIA*, 3 (1845–1847): appendix, pp. i–xv.

183   The review was, of course, anonymous (*Dublin University magazine*, 25, 98 (April, 1845): 379–96. For the attribution to Ferguson, see the checklist in Denman, *Samuel Ferguson*, pp. 195 ff. Ferguson had, it will be remembered, already championed Petrie's cause by savaging Betham's *Etruria Celtica* in *Blackwood's* (here, p. 253 notes 69, 70).

184   The review was reprinted in Kelly's *Dissertations chiefly on Irish church history*, ed. D. McCarthy (Dublin, 1864), pp. 137–219. There was also a positive review in the *Quarterly review*, 76 (1845): 354–87, by the Maynooth scholar Charles Russell (thus identified in the *Wellesley index*, 1), who praises Petrie's archaeological achievement generally for demonstrating the existence of ancient civility in Ireland.

185   Reprinted in Davis, *Prose writings*, pp. 90–103. There are striking parallels between the attitudes of Petrie and Davis on the subject of Irish antiquities; both argue strenuously that it is an imperative public duty to undertake a preservation campaign. Davis must have read with approval the sentiments expressed by Petrie in his

Preface: 'What, may I ask, would we know of the true greatness of the Greeks and Egyptians if we were unacquainted with their ancient monuments? What do we know of the Etruscans but what we have derived from this source?'; Davis, in essays like 'Historical Monuments of Ireland' and 'Irish Antiquities' voices similar concerns. The difference is, however, that Petrie wants to see ancient monuments preserved for scholarly reasons (the monuments give testable, positive information; their loss would give free rein to all sorts of errors and speculations concerning the past), whereas for Davis they are proof that Ireland has a national history and not just a provincial present. George Petrie, *The ecclesiastical architecture of Ireland, anterior to the Anglo-Norman invasion, comprising an essay on the origin and use of the Round Towers of Ireland, which obtained the gold medal and prize of the Royal Irish Academy* (Dublin, 1845), viii; Davis, *Prose writings*, pp. 80–9.

186 Quoted Stokes, *Life and labours of Petrie*, p. 210. This let both Petrie and the Academy off the hook.

187 For the social exclusivism and the élitism of learned (historical or antiquarian) societies in the mid-century, see Levine, *The amateur and the professional*, pp. 8–11, pp. 19–22. When the Irish Archaeological Society was founded in 1840, it envisaged only 'Noblemen and Gentlemen' as potential members, at a time when that terminology excluded, not only women, but also the non-professional middle classes (traders and employees).

188 Henry O'Neill, *The fine arts and civilization of ancient Ireland, illustrated with chromo and other lithographs and several woodcuts* (London and Dublin, 1863), p. 96. This handsome volume, with valuable illustrations by one of the outstanding draughts-men of the nineteenth century, contains three chapters on the Round Towers (pp. 80–112). O'Neill had been a collaborator of Petrie's, had fallen out with him over the question of inscriptions on the Cross of Cong, and wrote from a strong personal antipathy (he calls Petrie, sneeringly, 'the Doctor', throughout) combined with ardent national feeling. He recounts, in pugnaciously anti-English terms, the story of 'The decline of Irish civilization' (pp. 113–8), and developed the same nationalistic vision of Irish art history (great achievements before the arrival of the Normans, ruin and spoliation since then) in his *A descriptive catalogue of illustrations of the fine arts of ancient Ireland, serving to show that a truly national and beautiful style of art existed in Ireland from a remote period till some time after the Anglo-Norman invasion* (Dublin, 1855); in 1868 he published a pamphlet attacking landlordism, *Ireland for the Irish: a practical, peaceable, and just solution of the Irish land question* (London and Dundalk, 1868).

189 *Illustrated history of Ireland from the earliest period* (2nd ed.; New York & Kenmare, 1868, pp. 152–5). See also Archbishop Healy's pamphlet, published for the Catholic Truth Society: *The Round Towers of Ireland and holy wells of Ireland*. The publication is undated but was apparently occasioned by a masonic reprint of Henry O'Brien's book in 1898. Healy damns 'vain speculations regarding fanciful resemblances' and praises Petrie's 'careful and systematic' procedure, enabling him 'to prove his conclusions by unassailable evidence' (p. 17). A third example of attempts to cure the middle-class reading public of their fancies is 'S.J.' [i.e. John Salmon] *The Round Towers of Ireland: Their origins and uses* (Belfast 1886), an essay originally read before the Belfast Young Ireland Society. Salmon was one of the first to assert in print that Father Prout, 'in expressing an extravagant admiration of O'Brien's conjecture, was only playing off one of his numerous hoaxes upon public credulity' (p. 42).

190 Witness Caleb Palmer in *The Irish builder*, 12 (1870): 255–6, who invokes 'our only living national poet, whose poem on the "Pillar Towers of Ireland" coincides with my Baalist views'. Bourke, in *The Aryan origin of the Gaelic race and language* (Dublin, 1875), quotes the poem twice (pp. 344–5, pp. 378–9) to support his case for a pre-Christian origin.

191 Dunraven was a friend of Petrie; both were instrumental in 1840 in setting up, together with Todd, the Irish Archaeological Society. His sumptuous *Notes on Irish architecture*, ed. M. Stokes (2 vols.; London, 1875–77) essentially endorsed Petrie's case, as did, with minor modifications, Margaret Stokes's own *Early Christian architecture in Ireland* (London, 1878). It is this last work most of all which has settled the question as to the origin and dating of the Round Towers.

192 Such appointments proved hollow. Irish was not a full subject for any degree course, the emoluments were minimal, and very few students presented themselves – indeed, not a single one, ever, in Belfast. These chairs, which had been established for 'token, symbolic value' rather than from a 'desire to give [Irish] full-blown academic expression' were allowed to lapse after a negative assessment by a Royal Commission in 1857. C.f. Cornelius G. Buttimer, 'Celtic and Irish in College, 1849–1944', *Journal of the Cork historical and archaeological society*, 94 (1989): 88–112, esp. 89–91. A slightly expanded version of this article in Irish is in *The Irish review*, 17/18 (1995): 51–65.

193 For an example, see 'Early vestiges of the Gael', *Dublin University magazine*, 65, 388 (April, 1865): 466–80.

194 One correspondent is named as Connor Mac Sweeny, who subscribes to O'Brien's theory; another believer in phallicism is 'that old Catholic twaddle, Devereux of Carrickmannan'; in January and April 1845, Moore corresponds with John Windele of Cork on the subject of the pagan origin of the Round Towers (*Journal*, 4:1655–1656; 5:2222, 2227, 2240). Is it this correspondence which cooled Moore's 1838 endorsement of Petrie? Moore never publicly retracted the Orientalism proclaimed in vol. 1 of the *History of Ireland*, and accordingly Petrie classes Moore, without much palliative comment, among the ignoramuses in his *Ecclesiastical architecture*. The cordial understanding of the 1838 visit appears not to have lasted until 1845.

195 Hargrave Jennings, *The Rosicrucians, their rites and mysteries* (London, 1870), pp. 146–51; Anna Wilkes, *Ireland: Ur of the Chaldees* (London 1873); Daniel O'Byrne, *The history of the Round Towers of Ireland* (Kilkenny, 1877); James Bonwick, *Irish druids and old Irish religions* (London, 1894); John H. Edge, *An Irish Utopia: a story of a phase of the land problem. New edition with a special introduction (now first published) dealing with the subject of the Irish Round Towers* (Dublin, 1910).

196 O'Neill, *Fine arts and civilization of ancient Ireland*, pp. 111–2.

197 In addition to these two must be mentioned some correspondents of local archaeology journals and of the *Irish builder*. Regional archeologist like John Windele of Cork found followers in the pages of the *Ulster archaeological journal* (in the 1850s), in the *Kilkenny and South-East of Ireland Archaeological Society journal*; foremost among them were Richard Rolt Brash and Hodder M. Westropp. Brash, who published his ideas in book form as *The ecclesiastical architecture of Ireland to the close of the twelfth century* (Dublin, 1874), saw Round Towers, like Petrie, as Romanesque structures, but did allow for traces of an ancient fertility cult in the Sheela-na-Gigs, and gave some credit to the historicity of the mythical Goban

Saer-archbuilder. Westropp speculated that Round Towers were guiding beacons in churchyards (*fanaux de cimetière*) but may have held more outlandish views than he let on to: in 1885 he published a book called *Primitive symbolism as illustrated in phallic worship or the reproductive principle* (mentioned by G.S. Rousseau, *Perilous Enlightenment*, p. 103n). Their insidious anti-Petrie revisionism was frequently published or reprinted in *The Irish builder*, which kept the contrversy alive in the years 1868–1871. Its pages in those years were also dominated by an O'Brienesque eccentric named Caleb Palmer. Again, in 1875, a series of articles 'The literature of gothic architecture in Ireland' commenced in *The Irish builder*, containing repeated attempts to undercut the prominence of Petrie and to play up underdog sympathy for O'Brien. 'Poor Henry O'Brien's Phallic theory met with rough usage at the hands of his Christian countrymen [. . .] Notwithstanding, he has impregnated others with his views, and has still disciples and fellow-countrymen who uphold his opinions in part, and preach them. Dr. Petrie's work was, somewhat unfortunately, on its appearance accepted as a satisfactory settlement of the vexed question [. . .] Petrie, like others, during his life lived to find he had opponents who were not satisfied with his theory, and since his death the opposition has grown stronger' (17 (1875): 131). Again, the series was concluded by an editorial postscript which, after quoting Thomas Davis's dismissal of O'Brien, went on to say that 'had Davis lived a few years longer he would have found that O'Brien's theory had met painstaking and enthusiastic adherents among his own countrymen' (17 (1875): 253). The series attracted numerous incidental correspondents, among whom the silly Rev. Richard Smiddy gained some prominence and authority: 17 (1875): 229–230; 18 (1876): 76–79, 122; 19 (1877): 31–32. All this peripheral and ephemeral material indicates how widespread and tenacious the resistance against Petrie's factualism was in non-academic circles.

198 When Petrie had been forced in 1840 to shoulder the entire financial responsibility for the publication of his Round Towers essay, the woodcuts became his property. They were apparently bought by Keane. This was in itself enough to set speculations racing; c.f. W.J. Fitz-Patrick, *Irish wits and worthies, including Dr. Lanigan, his life and times, with glimpses of stirring scenes since 1770* (Dublin, 1873), p. 240.

199 Marcus Keane, *The towers and temples of ancient Ireland; their origin and history discussed from a new point of view* (Dublin, 1867), 37n. Molly Astore: 297. Another sample of Keane etymology: 'Devil in Irish is "Dia Bal" (literally, the God Baal)' (53; the Irish for 'devil' is, of course, *diabhal* fr. Latin *diabolus*). For Keane's reflections on the Sheela-na-Gig figure ('which there is reason to believe was sacred to the goddess Ana, as mother of the gods', 69), see p. 335, p. 372.

Keane's book met with mixed reviews, from the scathing to the reticent. The *Irish ecclesiastical record*, 5 (1869): 375–384) saw it as a regrettable throwback to the absurdities of Vallancey and O'Brien, but the *Dublin University magazine* was surprisingly mild: 'Though extreme in his theory [. . .] his mode of asserting his opinions is singularly modest' (*Dublin University magazine*, 71 (1871): 106–15; 328–35). Keane's work evidently came out of the antiquarian establishment and was as such respectable and worthy of serious treatment. There is evidence that Richard Rolt Brash was involved in the preparation (he mentions having seen the work in MS in 1866, c.f. *Notes and queries*, 9 (1866): 497).

200 For this reason he rejects Keane, who had traced history back, not to Japhet but to Japhet's brother Ham (p. 346). Bourke, a good Gaelic scholar, also ridiculed

Keane's preposterous etymologies, e.g. the 'Molly Astore' blunder (p. 438). He is similarly dismissive of his latest forerunner in the anti-Petrie camp, the Rev. Smiddy (p. 368n.).

201 Fifth and sixth unpaginated page after the title page. Bourke later reiterated his Aryan-cum-Milesian theory in explicitly pedagogical form, in the question-and-answer catechism entitled *Pre-Christian Ireland* (Dublin, 1887), esp. pp. 192–204 (chapter 21).

202 Proinsias Ó Maolmhuaidh, *Uilleog de Búrca: 'Athair na athbheochana'* (Dublin: Foilseachán Náisiúnta, 1981). For a good sketch of the wider background, including a valuable account of the influence of MacHale, see Cathal Ó Hainle, *Promhadh pinn* (Má Nuad: An Sagart, 1978), pp. 130–52.

203 C.f. Sheehy, *The rediscovery of Ireland's past*; Alter, 'Symbols of Irish nationalism'.

204 J. Windele, *Notices of Cork and vicinity*, p. 246; Sheehy, *The rediscovery of Ireland's Past*, pp. 62–3.

205 C.f. the communication by James Coleman, *Cork historical and archaeological society journal*, 3 (1894): 177–82, and Horace Fleming's letter corroborating Coleman, ibid. 267–8.

206 *Catalogue of a rare, curious, and interesting collection of new and second-hand books and tracts on Ireland, some of which are unique, now on sale for ready money by John O'Daly*, 10 (October 1855): 4, item 105. O'Daly adds: 'I never saw another copy of this curious old book.' The existence of such a book was cited as conclusive proof in favour of O'Brien's theory by Hargrave Jennings, *The Rosicrucians*, p. 149; Jennings states that the book ('which there is no doubt is genuine') turned up 'very unexpectedly'.

   Similarly, one Mr Graves was reported by the *Historical and Archaeological Association of Ireland journal*, 1, 2 (1869): 275–8 as presenting an account of a MS entitled *Hierographia Hiberniae* by Bishop David Rothe from the 1640s, describing the 'turra alta, et angusta, figurae rotundae' at St Canice's Cathedral in Kilkenny, adding 'Schematis ejusmodi turres passim in hoc regno reperiuntur, plerumque templis adstructae, sive in ornamentum sive in defensionem nescio, non enim inter antiquarios nostris convenit, quorsum vel a quibus fabricatae sunt [. . .]' (p. 276). Graves claimed he had this from Lynch, who incorporated this account into his unpublished *De praesulibus Hiberniae* of which Graves had consulted a copy in the Bodleian.

207 Petrie's letter to J. O'Kelly of the O'Connell Monument Commission, 31 October 1857, quoted Stokes, *Life and labours of Petrie*, p. 371. See also the account in Sheehy, *The rediscovery of Ireland's past*, pp. 58–60.

208 Stokes, *Life and labours of Petrie*, pp. 372–3.

209 Generally, both on the O'Connell funeral and on the later political usage made of Glasnevin as a *lieu de mémoire*, see Pauric Travers, '"Our Fenian dead": Glasnevin cemetery and the genesis of the republican funeral', in *Dublin and Dubliners. Essays on the history and literature of Dublin city*, ed. J. Kelly and U. Mac Gearailt (Dublin: Helicon, 1990), pp. 52–72; specifically, on Petrie's monument, p. 56.

210 *Ritual of the Ancient Order of Hibernians in America, arranged by the National Board. For the guidance of officers in the management of divisions, explaining the methods of conducting meetings, modes of installation and initiatory ceremonies* (Saratoga, N.Y.: 1906). Kindly brought to my attention by Professor David Fitzpatrick, who provided me with a copy of the text. The induction ceremony, called 'Lesson of the Tower', is on pp. 22–31.

211   It would be stating the obvious to denounce this as a silly 'invention of tradition'; more to the purpose would be to look at the modality in which this tradition is invented, and the type of needs and ideas this contrivance bespeaks. Ideally, such latter-day, archaizing quasi-hieratic rituals, from freemasonry to Royal Weddings, should be analysed according to the structural-syntactical method heralded by the anthropologist Frits Staal.

212   O'Curry, *Manners and customs*, 3: 52. O'Curry had previously dismissed scathingly all enthusiastic speculators: 'Some writers, again, whose want of acquaintance with the ancient language, and whose ignorance of the genuine history and archaeology of the Gaedhils, betray them into so many fanciful speculations, nay, even into the assumption of theoretic facts, if I may so call such inventions, accept the *Gobban Saer* indeed as a personage who had a real existence, but, in order to assist in supporting a whole series of false theories concerning the history and the life of our remote ancestors, refer back his era, together with that of the Round Towers, to pre-historic times' (3: 39–40).

213   The error ('the first result of a false translation of these annals in your excellent poem!') lay in a genealogical mix-up between the MacDonnells and the O'Donnells. The letter (which O'Donovan requested to be burnt) is bound up in a volume of pamphlets with the bookplate of D.F. MacCarthy, National Library P 2407. On the rivalry between O'Donovan and Connellan, see here, p. 137.

214   Stephen J. Brown, *Ireland in fiction. A guide to Irish novels, tales, romances and folklore* (reprint ed. Shannon: Irish University Press, 1969), p. 121.

215   Gerald Griffin, *The invasion* (Dublin, n.d. [c. 1870]), p. 401. It is in itself unusual that Irish novels should be considered to stand in need of such updatings, as if they were implicated in the development of scientific knowledge. For a similar anomaly in, conversely, the resistance of Irish narrative histories to scholarly revision, see here, pp. 111–113. In both instances we see a perplexity, which is peculiar to the Irish nineteenth-century reading culture, as to the distinction between the working conventions of fiction and historiography.

216   Griffin, *The invasion*, pp. 401–19.

217   It is indicative that (as the work of the Coinage Commission illustrates) the independent Free State avoided the whole nineteenth-century iconographical stock-in-trade, from wolfhounds and high crosses to shamrocks and Round Towers. C.f. *The Senate speeches of W.B. Yeats*, ed. D.R. Pearce (London: Faber & Faber, 1960), pp. 161–7.

218   Charles Gavan Duffy, *Young Ireland: A fragment of Irish history, 1840–1850* (London, 1880), pp. 561–2. The note from O'Brien to Davis dates from 1844. In early 1845, O'Donovan did briefly teach an Irish class at the Royal Irish Academy involving Smith O'Brien and Davis. C.f. Pádraig de Brún, 'An Irish class of 1845', *Éigse*, 17, (1977–1978): 214. De Brún ventures the guess that this Irish class may have brought the future instigators of the Celtic Society together.

219   Edward Walsh's 'The songs of The nation', in *The spirit of the nation: Ballads and songs by the writers of 'The nation'* (1845; new ed. Dublin, 1882), pp. 137–8.

220   Gavan Duffy, *Young Ireland*, 562–563; also quoted in Desmond Ryan, *The sword of light: From the Four Masters to Douglas Hyde, 1638–1938* (London, 1938), p. 147; c.f. *The spirit of the nation*, p. 80. Gavan Duffy had obviously missed the aspiration-dots.

221   Gavan Duffy, *Young Ireland*, 181. On the filiation between Moore and *The nation*, see also Thuente, *The harp re-strung*, esp. pp. 201–5. To be sure, the main thrust of

Thuente's argument is to show that Young Ireland picked up songs and themes of a United Irish provenance (pp. 206–30); but then again, Young Ireland picked up themes from all periods of the Irish past – it would have been odd had they left United Ireland out.

222   Matthew O'Conor was a brother of Charles O'Conor of Stowe; his military history appeared posthumously and was re-issued in 1855 as *The Irish brigades, or, memoirs of the most eminent Irish military commanders*. O'Callaghan was a regular contributor to *The nation*.

223   Davis, *Prose writings*, pp. 155–7.

224   Davis, *Prose writings*, pp. 192–200; c.f. also Denman, *Samuel Ferguson*, p. 55.

225   'A ballad history of Ireland', *Prose writings*, pp. 201–7.

226   John MacHale must be seen as one of the most important figures in Irish ideological history of the nineteenth century. From Mayo, hedge-school educated, native speaker of Irish, and radicalized by the famines he witnessed in his diocese of Killala and his archdiocese of Tuam, MacHale was an important supporter of (and influence on) Daniel O'Connell. MacHale's stance was nativist and Catholic exclusivist; his influence did much to turn Parnellite and even Fenian-style nationalism into a predominantly Catholic movement, and to give Ireland's Catholic population a prestigious example of the respectability of nationalism. He was also a figure of major importance in the mid-century cultivation of the Irish language, with his famous Gaelic translations of Homer and Moore's melodies, and his endorsement of the activities of Canon Ulick Bourke. MacHale's particularism is reflected in his resistance to the ultramontanist endeavours of Cardinal Cullen, and in his reservations about the dogma of papal infallibility. His combined anti-centralism and nationalism culminated, not only in his petty opposition to Newman as rector of the Catholic University (Newman was an intolerable choice for MacHale solely because he was English), but also in his refusal to denounce the Fenians as a secret society. Such 'national' secret societies were obnoxious to the papal authorities since it was groups like the Carbonari and Young Italy who had deprived the pope of his worldly dominions, and Cullen accordingly attempted, in line with papal policy, to suppress Catholic support for the Fenians. He was thwarted in this design by MacHale's refusal to toe the line. For an appropriately flamboyant biography of MacHale, see the Rev. Bernard O'Reilly's *John MacHale*, which in characteristic fashion is dedicated 'To the sacred memory of the dead, who, in prison, on the scaffold, on the battle-field, in exile, through the long sufferings of centuries, and the starless night of famine after famine, have perished, martyrs to their love for Ireland, and looking in vain for the dawn of her resurrection morn; – to the generous spirits of the living, the sons and daughters of Ireland at home and abroad who still suffer and labour and hope against hope for the redemption of Erin; – to the brave hearts of Irish soil whose heroic resolves no tyranny can change, whose fidelity to the hallowed cause of national right no bribe, no torture can move; – to the friends of Ireland, of every race and creed, in every civilized country.'

227   Lyons, *Ireland since the Famine*, p. 89. National schools banned standard patriotic fragments of poetry such as 'Breathes there a man with soul so dead' or 'Freedom shrieked when Kisciusko fell'. This indicates why education was such an important arena for political debate and political action up to and including Pearse.

228   Quoted in Alf MacLochlainn, 'Gael and peasant', p. 21. A good survey, indicative also of what could later become a trend towards Fenian sympathies, is given by

Barry Coldrey, *Faith and fatherland: The Christian Brothers and the development of Irish nationalism, 1838–1921* (Dublin: Gill & Macmillan, 1988), esp. chapter 6, 'The Christian Brothers' teaching of Irish history', p. 113–49.

229 C.f. E.R.R. Green, 'Charles Joseph Kickham and John O'Leary', in *The Fenian movement*, ed. T.W. Moody (Cork: Mercier, n.d.), pp. 77–88 (esp. pp. 80–1).

230 C.f. the chapter '"The dead generations": Irish history and historical fictions', in Philip O'Leary, *The prose literature of the Gaelic revival, 1881–1921. Ideology and innovation* (Pennsylvania State University Press, 1994), pp. 163–221.

231 Roy Foster, *The story of Ireland. An inaugural lecture delivered before the University of Oxford on 1 December 1994* (Clarendon Press, 1995).

232 Rigney, *Rhetoric of historical representation*, and 'Time for visions and revisions'.

233 Stephen Brown's 1919 checklist *Ireland in fiction* lists many hundreds of popular historical fictions set in Ireland at various periods in the past.

234 *History of Ireland: Critical and philosophical* (London/Dublin, 1881), p. iii.

235 *History of Ireland, 1: The heroic period* (1878), p. iii. 'It is a common-place that the true function of the historian is to give a clear and vivid picture of the past; but, although the principle is recognised in theory, it is practically set aside, and pure historical composition relegated to the novelist and romancer, whose audience, as they desire merely amusement, make no very stern demands on the veracity and historical faithfulness of the writer. In fact, the province of archaeology has so extended its frontiers, as to have swallowed up the dominion of pure history altogether. Nearly every work which one takes up affecting to treat of the past in a rigid and conscientious spirit, is merely archaeological. It is an accumulation of names, dates, events, disquisitions, the balancing of probabilities, the testing of statements and traditions, categorical assertions concerning laws and customs. All works of this character are of the nature of archaeology; they are the material of history, not history itself. [. . .] In history, there must be sympathy, imagination, creation. [. . .] History is the flower of archaeology; it justifies, rewards and crowns the obscure toil of those patient and single-minded excavators of the buried past' (pp. iii –iv).

236 Quoted in Mc Cormack, *From Burke to Beckett. Ascendancy, tradition and betrayal in literary history* (Cork University Press, 1994), p. 233. O'Halloran wrote, of course, in the late eighteenth century, after and during the rise of the Vallancey school.

237 Sister Mary Frances Cusack, in her *Illustrated history of Ireland* (1868), praises the Fenian movement as a wholesome influence in Ireland's intellectual life (p. 8). The Rev. P.L. O'Toole, in his *History of the Clan O'Toole (Ui Thuathail) and other Leinster septs* (Dublin, 1890) glorifies 'the independent policy of Parnell and his heroic band in fighting the grand fight' as a latter-day continuation of 'the indomitable spirit of the O'Tooles in the days of Elizabeth' (p. 285). The Rev. Bernard O'Reilly mentions, in the preface to his *John MacHale*, 'Parnell, and the men who with him are ready to sacrifice everything, even life itself, who brave everything, endure everything for the cause of Ireland' (1: viii).

238 *The history of Ireland, ancient and modern, taken from the most authentic records and dedicated to the Irish brigade, by the abbé Mac-Goeghegan* [sic]. *With a continuation from the treaty of Limerick to the present time by John Mitchel* (New York & Montreal, n.d. [1865–1868]). Fittingly, the motto on the title-page is the first stanza of Thomas Moore's 'Let Erin remember'.

239 Martin Haverty's popular *History of Ireland, ancient and modern*, originally published in 1860, went through many reprints. As its subtitle announces, Haverty's

History relies on a combination of 'our native annals', 'the most recent researches of eminent Irish scholars and antiquaries' and generally on 'all the resources of Irish history now available'. [Kindly brought to my attention by Luke Gibbons. J.L.]

240 James and Freeman Wills, *The Irish nation: its history and biography* (Edinburgh/London, [1845]), 3. Gibbons, *Transformations in Irish culture*, pp. 165–9, comments on this passage that its disjointed, oneiric sense of history corresponds to Eisenstein's theory of filmic *montage* (the cross-cutting of diverse images), and so foreshadows the fragmented construction of *Ulysses*. C.f. below, here, p. 228.

241 Dion Boucicault, *The fireside story of Ireland* (2nd ed.; London, 1881).

242 Sigmund Freud, 'The "Uncanny"' (1919), in id., *Art and literature*, ed. A. Dickson (The Pelican Freud library, ed. and trans. J. Strachey; Harmondsworth: Penguin, 1985), pp. 335–76.

The Presence of the Past

1 Roy Foster, *Paddy and Mr. Punch*, p. 5.

2 The Irish Archaeological Society had close ties with the Royal Irish Academy and got into financial difficulties as an indirect result of the Famine. The report read at the AGM of December 1847 regrets a general antiquarian apathy and a pressing lack of subscriptions, adding that 'the unparallelled season of distress with which we have been visited during the last year, and the many calls upon the sympathies of the public, may, in part, account for this fact' (*Leabhar Breathnach*, ed. J.H. Todd (Dublin, 1848), appendix, p. 13). The Irish Archaeological Society merged in 1853 with the Celtic Society, founded in 1845 by John O'Daly. A breakaway element of that Celtic Society called itself the Ossianic Society from 1853 onwards; its membership was composed of more nationalistically minded figures, although the rules still held to the principle 'That all matters relating to the Religious and Political differences prevailing in this country, be strictly excluded from the meetings and publications of the Society' (*Transaction of the Ossianic Society*, 1 (1854): 4). The Ossianic Society was active under the aegis of Owen Connellan and John O'Daly until 1860; its members included Canon Bourke, John O'Donovan, Standish Hayes O'Grady, Smith O'Brien and the nationalist publisher James Duffy.

3 *Transactions of the Iberno-Celtic Society*, 1820: p. vii.

4 *Ancient Ireland*, first prospectus (bound with the copies of the actual journal in the National Library of Ireland). The cover to the fourth issue (April, 1835), reiterates this: 'Politics and Polemics are to be totally excluded from the pages of this magazine – it is to be purely historical and literary.' On Barron and *Ancient Ireland*, see Ryan, *The sword of light*, pp. 111–52.

5 C.f. Patrick Power, 'The Gaelic Union: A nonagenarian retrospect', *Studies*, 38 (1949): 413–8.

6 *Gaelic journal*, 2, 13 (January 1884): 223.

7 He reiterated his anti-political views forcefully on that occasion, in the pamphlet *The Gaelic League and politics* (Dublin: Gaelic League, 1914).

8 Pearse, 'The coming revolution' (1913), quoted in Gareth W. Dunleavy, *Douglas Hyde* (Bucknell University Press,1974), p. 50.

9 The national school system was supported by Cardinal Cullen but opposed by Archbishop McHale because of its secular and (it was feared) anti-Catholic nature

(see here, pp. 161–162). The debate gave rise to a tell-tale anticolonialist pun on the primate's name: what was feared was a new 'Cullenization' of Ireland. The difference between Ireland and other European countries was that there was a cultural as well as a social divide at work: it was not that the Gaelic peasantry lacked any notion of a higher civilization, but rather that this notion was bound up with the older high Gaelic culture (which, though smothered in the past two centuries, was still remembered) rather than with the Victorian values of the metropolitan upper middle classes.

10 Levine, *The amateur and the professional*, p. 14, p. 19, p. 50.

11 Zimmermann, *Songs of Irish rebellion*.

12 As John Hewitt has pointed out, Allingham's broadsheets 'pioneered a mode and technique which had its lasting triumphs in the hands of Yeats, Colum and Joseph Campbell' ('Introduction', in *The poems of William Allingham*, ed. J. Hewitt; Dublin: Dolmen, 1967, p. 11). The appeal of popular print was not limited to Ireland; popular prints and printed books have intrigued men of letters since the days of Goethe and his preoccupation with *Volksbücher*; Flemish authors like Felix Timmermans and Maurice Maeterlinck also invoked folk publications (*Het Kindeke Jezus in Vlaanderen*, 'Six chansons de pauvre homme pour célébrer la semaine de Flandre') much as Yeats did: like Yeats, they invoked an 'authenticité populaire' and attempted to regenerate poetry by tapping these 'sources profondes et lointaines': Jeannine Paque, *Le symbolisme belge* (Bruxelles: Labor, 1989), 30. The parallel between Ireland and Belgium (both diglossic, bicultural countries) is far from fortuitous; I have explored it more fully in my 'Literaruur op de landkaart'.

13 William Carleton, *Traits and stories of the Irish peasantry*, new ed. (2 vols. Dublin, 1843), 1: viii–x.

14 Curtin: *Myth and folk-lore of Ireland*, 1889; *Hero-tales of Ireland*, 1894; *Tales of the fairies and of the ghost world, collected from oral tradition in south-west Munster*, 1895. Kennedy: *Legends of Mount Leinster* (under the pseudonym 'Harry Whitney', 1855); *Fictions of our forefathers: Fion Mac Cumhail and his warriors* (serialized in the *Irish quarterly review*, 1859); *Legendary fictions of the Irish Celts*, 1866; *The fireside stories of Ireland*, 1870; *The bardic stories of Ireland*, 1871. Jacobs: *Celtic fairy tales*, 1892; *More Celtic fairy tales*, 1894. Larminie: *West Irish folk-tales and romances* (1893). Hyde: *Leabhar sgeulaigheachta*, 1889; *An sgeuluidhe Gaodhalach*, 1895.

15 A 'recycling' principle is present here as much as in the case of the popular histories mentioned here, p. 153. A cumulated edition of Crofton Croker and Lover, *Legends and tales of Ireland*, appeared in 1870, a volume of *Tales and stories of Ireland by Carleton, Lover and Mrs Hall* in 1852. W.B. Yeats's collections *Representative Irish tales* (1891), *Fairy and folk tales of the Irish peasantry* (1888) and *Irish fairy tales* (1892) are wholly cannibalized from earlier literary or folkloristic texts. C.f. Mary Helen Thuente's source lists in W.B. Yeats, *Representative Irish tales* (Gerrards Cross: Colin Smyth, 1979), pp. 21–3 and W.B. Yeats, *Fairy and folk tales of Ireland* (4th ed.; Gerrards Cross: Colin Smythe, 1992), pp. xvii–xxi.

16 For a discussion, see Luke Gibbons, 'The sympathetic bond: Ossian, Celticism and colonialism', in *Celticism*, ed. T. Brown (Amsterdam: Rodopi, 1996), pp. 273–91.

17 And commonplace it largely is. To be sure, there is an objective 'real' trend towards modernization which is rarely put in reverse, and to that extent the traditional life of the countryside is indeed shrinking; and cataclysms like the Famine did in actual fact wipe out much folk culture. Yet on the other hand, the way in which

Yeats and lady Gregory describe harvesting folk wisdom from the lips of a diminishing peasantry follows, in true commonplace fashion, the same register as Carleton a half-century earlier.

18 For a closer scrutiny, specifically of the German country idyll, see my 'Identity and self-image: German auto-exoticism as escape from history', in *Komparatistik und Europaforschung. Perspektiven vergleichender Literatur- und Kulturwissenschaft*, ed. H. Dyserinck and K.U. Syndram (Bonn/Berlin: Bouvier, 1992), pp. 117–36.

19 Henry Sumner Maine, *Village-communities in the east and west* (London, 1871), pp. 27–8.

20 In English, one of the first to propound this idea (with explicit reference to Vico) was Dr Thomas Arnold (c.f. 'On the social progress of states', 1830, in *Miscellaneous works*, p. 82). In France, it led to a romantic re-writing of French history from Clovis to the Revolution, in terms of an ethnic master-conflict between conquered Gauls and oppressive Franks. That scheme was first adopted by Thierry, refined by Michelet (who had begun his career by translating Vico) and taken to extravagant heights by Henri Martin. The repercussion of this line of thought in conservative social thought has been famously demonstrated in Louis Chevalier, *Classes laborieuses et classes dangéreuses à Paris pendant la première moitié du XIXe siècle* (Paris: Plon, 1958).

21 Sometimes erroneously credited to D'Arcy McGee. *The spirit of the nation*, pp. 296–8.

22 Alan Warner, *William Allingham* (Bucknell University Press, 1975), p. 38.

23 These poems date from *c.* 1833; c.f. Denman, *Samuel Ferguson*, pp. 14–5.

24 From the days of medieval romance, the hunt has been heavily invested with symbolical and narrative resonance as the one pursuit that brings the ordered world face to face with wild nature. Seen in that light, it is remarkable that J.M. Synge's vitalistic, populist rejection of the Celtic Twilight's fairy cult returned to the notion of hunting, or, more appropriately, poaching, as a signal of shared identity with the untamed parts of the country and its inhabitants:

> Adieu, sweet Angus, Maeve and Fand
> Ye plumed yet skinny Shee
> That poets played with hand in hand
> To learn their ecstasy.
>
> We'll search in Red Dan Sally's Ditch
> And drink in Tubber fair,
> Or poach with Red Dan Philly's bitch
> The badger and the hare.

25 London 1870. Doyle, a well-known painter and illustrator, was an uncle of Arthur Conan Doyle, who in later life was to become a convinced spiritualist and was to attract ridicule by defending the authenticity of fraudulent photographs purporting to depict fairies.

26 The fairy-tradition obviously became an important influence in the Celtic Twilight. For non-Yeatsian examples, see Jane Barlow's extravaganza *The end of Elfintown*.

27 From the collection *Blackberries*; quoted in Hans Kropf, *William Allingham im Lichte der irischen Freiheitsbewegung* (Biel: Andres, 1928), p. 54n. On Allingham, see Terence Brown, 'William Allingham: Cultural confusion', in id., *Northern voices: Poets from Ulster* (Dublin: Gill & Macmillan, 1975), pp. 42–54.

28 Quoted Kropf, *Allingham*, pp. 53–4.

29 Most famously, of course, in the closing line of 'A nation once again', but also in his essay on 'Irish antiquities', where he explains the lack of historical consciousness in Ireland (as opposed to the national cultivation of ancient monuments in England, France and Germany) from the fact that 'This island has been for centuries either in part or altogether a province' (Davis, *Prose writings*, p. 84). For Davis, as for Allingham, provicialism or regionalism strips Ireland of its historical and political awareness. For the nationalist Davis, that is a cultural lobotomy; for the unionist Allingham, a redemption from violence.

30 A letter from 1854 to Lady Ferguson: 'Let me not, however in my rural rapture, pretend that I never sigh for city life.'

31 *William Allingham's diary*, ed. G. Grigson (Fontwell, Sussex: Centaur, 1967), pp. 297–8. There might have been an ironic undertone of good-humoured banter involved, and a dose of 'goading the Paddy' on Tennyson's part. There are various altercations of this sort lovingly recorded in Allingham's diary.

> T. 'Ireland's a dreadful country! I heartily wish it was in the middle of the Atlantic Ocean.'
>
> 'Below the surface?' I asked.
>
> 'No, no, a thousand miles away from England. I like the charm of their manners – but they're a fearful nuisance.'
>
> 'Very troublesome,' I admitted, 'but there's some truth in the popular Irish notion that nothing can be got from England except by agitation.' (p. 293)

Views like Tennyson's were shared by the English establishment at large. For an interesting selection of bigoted press voices, see Ned Lebow, 'British images of poverty in pre-Famine Ireland', in *Views of the Irish peasantry*, eds. D.J. Casey and R.E. Rhodes (Hamden, CT: Archon, 1977), pp. 57–85, as well as Roy Foster, *Paddy and Mr. Punch*, pp. 171–94.

32 *New Ireland review*, 8 (1897/8): 66.

33 C.f. MIFG, pp. 35–53, and my 'Wildness and Wilderness'.

34 A typology of *Punch's* offensively anti-Irish caricatures has been memorably given by Curtis, *Apes and angels*.

35 C.f. the analysis in MIFG, 129–36, especially as regards the contradistinction between Irish and French characters.

36 Edward Bunting, *The ancient music of Ireland, arranged for the pianoforte, to which is prefixed a dissertation on the Irish harp and harpers, including an account of the old melodies of Ireland* (Dublin, 1840), p. 5. Bunting's irritation with Moore may have been heightened by Moore's contention that ancient Irish music was monodic. Bunting insists on the ancient use of bourdon harmony against the 'ingenuity or dogmatism, whether of Mr. Moore or Mr. Pinkerton' (p. 8).

37 Edward Bunting, *A general collection of the ancient music of Ireland, arranged for the piano forte; some of the most admired melodies are adapted for the voice, to poetry chiefly translated from the original Irish songs, by Thomas Campbell Esq and other eminent poets, to which is prefixed a historical & critical dissertation on the Egyptian, British and Irish harp* (London, n.d., [1809]), p. 30.

38 Zimmermann, *Songs of Irish rebellion*, p. 281.

39 As a popular instrument, the harp has ceded to the fiddle, accordeon and guitar. There have been some mid-century attempts at revival, most prominently by Mary O'Hara, but these have smacked of Bunratty-style folklorism, and the instrument

has remained marginal to everyday practice in folk music. An important exception to this trend was the harp revival as instigated in the 1970s by the Breton Celticist musician Alan Stivell. How widespread the harp was as a folk instrument in the nineteenth century may be gathered from the fact that there is an old mendicant harp-player roaming Germany in Goethe's *Wilhelm Meisters Lehrjahre* (1795), and that in Hector Malot's sentimental novel *Sans famille* (1878), the young vagrant foundling Rémy still roams France with a harp.

40   The tendency for anthologies to anthologize selections from earlier anthologies was marked from the beginning: Henry R. Montgomery's *Specimens of the early native poetry of Ireland* (1846, 2nd ed. 1892) was culled from other collections.

41   On the oral appeal of Irish nineteenth-century ballad and verse (be it collected from anonymous folk sources or cultivated as a genre by metropolitan poets, often under pseudonym) see the interesting comments by Seamus Deane, in FDA, 2: 1–9.

42   Gibbons, *Transformations in Irish Culture*, pp. 134–7, has given an elegant interpretation of this, juxtaposing Gretta's response to a heard song with Gabriel Conroy's journalistic preoccupations. Gibbons reads that opposition in terms of the oral exchange that characterizes a pre-modern, pre-national community versus the media and print culture which provide the modern nation with its 'imagined community'.

43   James Hardiman, *Irish minstrelsy, or bardic remains of Ireland; with English poetical translations* (2 vols.; London, 1831).

44   Hardiman, *Irish minstrelsy*, 1: xxi; 2: 3–9. The explanatory notes on 2: 117–69 are also replete with anti-English denunciations.

45   MacDonagh, *States of mind*.

46   quoted Roy Foster, *Paddy and Mr. Punch*, p. 180.

47   *Dublin University magazine*, 3 (1834): 465–78; 4 (1834): 152–67; 447–67; 514–30, with a selection of translations subjoined, pp. 530–42. As can be seen, the review on the Jacobite section is twice as long as the others.

48   Among the translations furnished by Ferguson figure much-anthologized classics such as 'O'Byrne's bard to the clans of Wicklow', 'Molly Astore', 'Pastheen Finn', 'Cashel of Munster', two version of 'The Coolun', 'Kitty Tyrrell', 'Grace Nugent', 'Drimin dhu' and 'The fair hills of Ireland'.

49   'The contrast between the native songs and the lyrics of Moore, is indeed strangely striking – as strange as uncouthness can present in juxtaposition with politeness' (p. 153).

50   Ibid. Elsewhere, there is a sour reference to D'Alton as someone who publishes his local history by subscription, and who is therefore, by implication, something of a hack (p. 522).

51   P. 159. There is another snipe at celibacy and perfidy in the popish clergy, pp. 524–8; such Protestant assertiveness was very much in line with the general tone of the *Dublin University magazine*, which, for all that it offered a forum for mid-century Irish literature, was deeply bigoted in its religious and social politics.

52   pp. 528–9. Ferguson was later to patch things up with Hardiman, whom he came to appreciate as a historian.

53   p. 167; the phrase is used twice when referring to the practice of early marriages and numerous offspring. Uncannily, ten years before the Famine, Ferguson is noting the great population increase among the poorer peasantry that created such a large group of Famine victims.

54 Quoted in Allingham, *Diary*, p. 298.

55 The first installment appeared in the December issue of 1834, pp. 674–90.

56 See also the perceptive sketch of Ferguson in Cairns and Richards, *Writing Ireland*, pp. 25–31, as well as Terence Brown, 'Samuel Ferguson: Cultural nationalism', in id., *Northern Voices*, 29–41.

57 In a letter to Davis, written in 1845, Ferguson stated his hope 'to see Dublin at least a better Edinburgh' (Denman, *Samuel Ferguson*, p. 63). The phraseology 'western Gael' in the title of his poetry collection likewise implies a Scots-Gaelic counterpart; Hardiman would like to see the native peasantry as an Edinburgh patrician would regard Highlanders.

58 'The Celto-Scythic progresses', *Dublin University magazine*, 39 (1852): 271–91. For the attribution to Ferguson, see the checklist in Denman, *Samuel Ferguson*, pp. 195 ff.

59 W.B. Yeats, 'William Allingham, 1824–1889' (1892), in id., *Uncollected prose*, ed. J.P. Frayne and C. Johnson (2 vols.; London: Macmillan, 1970–75), 1: 258–61. Even here, Yeats goes on to intimate, in Blakean terms, where he hopes to *differ* from his sentimental precursor: '[Allingham] saw neither the grand unities of God or of man, of his own spiritual life or of the life of the nation about him, but looked at all through a kaleidoscope full of charming accidents and momentary occurrences. In greater poets everything has relation to the national life or to profound feeling; nothing is an isolated artistic moment; there is a unity everywhere, everything fulfils a purpose that is not its own; the hailstone is a journeyman of God, and the grass blade carries the universe upon its point. But, then, if Allingham had had this greater virtue, he might have lost that which was peculiar to himself' (p. 260). Similar criticisms occur in other essays on Allingham from the period 1890–1891, regretting his lack of national feeling ('there is no great literature without nationality, no great nationality without literature'; *Uncollected Prose*, 1: 104) and contrasting him unfavourably with poets who felt 'Ireland as a whole' and who wrote 'of the joys and sorrows of the Irish people, as Davis, and Ferguson, and Mangan have done' (1: 212).

60 Allingham, *Diary*, p. 17.

61 'Lorsqu'en voyageant dans la presqu'île armoricaine on dépasse la région [. . .] de la Normandie et du Maine [. . .] le plus brusque changement se fait sentir tout à coup. Un vent froid, plein de vague et de tristesse, s'élève et transporte l'âme vers d'autres pensées; le sommet des arbres se dépouille et se tord; la bruyère étend au loin sa teinte uniforme; le granit perce à chaque pas un sol trop maigre pour le revêtir; une mer presque toujours sombre donne à l'horizon un cercle d'eternels gémissements.' Ernest Renan, 'La poésie des races celtiques' (1859), in id., *Oeuvres complètes*, ed. H. Psichari (Paris: Pléiade, 1948), 2: 252. Renan himself explicitly draws a parallel with similar Celtic regions: the transition from England to Wales, from the Lowlands into the Highlands, from anglicizied Ireland into the still Gaelic west. See, generally, T. Brown, ed. *Celticism* (Amsterdam: Rodopi, 1996).

62 'At last one turns around and looks westward. Everything is changed. Over the mouth of the Conway and its sands is the eternal softness and mild light of the west; the low line of the mystic Anglesey, and the precipitous Pemmaenmawr, and the great group of Carnedd Llewellyn and Carnedd David and their brethren fading away, hill behind hill, in an aerial haze, make the horizon; between the foot of Penmaenmawr and the bending coast of Anglesey, the sea, a silver stream,

disappears one knows not whither. On this side Wales – Wales, where the past still lives, where every place has its tradition, every name its poetry, and where the people, the genuine people, still knows this past, this tradition, this poetry, and lives with it, and clings to it; while, alas, the prosperous Saxon on the other side, the invader from Liverpool and Birkenhead, has long ago forgotten his.' Arnold, *On the study of Celtic literature*, pp. 13–14. The remarkable syntax, with its long enumerative sentences generating clause after additional clause, dilutes grammatical coherence in favour of evocation and incantation and thus stylistically matches Arnold's imagery. Both Arnold and Renan see the mainland (France/England) as sites of human activity, and the western fringe (Brittany/Wales) as largely unpeopled landscapes consisting mainly of empty nature.

63 Witness John V. Kelleher's famous analysis 'Matthew Arnold and the Celtic revival', in *Perspectives in criticism*, ed. H. Levin (Harvard University Press, 1950), pp. 197–221.

64 Honoré de Balzac, *Les chouans* (1829), ed. M. Regard (Paris: Garnier, 1964), pp. 23–4. Balzac goes on to describe Brittany as an *absence* of civilisation and ends up comparing it to their neighbours across the Atlantic, the Indians of North America – a simile which had been rendered popular by the success of the novels of James Fenimore Cooper, and which we have also encountered with Carlyle. 'L'absence complète de nos lois, de nos moeurs, de notre habillement, de nos monnaies nouvelles, de notre langage [. . .] s'accordent à rendre les habitants de ces campagnes plus pauvres de combinaisons intellectuelles que ne le sont les Mohicans ou les Peaux rouges de l'Amérique septentrionale.'

65 A similar telescoping trajectory penetrating stage-by-stage deeper into the outer periphery is used by the opening passages of Renan and Arnold. It is also to be found in the Scottish novels of Sir Walter Scott: Young Osbaldistone, in *Rob Roy*, moves first to Northumberland, then flees across the Scottish border, and gradually progresses into the wild haunts of the Highlands beyond Glasgow. Similarly, young Edward Waverley, in *Waverley*, moves from England to Bradwardine Hall, thence into the Highlands, and deeper yet towards MacIvor's hall, from where Flora takes his quest for pristine Scottishness to its culmination: along a river, through a chasm, into a romantic amphitheatre where, posed with a harp beside a waterfall, she sings a Gaelic poem for him. See here, pp. 40–1, and my 'Over de ontologische status van imagotypen'.

66 Anon. 'The west's awake', *Celtia*, 2, (September, 1902): 129.

67 E.W. Lynam, 'The O'Flaherty country', *Studies*, 3 (1914): 13.

68 Francis Shaw, 'The Celtic twilight', *Studies*, 23 (1934): 25–41, 260–78. Malcolm Chapman, *The Gaelic vision in Scottish culture* (London: Croom Helm, 1978); id., *The Celts: The construction of a myth* (Basingstoke: Macmillan, 1992); George Watson, 'Celticism and the annulment of history', in *Celticism*, ed. T. Brown, pp. 207–20.

69 For an interesting study on the French case, see Charles Rearick, *Beyond the Enlightenment. Historians and folklore in nineteenth-century France* (Indiana University Press, 1974). Rearick links the rise of folkore (as an offshoot of the historical sciences) to the rise of statistical ethnographical methods, as exemplified in Ireland by the Ordnance Survey.

70 Witness, not only collections like *The Celtic twilight* or the ones mentioned in footnote 15, p. 274, but also his shorter pieces of the period 1886–93, as gathered

by J.P. Frayne in *Uncollected prose*, vol. 1. See also Mary Helen Thuente, *W.B. Yeats and Irish folklore* (Dublin: Gill & Macmillan, 1980), and the analysis by John Wilson Foster, 'The death of Anshgayliacht, the rise of folklore studies – Douglas Hyde, William Larminie', in id., *Fictions of the Irish literary revival: A changeling art* (Syracuse University Press, 1987), pp. 219–35.

71 W.B. Yeats, *Fairy and folk tales*, p. 5.

72 W.B. Yeats, *Mythologies* (London: Macmillan, 1962), 15; the evocation continues: 'My ghosts inhabit the village of H—, in Leinster. History has in no manner been burdened by this ancient village [. . .]'

73 'The Celtic element in literature', in W.B. Yeats, *Essays and introductions* (London: Macmillan, 1961), 173–188 (187).

74 A remarkable instance is contained in 'The seven sages', celebrating Swift, Goldsmith, Berkeley, Burke and the whole familiar Anglo-Irish patriarchy so dear to Yeats's heart, by stating that 'They understood that wisdom comes of beggary', *Collected poems* (2nd ed.; London: Macmillan, 1950), pp. 271–3.

75 Roy Foster, *Paddy and Mr. Punch*, p. 228. Foster goes on to argue, no less astutely: 'The lost world of childhood also stands for a long-lost world of social dominance. Folklore also asserted another identity: the gentry's liking for the disappearing type of "pure" Irish peasant [. . .]'.

76 'Nationality in literature' (1893), in *Uncollected prose*, 1: 266–75.

77 *Collected poems*, p. 271. This poem forms part of a little sequence which tries to capture the decline of literature and culture, from Shakespeare to the present, in the simile of retreating water. It comes close to echoing Arnold's simile in 'Dover Beach' – c.f. 'The nineteenth century and after'.

78 Just how effective, can be judged from the fact that a similar conceptualization of literary emancipation was reached in different circumstances by different authors from marginal literatures. The Cameroon critic Bernard Fonlon discussed the viability of postcolonial African literature in strikingly similar terms: 'The greatest dramatic works that the world has seen, from Sophocles to Shakespeare, were built up from tales, legends and History. [. . .] It is precisely here that the African writers of to-day have their chance. Theirs is the unique advantage that, whereas European traditions, for the most part, have been exploited and exhausted and the European arts are at a loss what to do with themselves, where to turn for new inspiration, the African past, as a source of material for creative writing, is largely untouched.' Bernard Fonlon, 'A word of introduction', *Abbia*, 14–15 (1966): 9. For a closer analysis of the parallel, see my '"The cracked lookingglass of a servant": Cultural decolonization and national consciousness in Ireland and Africa', in *Europa und das nationale Selbstverständnis. Imagologische Probleme in Literatur, Kunst und Kultur des 19. und 20. Jahrhunderts*, ed. H. Dyserinck and K.U. Syndram (Bonn: Bouvier, 1988), pp. 103–18.

79 Witness Yeats's article on 'The de-anglicizing of Ireland' (1892), extolling Irish potential over both decrepit England and immature America: 'America, with no past to speak of, a mere "parvenue" among nations, is creating a national literature which in its most characteristic products differs almost as much from English literature as does the literature of France. [. . .] It should be more easy for us, who have in us this wild Celtic blood, the most un-English of all things under heaven, to make such a literature' (*Uncollected prose*, 1: 255–6).

80 Quoted in *Ancient Ireland*, 2 (10 January 1835): cover page.

81 Quoted in *Gaelic journal*, 4, 42 (July 1892): 160.

82 Philip O'Leary, *The prose literature of the Gaelic revival, 1881–1921. Ideology and innovation* (Pennysylvania State University Press, 1994), esp. pp. 45–52.

83 There are earlier examples of this attitude. In the first issue of Philip Barron's weekly magazine *Ancient Ireland* (January 1835), a correspondent is quoting as stating 'I have, for the last two years, thrown away the English language with contempt, and taken to our own language again' (p. 4).

84 I here quote the English translation of the Irish dialogue between 'An seanduine agus an sglabhaidh', as given in the original on facing pages (pp. 100–3).

85 This attempt to enlist the native Irish-speaking peasantry by handing out baubles (not unlike the beads and mirrors used to propitiate natives in Africa) was already formulated by Douglas Hyde, when he proposed 'some system of giving medals or badges of honour to every family who will guarantee that they have always spoken Irish amongst themselves during the year', *Necessity of de-anglicising Ireland*, p. 17.

86 Witness the analysis by John Wilson Foster, in *Fictions of the Irish literary revival*, pp. 203–18.

87 Cecile O'Rahilly, ed. and trans., *Táin Bó Cúalnge from the Book of Leinster* (Dublin: Dublin Institute for Advanced Studies, 1967), p. 171; in the original p. 32 'do thócbáil a nnochta & a nnáre dó'.

88 Lady Gregory in a letter to Yeats as quoted by Gerard Murphy, in his preface to Augusta Gregory, *Cuchulain of Muirthemne. The story of the men of the Red Branch of Ulster arranged and put into English* (5th ed.; Gerrards Cross: Colin Smythe, 1970), pp. 8–9.

89 Thomas Kinsella, *The Táin, translated from the Irish epic Táin Bó Cuailnge* (Dublin: Dolmen, 1970), p. vii.

90 Le Brocquy's comment, in Kinsella, *Táin*, p. viii.

91 In his poem 'The route of the Táin', Kinsella speaks of aiming to 'enrich the present / honouring the past'. *New poems 1973* (Dublin: Dolmen, 1973), p. 57.

92 Gregory, *Cuchulain*, p. 150, p. 170. O'Rahilly, in her presentation of the original, collates different MSS into the phrase 'A long sword, as long as a ship's rudder, firmly fixed and resting on the two thighs of the great, proud warrior who is within the chariot' (*Claideb fata sithlaí co n-ecrasaib serrda for díb sliastaib sudigthi dond óclaíg móir borrfaid fail isin charput ar medón*): *Táin*, pp. 11, 43.

93 For the episodes in question, see Gregory, *Cuchulain*, p. 174, p. 143, p. 204; Kinsella, *Táin*, pp. 55, 169, 250; O'Rahilly, *Táin*, pp. 3, 72, 133, 140, 212, 269, 277.

94 Kinsella, *Táin*, 2. Original: 'Asberat alaili imorro isdoSenchán adchaos iartroscud frinoebu síl Fergus & nibo machthad cidsamlaid nobeth' (*Zeitschrift für Vergleichende Sprachforschung*, 28 (1887): 433–4).

95 O'Rahilly, *Táin*, 272. In the original, 'Bendacht ar cech óen mebraigfes go hindraic Táin amlaid seo & ná tuillfe cruth aile furri' (p. 136).

96 John Wilson Foster, *Fictions of the Irish literary revival*, p. 25.

97 The same attitude is noticeable in Maud Gonne, whose combative posture to speak up for the downtrodden masses of Ireland was at the same time intended to proclaim her own self-appointed spokesmanship. Gonne claims to speak on the peasantry's behalf although no formal or implied mandate to that effect had ever been given to her. 'I will be the voice of these helpless victims of England's policy, I will speak for them before the world, even if it be but to call down the execration

of mankind upon England's civilisation and England's government, which is responsible for all this ruin and misery' (Maud Gonne, 'Famine in the west', *Irish daily independent*, 10 March 1898).

98 Roy Foster, *Paddy and Mr. Punch*, pp. 262–3.

99 The terms are Philip O'Leary's, *The prose literature of the Gaelic revival*.

100 Long-lived, of course, only by virtue of constant rebirths and transformations. The activities of the dramatic movement around Yeats begin with the establishment of the National Literary Society in 1892, spawning the Irish Literary Theatre in 1899. The departure in 1902 of Edward Martyn (who went on to establish the Players' Group) and a fusion with the Fay brothers' Irish National Dramatic Company saw the Irish Literary Theatre transformed, in 1903, into the Irish National Theatre Society, which in 1905 (after the breakaway of the Theatre of Ireland) rechristened itself into the National Theatre Company (still in existence today as the resident company in the Abbey Theatre; a breakaway in 1918, the Dublin Drama League, went on to found the Gate Theatre).

There were various other rivalling theatre groups besides the breakaway ones given above: An Irish Theatre Company, with Griffith's nationalist Cumann na nGaedhal and the nationalist women's group Inghinidhe na hÉireann for sponsors, merged in 1903 into the National Players Society which had a strong Gaelic League backing; that company remained in existence until 1907.

These developments have been cumulated from the outstanding and invaluable collection by Robert Hogan and James Kilroy et al. ed. *The modern Irish drama, a documentary history* (6 vols., Dublin: Dolmen; Gerrards Cross: Colin Smythe, 1975–1992; hereinafter referred to as MID). The following treatment of the literary and political ideals surrounding Yeats and Synge has benefited from David Cairns and Shaun Richards, 'Reading a riot: The "reading formation" of Synge's Abbey audience', *Literature and history*, 13 (1987): 219–37, and Louis Dieltjens, 'The Abbey Theatre as a cultural formation', in *History and violence in Anglo-Irish literature*, ed. J. Duytschaever and G. Lernout (Amsterdam: Rodopi, 1988), pp. 47–65.

101 'The Irish literary theatre' (1899), *Uncollected prose*, 2: 163.

102 Ibid, p. 141. In 1895, Yeats had already written 'When once a country has given perfect expression to itself in literature, has carried to maturity its literary tradition, its writers, no matter what they write of, carry its influence about with them, just as Carlyle remained a Scotsman when he wrote of German kings or French revolutionists, and Shakespeare an Elizabethan Englishman when he told of Coriolanus or of Cressida' ('Irish national literature', 1896, *Uncollected prose*, 2: 360).

103 *Uncollected prose*, 1: 224, 250; *L'Irlande libre*, 2, 4 (1 April 1898), 1. There is, possibly, some pandering here to the naive Gallo-Celtic enthusiasms evinced throughout the pages of Maud Gonne's activist periodical pamphlet (*Organe de la colonie irlandaise à Paris*), in which the suffering Irish were glorified as 'des Celtes, comme les plus nobles d'entre nos aïeux, des Celtes au coeur de héros, à l'âme d'enfant, aux lèvres ingénues, faites pour la prière et l'ode, avec grands yeux clairs fleuris de mirages' (Jean Richepin, 'Approbation', *L'Irlande libre* 1, 1 (1 May 1897), 1).

104 Witness his address to an audience of IRB sympathizers, 'Emmet the apostle of Irish liberty', in *Uncollected prose*, 2: 310–27.

105 The first version appeared in the *North American review*, the second in lady Gregory's collection *Ideals in Ireland*. Both versions are in *Uncollected prose*, 2: 184–96.

106 *Uncollected prose*, 2: 236–42. Witness also a word of praise for the Gaelic League at a luncheon speech in 1900, quoted in MID, 1:80–81.

107 C.f. generally the excellent chapter 'Uneasy alliance: The Gaelic revival and the "Irish" renaissance', in O'Leary, *The prose literature of the Gaelic revival*, pp. 281–354. Hyde later, in 1903, contributed another play, entitled *Pleusgadh na bulgóide*. The English titles of Hyde's play tended to abandon a properly idiomatic translation of the noun-phrases ('Twisting the rope', 'How the bubble burst') in favour of the more racy-sounding 'The twisting of the rope', 'The bursting of the bubble' – an unconscious echo, perhaps, of 'The rising of the moon'. The locution (a verbal noun with a genitive) became a favourite with Anglo-Irish authors wishing to invoke a 'Gaelic' flavour. Titles on the pattern 'The something of the other' ('The bending of the bough', 'The dreaming of the bones', 'The hosting of the Shee', etc.) occur with remarkable frequency throughout the Celtic Twilight, and are that period's equivalent to the mavrones and machrees of earlier Anglo-Irishism.

108 Quoted MID 1:110. It was this populist bigotry which young James Joyce attacked in *The day of the rabblement*.

109 Frank Hugh O'Donnell, *Souls for gold! Pseudo-Celtic drama in Dublin* (London, 1894), p. 5. On O'Donnell, see Áine Ní Chonghaile, *F.H. O'Donnell, 1848–1916: A shaol agus a shaothar* (Dublin: Coiscéim, 1992).

110 C.f. the section 'Belief and unbelief', *The Celtic twilight* (London, 1893), pp. 11–4. It is perhaps because of O'Donnell's blistering attack that Yeats 'left out a few passages' when he re-issued *The Celtic twilight* as part of his *Mythologies* in 1925; W.B. Yeats, *Mythologies* (London: Macmillan, 1962), p. 1. There had also been some theosophical elucubrations by Yeats on Irish fairies (*Uncollected prose*, 1: 130–7; 245–7).

111 Thus, in a moderately favourable review of *On Baile's strand* in late 1904, Griffith's *United Irishman* added that, if the Abbey were to thrive, 'it must also be moulded by the influences which are moulding National life at present' (MID, 2: 131) – a direct quotation of Yeats's own words as expressed in 'First principles', *Samhain* 1904: '[National literature] [. . .] is the work of writers who are moulded by the influences that are moulding their country, and who write out of so deep a life that they are accepted there in the end' (*Explorations*, p. 156).

112 Thus the comment of Robert Hogan and James Kilroy in MID, 1: 30. Witness the condemnation of the play by Cardinal Logue (MID 1: 43), or the exhortation in the *Daily nation*, 8 May 1899, to protest against the staging of *The Countess Cathleen* 'in the names of morality and religion, and Irish nationality [. . .] And we hope very earnestly that [. . .] those Irish Catholics, who may form a portion of the audience, will so give expression to their disapproval as to effectually discourage any further ventures of a similar kind' (quoted MID, 1: 38).

113 For such literary dialectics, c.f. the model as advanced by Hans Robert Jauss in his classical essay 'Literaturgeschichte als Provokation der Literaturwissenschaft' (in Jauss's *Literaturgeschichte als Provokation*, Frankfurt: Suhrkamp, 1970, pp. 168–206). In Jauss's model, innovative texts stretch the reader's 'horizon of expectation' and can therefore provoke the readership and cause scandal. However, innovation-

oriented models such as Jauss's hermeneutic historicism conflate artistic innovation and social nonconformism: in Jauss's model, 'important' texts (Jauss's own
example being *Madame Bovary*) challenge both the literary conventions and
the social complaceny of the reader. Jauss fails to provide an argument, however,
whether or not there is a structural overlap between these aesthetic and ideological
aspects; nor does he justify his implicit endorsement and positive valorization of
innovativeness.

114   *Gaelic journal*, 11 no. 128 (May, 1901): 95. The article in question was 'The last
fortress of the Celt', which had appeared in *The Gael* (April, 1901).

115   'Plans and methods' (1899), in *Uncollected prose*, 2: 159–62.

116   MID 2: 14. The play was performed behind a gauze, in green light, so as to get a
dreamlike, otherworldly atmosphere; the strategy was taken from a production of
Maeterlinck's *Pelléas et Mélisande* by Lugné-Poë's Théâtre de l'Oeuvre (MID 2: 41).

117   In *Samhain*, 1902; again in W.B. Yeats, *Explorations* (London: Macmillan, 1962),
p. 96.

118   Annie Horniman, a tea heiress with a number of artistic and theatrical interests,
had met Yeats in the Order of the Golden Dawn, and became the most important
financer of the Abbey after 1905; her influence was deeply marked by élitist
exclusivism and that *fin-de-siècle* aestheticism which aimed only at the 'elect'; as
such, her influence on Yeats marked a sharp change from the nationalist activism
of Maud Gonne.

119   MID 3: 34–5; see also the comments by Yeats, Horniman and Lady Gregory
quoted MID 3: 58, 59, 61. Synge's reaction is interesting: 'I object to giving Miss
Horniman any control over the company whatever. If she is given power it ceases
to be an Irish movement worked by Irish people to carry out their ideas [. . .] I
object to Miss Horniman's control not because she is English, but because I have
no confidence in her ideals' (p. 88). One immediate bone of contention was
Horniman's wish to limit the cheap (sixpence) seats in the house so as not to lower
the tone of the establishment. D.P. Moran fulminated against this exclusivism in
The Leader throughout 1905; c.f. James W. Flannery, *Miss Annie F. Horniman and
the Abbey Theatre* (Dublin: Dolmen, 1970), pp. 16–7.

120   Audience reactions to *The playboy of the western world* have been collected by
James Kilroy in his *The 'Playboy' riots* (Dublin: Dolmen, 1971); here: pp. 7, 13, 15.

121   For a similar affair in the case of Sheridan's *The rivals*, see MIFG, 144–48.

122   Kilroy, *Playboy riots*, pp. 13–14. These excerpts, crudely picked from their context,
do no justice to the review as a whole, which in fact is sane and well-argued – more
or less along the lines of Corkery's comments in *Synge and Anglo-Irish literature*.

123   Gérard Genette, 'Vraisemblance et motivation', in id., *Figures II. Essais* (Paris: Seuil,
1969), p. 73 (my trans.). Genette takes the phrase 'tout ce qui est conforme à
l'opinion du public' from Rapin's *Poétique* of 1639. However, the underlying
insight can already be found in Aristotle's *Poetics*. Aristotle says that plausible
inventions are better than implausible truths, and points out that things should be
represented 'as they are, or else as people think they are, or else as people think
they ought to be'. In other words: realism, indeed mimesis itself, is something that
functions under the pragmatic conventions of recognizability (*Poetics* 1454^a;
1460^{b}5–12; 1461^{b}10–12).

124   See here, p. 212. Yeats helpfully described *Maeve*, with its hamfisted allegories, as
'a symbolic expression of clashing Irish and English ideals' – as if the point could

possibly be missed. 'The Celtic element in literature' (1897), in *Essays and introductions*, p. 187.

125 Kilroy, *Playboy riots*, p. 7. A similar note was sounded in 1905 in the *Freeman's journal* concerning *The well of the saints*: 'Mr. Synge's plays are somewhat baffling. How are they to be interpreted? Are they designed as a contribution to Irish national drama, and if so, what is meant by Irish national drama? Is it an attempt to hold the mirror up to Irish nature? Are we to look to it for a treatment of the facts of Irish life, present or past, in accordance with the commonly accepted Irish ideals?' (quoted MID 3: 19).

126 Kilroy, *Playboy riots*, p. 13. This sense of genre ambiguity is well attested. Synge was asked by a reporter if he had intended to create naturalistic verisimilitude or symbolical applicability, 'to represent Irish life as it is lived [. . .] holding up the mirror to nature'; Synge denied this emphatically and issued a press statement saying, among other things, '*The playboy of the western world* is not a play with "a purpose" in the modern sense of the word, but although parts of it are, or are meant to be, extravagant comedy, still a great deal that is in it, and a great deal more that is behind it, is perfectly serious, when looked at in a certain light. That is often the case, I think, with comedy, and no-one is quite sure to-day whether Shylock or Alceste should be played seriously or not. There are, it may be hinted, several sides to *The Playboy*' (Kilroy, *Playboy riots*, p. 41).

127 The following altercation between Yeats and Griffith has been gleaned from MID 2: 79–81.

128 On that theme, c.f. Cyrus Hoy, 'The widow of Ephesus', in id., *The hyacinth room: An investigation into the nature of comedy, tragedy, and tragicomedy* (London: Chatto & Windus, 1964), pp. 3–20. Kindly brought to my attention by Ton Hoenselaars.

129 Griffith levelled a similar charge at *The well of the saints*: 'The story – a well known one – has been treated in our own time by an English novelist. Mr. Synge's localisation of it is a failure, and his dramatisation disappointing. His peasants are not Irish, and the language they use in strife is pure Whitechapel [. . .] What there is "Irish", "national" or "dramatic" about it even Oedipus might fail to solve. How is it that the Irish National Theatre which started so well, can now only alternate a decadent wail with a Calvinistic groan' (quoted MID 3: 19–20).

130 'The reform of the theatre' (1903), in *Explorations*, p. 107.

131 'The Irish National Theatre and three sorts of ignorance', *Uncollected prose*, 2: 307–8. Earlier, in the *New Ireland review* for 1895, one William Barrett had already voiced exasperation with the 'fancy green frock-coat, red coats, heroes of the *Shaughraun* type, villains of the Mickey Feaney class, and all the other familiar *dramatis personae*' which were 'too trite as well as too vulgar to be further appreciated'. Barrett savagely mocked the pious clichés of Boucicault-style drama: 'a background of soldiers or policemen, four principal "good" people, consisting of a high-minded young Irish gentleman in tight trousers, a faithful retainer, whose name should be Larry or Thade, the charming *fiancée* of the young gentleman, and the merry sweetheart of the faithful retainer; and two principal "bad" people – generally a wicked landlord and a hireling spy'. William Barrett, 'Irish drama?', *New Ireland review*, 8 (1895): 38–41.

132 MID 2: 81. The formula was a favourite with Yeats at the time; he appears to have picked it up from Goethe. He uses it in a letter to Frank Fay in August 1904, attacking theatrical realism: 'Art is art because it is not nature'; quoted in Hugh

Hunt, *The Abbey Theatre. Ireland's national theatre 1904–1979* (Dublin: Gill & Macmillan, 1979), p. 8.

133   Witness Maud Gonne's intervention in the debate: 'A National theatre [. . .] must have its roots deep down in the centre of national life. In Ireland it must draw its vitality from that hidden spring from which the seven fountains of Gaelic inspiration flow [. . .] otherwise its branches will not have the strength to blossom under the blighting wind of foreign civilisation and thought which has blown so long over Ireland. [. . .] Mr. Yeats asks for freedom for the Theatre, freedom even from patriotic captivity. I would ask for freedom for it from one thing more deadly than all else – freedom from the insidious and destructive tyranny of foreign influence' (MID 2: 81).

134   Ironically, when Yeats in 1906 abandoned Maud Gonne's nationalism and embraced Annie Horniman's élitist aestheticism, and was about to turn the Abbey into a straightforward art theatre, it was Synge himself who objected: 'National dramas have never been created by such theatres. Goethe at the end of his life said that he and Schiller had failed to make a German drama at Weimar because they had confused their audiences with, one day, Shakespeare, one day Calderon, one day Sophocles and another Racine. If we do the same we are doomed' (MID 3: 88).

135   *Béaloideas*, 58 (1990): 141–80. C.f. also Declan Kiberd, *Synge and the Irish language* (London: Macmillan, 1979), pp. 151–75 (esp. pp. 152–9), and John Wilson Foster, *Fictions of the Irish literary revival*, p. 234.

136   'Among the audience of the last performance of *On Baile's Strand* there was a famous German scholar who had just edited the old German version of the world-wide story of the king who fights with his own son. Yet, no man can say whether that story came from Ireland to Germany or from Germany to Ireland, or whether to both countries from some common source.' Again, Yeats outlines various alternative lines of descent for Synge's theme in the *Shadow*, from eastern tales to Hyde's *Love songs of Connacht* (MID 3: 10, 12).

137   The matter has been the subject of various publications, notably by James Stewart ('Boccaccio in the Blaskets', *Zeitschrift für Celtische Philologie*, 43 (1989): 125–40) and Bo Almqvist ('The mysterious Mícheál Ó Gaoithín, Boccaccio and the Blasket tradition', *Béaloideas*, 58 (1990): 75–140.

138   Interestingly, the revision of that assumption also forces one to see 'folk' less in amorphous, collective terms and to take account of the individuality of the people involved: in assessing the case of the Blasket Boccaccio, Almqvist (op. cit.) was forced to pay special attention to the personality and the motivations of one important adapter of *Decameron* material, Mícheál Ó Gaoithín; thus the one-size-fits-all authorship of a collective 'folk' provenance yields to the nuclear notion of individual creation and driving concerns which is properly the sphere of literary criticism.

139   An interesting parallel is that of eighteenth-century Germany. Authors like Lessing, Herder and young Goethe attacked the prevalent fashion of classicism, not only because it went against their (pre-)romantic sensibilities, but also because it was considered both alien and élitist. Classicism was the taste of the courts, was French-imported, was unrooted in the national culture and (as a result) of doubtful morality. Hence, the national revival programme that these men of letters proposed was at the same time romantic (anti-classicist), national (against the francophilia and cosmopolitanism of court culture) and populist (against the élitism of court

culture); accordingly, the German romantics drew on the native values of honest burghers and pleasant peasants, on folktales and chapbooks, on a culture which was *Deutsch*, vernacular in the double sense of 'homegrown' and 'demotic'. Indeed, the German case is more than a parallel: it is the prototype for such movements in Europe. The underlying commonplace, operative from the Enlightenment to the present day, is that élite culture has no national roots and is therefore morally flawed; while, conversely, the plain people (in whom the nation manifests its particular character most clearly) may be less refined but have a stronger sense of honest morality. The reader will have no problems to find instances of that widespread link between populism and nationalism, from the French Revolution to Fianna Fáil.

140 Kilroy, *Playboy riots*, p. 13.

141 The second time that Mahon senior turns out to have survived his son's lethal blows marks, of course, a much more positive turn of events, and marks a reconciliation between father and son – a mature transcendence of earlier Oedipal rivalry.

142 It would be possible to extend this pattern to Synge's other plays. *Deirdre* is, of course, one long parable on the tyranny of old power over young love. *At the hawk's well* shows that a magic cure does not cleanse away the inheritance of ingrained attitudes; and in *Riders to the sea*, the audience and the reviewers showed themselves deeply troubled by the relentless on-stage presence, through much of the action, of a corpse which for once did *not* rise from the dead – that of a young man who had predeceased his old mother. Throughout Synge's plays, and contrary to comic or propagandist convention, youth is fey and vulnerable, outlived or outwitted by old age. Moreover, Synge's reply to the *Playboy's* critics is illustrative. Entitled 'Can we go back into our mother's womb?', it is directly concerned with the irreversibility of historical development, and rhetorically merges the opposition between national narrowmindedness and European cosmopolitanism with the one between decrepit old age and energetic youth. Irish isolationism is likened to 'the hysteria of old women's talk', while Synge looks forward to the day when a 'young man will teach Ireland again that she is part of Europe' (J.M. Synge, *Collected works*, 2: *Prose*, ed. A. Price (Oxford University Press, 1966), pp. 399–400.

143 Idman, *Charles Robert Maturin*, p. 100.

144 There are undead presences in *The land of heart's desire* and *The shadowy waters* (Roy Foster, *Paddy and Mr. Punch*, 219–221). In the later Yeats, there is the short poem 'Oil and blood'. In the *Collected poems* it follows 'Blood and the moon', from which it takes added resonance.

> In tombs of gold and lapis lazuli
> Bodies of holy men and women exude
> Miraculous oil, odour of violet.
>
> But under heavy loads of trampled clay
> Lie bodies of vampires full of blood;
> Their shrouds are bloody and their lips are wet.

145 On *Purgatory* and its preoccupation with the ghostly 'burden of the past', see W.J. Mc Cormack's treatment in *From Burke to Beckett*, pp. 341–47. Mc Cormack's tone is set by a very aptly-chosen quotation from Karl Marx's *The eighteenth brumaire of Louis Bonaparte*: 'The tradition of the dead generations weighs like a nightmare on

the minds of the living. And, just when they appear to be engaged in the revolutionary transformation of themselves and their material surroundings [. . .] they timidly conjure up the spirit of the past to help them' (p. 328).

146 Moynahan, *Anglo-Irish*, p. 135.

147 'Awaking from the dead' has continued to be a fruitful topic in the Irish literary imagination: witness its ironic-lyrical treatment in Niall Williams's play, produced in 1995 at the Peacock Theatre, *A little like paradise*.

Conclusion

1 Immanuel Kant, *Critique of pure reason*, trans., J.M.D. Meiklejohn (London: Dent, 1934), p. 145.

2 Gibbons, *Transformations in Irish culture*, pp. 134–47. John Wilson Foster, *Fictions of the Irish literary revival*, p. 157. C.f. also Mc Cormack, *From Burke to Beckett*, 259–62. The extent to which *Dubliners'* paralysis corresponds to Dublin's socio-economic and political situation at the time is described in James Fairhall, *James Joyce and the question of history* (Cambridge University Press, 1995), pp. 64–105.

3 One occasionally hears counter-interpretations to the effect that the 'journey westward' which Gabriel finds himself forced to undertake is a 'Good Thing', a necessary return to reflect on first principles. This attempt to give a more positive nationally Irish reading to Joyce appears distortive. It turns the story at cross-purposes, against the general theme of *Dubliners*, against Joyce's penchant for a masochistically sentimental indulgence in marital jealousy, against his Ibsenitish enthusiasm evinced at the time, against his endorsement of Synge against the Miss Ivorses in the Abbey audience in 'The day of the rabblement', and against feelings as expressed in his Trieste lectures that Ireland should be finished once and for all with its morbid and jejune invocation of a dead past. The 'journey westward' was eloquently rejected by Joyce himself in his decision to head for the Continent. In that respect, the reading as advanced by John Wilson Foster, *Fictions of the Irish literary revival*, pp. 142–74, still holds good, despite different recent interpretations by Luke Gibbons and Emer Nolan. Gibbons sees the final epiphany in 'The dead' as an acceptance, by this most urban of writers, of Ireland's rural, communitarian background; Gibbons juxtaposes Gabriel's modern, journalistic preoccupations with Gretta's more communitarian involvement in song and oral communication (Gibbons, *Transformations in Irish culture*, pp. 134–47). Nolan revalorizes Gabriel's 'swoon' as a redemption from his self-centered masculinity, the admission of feminine affect, and a concomitant 'resurgence of tradition' relayed 'through the figure of the woman and her illicit passion'; *James Joyce and nationalism* (London: Routledge, 1995), pp. 24–36.

4 'Joyce wrote "The Wandering Rocks" with a map of Dublin before him on which were traced in red ink the paths of the Earl of Dudley and Father Conmee. He calculated to a minute the time necessary for his characters to cover a given distance of the city'. Frank Budgen, *James Joyce and the making of 'Ulysses'* (London: Grayson & Grayson, 1934), pp. 124–5.

5 Gibbons, *Transformations in Irish culture*, pp. 165–9.

6 C.f. Udaya Kumar, *The Joycean labyrinth: Repetition, time and tradition in 'Ulysses'* (Clarendon Press, 1991), esp. pp. 69–70.

7 James Joyce, *Ulysses, the corrected text*, ed. H. Gabler (London: Bodley Head, 1986), p. 96. The hoarse timekeeper is an interesting analogue to Father Conmee. C.f. also Fairhall, *James Joyce and the question of history*, p. 197.

8 Stephen muses on Lessing's terms: 'You are walking through it howsomever. I am, a stride at the time. A very short space of time through very short times of space. Five, six, the *Nacheinander*.' (*Ulysses*, p. 31). C.f. also Kumar, *The Joycean labyrinth*, pp. 50 ff.

9 *From Burke to Beckett*, p. 275.

BIBLIOGRAPHY

note: In the case of university presses, the place of publication has been omitted; publishers are named only for post-1900 publications.

'Albert, L.' – *see* Herrmann, L.

Allingham, William, *Diary*, ed. G. Grigson (Fontwell, Sussex: Centaur, 1967).

Allingham, William, *Poems*, ed. J. Hewitt (Dublin: Dolmen, 1967).

Almqvist, Bo, 'The mysterious Mícheál Ó Gaoithín, Boccaccio and the Blasket tradition', *Béaloideas*, 58 (1990): pp. 75–140.

Alter, Peter, *Nationalismus* (Frankfurt: Suhrkamp, 1985).

Alter, Peter, 'Symbols of Irish nationalism', *Studia hibernica*, 14 (1974): pp. 104–23.

Anderson, Benedict, *Imagined communities: Reflections on the origin and spread of nationalism* (London: Verso, 1983).

Anderson, Christopher, *Brief sketch of various attempts which have been made to diffuse a knowledge of the holy scriptures through the medium of the Irish language* (Dublin, 1818).

Anderson, Christopher, *Historical sketches of the native Irish and their descendants* 2nd ed. (Dublin, 1821).

Andrews, John. *A paper landscape: The Ordnance Survey in nineteenth-century Ireland* (Clarendon Press, 1975).

Arnold, Matthew, *On the study of Celtic literature* (London: Dent (Everyman ed.) 1910).

Arnold, Thomas, *Miscellaneous works* (London, 1845).

Bakhtin, Mikhail, *The dialogic imagination: Four essays*, ed. M. Holquist. (University of Texas Press, 1981).

Balzac, Honoré de, *Les chouans* (1829), ed. M. Regard (Paris: Garnier, 1964).

Banim, John, *The Anglo-Irish of the nineteenth century. A novel*, 3 vols. (London, 1828).

Banton, Michael, *Racial theories* (Cambridge University Press, 1987).

Barrow, George Lennox, *The Round Towers of Ireland* (Dublin: Academy Press, 1979).

Beaufort, N.N. [Miss], 'The state of architecture and antiquities, previous to the landing of the Anglo-Normans in Ireland', *Transaction RIA*, 15 (1828): pp. 101–241.

Beaufort, Daniel Augustus, *Memoir of a map of Ireland* (Dublin, 1792).

Beer, Gillian, *The romance* (London: Methuen, 1969).

Benstock, Shari, 'At the margin of discourse: Footnotes in the fictional text', *PMLA*, 98 (1983), pp. 204–25.

Betham, William, *Etruria Celtica. Etruscan literature and antiquities investigated; or, the language of that ancient and illustrious people compared and identified with the Iberno-Celtic, and both shown to be Phoenician*, 2 vols. (Dublin, 1842).

Betham, William, *Letter to Sir William Rowan Hamilton, president of the Royal Irish Academy* (Dublin, 1840).

Blaas, Piet, *Anachronisme en historisch besef: Momenten uit de ontwikkeling van het Europees historisch bewustzijn* (The Hague: Nijgh & Van Ditmar, 1988).

Blacker, Valentine, *Ardmagh, a chronicle; The fire towers; Carmel; The goldsmith – an Indian tale; and The fourth sword* (Armagh, 1848).

Bonwick, James, *Irish druids and old Irish religions* (London, 1894).

Bopp, Franz, 'Über die celtischen Sprachen vom Gesichtspunkte der vergleichenden Sprachforschung', in id., *Kleine Schriften zur vergleichenden Sprachwissenschaft. Gesammelte Berliner Akademieabhandlungen 1824–1854* (Leipzig: Zentralantiquariat der DDR, 1972), pp. 149–234.

Boucicault, Dion, *The fireside story of Ireland*, 2nd ed. (London, 1881).

Bourke, Ulick, *The Aryan origin of the Gaelic race and language* (Dublin, 1875).

Bourke, Ulick, *Pre-Christian Ireland* (Dublin, 1887).

Bowen, Desmond, *The Protestant crusade in Ireland, 1800–1870: A study of Protestant-Catholic relations between the Act of Union and disestablishment* (Dublin: Gill and Macmillan, 1978).

Boyce, D.G. *Nationalism in Ireland*, 3rd ed. (London: Routledge, 1995).

Brash, Richard R, *The ecclesiastical architecture of Ireland to the close of the twelfth century* (Dublin, 1874).

Brooks, Peter, *The melodramatic imagination: Balzac, Henry James, melodrama and the mode of excess* (Columbia University Press, 1984).

Brown, Malcolm, *The politics of Irish literature. From Thomas Davis to W.B. Yeats* (London: George Allen and Unwin, 1972).

Brown, Stephen J., *Ireland in fiction: A guide to Irish novels, tales, romances and folklore* (reprint ed., Shannon: Irish University Press, 1969).

Brown, Terence, ed., *Celticism* (Amsterdam: Rodopi, 1996).

Brown, Terence, *Northern Voices: Poets from Ulster* (Dublin: Gill and Macmillan, 1975).

Bryant, Jacob, *Analysis of antient mythology*, 1775, 3 vols. (new ed. London, 1806).

Budgen, Frank, *James Joyce and the making of 'Ulysses'* (London: Grayson and Grayson, 1934).

Bunting, Edward, *A general collection of the ancient music of Ireland, arranged for the piano forte; some of the most admired melodies are adapted for the voice, to poetry chiefly translated from the original Irish songs, by Thomas Campbell Esq and other eminent poets, to which is prefixed a historical & critical dissertation on the Egyptian, British and Irish harp* (London, [1809]).

Bunting, Edward, *The ancient music of Ireland, arranged for the pianoforte, to which is prefixed a dissertation on the Irish harp and harpers, including an account of the old melodies of Ireland* (Dublin, 1840).

Burke, Martin J., 'The politics and poetics of nationalist historiography: Mathew Carey and the *Vindiciae Hibernicae*', in *Forging in the smithy: National identity and representation in Anglo-Irish literary history*, ed. J. Leerssen, A.H. van der Weel and B. Westerweel (Amsterdam: Rodopi, 1995), pp. 183–94.

Bush, Douglas, *Matthew Arnold: A survey of his poetry and prose* (London: Macmillan, 1971).

Buttimer, Cornelius G. 'Celtic and Irish in college 1849–1944', *Journal of the Cork Historical and Archaeological Society*, 94 (1989): 88–112.

Cairns, David and Shaun Richards, 'Reading a riot: The "reading formation" of Synge's Abbey audience', *Literature and history*, 13 (1987): 219–37.

Cairns, David and Shaun Richards, *Writing Ireland* (Manchester University Press, 1988).

Campbell, Mary, *Lady Morgan: The life and times of Sydney Owenson* (London: Pandora, 1988).

Carey, Mathew, *Vindiciae Hibernicae* (Philadelphia 1819).

Carleton, William, *Traits and stories of the Irish peasantry*, new ed., 2 vols. (Dublin, 1843).

Carlyle, Thomas, 'Repeal of the Union', in id. *Rescued essays*, ed. P. Newberry (London, 1892), pp. 17–52.

Chapman, Malcolm, *The Celts: The construction of a myth* (Basingstoke: Macmillan, 1992).

Chapman, Malcolm, *The Gaelic vision in Scottish culture* (London: Croom Helm, 1978).

Chevalier, Louis, *Classes laborieuses et classes dangéreuses à Paris pendant la première moitié du XIXe siècle* (Paris: Plon, 1958).

Cloncurry, Valentine (Lord), *Personal recollections of the life and times, with extracts from the correspondence, of Valentine Lord Cloncurry* (Dublin, 1849).

Coldrey, Barry, *Faith and fatherland: The Christian Brothers and the development of Irish nationalism, 1838–1921* (Dublin: Gill and Macmillan, 1988).

Colley, Linda, *Britons: Forging the nation, 1707–1837* (Yale University Press, 1992).

Connellan, Thaddeus, *The king's letter, in Irish and in English; with an introduction to the Irish language, and reading lessons for the use of his majesty's Irish subjects* (Dublin, 1822).

Connolly, S.J., *Religion, law and power: The making of Protestant Ireland, 1660–1760* (Oxford: Clarendon Press, 1992).

Croker, Thomas Crofton, *Researches in the south of Ireland, illustrative of the scenery, architectural remains, and the manners and superstitions of the peasantry. With an appendix containing a private narrative of the rebellion of 1798* (London, 1824).

Curran, William Henry, *Life of the right honourable John Philpot Curran* (2nd ed. Edinburgh, 1822).

Curtis, L.P., *Apes and angels: The Irishman in Victorian caricature* (Washington: Smithsonian Institution, 1971).

Curtis, L.P., *Anglo-Saxons and Celts: A study of Anglo-Irish prejudice in Victorian England* (University of Bridgeport, CT: Conference on British Studies, 1968).

[Cusack, Mary Frances], *An illustrated history of Ireland from the earliest period*, 2nd ed. (Kenmare and New York, 1868).

D'Alton, John, 'Essay on the ancient history, religion, learning, arts, and government of Ireland', *Transactions RIA*, 16 (1830): 1–380.

D'Alton, John, *The history of Ireland, from the earliest period to the year 1245, when the Annals of Boyle, which are adapted and embodied as the running text authority, terminate; with a brief essay on the native annalists, and other sources for illustrating Ireland, and full statistical and historical notices of the barony of Boyle*, 2 vols. (Dublin, 1845).

Dann, Otto, *Nation und Nationalismus in Deutschland, 1770–1990* (München: Beck, 1993).

Davis, Thomas, *Prose writings: Essays on Ireland* (London, 1889).

Deane, Seamus, 'Edmund Burke and the ideology of Irish liberalism', in *The Irish mind: Exploring intellectual traditions*, ed. R. Kearney (Dublin: Wolfhound Press, 1985), pp. 141–56.

Deane, Seamus, 'Irish national character 1790–1900', in *The writer as witness: Literature as historical evidence*, ed. T. Dunne (Cork University Press, 1987), pp. 90–113.

Deane, Seamus, gen. ed. *The Field Day anthology of Irish writing*, 3 vols. (Derry: Field Day Company, 1991).

De Brún, Pádraig, 'An Irish class of 1845', *Éigse*, 17 no. 2 (1977–1978): 214.

De Brún, Pádraig, 'The Irish Society's bible teachers, 1818–27', *Éigse*, 19, no. 2 (1983): 281–332; 20 (1984): 34–92; 21 (1986): 72–149; 22 (1987): 54–106; 24 (1990): 71–120; 25 (1991): 113–149; 26 (1992): 131–172.

Delany, Matthew, *An answer to Mr. Flanagan's extravagant assertions respecting the Round Towers of Ireland; with some original views as to their real origin and uses, and certain singular particulars on the one at Clondalkin, worthy the attention of the curious* (Carlow, 1843).

Denman, Peter, *Samuel Ferguson: The literary achievement* (Gerrards Cross: Colin Smythe, 1990).

Dieltjens, Louis, 'The Abbey Theatre as a cultural formation', in *History and violence in Anglo-Irish literature*, ed. J. Duytschaever and G. Lernout (Amsterdam: Rodopi, 1988), pp. 47–65.

Dittrich, Z.R. et al., *Knoeien met het verleden* (Utrecht and Antwerpen: Spectrum, 1984).

Donnelly, James S., 'Pastorini and captain Rock: Millenarianism and sectarianism in the Rockite movement of 1821–4', in *Irish peasants: Violence and political unrest, 1780–1914*, ed. S. Clark and J.S. Donnelly (Manchester University Press, 1983), pp. 102–39.

Dowling, P.J., 'Patrick Lynch, schoolmaster, 1754–1818', *Studies*, 20 (1931): 461–71.

Doyle, Richard, *In fairyland: A series of pictures from the elf-world* (London, 1870).

Droixhe, Daniel, *La linguistique et l'appel de l'histoire, 1600–1800. Rationalisme et révolutions positivistes* (Genève: Droz, 1978).

Duffy, Charles Gavan, *Young Ireland: A fragment of Irish history, 1840–1850* (London, 1880).

Dunleavy, Gareth W., *Douglas Hyde* (Bucknell University Press, 1974).

Dunne, Tom, 'The best history of nations: Lady Morgan's Irish novels', *Historical studies*, 16 (1987): 133–59.

Dunne, Tom, 'Haunted by history: Irish romantic writing, 1800–1850', in *Romanticism in national context*, ed. R. Porter and M. Teich (Cambridge University Press, 1988), pp. 68–91

Dunraven (Lord), *Notes on Irish architecture*, ed. M. Stokes, 2 vols. (London, 1875–77).

Dyserinck, Hugo, 'Komparatistische Imagologie: Zur politischen Tragweite einer europäischen Wissenschaft von der Literatur', in *Europa und das nationale Selbstverständnis. Imagologische Probleme in Literatur, Kunst und Kultur des 18. und 19. Jahrhunderts*, ed. H. Dyserinck and K.U. Syndram (Bonn: Bouvier, 1988), pp. 13–37

Eagleton, Terry, *Heathcliff and the great hunger. Studies in Irish culture* (London: Verso, 1995).

Edge, John H., *An Irish utopia: A story of a phase of the land problem. New edition with a special introduction (now first published) dealing with the subject of the Irish Round Towers* (Dublin, 1910).

Edgeworth, Maria, *Castle Rackrent*, ed. George Watson (Oxford University Press, 1964).

Even-Zohar, Itamar, 'Polysystem theory', *Poetics Today*, 1 (1979): 287–310.

Fabian, Johannes, *Time and the other: How anthropology makes its object* (Columbia University Press, 1983).

Fairhall, James, *James Joyce and the question of history* (Cambridge University Press, 1995).

Faverty, Frederic E., *Matthew Arnold the ethnologist* (Northwestern University, 1951).

Ferguson, Mary Catharine (Lady), *Sir Samuel Ferguson in the Ireland of his day*, 2 vols. (London/Edinburgh, 1896).

Ferguson, Samuel, 'The Celto-Scythic progresses', *Dublin University magazine*, 39 (1852): 271–91.

Ferguson, Samuel, 'Hardiman's Irish minstrelsy', *Dublin University magazine*, 3 (1834): 465–78; 4 (1834): 152–67; 447–67; 514–30.

Ferguson, Samuel, *Lays of the western Gael and other poems* (London, 1865).

Ferguson, Samuel [?], 'Ordnance Survey in Ireland', *Dublin University magazine*, 23 (1844): 494–500

Fink, Zera S. *The classical republicans: An essay in the recovery of a pattern of thought in seventeenth-century England*, 2nd ed. (Northwestern University, 1962).

Fitzmaurice, S.H., 'Hervey de Montmorency', *Journal of the Old Wexford Society*, 2 (1969): 19–25.

Fitz-Patrick, W.J., *Irish wits and worthies, including Dr. Lanigan, his life and times, with glimpses of stirring scenes since 1770* (Dublin, 1873).

Flanagan, John, *A discourse of the Round Towers of Ireland; in which the errors of the various writers on that subject are detected and confuted, and the true cause of so many differences among the learned, and the question of their use and history, is assigned and demonstrated* (Kilkenny, 1843).

Flanagan, John, *Delany confuted; or, an exposure of the flagitious frauds of the writer of that name in forging evidence to prove the existence of a Round Tower at Clondalkin, in the county of Dublin. With some further observations on the ancient Phoenician smelting furnace in Sancanathice, in Kilkenny* (Kilkenny, 1843).

Flanagan, Thomas, *The Irish novelists 1800–1850* (Columbia University Press, 1959).

Flannery, James W., *Miss Annie F. Horniman and the Abbey Theatre* (Dublin: Dolmen, 1970).

Foster, John Wilson, *Fictions of the Irish literary revival. A changeling art* (Syracuse University Press, 1987).

Foster, Roy, *Modern Ireland, 1600–1972* (London: Penguin, 1988).

Foster, Roy, *Paddy and Mr. Punch: Connections in Irish and English history* (London: Penguin, 1993).

Foster, Roy, *The Story of Ireland: An inaugural lecture delivered before the University of Oxford on 1 December 1994* (Clarendon Press, 1995).

Freud, Sigmund, 'The "Uncanny"', in id., *Art and Literature*, ed. A. Dickson (Pelican Freud library, ed. and trans. J. Strachey, 14; Harmondsworth: Penguin, 1985), pp. 335–77.

Gavan Duffy, Charles, *A short life of Thomas Davis* (London, 1895).

Gellner, Ernest, *Nations and nationalism* (Oxford; Blackwell, 1983).

Genette, Gérard, *Figures II. Essais* (Paris: Seuil, 1969).

Genette, Gérard, *Seuils* (Paris: Seuil, 1987).

Gerrard, Christine, *The Patriot opposition to Walpole: Politics, poetry and national myth, 1725–1742* (Oxford: Clarendon Press, 1995).

Gibbons, Luke, 'The sympathetic bond: Ossian, Celticism and colonialism', in *Celticism*, ed. T. Brown (Amsterdam: Rodopi, 1996), pp. 273–91.

Gibbons, Luke, *Transformations in Irish culture* (Cork University Press, 1996).

[Gilbert, J.T.], *On the life and labours of John O'Donovan, LL.D.* (London, 1862).

Girardet, Raoul, *Mythes et mythologies politiques* (Paris: Seuil, 1986).

Gleeson, Dermot F., 'Peter O'Connell: Scholar and scribe, 1755–1826', *Studies*, 33 (1944): 342–348.

Goodwin, Albert, *The friends of liberty: The English democratic movement in the age of the French revolution* (London: Hutchinson, 1979).

Gould, Stephen Jay, *The mismeasure of man* (New York: Norton, 1981).

Greene, David, *Makers and forgers* (G.J. Williams Memorial lecture; University of Wales Press, 1975).

Gregory, Augusta (Lady), *Cuchulain of Muirthemne. The story of the men of the Red Branch of Ulster arranged and put into English*, 5th ed. (Gerrards Cross: Colin Smythe, 1970).

Grell, Ch. and Chr. Michel, eds., *Primitivisme et mythes des origines dans la France des Lumières* (Université de Paris-Sorbonne, 1989).

Grierson, Herbert, 'History and the novel', in Herbert Grierson, Edwin Muir, G.M. Young and S.C. Roberts, *Sir Walter Scott lectures 1940–1948* (Edinburgh: At the University Press, 1950) pp. 31–51.

Griffin, Gerald, *The invasion* (Dublin: Duffy, n.d. [*ca.* 1870]).

Haitsma Mulier, E.O.G., 'De geschiedschrijving over de Patriottentijd en de Bataafse Tijd', in *Kantelend geschiedbeeld. Nederlandse historiografie sinds 1945*, ed. W.W. Mijnhardt (Utrecht/Antwerpen: Spectrum, 1983), pp. 206–227.

Haliday, William, *Úraicecht na Gaedhilge: A grammar of the Gaelic language* (Dublin, 1808).

Hardiman, James, *History of the city and the county of Galway* (Dublin, 1821).

Hardiman, James, *Irish minstrelsy, or bardic remains of Ireland; with English poetical translations*, 2 vols. (London, 1831).

Haverty, Martin, *The history of Ireland, ancient and modern, derived from our native annals, from the most recent researches of eminent Irish scholars and antiquaries, from the state papers, and from all the resources of Irish history now available* (Dublin, 1860).

Hayden, John, ed., *Scott: The critical heritage* (London: Routledge and Kegan Paul, 1970).

Healy, John (Archbishop), *The Round Towers of Ireland and holy wells of Ireland* (Dublin, n.d. [*c.* 1898]).

Herrmann, L. ['L. Albert'], *Six thousand years of Gaelic grandeur unearthed. The most ancient and truthful chronicles of the Gael, vol. 1, 5357 to 1004 BC, with a preface, containing history of the discovery, and a dissertation presenting numerous proofs of authenticity and antiquity* (London, Foyle, n.d. [1936]).

Herrmann, L. ['L. Albert'], *The buried-alive chronicles of Ireland: An open challenge to the Celtic scholars of Breo-tan and Er-i* (London: Foyle, 1938).

Higgins, Godfrey, *Anacalypsis, an attempt to draw the veil of the Satic Isis; or, an inquiry into the origin of languages, nations, and religions*, 2 vols. (London, 1836).

Higgins, Godfrey, *The Celtic druids; or, an attempt to shew that the druids were the priests or oriental colonies who emigrated from India, and were the introducers of the first or Cadmean system of letters, and the builders of Stonehenge, of Carnac, and of other Cyclopean works, in Asia and Europe*, 2nd ed. (London, 1829).

Hill, Jacqueline, '1641 and the quest for Catholic emancipation, 1691–1829', in *Ulster 1641: Aspects of the rising*, ed. B. Mac Cuarta (Queen's University, Belfast, 1993), pp. 159–72.

Hoare, Richard Colt, *Journal of a tour in Ireland AD 1806* (London, 1807).

Hobsbawm, Eric. *Nations and nationalism since 1780: Programme, myth, reality* (Cambridge University Press, new ed. 1992).

Hobsbawm, Eric and Terence Ranger, eds. *The invention of tradition* (Cambridge University Press, 1983).

Hogan, Robert and James Kilroy, eds., *The Irish literary theatre, 1899–1901* MID, 1 (Dublin: Dolmen, 1975).

Hogan, Robert, and James Kilroy, eds., *Laying the foundations, 1902–1904* MID, 2 (Dublin: Dolmen, 1976).

Hogan, Robert, and James Kilroy, eds., *The Abbey Theatre: The years of Synge, 1905–1909* MID, 3 (Dublin: Dolmen, 1978).

Hoy, Cyrus, 'The widow of Ephesus', in id. *The hyacinth room. An investigation into the nature of comedy, tragedy, and tragicomedy* (London: Chatto & Windus, 1964).

Hunt, Hugh, *The Abbey Theatre: Ireland's national theatre 1904–1979* (Dublin: Gill & Macmillan, 1979).

Hyde, Douglas, *The necessity for de-anglicising Ireland* (1892; Leiden: Academic Press, 1994).

Idman, Niilo, *Charles Robert Maturin: His life and works* (Helsingfors: Central-tryckeri, 1923).

Im Hof, Ulrich, *Mythos Schweiz: Identität, Nation, Geschichte, 1291–1991* (Zürich: Neue Zürcher Zeitung, 1991).

Jauss, Hans Robert, 'Literaturgeschichte als Provokation der Literaturwissenschaft', in id. *Literaturgeschichte als Provokation* (Frankfurt: Suhrkamp, 1970), pp. 168–206.

Jennings, Hargrave, *The rosicrucians, their rites and mysteries* (London, 1870).

Jourdan, A. & J. Leerssen, eds., *Remous révolutionnaires. Armée française, république batave* (Amsterdam University Press, 1996).

Joyce, James, *Dubliners* (New York: Random house, n.d.).

Joyce, James, *Ulysses, the corrected text*, ed. H. Gabler (London: Bodley Head, 1986).

Kane, Eileen, 'Stereotypes and Irish identity: Mental illness as a cultural frame', *Studies*, 75 (1986): 539–51.

Kant, Immanuel, *Critique of pure reason*, trl. J.M.D. Meiklejohn (London: Dent, 1934).

Keane, Marcus, *The towers and temples of ancient Ireland; their origin and history discussed from a new point of view* (Dublin, 1867).

Kelleher, John V., 'Matthew Arnold and the Celtic revival', in *Perspectives in Criticism*, ed. H. Levin (Harvard U.P., 1950), pp. 197–221.

Kelly, Matthew, *Dissertations chiefly on Irish church history*, ed. D. McCarthy (Dublin, 1864).

Keogh, Dáire, *The French disease: The Catholic Church and Irish radicalism, 1790–1800* (Blackrock: Four Courts Press, 1993).

Kiberd, Declan, *Synge and the Irish language* (London: Macmillan, 1979).

Kilroy, James, *The 'Playboy' riots* (Dublin: Dolmen, 1971).

Kinsella, Thomas, *The Táin, translated from the Irish epic Táin Bó Cuailnge* (Dublin: Dolmen, 1970).

Kinsella, Thomas, *New poems 1973* (Dublin: Dolmen, 1973).

Kliger, Samuel, *The Goths in England: A study in seventeenth- and eighteenth-century thought* (Harvard University Press, 1952).

Kropf, Hans, *William Allingham im Lichte der irischen Freiheitsbewegung* (Biel: Andres, 1928).

Kumar, Udaya, *The Joycean labyrinth: Repetition, time, and tradition in 'Ulysses'* (Clarendon Press, 1991).

Lanigan, *Ecclesiastical history of Ireland, from the first introduction of Christianity among the Irish to the beginning of the thirteenth century, compiled from the works of the most esteemed authors, foreign and domestic, who have written and published on matters connected with the Irish church; and from Irish annals and other authentic documents still existing in manuscript*, 4 vols. (Dublin, 1822).

Lebow, Ned. 'British images of poverty in pre-Famine Ireland', in *Views of the Irish Peasantry*, ed. D.J. Casey and R.E. Rhodes (Hamden, CT: Archon, 1977), pp. 57–85

Leeb, I. Leonard, *The ideological origins of the Batavian revolution: History and politics in the Dutch Republic 1747–1800* (The Hague: Martinus Nijhoff, 1973).

Leerssen, J.Th., 'Identity and self-image: German auto-exoticism as escape from history', in *Komparatistik und Europaforschung. Perspektiven vergleichender Literatur- und Kulturwissenschaft*, ed. H. Dyserinck and K.U. Sydram (Bonn/Berlin: Bouvier, 1992), pp. 117–36.

Leerssen, J.Th., '"The cracked lookingglass of a servant": Cultural decolonization and national consciousness in Ireland and Africa', in *Europa und das nationale Selbstverständnis. Imagologische Probleme in Literatur, Kunst und Kultur des 19. und 20. Jahrhunderts*, ed. H. Dyserinck and K.U. Syndram (Bonn: Bouvier, 1988), pp. 103–18.

Leerssen, J.Th., 'Echoes and images: Reflections upon foreign space', in *Alterity, Identity, Image: Selves and others in society and scholarship*, ed. R. Corbey and J.Th. Leerssen (Amsterdam: Rodopi, 1991), pp. 123–38.

Leerssen, J.Th., 'Europe as a set of borders', *Yearbook of European studies*, 6 (1993): 1–14.

Leerssen, J.Th., 'Literatuur op de landkaart: Taal, territorium en culturele identiteit', *Forum der letteren*, 34 (1993): 16–28.

Leerssen, J.Th., *Mere Irish and Fíor-Ghael: Studies in the idea of Irish nationality, its development and literary expression prior to the nineteenth century*, 2nd ed. (Cork University Press, 1996).

Leerssen, J.Th., 'Over de ontologische status en tekstuele situering van imagotypen: Exotisme en Walter Scotts *Waverley*', in *Deugdelijk Vermaak. Opstellen over literatuur en filosofie in de negentiende eeuw*, ed. E. Eweg (Amsterdam: Huis aan de Drie Grachten, 1987).

Leerssen, J.Th., 'Wildness, wilderness, and Ireland: Medieval and early-modern patterns in the demarcation of civility', *Journal of the history of ideas*, 56 (1995): 25–39.

Levine, Philippa, *The amateur and the professional: Antiquarians, historians and archaeologists in Victorian England, 1838–1886* (Cambridge University Press, 1986).

van der Linden, H., 'Histoire de notre nom national' *Académie royale de Belgique, Bulletin de la classe des lettres*, 5e série, 16 (1930): 27–40.

Lynch, Patrick, *For-oideas ghnaith-Ghaoighilge na h-Eireand. Introduction to the knowledge of the Irish language as now spoken* (Dublin, 1815).

Lyons, F.S.L., *Ireland since the Famine* (London: Fontana/Collins, 1973).

McCarthy, Justin and Justin Huntly McCarthy, *A history of the four Georges* (4 vols.; London: Chatto & Windus, 1901).

MacCartney, Donald, 'The writing of history in Ireland, 1800–1830', *Irish Historical Studies*, 10, 40 (Sept. 1957): 347–362.

Mc Cormack, W.J., *Ascendancy and tradition in Anglo-Irish literary history from 1789 to 1939* (Clarendon Press, 1985). re-edited as:

Mc Cormack, W.J., *From Burke to Beckett. Ascendancy, tradition and betrayal in literary history* (Cork University Press, 1994).

MacDonagh, Oliver, *O'Connell. The life of Daniel O'Connell, 1775–1847* (London: Weidenfeld & Nicolson, 1991).

MacDonagh, Oliver, *States of mind: A study of Anglo-Irish conflict 1780–1980* (London: George Allen and Unwin, 1983).

[MacDonald, W.R.], *The Dublin mail; or, intercepted correspondence*, 4th ed. (London, 1822).

MacDougall, Hugh A., *Racial myth in English history: Trojans, Teutons, and Anglo-Saxons* (University Press of New England, 1982).

MacGeoghegan, Abbé James. *The history of Ireland, ancient and modern, taken from the most authentic records and dedicated to the Irish brigade, by the abbé Mac-Goeghegan [sic]. With a continuation from the treaty of Limerick to the present time by John Mitchel* (New York and Montreal, n.d. [1865–1868]).

MacLochlainn, Alf, 'Gael and peasant – a case of mistaken identity?', in *Views of the Irish peasantry, 1800–1916*, ed. D.J. Casey and R.E. Rhodes (Hamden, CT: Archon, 1977), pp. 17–36.

Madden, R.R., *The United Irishmen, their lives and times with several additional memoirs, and authentic documents, heretofore unpublished; the whole matter newly arranged and revised*, 2 vols. (Dublin, 1858).

[Mahony, Francis Sylvester], *Reliques of Father Prout* (London, 1859).

Maine, Henry Sumner, *Village-communities in the east and west* (London, 1871).

Maturin, Charles Robert ('Dennis Jasper Murphy'), *The wild Irish boy*, 2 vols. (New York, 1808).

Maturin, Charles Robert, *The Milesian Chief*, 4 vols. (London, 1812).

Michelet, Jules, *Histoire de la Révolution française*, ed. G. Walter, 2 vols (Paris: Pléiade, 1952).

Mitchel, John – *see* MacGeoghegan, abbé.

Molony, John N., *A soul came into Ireland. Thomas Davis, 1814–1845* (Dublin: Geography, 1995).

Momigliano, Arnaldo, 'Ancient history and the antiquarian', in id. *Contributo alla storia degli studi classici* (Roma: Edizioni de Storia e Letteratura, 1955), pp. 67–106

Montmorency-Morres, Hervé, *Historical and critical inquiry into the origin and primitive uses of the Irish pillar-tower* (Dublin, 1821).

Moody, T.W., ed., *The Fenian movement* (Cork: Mercier, n.d.).

Moore, Thomas, *History of Ireland*, 4 vols. (London: 1835–1845).

Moore, Thomas, *Moore's Irish melodies, with symphonies and accompaniments by Sir John Stevenson and Sir Henry Bishop* (Dublin, n.d. [1879]).

Moore, Thomas, *The journal of Thomas Moore*, ed. W.S. Dowden, 6 vols. (University of Delaware Press, 1983–1991).

Moore, Thomas, *The letters of Thomas Moore*, ed. W.S. Dowden, 2 vols. (Clarendon Press, 1964).

Moore, Thomas, *Life and death of Lord Edward Fitzgerald*, 2 vols. (London, 1831).

[Moore, Thomas], *Memoirs of Captain Rock, the celebrated Irish chieftain, with some account of his ancestors. Written by himself* (London, 1824).

[Moore, Thomas] *Travels of an Irish gentleman in search of religion* (Dublin, 1833).

Morgan, Sydney (Lady), *The lay of an Irish harp; or, metrical fragments, by Miss Owenson* (London, 1807).

Morgan, Sydney (Lady), *O'Donnel: A national tale*, 3 vols. (London, 1814).

Morgan, Sydney (Lady), *The O'Briens and the O'Flahertys: A national tale*, 4 vols. (London, 1827).

Morgan, Sydney (Lady), *Patriotic sketches written in Connaught*, 2 vols. (Dublin, 1807).

Morgan, Sydney (Lady), *St. Clair, or, the heiress of Desmond* (Philadelphia, 1807).

Morgan, Sydney (Lady), *The wild Irish girl* (London and New York: Pandora, 1986).

Moynahan, Julian, *Anglo-Irish: The literary imagination in a hyphenated culture* (Princeton University Press, 1995).

Nederveen Pieterse, Jan, *White on black: Images of Africa and blacks in western popular culture* (Yale University Press, 1992).

Neilson, William, *An introduction to the Irish language* (Dublin, 1808).

Ní Chonghaile, Áine, *F.H. O'Donnell, 1848–1916: A shaol agus a shaothar* (Baile Átha Cliath: Coiscéim, 1992).

Ní Dhuibhne-Almqvist, Éilís, 'Synge's use of popular material in *The shadow of the glen*', *Béaloideas*, 58 (1990): 141–180.

Nolan, Emer, *James Joyce and nationalism* (London: Routledge, 1995).

Nora, Pierre, ed., *Les lieux de mémoire* 3 vols. in 5 (Paris: Gallimard, 1988–1993).

O'Brien, Henry, *The Round Towers of Ireland, or the history of the Tuath-De-Danaans for the first time unveiled*, 2nd ed. (London and Dublin, 1834), originally published Dublin, 1834, under the title *The Round Towers of Ireland, or the mysteries of freemasonry, of sabaism, and of budhism, now for the first time unveiled*.

O'Brien, Paul, *A practical grammar of the Irish language* (Dublin, 1809).

O'Byrne, Daniel, *The history of the Round Towers of Ireland* (Kilkenny, 1877).

O'Callaghan, John Cornelius, *History of the Irish brigades in the service of France* (Dublin, 1854).

O'Connell, Daniel, *A memoir on Ireland native and Saxon, vol. 1: 1172–1660* (Dublin, 1843).

O'Connor, Roger, *The chronicles of Eri, or the history of the Gaal Scot Iber: or, the Irish people translated from the original manuscripts in the Phoenician dialect of the Scythian language* (Dublin, 1822).

[O'Connor, Roger], *Letters to his majesty, King George the fourth, by Captain Rock* (Dublin, 1828).

O'Conor, Charles, *Rerum Hibernicarum scriptores veteres* 4 vols. (Buckingham, 1814–1826).

O'Conor, Matthew, *Military history of the Irish nation, comprising a memoir of the Irish brigades in the service of France* (Dublin, 1845).

O'Curry, Eugene, *Lectures on the manuscript materials of ancient Irish history* (Dublin, 1861).

O'Curry, Eugene, *On the manners and customs of the ancient Irish*, ed. W.K. O'Sullivan, 3 vols. (London, Dublin, New York, 1873).

O'Donovan, John, *A grammar of the Irish language, published for the use of the senior classes of the college of St. Columba* (Dublin, 1845).

Ó Dúill, Greagóir, *Samuel Ferguson: Beatha agus saothar* (Dublin: Clóchomhar, 1993).

O'Flaherty, John T. 'A sketch of the history and antiquities of the southern islands of Arran, lying off the west coast of Ireland, with observations on the religion of the Celtic nations, pagan monuments of the early Irish, druidic rites &c.', *Transactions RIA*, 14 (1825).

O'Grady, Standish, *History of Ireland, 1: The heroic period; 2: Cuchulain and his contemporaries* (London, 1878–1880).

O'Grady, Standish, *History of Ireland: Critical and philosophical* (London & Dublin, 1881).

O'Grady, Standish, *The story of Ireland* (London, 1894).

Ó Hainle, Cathal, *Promhadh pinn* (Maynooth: An Sagart, 1978).

O'Halloran, Clare, 'Golden ages and barbarous nations: Antiquarian debate on the Celtic past in Ireland and Scotland in the eighteenth century' (Ph.D. thesis; Cambridge, 1991).

O'Halloran, Sylvester and A.M. Sullivan, *The pictorial history of Ireland, from the landing of the Milesians to the present time; detailing, in chronological order, all the important events of the reigns of the kings and chieftains, and embracing authentic accounts of their several wars with the Romans, Britons, Danes and Normans; with graphic descriptions of the battle of Clontarf; Strongbow's invasion; the death of king Roderick O'Connor; crowning of Edward Bruce king of Ireland; war of the O'Neills and O'Donnells against England; confiscation of Ulster; Cromwell's invasion; persecution of the catholics; war between king James and William of Orange; siege of Derry and battle of the Boyne; siege of Athlone; battle of Aughrim; siege and treaty of Limerick; penal laws; the Volunteers; the United Irishmen; rebellion of '98; the Union; Catholic Emancipation and Repeal; the Young Irelanders; the Fenian insurrection; the Land League, etc. etc.* (Boston, 1884).

O'Leary, J., *Ireland among the nations: or, the faults and virtues of the Irish compared with those of other races* (New York and Boston, 1874).

O'Leary, Philip, *The prose literature of the Gaelic revival, 1881–1921. Ideology and innovation* (Pennsylvania State University Press, 1994).

Ó Maolfhabhail, Art, 'Eoghan Ó Comhraí agus an tSuirbhéaracht Ordanáis', in *Ómós do Eoghan Ó Comhraí*, ed. P. Ó Fiannachta (An Daingean: An Sagart, 1995), pp. 145–82.

Ó Maolmhuaidh, Proinsias, *Uilleog de Búrca: 'Athair na hathbheochana'* (Dublin: Foilseachán Náisiúnta, 1981).

O'Neill, Henry, *A descriptive catalogue of illustrations of the fine arts of ancient Ireland, serving to show that a truly national and beautiful style of art existed in Ireland from a remote period till some time after the Anglo-Norman invasion* (Dublin, 1855).

O'Neill, Henry, *The fine arts and civilization of ancient Ireland, illustrated with chromo and other lithographs and several woodcuts* (London and Dublin, 1863).

O'Neill, Henry, *Ireland for the Irish: A practical, peaceable, and just solution of the Irish land question* (London and Dundalk, 1868).

O'Neill, Henry, *The Round Towers of Ireland* (Dublin, 1877).

O'Rahilly, Cecile, ed. and trans., *Táin Bó Cúalnge from the Book of Leinster* (Dublin: Dublin Institute for Advanced Studies, 1967).

O'Reilly, Bernard, *John MacHale, archbishop of Tuam. His life, times, and correspondence*, 2 vols. (New York & Cincinnati, 1890).

O'Reilly, Edward, 'An essay on the nature and influence of the ancient Irish institutes, commonly called the Brehon Laws, and of the number and authenticity of the documents whence information concerning them may be derived; accompanied by specimens and translations from some of their most interesting parts; with an appendix, containing a catalogue of the principal ancient Irish Laws, to be found in the MSS library of Trinity College, and other libraries', *Transactions RIA* 14 (1825): 141–223.

O'Reilly, Edward, 'Chronological account of Irish writers, and descriptive catalogue of such of their works, as are still extant in verse or prose', *Transactions of the Iberno-Celtic Society*, 1 (1820): xi–ccxxxvii.

O'Reilly, Edward, *Sanas Gaoidhilge – Sags-Bhéarla. An Irish-English dictionary with numerous comparisons of Irish words with those of a similar orthography, sense or sound in the Welsh and Hebrew languages, to which is annexed a compendious Irish grammar* (Dublin, 1817, 2nd. ed. 1821).

Orpen, C.E.H., *The claim of millions of our fellow-countrymen of present and future generations, to be taught in their own and only language: the Irish. Addressed to the upper classes in Ireland and Great Britain* (Dublin, 1829).

[O'Sullivan, Mortimer], *Captain Rock detected: or, the origin and character of the recent disturbances, the causes, both moral and political, of the present alarming condition of the south and west of Ireland, fully and fairly considered and exposed by a Munster farmer* (London, 1824).

O'Toole, P.L., *History of the Clan O'Toole (Ui Thuathail) and other Leinster septs* (Dublin, 1890).

Owenson, Sydney – see Morgan, Sydney (Lady).

Palmer, R.R., *The age of the democratic revolution. A political history of Europe and America, 1760–1800*, 2 vols. (Princeton University Press, 1959).

Paque, Jeannine, *Le symbolisme belge* (Bruxelles: Labor, 1989).

Payne Knight, Richard, *A discourse on the worship of Priapus and its connexion with the mystic theology of the ancients* (1786; reprinted, together with Thomas Wright, *The worship of the generative powers during the middle ages of western Europe* (1866); New York: Dorset Press, 1992).

Peardon, Thomas, *The transition in English historical writing: 1760–1830* (New York: AMS, 1966).

Perry, F.T., *The chronicles of Eri, or the ancient Irish, who they were, and their connections with the coronation stone* (London: Stockwell, n.d. [1939]).

Petrie, George, 'On the history and antiquities of Tara Hill', *Transactions RIA*, 18 (1839), pt. 2.

Petrie, George, *The ecclesiastical architecture of Ireland, anterior to the Anglo-Norman invasion, comprising an essay on the origin and use of the Round Towers of Ireland, which obtained the gold medal and prize of the Royal Irish Academy* (Dublin, 1845).

Petrie, George, *Letter to Sir Willam R. Hamilton, LL.D., royal astronomer of Ireland, and president of the Royal Irish Academy: in reply to certain charges made against the author by Sir William Betham, in two letters recently published* (Dublin, 1840).

Phallic objects, monuments and remains, illustrations of the rise and development of the phallic idea (sex worship) and its embodiment in works of nature and art (n.pl., privately printed, 1889).

Pictet, Adolphe, *De l'affinité des langues celtiques avec le sanscrit. Mémoire couronné par l'Institut (Académie royale des inscriptions et belles-lettres)* (Paris, 1837).

Pinkerton, John, *Literary correspondence* 2 vols. (London, 1830).

Poliakov, Léon, *Le mythe aryen. Essai sur les sources du racisme et des nationalismes* new ed. (Bruxelles, 1987).

Popper, Karl, *The open society and its enemies*, 2 vols. (London: Routledge and Kegan Paul, 1945).

Power, Patrick, 'The Gaelic Union: A nonagenarian retrospect', *Studies*, 38 (1949): 413–418.

Prichard, J.C., *The eastern origin of the Celtic nations proved by a comparison of their dialects with the Sanskrit, Latin, and Teutonic languages: Forming a supplement to Researches into the physical history of mankind*, ed. R.G. Latham (London, 1857).

Prichard, J.C., *Researches into the physical history of man*, ed. G.W. Stocking (University of Chicago Press, 1973).

Rearick, Charles, *Beyond the Enlightenment. Historians and folklore in nineteenth-century France* (Indiana University Press, 1974).

Reizov, Boris, *L'historiographie romantique française, 1815–1830* (Moscow: Editions en langues étrangères, n.d. [1962]).

Renan, Ernest, 'La poésie des races celtiques' (1859), in *Oeuvres complètes*, ed. H. Psichari (Paris: Pléiade, 1948), 2: 252–301

Ricoeur, Paul, *Soi-même comme un autre* (Paris: Seuil, 1990).

Rigney, Ann, 'Relevance, revision and the fear of long books', in *A New Philosophy of History*, ed. F. Ankersmit & H. Kellner (London: Reaktion, 1995), pp. 127–47.

Rigney, Ann, *The rhetoric of historical representation: Three nineteenth-century histories of the French Revolution* (Cambridge University Press, 1991).

Rigney, Ann, 'Time for visions and revisions: Interpretative conflict from a communicative perspective', *Storia della storiografia*, 22 (1992): 85–92.

Ritual of the Ancient Order of Hibernians in America, arranged by the national board. For the guidance of officers in the management of divisions, explaining the methods of conducting meetings, modes of installation and initiatory ceremonies (Saratoga, N.Y.: 1906).

Robbins, Caroline, *The eighteenth-century commonwealthman. Studies in the transmission, development and circumstance of English liberal thought from the restoration of Charles II until the war with the Thirteen Colonies* (Harvard University Press, 1959).

Rousseau, G.S., 'The sorrows of Priapus', in id., *Perilous Enlightenment. Pre- and post-modern discourse: sexual, historical* (Manchester University Press, 1991), pp. 65–108.

Rowse, A.L., *Matthew Arnold: poet and prophet* (London: Thames and Hudson, 1976).

Ryan, Desmond, *The sword of light: From the Four Masters to Douglas Hyde, 1638–1938* (London: Barker, 1938).

Said, Edward, *Orientalism* (London: Routledge and Kegan Paul, 1978).

Said, Edward, *Culture and imperialism* (New York: Knopff, 1993).

Sainsbury, John, *Disaffected Patriots: London supporters of revolutionary America, 1769–1782* (McGill-Queen's University Press, 1987).

[Salmon, John], *The Round Towers of Ireland: Their origins and uses* (Belfast, 1886).

Samuels, Raphael, ed., *Patriotisms: The making and unmaking of British national identity*, 3 vols. (London: Routledge, 1989).

Schutte, G.J., 'Van verguizing naar eerherstel. Het beeld van de Patriotten in de negentiende en twintigste eeuw', in *Voor vaderland en vrijheid. De revolutie van de Patriotten*, ed. F. Grijzenhout et al. (Amsterdam: De Bataafsche Leeuw, 1987), pp. 177–92

Scott, Walter, *Essays on chivalry, romance and the drama* (Chandos classics; London, n.d.).

Scott, Walter, *Waverley, or 'tis sixty years since*, ed. Clare Lamont (Oxford: Clarendon Press, 1981).

Scurry, James, 'Remarks on the Irish language, with a review of its grammars, glossaries, vocabularies and dictionaries', *Transactions RIA*, 15 (1828): pp. 1–86.

Shannon-Mangan, Ellen, *James Clarence Mangan: A biography* (Blackrock, Co. Dublin: Irish Academic Press, 1996).

Shaw, Francis, 'The Celtic Twilight', *Studies*, 23 (1934): pp. 25–41, pp. 260–78.

Sheehy, Jeanne, *The rediscovery of Ireland's past: The Celtic revival, 1800–1830* (London: Thames and Hudson, 1980).

Shils, Edward, *Center and periphery: Essays in macrosociology* (University of Chicago Press, 1975).

Shils, Edward, *Tradition* (University of Chicago Press, 1981).

Sloan, Barry, *The pioneers of Anglo-Irish fiction, 1800–1850* (Gerrards Cross: Colin Smythe; Totowa, N.J.: Barnes and Noble, 1986).

Smiddy, Richard, *An essay on the druids, the ancient churches, and the Round Towers of Ireland* (Dublin, 1871).

Smith, I. Webber, *An essay on the Round Towers of Ireland as compared with other monuments* (Dublin, 1838).

Snyder, Edward, *The Celtic revival in English literature, 1760–1800* (Harvard University Press, 1923).

Spender, Dale, 'Lady Morgan and political fiction', in id., *Mothers of the novel. 100 good women writers before Jane Austen* (London and New York: Pandora, 1986), pp. 301–14.

The spirit of the nation. Ballads and songs by the writers of 'The nation' (1845; new ed. Dublin, 1882).

Stanley, A.P., *The life and correspondence of Thomas Arnold, DD* 2 vols. (London, 1881 ed.).

The statutes at large passed in the parliaments held in Ireland 13 vols. (Dublin, 1786).

Stepan, Nancy, *The idea of race in science: Great Britain, 1800–1960* (London: Macmillan, in association with St Antony's College, Oxford, 1982).

Stevenson, Lionel, *The wild Irish girl. The life of Sydney Owenson, Lady Morgan (1776–1859)* (London: Chapman and Hall, 1936).

Stewart, James, 'Boccaccio in the Blaskets', *Zeitschrift für Celtische Philologie*, 43 (1989): 125–40

Stokes, Margaret, *Early Christian architecture in Ireland* (London, 1878).

Stokes, William, *The life and labours in art and archeology of George Petrie, LL.D.* (London, 1868).

Sullivan, A.M., – *see* O'Halloran, Sylvester.

Sullivan, A.M., *The story of Ireland; or, A narrative of Irish history, from the earliest ages to the present time, written for the youth of Ireland* (Dublin, 1867).

Synge, J.M., *Collected works*, 2: *Prose*, ed. A. Price (Oxford University Press, 1966).

Sznycer, Maurice, *Les passages puniques en transcription latine dans le 'Poenulus' de Plaute* (Paris: Klincksieck, 1967).

Thuente, Mary Helen, *The harp re-strung: The United Irishmen and the rise of Irish literary nationalism* (Syracuse Univ. Press, 1994).

Thuente, Mary Helen, *W.B. Yeats and Irish folklore* (Dublin: Gill and Macmillan, 1980).

Tracy, Robert, 'Maria Edgeworth and Lady Morgan: Legality versus legitimacy', *Nineteenth-century Fiction*, 40 (1985–6), pp. 1–22.

Travers, Pauric, '"Our Fenian dead": Glasnevin cemetery and the genesis of the republican funeral', in *Dublin and Dubliners. Essays in the history and literature of Dublin city*, ed. J. Kelly and U. Mac Gearailt (Dublin: Helicon, 1990), pp. 52–72.

Ua Casaide, Séamus, 'Richard McElligott, honorary member of the Gaelic Society', *Journal of the North Munster Archaeological Society*, 3 (1913–15), pp. 362–70.

Vance, Norman, 'Celts, Carthaginians and constitutions: Anglo-Irish literary relations, 1780–1820', *Irish historical studies*, vol. 22, no. 87 (March, 1981): 216–38.

Venturi, Franco, *Utopia and reform in the Enlightenment* (Cambridge University Press, 1971).

Viallaneix, P. and P. Ehrard, eds., *Nos ancêtres les Gaulois* (University of Clermont-Ferrand, 1982).

Villanueva, Joaquín, *Ibernia phoenicea, seu phoenicum in Ibernia incolatus, ex ejus priscarum coloniarum nominibus, et earum idolatrico cultu demonstratio* (Dublin, 1831).

[Villanueva, Joaquín], *Phoenician Ireland. Translated and illustrated with notes, plates, and Ptolomey's map of Erin made modern, by Henry O'Brien, Esq., B.A., author of the 'prize essay' upon the 'Round Towers' of Ireland* (Dublin, 1833).

Villanueva, Joaquín, *Poesias escogidas* (Dublin, 1833).

Villanueva, Joaquín, *Sancti Patricii, Ibernorum apostoli, synodi, canones, opuscula et scriptorum quae supersunt, fragmenta scholiis illustrata* (Dublin, 1835).

Viroli, Maurizio, *For love of country: An essay on patriotism and nationalism* (Clarendon Press, 1995).

Walker, J.C., 'On the origin of romantic fabling in Ireland', *Transactions RIA*, 10 (1808).

Warburton, J., J. Whitelaw and R. Walsh. *History of the city of Dublin*, 2 vols. (London, 1818).

Warner, Alan, *William Allingham* (Bucknell University Press, 1975).

Weld, Isaac, *Illustrations of the scenery of Killarney and the surrounding country* (London, 1807).

The Wellesley index to Victorian periodicals, 1824–1900, ed. W.E. Houghton et al. 5 vols. (University of Toronto Press, 1966).

Wes, M.A. 'Van Hermann tot Hitler', in id., *Verslagen verleden. Over geschiedenis en oudheid* (Amsterdam: Wetenschappelijke uitgeverij, 1980), pp. 124–208.

Wilkes, Anna, *Ireland: Ur of the Chaldees* (London 1873).

Wills, James and Freeman Wills. *The Irish nation: its history and its biography* (Edinburgh, n.d.).

Windele, John, *Historical and descriptive notices of the city of Cork and its vicinity* (Cork, 1840).

Wiseman, Nicholas (Cardinal), *Twelve lectures on the connexion between science and revealed religion, delivered in Rome* (new ed.; Dublin, 1866).

Wood, Thomas, 'On the mixture of fable and fact in the early annals of Ireland, and on the best mode of ascertaining what degree of credit the ancient documents are justly entitled to', *Transactions RIA*, 13 (1818): 3–80.

van der Woud, Auke. *De Bataafse hut. Verschuivingen in het beeld van de geschiedenis (1750–1850)* (Amsterdam: Meulenhoff, 1990).

Wright, Thomas, *see* Payne Knight, Richard.

Yeats, W.B., *Collected poems* 2nd ed. (London: Macmillan, 1950).

Yeats, W.B., *Essays and introductions* (London: Macmillan, 1961).

Yeats, W.B., *Explorations* (London: Macmillan, 1962).

Yeats, W.B., *Fairy and folk tales of Ireland*, 4th ed. (Gerrards Cross: Colin Smythe, 1992).

Yeats, W.B., *Mythologies* (London: Macmillan, 1962).

Yeats, W.B., *Representative Irish tales* (Gerrards Cross: Colin Smythe, 1979).

Yeats, W.B., *Senate speeches*, ed., D.R. Pearce (London: Faber and Faber, 1960).

Yeats, W.B., *Uncollected prose*, ed. J.P. Frayne and C. Johnson, 2 vols. (London: Macmillan, 1970–1975).

Zaal, Wim, *De verlakkers. Literaire vervalsingen en mystificaties* (Amsterdam: Amber, 1991).

Zimmermann, Georges-Denis, *Songs of Irish rebellion. Political street ballads and rebel songs 1780–1900* (Hatboro, Pa.: Folklore Associates, 1967).

INDEX